# Sports Events, Society and Culture

This innovative and timely volume moves beyond existing operational and pragmatic approaches to events studies by exploring sports events as social, cultural, political and mediatised phenomena. As the study of this area is developing there is now a need for critical and theoretically informed debate regarding conceptualisation, significance and roles.

This edited collection explores the core themes of consumption, media technologies, representation, identities and culture to offer new insight into how sports events contribute to generation of individual and shared meaning over personal, community and national identities, as well as the associated issues of conflict, resistance and power. Chapters promote a critical (re)evaluation of emerging empirical research from a diverse range of sports events and locations from the international to local level. A multi-disciplinary approach is taken with contributions from areas including sports studies, media studies, sociology, cultural studies, communications, politics, tourism and gender studies.

Written by leading academics in the area, this thorough exploration of the contested relationship between sports events, society and culture will be of interest to students, academics and researchers in Events, Sport, Tourism and Sociology.

**Katherine Dashper** (PhD) is a Senior Lecturer at Leeds Metropolitan University. Her research interests include gender and sexuality within sport and leisure practices, with a particular focus on equestrianism and rural recreation. She is editor of *Rural tourism: An international perspective* (Cambridge Scholars Press, 2015).

**Thomas Fletcher** (PhD) is Senior Lecturer at Leeds Metropolitan University. His research interests include 'race'/ethnicity, social identities, families and pets, and equity and diversity in sport and leisure. He is editor (with Katherine Dashper) of *Diversity, equity and inclusion in sport and leisure* (Routledge, 2014).

**Nicola McCullough** is Senior Lecturer at Leeds Metropolitan University. She is Course Leader for the MSc in Sports Events Management. Her research interests are broadly concerned with governance and major sporting events and the importance of professionalism within the global sports events industry.

**Routledge advances in event research series**
Edited by Warwick Frost and Jennifer Laing
*Department of Marketing, Tourism and Hospitality,*
*La Trobe University, Australia*

**Events, Society and Sustainability**
*Edited by Tomas Pernecky and Michael Lück*

**Exploring the Social Impacts of Events**
*Edited by Greg Richards, Maria deBrito and Linda Wilks*

**Commemorative Events**
*Warwick Frost and Jennifer Laing*

**Power, Politics and International Events**
*Edited by Udo Merkel*

**Event Audiences and Expectations**
*Jo Mackellar*

**Event Portfolio Planning and Management**
A holistic approach
*Vassilios Ziakas*

**Conferences and Conventions**
A research perspective
*Judith Mair*

**Fashion, Design and Events**
*Edited by Kim M. Williams, Jennifer Laing and Warwick Frost*

**Food and Wine Events in Europe**
*Edited by Alessio Cavicchi and Cristina Santini*

**Event Volunteering**
*Edited by Karen Smith, Leonie Lockstone-Binney, Kirsten Holmes and Tom Baum*

**The Arts and Events**
*Hilary du Cros and Lee Jolliffe*

**Sports Events, Society and Culture**
*Edited by Katherine Dashper, Thomas Fletcher and Nicola McCullough*

Forthcoming:
**The Future of Events and Festivals**
*Edited by Ian Yeoman, Martin Robertson, Una McMahon-Beattie, Elisa Backer and Karen Smith*

**Exploring Community Events and Festivals**
*Edited by Allan Jepson and Alan Clarke*

**Event Design**
*Edited by Greg Richards, Lénia Marques and Karen Mein*

**Rituals and Traditional Events in the Modern World**
*Edited by Warwick Frost and Jennifer Laing*

**Approaches and Methods in Events Studies**
*Tomas Pernecky*

# Sports Events, Society and Culture

Edited by Katherine Dashper,
Thomas Fletcher and Nicola McCullough

Routledge
Taylor & Francis Group

LONDON AND NEW YORK

First published 2015
by Routledge
2 Park Square, Milton Park, Abingdon, Oxon OX14 4RN

and by Routledge
711 Third Avenue, New York, NY 10017

First issued in paperback 2017

*Routledge is an imprint of the Taylor & Francis Group, an informa business*

*British Library Cataloguing in Publication Data*
A catalogue record for this book is available from the British Library

*Library of Congress Cataloging in Publication Data*
Sports events, society and culture / edited by Katherine Dashper, Thomas
Fletcher and Nicola McCullough.
  pages cm. – (Routledge advances in event research series)
  Includes bibliographical references and index.
  1. Sports –Social aspects –Case studies. 2. Sports –Psychological aspects
  –Case studies. 3. Mass media and sports –Case studies. I. Dashper,
  Katherine, author, editor of compilation. II. Fletcher, Thomas, author,
  editor of compilation. III. McCullough, Nicola, author, editor of
  compilation.
  GV706.5.S7399 2014
  306.4′83–dc23                                   2014001478

ISBN 13: 978-1-138-08250-2 (pbk)
ISBN 13: 978-0-415-82675-4 (hbk)

Typeset in Times New Roman
by Wearset Ltd, Boldon, Tyne and Wear

This book is dedicated to Ian, Amanda, William, Matt, Samuel and Abigail

# Contents

# Contributors

**Harpreet Bains** (PhD) is a freelance academic within the field of South Asian Studies. Her research interests include ethnicities, masculinities, patriarchy, feminism and sport within the South Asian community in the UK. She has worked at Sheffield University, Edinburgh University and Newham College University Centre teaching modules on Sociology of Sport, Feminism and Masculinities and Race and Racism.

**Andrew Bradley** (PhD) is a Senior Lecturer in Events Management at the University of Gloucestershire. He has published extensively on a range of event related topics such as the decision making process in the choice of event venue, the creation of an event experience and the tensions that exist between event theory and event practice. His principal research interest, however, is in relation to the media coverage of local events in terms of the form that this coverage takes, how event managers have sought to manipulate the media coverage of their events and what impacts this coverage has upon a range of local communities.

**Katherine Dashper** (PhD) is a Senior Lecturer in Events Management at Leeds Metropolitan University. Her research interests include gender and sexuality within sport and leisure practices, with a particular focus on equestrianism and rural recreation. Her current research focuses on the interactions between humans, animals and the natural environment within sport and active leisure. She is editor of *Rural tourism: An international perspective* (Cambridge Scholars Press, 2015) and *Diversity, equity and inclusion in sport and leisure* (with Thomas Fletcher, Routledge, 2014) and has published in a range of international journals.

**Suzanne Dowse** (PhD) is a Senior Lecturer in Events Management at Canterbury Christ Church University. Prior to this position she was the Research Development Manager for the Centre for Sport, Physical Education and Activity Research (SPEAR) at Canterbury Christ Church University. She has been involved in research exploring the politics, policy and education lessons learnt from hosting sport events, including, for example, Olympic sport and health legacies. Her research interests are broadly concerned with the links between international relations and sport, and the political and social implications of hosting sport events.

**Rebecca Finkel** (PhD) is an urban cultural geographer and is currently Programme Leader and Lecturer, Events Management, in the School of Arts, Social Sciences and Management at Queen Margaret University, Edinburgh. Her main field of study centres on gender, social justice and events management. Her main research interests include the strategic analysis of government socio-economic policies for funding and development, with specific focus on social capital and social equality. Her most recent research is framed within conceptualisations of cultural identity, symbolic boundaries and resistance to globalisation, as well as mapping human rights and mega sporting events. She is currently focusing on the links between sex work, human trafficking and the Olympic Games.

**Thomas Fletcher** (PhD) is a Senior Lecturer in Events Management at Leeds Metropolitan University. His research interests include: "race"/ethnicity, social identities, families and pets, and equity and diversity in sport and leisure. Thomas has published in a range of peer review journals including *Ethnic and Racial Studies, Sociological Research Online, International Review for the Sociology of Sport* and *Leisure/Loisir.* He is editor (with Katherine Dashper) of *Diversity, equity and inclusion in sport and leisure* (Routledge, 2014). He is currently guest editing a special issue of the journal *Identities* entitled *Cricket, migration and diasporic communities* (publication late 2014/early 2015). He is also Secretary for the Leisure Studies Association.

**Frances Harkin** is a PhD candidate at the Institute of Irish Studies, Queen's University of Belfast. Her doctoral thesis focuses upon London's Irish diasporic community and the ways in which different members of this community engage with the Gaelic Athletic Association. It also considers the different modalities of Irish identity articulated through the medium of sport. Frances also holds a Master's degree in Irish Studies from Queen's University, Belfast and a Bachelor of Arts degree from St Mary's University College in London. Her wider research interests include multigenerational identities and the Irish diaspora, with particular reference to Irish migration to London and the role of Irish sporting and cultural practices in Irish diasporic communities.

**Dağhan Irak** is a researcher and sports journalist from Istanbul, Turkey. He holds a bachelor's degree in Journalism from Galatasaray University, and a master's in Modern Turkish History from Boğaziçi University. His master's thesis 'The transformation of football fandom in Turkey since the 1970s was a comparison of British and Turkish football scenes in terms of hyper-commodification and social change. He has two published books, *Türkiye ve Sosyal Medya* (*Turkey and social media*, with Onur Yazıcıoğlu), and *Hükmen Yenik!: Türkiye'de ve İngiltere'de Futbolun Sosyo-Politiği* (*Lost by default: The socio-politics of* *football in Turkey and England*). His research interests are primarily related to socio-political aspects of sports, politics, and conventional and new media. He is currently pursuing a double-PhD at the University of Strasbourg (in sports sociology) and Galatasaray University (in media studies).

**Iain Lindsay** (PhD) is an international consultant and researcher within the sport for development, safeguarding and the security sectors. He also lectures on the Sport Science and Sociology undergraduate and post-graduate courses at Brunel University, UK. He has a specific interest in sport in the development context (including society, history, culture, religion, economy and politics) and has recently published research regarding the politics of sporting mega-events, mega-event delivery and security, urban regeneration and the role of sport in society. His other research includes work that addresses the influencing factors on sport participation, child protection, safeguarding, urban ethnography and gang-related projects. Dr Lindsay's current/recent research includes 'Serious youth violence: Gangs in the post-2012 Olympic City', 'The health and sport engagement project' (SportEngland), 'Understanding the value of sport and physical activity in tertiary education' (SportScotland) and 'Child protection and the 2014 FIFA World Cup' (Oak Foundation).

**Nicola McCullough** is a Senior Lecturer in Events Management at Leeds Metropolitan University. She is Course Leader for the MSc in Sports Events Management. Prior to this position she has worked extensively on an international level within the events industry including specific roles working with host nations in securing sporting events. She is currently involved in research investigating the cultural complexities of delivering major sporting events within emerging nations. Her research interests are broadly concerned with how the role of governance influences the hosting of major sporting events and the importance of professionalism within the global sports events industry.

**Jim O'Brien** (PhD) is Senior Lecturer in Journalism and Sports Journalism at Southampton Solent University. He has also held senior academic posts in the Netherlands and Greece. In the past his research interests have embraced political communication and international education. More recently his research has focused on football, particularly in Spain and Italy, undertaking several projects on the relationship between Spanish football and history, politics, media and culture in Spain. He has written about football in Catalona and Andalucia, and in respect of the Spanish national team. He is currently completing a major study of Spanish football entitled 'From La Furia to La Roja; Football, politics and culture in Spain'. As a fluent speaker of Spanish, he has travelled extensively in Catalonia, the Basque Country, Spain and Latin America.

**Noëlle O'Connor** (PhD) is Senior Lecturer in Tourism and Hospitality Studies in Limerick Institute of Technology (Ireland) and is also a MBA Online Lecturer at Glion University (Switzerland). Noëlle has industrial experience in the Irish, British, French and Austrian hospitality industries and has gained much external examining experience in Ireland, Nepal, Switzerland and the

UK. Noëlle's research focuses on the areas of film induced tourism, destination branding and tourism education. Noëlle has also edited the books *Tourism and hospitality research in Ireland* (2007) and *A film marketing action plan for film induced tourism destinations: Using Yorkshire as a case study* (2010).

**Karl Russell** (PhD) is a Senior Lecturer in Hospitality Management at the University of Sunderland, UK. He is a professional member of the Institute of Hospitality Management, a Fellow of the Higher Education Academy and has held teaching posts in England, Scotland, Switzerland, United Arab Emirates and Iran. His research interests and teaching areas are within strategic hospitality management, hotel brand growth strategies and hospitality competitive advantage within emerging markets and Islamic hospitality. He has extensive research and consultancy experience in the UK, Switzerland and the Middle East. Karl's co-authored paper: 'Islamic hospitality in the UAE: Indigenization of products and human capital', which was published in the *Journal of Islamic Marketing* (2010) was a 'Highly Commended Award Winner' at the Emerald Literati Awards for Excellence, 2011.

**Daniel Schulze** studied International Cultural and Business Studies at Passau University, Germany (graduated 2011); he also studied Text and Performance Studies at King's College London and the Royal Academy of Dramatic Art (graduated 2008). He worked as personal assistant to the director and play-wright Robert Wilson from 2008 to 2009. He is currently a PhD candidate and teaching fellow at Würzburg University (Germany). His PhD thesis is on the subject of 'The Aesthetics of lying and authenticity in contemporary theatre and performance'.

**Damion Sturm** (PhD) is a Research Associate with the Screen and Media Studies Department, University of Waikato, Hamilton, New Zealand. With a specialisation in global media cultures (inclusive of sport, celebrity, fan and material cultures), he has recently co-authored *Media, masculinities and the machine* with Professor Dan Fleming, as well as articles on male fan-star relationships, new media fandom, nation-building and autoethnographic fan representations. His PhD explored fan engagements with Formula One motor-racing ('Being Jacques Villeneuve: Formula One, "agency" and the fan').

**Mark Turner** is a Senior Lecturer in Sport Sociology at Southampton Solent University, UK. He is a member of the Southampton Solent Centre for Health, Exercise and Sport Science (CHESS) research cluster. Mark was awarded a BSc Sport Studies from the University of Lancaster and an MA Sport, Culture and Society from the University of Brighton. Mark is currently studying for his PhD. This project aims to investigate the impact of electronic cultures on football fan behaviours, identities and issues. His expertise focuses on the changing social, cultural and political significance of football goal celebrations and the virtual spaces and places at which football fans are now interacting.

**Lawrence A. Wenner** (PhD) is the Von der Ahe Professor of Communication Ethics in the College of Communication and Fine Arts and the School of Film and Television at Loyola Marymount University in Los Angeles. Dr. Wenner's research includes eight books and over 100 journal articles and chapters. His most recent books include *Sport, beer, and gender: Promotional culture and contemporary social life* (with Steven Jackson; Peter Lang, 2009) and *Fallen sport heroes, media, and celebrity culture* (Peter Lang, 2013) He currently serves as Editor of two scholarly journals, the *International Review for the Sociology of Sport* and *Communication and Sport*.

**Donna Wong** (PhD) is a Research Fellow in the Centre for the International Business of Sport at Coventry Business School. Her research interests relate to various aspects of sport, including media, youth participation and social trends. Being an active researcher, she has published widely in a range of peer review journals and book chapters. Recent publications include (with I. Kuroda and J. Horne) 'Sport, broadcasting and cultural citizenship in Japan', in J. Scherer and D. Rowe (eds) *Sport, public broadcasting, and cultural citizenship: Signal lost?* (Routledge, 2013). She is currently serving as an Executive Board Member in the Leisure Studies Association.

# Acknowledgements

We would like to thank our colleagues within the International Centre for Research in Events, Tourism and Hospitality at Leeds Metropolitan University for providing a stimulating working environment. In particular, we wish to thank Professor Rhodri Thomas for his unwavering support and commitment to critical scholarship.

We thank all of the contributors for their hard work throughout the genesis of the project.

Finally, we would like to thank Routledge, in particular Philippa Mullins, for advice and encouragement.

# Introduction

## Sports events, society and culture

*Katherine Dashper, Thomas Fletcher and
Nicola McCullough*

### The sports event field

Sports events contribute to the generation of individual and shared meanings in relation to personal, community and national identities (Hayes and Karamichas, 2012). But they are also sources of conflict and resistance, and act as sites for the negotiation of individual and collective power struggles. As Dashper and Fletcher (2013: 1227) have previously argued, sport continues to be cited as an exemplar par excellence of an agent of personal and social change. Numerous studies articulate the possibility of sport acting as a legitimate space for political struggle, resistance and change, and as a modality for "self-actualisation and the reaffirmation of previously abject identities" (Carrington, 2012: 36). However, we argue that, currently, much of the literature surrounding sports events does not account sufficiently for the events' deeply socio-political dimensions.

In his formulation of the field of event studies, Getz (2007) advocates moving beyond praxis, i.e. planning and management, towards a more holistic appreciation of the roles, meanings and experiences of events. Getz makes the distinction between event studies, which he defines as "the academic field devoted to creating knowledge and theory about planned events", and events management, which he describes as "the applied field of study and area of professional practice that draws upon knowledge and theory from Event Studies" (p. 2). According to Thomas and Bowdin (2012), this distinction that Getz (2007) puts forth has not stimulated the level of discussion that it deserves, but it is a distinction that we find useful. We situate this volume broadly within the field of event studies, as opposed to event management, in that contributions focus less on the business and management side of sports events and more on using theory and empirical research to try and understand events as socio-cultural constructions. Our motivation for focusing the collection in this way builds on emerging critiques of the "mainstream" events management literature, as put forward by Getz (2007), Jago (2012) and Rojek (2012, 2013), amongst others, which argues that event-related research needs to become more theoretical and critical.

According to Jago (2012: 220):

> One of the criticisms levelled at event researchers is that they make little effort to add to knowledge per se and tend to focus on the very mundane

operational dimensions of events.... They tend to focus on the specifics of a single event and they make little if any attempt to apply the learnings from the research to the broader field.

He cautions that this issue must be addressed if the field is to obtain external credibility, thereby enabling it to realise its potential. Rojek (2013: 18) continues this argument in *Event Power*, where he argues that "in focusing on the operational, technical aspects of event design, publicity and management, event professionals unwittingly obscure the relationship of events to deeper, wider questions of history, power, personal gratification, control and resistance". For Richards and de Brito (2013: 234) critiques such as these justify the (emerging) belief that there is an argument for supplementing "the predominant management-based approach [to understanding events] with a broader social science view of how events articulate with social processes and structures". Indeed, we contend that, academically, the event itself (i.e. its production, setting, management) should not necessarily be the focus of analysis; rather the event must be thought of as a social milieu for the (re)articulation of other social issues, including, for example, social inclusion/exclusion, and expressions of individual and collective identities.

In pointing the way forward for future research in sports events, Jago (2012) suggests that there is a need to consider the holistic benefits of sports events. He identifies a contemporary tendency to examine economic, social (and cultural) and environmental impacts as silos when, perhaps, treating them as intersecting constituents would be a more effective approach (what Getz (2009) refers to as a triple-bottom-line approach). In so doing, he argues for scholars to uncover more effectively the benefits of events in order for practitioners to better maximise those benefits. We agree that there is a need to examine sports events holistically, but we would challenge the view of looking only for their *benefits*. We argue that sports events (and events generally) are all too often viewed through rose-tinted glasses, whereby their negative aspects/impacts are either overlooked, or treated as secondary to their benefits. This is not to say that critical research is not taking place. There are a host of authors currently engaged in critical research within the field of sports events (see, for example, Horne and Manzenreiter, 2006; Horne, 2007; Lenskyj, 2008; Darnell, 2012; Hayes and Karamichas, 2012; Sugden and Tomlinson, 2012; Palmer, 2013). However, these authors rarely identify themselves as "event" academics or "event managers". Rather, they are routinely sociologists (of sport), political scientists or economists. This supports Getz's (2007: 8) argument for the need for "more cross-disciplinary contributions both in theory and methods" in event-related research, and for greater dialogue between those that identify themselves, academically and institutionally, with event management (or event studies) and those researching events from different academic fields. Contributions in this volume go some way towards beginning to bridge this gap.

Chris Rojek (2013) calls for greater synergy between event-related research and other established fields, such as leisure studies, in order to encourage more critical scholarship that transcends the current field of events management/ studies. He argues that whilst event management literature is both diverse and profuse, it is united by self-congratulation, with a worrying tendency to glorify the positive impacts events can make. He warns that "the overwhelming, paramount assumption, propagated by Event Management Teams and network power, is that these events are an intrinsic social good" (Rojek, 2012: 5). Amongst other things these social goods include: bringing lasting social and economic benefits to host communities, enhancing community identity and image, regeneration and place (re)development, facilitating community cohesion and well-being, and promoting national identity (Sharpley and Stone, 2011: 352). However, the supposition that events are an unquestionable social good is flawed. Scholars of events are clearly astute enough to acknowledge this, but we argue that current critiques do not go far enough. The majority do accept that events produce both positive and negative impacts, but these are largely glossed over, and rarely do they respond with authority on what these impacts are, or how the negatives might be combated.[1] Moreover, in keeping with the technocratic criticisms outlined already, much of the literature identifies what are, arguably, quite mundane negative impacts, including for example, noise pollution, increased littering and additional traffic congestion. We are by no means dismissing the significance of these impacts, but we are suggesting that, in moving the research agenda forward, researchers may usefully extend their gaze to also focus attention on the more invidious impacts of sports events, rather than those that may be successfully 'managed' by hiring clean-up crews, temporarily closing roads or redirecting attendees.

Sports mega-events for example, are frequently associated with institutional corruption (Jennings, 2011), soaring economic costs (Gratton *et al.*, 2006), environmental cleansing (Palmer, 2013), terrorism and securitisation (Giulianotti and Klauser, 2012), gentrification (Watt, 2013), violence and human rights violations (COHRE, 2007) and human/sex trafficking (Frontline, 2009; Matheson and Finkel, 2013). More routinely, principally via media coverage, sports events remain a primary agonist in the (re)articulation of structural inequalities, along the lines of gender, sexuality, "race" and ethnicity, social class, disability and their intersections (Fletcher and Dashper, 2013). Nevertheless, Rojek believes that (currently at least) there is a reticence within the event management literature to fully deconstruct the utopian vision of events as an intrinsic social good. It is worth quoting him at length to appreciate the ferocity of critique put forth:

> When one looks at the social, cultural and economic outcomes claimed by the likes of Getz (1991, 1997, 2007) and Bowdin *et al.* (2011, p. 87), with their casual references to 'celebration spaces', 'cultural and economic benefits', 'building community pride', 'increasing environmental awareness' and 'introducing new and challenging ideas', it is above all, the audacity of the Event Management self-image that comes to mind. Questions of social control, economic inequality and moral regulation are scrupulously

marginalised. This reinforces the distinguishing feature of Event conscious-ness, which is to picture the world as a series of episodes, incidents and emergencies that require managerial intervention and technocratic remedies.

(Rojek, 2012: 8)

Other critiques of events-related literature (including sports events) also note that much of the work within events studies rarely uses events as generative of social theory and at best shows how concepts and ideas developed in other contexts can be applied to events. In so doing, events scholars are making little effort to contribute theoretical outcomes that can benefit other fields. This criticism is crystallised in the introduction to *Exploring the social impacts of events* (Richards *et al.*, 2013), another book in the Advances to Events Research series, to which this book belongs. In a section in the intro-duction to the collection entitled "Theoretical groundings", Wilks (2013) reflects on how events research, specifically social impact research, lies at the "crossroads of several disciplines" (p. 4). She then proceeds to list a range of sociological and cultural studies theories and concepts that would be useful for scholars of events research to engage with. Amongst these she cites social and cultural capital; social networks and theories of network society; com-munity and social cohesion; theories of "race", ethnicity and diaspora; identity theories, including those pertaining to tribes and neo-tribes; theories of place and space; power. With each of these suggestions Wilks provides the obliga-tory courtesy "nod" to the theoretical "power houses" in each area. In so doing we cannot help but think that she reinforces the parasitic perception of events-related research. Wilks is by no means alone in this. Indeed, as Getz (2007) suggests, this tendency to draw ideas from other fields may be inevitable. Due to the infancy of event studies as a field, some theoretical and conceptual bor-rowing is to be expected, although at times it can appear that "we are carving off a portion of their body of knowledge and giving it special status, but that is what happens when there is explosive growth in the value of, and interest in a particular phenomenon" (Getz, 2007: 5). That said, we would caution that, regardless of a field's infancy, theories and concepts borrowed from other fields should be rigorously applied and used to extrapolate the nuances and vagaries of events. We contend that the question should not really be over which theory(ies) researchers ought to use; rather the key concern must be on what we are trying to uncover, if anything, and how social theory(ies) can contribute to our broader understanding.

Events management literature is currently crying out for critical research that positions events (sports events included) at the heart of wider social, cultural, political and economic issues. Indeed, for Rojek (2013: 4):

The problem with these sound-bite concepts, and the rationale behind them, is that they confine Event consciousness to a vantage point that views the world as a series of incidents, emergencies and episodes rather than a con-junction of structures of power and causal sequences.

Rojek is clearly pessimistic about the current state of play of "professional" event management literature. This is not to say that he does not see the worth of events management as an academic field, or that he dismisses events as a valuable leisure pursuit. In fact, quite the contrary; he suggests that the proliferation of events management diplomas and degrees (he does not cite sports events management, although a number of specific sports event management degrees are now being developed at both undergraduate and postgraduate levels) in recent years as a measure of the importance of events in both income generation and influencing social consciousness. He goes so far as to say that "By some distance, they (academic courses) constitute the main front of student growth and arguably, innovation in the field" of leisure studies (Rojek, 2012: 1).

Thus, for Rojek and Jago amongst others, it is not the field(s) of events studies and/or events management that is the problem per se, rather it is: (1) the rigour of their theoretical application; and (2) the accuracy of claims over their positivity and negativity. Rojek attributes both of these criticisms to the collective naivety within the field(s). He argues that it is in the nature of new and emerging fields, such as events studies and events management, to make bold claims. Indeed, this is how new fields get noticed and evolve. However, for Rojek, the positive claims made by events studies and events management are excessive and reflect a "disturbing myopia about generations of critical study in the Social Sciences and Leisure Studies on questions of power, control and resistance" (Rojek, 2012: 8).

The fields of events studies and events management are not alone in receiving such criticism. It is ironic that much of the critical literature on (sports) events and (sports) events management are pointing towards scholars to engage with literature from the social sciences (of sport) because the social sciences of sport have similarly been battling for legitimacy within the "mainstream" social sciences literature over the last three to four decades. There are palpable similarities between current criticisms of event-related literature and those aimed at the sociology of sport during the late 1980s–early 1990s. Drawing on Bourdieu's (1988) early critique of the sociology of sport, Carrington (2012: 6) writes how "Sport both hyper-accentuates and finds itself on the wrong side of a supposedly insurmountable (and deeply 'classed') dualism between useless physicality and purposeful intellectualism". Carrington goes on to lament that the sociologist who takes sport as a starting point for sociological enquiry risks a certain professional disparagement, remarking that "It would be comforting to report that in the intervening years [following Bourdieu's critique] such a denouncement of intellectual snobbery on the one hand and of wilful intellectual refusal on the other has been overcome. Alas, it is not possible to do so." It is not unreasonable to say that events management is currently at a similar crossroads; often mocked within the academy as a "Mickey Mouse" subject, and frequently misunderstood as teaching students how to erect tents and form orderly queues.[2]

Crucially though, we would contend, rather than hindering the development of events-related research, these criticisms could be an opportunity. Utilising Carrington's (2012) analyses of sport, it could be suggested that the assumed apolitical nature of events allows researchers to situate them as social milieus for the articulation of wider political issues. Carrington (2012: 4) argues that it is sport's (event's)

> assumed innocence as a space ... and a place ... that is removed from everyday concerns of power, inequality, struggle and ideology, that has, paradoxically, allowed it to be filled with a range of contradictory assumptions that have inevitably spilled back over and into wider society.

He suggests that taking this contradiction seriously – that is *the political nature of the apolitical* – helps us towards a deeper and richer understanding of politics. Sport events and politics are inseparable, as continuing debates about sex workers and human trafficking in Vancouver (2010), controversies surrounding the question of gay rights in Russia (2014) and the rights of migrant workers in Qatar (2022) illustrate. These, and many other examples, show how sports events are not benign, whimsical leisure pursuits, devoid of political meaning; rather they are serious spaces which should encourage critical engagement with these issues.

Understanding events is a useful lens through which to understand elements of contemporary society; however, currently the argument *for* taking events seriously is not strong enough. We can learn from the experiences of academics within other fields, including sociologists of sport, who have advocated for their sub-discipline's legitimacy. It is worth drawing upon Carrington (2012: 10, emphasis in original) again here:

> The key for those who do not think that sport [in our case, *events*] constitutes an actual object of study and an important one at that, is to think through *why* sport [events] appears to be marginal to serious cultural critique and intellectual examination (without becoming overly defensive) while also demonstrating *what* sport [events] adds to our broader understandings of diverse sociological issues ... while avoiding assuming the de facto centrality of sports [events] to all issues at all times.

In this book we identify some of the "gaps" in existing research on events and sports events in order to highlight what types of enquiries might usefully be pursued to open up a critical dialogue between researchers, students and practitioners in the events and sports events fields. More specifically, the aim of this book is to move beyond existing operational and pragmatic approaches to event-related studies by exploring sports events as social, cultural, political and mediatised phenomena. We acknowledge that, as the study of sports events develops, there is need for critical and theoretically informed debate regarding their conceptualisation, significance and roles. This book is timely due to the increasingly globalised nature of the sports events industry and the concurrent democratisation of media; not to mention a bourgeoning interest in event studies and events management, with sports events representing a key part of this.

Contributors promote a critical (re)evaluation of emerging empirical research from a broad range of sports events and locations. The collection contains research on a diverse range of sports events, ranging from very small, localised contexts to mega-events, and considers these from an international perspective. Contributors to the collection also draw upon a range of different theoretical perspectives, thereby addressing some of the atheoretical criticisms frequently levelled at events-related research.

The book is divided into four key themes: inventing, packaging and consuming sports events; media and mediatisation; identities; mega-events. The collection is intentionally broad, and is in no way intended to be a "one-stop shop" for students, academics and practitioners working within the field of sports events. However, the contributions reflect the diversity of current research related to sports events, society and culture, and begin to address some of the gaps in current scholarship and, in doing so, identify potential future research agendas.

## Inventing, packaging and consuming sports events

According to Crawford (2009: 284) "sport is usually encountered and consumed in everyday life in fairly ordinary and mundane ways", including observing (or sometimes paying partial notice to) the myriad of television and news programmes and stories, billboard, television and press advertisements, clothing and other consumer items, and conversations of those around us. For Crawford (2004), the way we engage with and consume all of these sport-related signs and symbols contribute to the "everyday" and "ordinary" sport scene which, crucially, becomes "extraordinary" at certain times and in certain places (such as in sport stadiums or in pubs) (Crawford 2004, 2009; see also Chapter 2 in this volume).

The global nature of sport and how it is packaged and consumed owes a lot to the increasing sophistication of media technologies. In particular, technologies such as television, radio, the print media and the internet have increased the possibility for individuals to connect with sports in ways other than attending the live event. There has been a dramatic shift in the nature of world television over the past three decades. According to Miller (1999) this shift can be explained via two processes: (1) that television has moved from a comparatively scarce resource to a common one in most sections of the world; and (2) that it has changed from being a predominantly nation-based and state-run medium toward internationalism and privatisation (see Chapter 6 in this volume). Miller attributes these processes to bourgeoning interests in neoliberal ideologies towards: cutting down cross-ownership regulations (thereby encouraging capitalists to invest across media); reducing public-sector budgets (moving labour, product development and technological initiative(s) to profit-centred services); opening up terrestrial television to international corporations (undercutting local production); attacking the idea of public broadcasting as elitist and inefficient. The commingling of sport and television means that what we are seeing is a "televisualisation of sport" and a "sportification of television". How and/or whether these have impacted upon the "live" event viewing experience is discussed further below.

It is currently impossible to think about sports without also thinking about the triumvirate of globalisation, commercialisation and corporate capitalism. Linking these three concepts are media technologies which, according to Castells (1996), have created a shift away from an "industrial mode of development" towards an "informational mode of development". Accordingly:

> In the industrial mode of development, the main source of productivity lies in the introduction of new energy sources, and in the ability to decentralize the use of energy through the production and circulation processes. In the new, informational mode of development, the sources of productivity lie in the technology of knowledge generation, information processing, and symbolic communication.
>
> (Castells, 1996: 17)

For Postman (1993), new media technologies (including the internet), are seen to consolidate the position of consumer capitalism. Indeed, evidence to support the argument that the primary role of media technologies is to act as a medium to invent and gratify consumer needs for corporate capitalism can be found extensively in the world of sport.

This argument is taken up in the opening chapter by Lawrence Wenner, who presents a critical analysis of Superbowl advertisements, examining what he terms "the dirty logics" of the "Super Bowl *of* Advertising" and the "Super Bowl *in* advertising". Wenner argues that sporting events, in this case the Super Bowl, act as catalysts for the production of "commercial narratives that seek to fashion an event-to-advertising connection" (p. 35) that draws upon well-established sporting narratives (or "logics") that can be commodified and sold back to the consumer. Drawing on dirt theory and consumer culture theory, the chapter considers the dynamics of three "dirty narrative strategies" that build on: (1) Super Bowl hero dirt; (2) Super Bowl event dirt; (3) Super Bowl commercial dirt. Wenner advocates for scholarship to examine these event-to-advertising connections to "understand the cultural shadow of how sport and its logics permeate culture" and how "an essential part of that agenda will have to be focused on how sport [and its 'dirty logics'] is reappropriated in other settings" (p. 37).

Television remains highly influential for communicating dominant ideologies to the sporting public. Both Weed (2007) and Crawford (2009) document the growing tendency for sports events to be consumed via large-screen televisions in public houses. In this sense, the pub becomes representative of a new type of stadia – one that may be geographically detached from the "live" event venue, but provides a space for (mainly male) communal gatherings. Weed (2007) suggests that watching sport in pubs offers individuals the close social proximity often missing in a contemporary and increasingly fragmented society. For Crawford (2009), this "proximity" may be explained in both a social and physical sense, as sport fans in pubs are more willing to be crowded in with strangers, and have their "personal space" compromised, in ways reminiscent of the crowding of stadium terracing.

In saying this, the ways in which we consume sports and events *are* changing. Information and communication technologies have opened up new possibilities for sport. The growth of media technology(ies) and growing patterns towards digitisation have opened up channels, such as websites, blogs, podcasts, video streaming and mobile phone applications, all of which provide sports information and entertainment services instantly and "on demand".

Contemporarily, none of these technologies have been more influential than the internet. For Crawford (2004) the internet has proved a particularly effective way for teams and leagues to reach supporters, and both new and old "customers", in the privacy of their own homes without relying on the aid of other media sources such as television and the print press. The internet (along with other technologies) provides individuals with access to existing communities, but can also expand the scope of these and help create and nurture new ones, to the extent that "individuals can now connect and form affiliations and allegiances to sport via solely electronic means" (Crawford, 2004: 143). However, the internet has been criticised as both a consequence of, and contributor to, the individualisation of society. Postman (1993), for example, suggests that the internet dehumanises and isolates its users via negating the need to be physically present during social interaction(s). The internet has also been extensively criticised for what is seen as its key role in the proliferation of consumer culture (see above). Hence, as with other types of mass media, it is important to understand both the opportunities and limitations afforded by the internet.

Mark Turner takes up this debate in relation to the ways in which fans consume professional English football matches: live at the event; via television; via the internet. He critiques the concept of the "live" event by arguing that fans are consuming football via increasingly mediatised ways. In so doing, he argues that mediatised events are usurping the "live" event within the cultural economy. A number of researchers are suggesting that, due in part to the increased commercialisation and costs of attending live football events at stadia, more fans are turning to alternative spaces to consume and enjoy football, and sport more generally (Weed, 2007; Dixon, 2013). Turner (p. 50) draws on Redhead's reading of Baudrillard and Virilio, as theorists of hyper-reality and accelerated culture, to argue that due to the growing influence of

> global media communications and technologies, we are able to recognise the way(s) in which the experience of the live event at the stadium and the hyper real mediatised live have become so mixed up and intertwined that, in many ways, they now cannot be understood independent of each other.

Central to our understanding of this event mediatisation is how we conceptualise consumers/audiences. There is growing recognition that consumers of sport are becoming increasingly discerning and vocal. The contemporary pattern within English top-flight football towards foreign ownership and management of football clubs has led to a number of fan protests (see for example Nauright and Ramfjord, 2010). Therefore, we must begin to think about consumers of sport as active participants within the overall event narrative. Abercrombie and Long-hurst's (1998) concept of the "diffused audience" offers an appropriate applica-tion to sports events. Put simply, the diffused audience is a contemporary progression from "simple" audiences (direct observers at an event), through "mass" audiences (being an audience member to "mediated" texts such as tele-vision, cinema or sound recordings) to a contemporary situation, where in an increasingly spectacular and performative society we become both audience and performers in our everyday lives.

The assumption that social actors act as both audience and performers is at the heart of Daniel Schulze's Chapter 3 on the spectacle and drama of profes-sional wrestling. Schulze argues that professional wrestling invites the participa-tion of the audience, suggesting that "matches are not a matter of quiet spectating; rather audiences *experience* a wrestling match with their whole bodies, and they externalise their emotions immediately by booing, heckling or cheering" (p. 59). Schulze explains how wrestling can be understood as a micro-cosm of American society and draws on problematic narratives including dys-functional families, prolonged adolescence, sexism and homophobia, which are infused within the soap opera style storylines invented and packaged to appeal to wrestling's predominantly (young) male audience. Schulze points out that fans are not passive consumers of these storylines, rather they are influential in their creation. However, in spite of this consumer participation, Schulze is critical of the content of these stories and the ways in which "professional wrestling delights in pushing the boundaries of what is socially acceptable and in good taste, while at the same time displaying very conservative, heteronormative values" (p. 64).

The creation of a sporting spectacle is central to Damion Sturm's Chapter 4 on Formula One. Due to Formula One's economic and technological inaccess-ibility, the sport is almost "other worldly" and is thus (re)packaged and projected as a "spectacular and seductive" global media spectacle (Kellner, 2003). For Sturm, Formula One's commercialism, innovative mediation, prestige and popular global status reveal the complexities and interconnections of the ways in which sports events are packaged and produced within contemporary consumer culture. Sturm argues that Formula One is constructed as "a glamorous and high-tech global spectacle of speed" which is constantly reinforced through the use of exotic locations, futuristic machines and the promotion of an "expensive, con-sumerist, jet-setting lifestyle", the latter of which is epitomised through the drivers who are "an embodiment of the sport's glamour ... through their globe-trotting displays of masculine bravado and apparently luxurious lifestyles" (p. 70). Problematically, however, the mediatised spectacle that is created is "essentially homogenous and Eurocentric" (p. 80) in that it "reproduces a version of cultural imperialism, whereby the host nations have Formula One's homoge-nous global commodity spectacle imposed upon them, seemingly with little regard for the specifics of the country or culture" (p. 76).

## Media and "mediatisation"

As the contributions in the previous section indicate, sports events and media are intimately connected; indeed, it is impossible to imagine one without the other (Rowe, 2009). From early sensational reports in local newspapers, to saturation of television channels and the proliferation of subscription-based services, to the explosion in online discussions, blogs and user-generated content, sport provides stories, drama, joy and anguish to fill media channels and attract large, committed audiences. Media has been essential to the development of sport from locally practised games and contests to mass spectator, global spectacles (Horne and Manzenreiter, 2006). Many sports events have been willing to adapt their format, rules and structure to accommodate better the needs of commercial media, in order to reap the associated benefits of greater exposure, increased (global) audiences and commercial investment and sponsorship (Boyle and Haynes, 2009). For most consumers of sport, be they avid, dedicated fans or more passive, occasional viewers, their predominant relationship with sports events is not through direct viewing of the "live" event, but rather through a mediated and mediatised form that is (re)produced, (re)packaged and (re)presented for media audiences (see Chapters 1 and 2 in this volume). As a consequence, sports events have become "mediatised" through "a relentless process of convergence and intertwining" (Rowe, 2009: 543) between the powerful institutions of sport and the media, two key elements of popular culture.

Wenner (1998: xiii) argues that such is the importance of the sport-media relationship in the modern era that it is more appropriate to use the conflated term "MediaSport" to reflect the "cultural fusing of sport with communication". However, although the relationship between sport and media is clearly close and symbiotic, Blain (2002) cautions against losing sight of the fact that sport and media are analytically distinct, and that the interrelationships between various sporting practices and different media forms remain highly differentiated. As the contributions in this collection illustrate, analyses of sports events and media reveal how these interactions can be empowering or restrictive, progressive or reactionary, commercially dominated or more democratic and fan-based (see Chapters 5, 6 and 7 in this volume). What the growing body of research focusing on the interrelationships between media and sport all agree on, however, is the importance of unpacking, deconstructing and critiquing the ubiquitous mediatisation of sport and sports events.

One of the pre-eminent theorists of the sports-media relationship, David Rowe (2009: 548–549), argues that

> there is a clear potential for media sport texts to perpetuate and reinforce ideologies of domination already present within the social institution of sport, and also to reproduce, exacerbate and amplify them through the presentational routines of the media sport spectacle.

Analyses of media representations of sports events have revealed the prevalence of discourses related to gender, race, class, sexuality and nation, and the various ways in which "the content, focus and style of media sports reporting often reflects deep-rooted inequalities and reinforces negative stereotypes of marginal and under-represented groups" (Fletcher and Dashper, 2013). In this collection, Rebecca Finkel's Chapter 5 illustrates how, although media are complicit in the production and reproduction of inequalities through sport, media representations can also be instrumental in beginning to challenge deep-rooted prejudices and stereotypes. Finkel's analysis of media reporting on women's boxing at the 2012 Olympic Games shows how positive media reports played an important role in challenging long-held assumptions that women are physically weak and need to be protected from (masculine) violence, as manifest through boxing. Finkel argues that media reactions to women's boxing played an important role "in improving the collectively recognised legitimacy of women's boxing and providing an arena for the global consumption of women's violent sport" (p. 86). Although Finkel acknowledges these positive representations were still framed within a dominant masculinist framework in which women's sporting participation remains marginalised and under-represented (see Donnelly and Donnelly, 2013), she argues that media responses to women's boxing at the 2012 Games "set about an incremental shift in how the sport is viewed, and has, to some extent at least, altered (or challenged) the meanings associated with women's participation in combat sports" (p. 96).

To date, the focus of most sports media has tended to be western markets; however, these markets are now largely saturated and attention is turning to the Asia-Pacific region, which is seeing growing interest in and consumption of sports events and sports media (Horne, 2005; Rowe and Gilmour, 2010). In this collection, Donna Wong introduces the context of Singapore, a city-state that is establishing itself as Asia's global media city and sports hub. Wong traces the development of the relationship between media and sport in Singapore and considers the challenges facing the regulator of trying to balance commercial interests of pay-TV providers with the public interest to be able to view sports events at no, or minimal, cost. Within the context of Singapore, Wong argues that the government should "get involved in the defence, maintenance and extension of the rights of the cultural citizenship associated with broadcast sport, in recognition of the increased standing of sport events within public culture" (p. 112).

In Chapter 7, from Dağhan Irak, turns attention towards "new" forms of media that use the internet to enable (some) fan involvement in sports events mediatisation. McGillivray (2013: 1) argues that "the mass availability of everyday digital technologies democratises media making, changing the way events are conceived, planned, mediatised and reported". Indeed, participation in media production is now an everyday leisure activity. This has no doubt been made possible through the proliferation of social media and other technologies which allow social agents to "feed the sporting event discourse" (McGillivray, 2013: 5). Miah and Jones (2012) argue that new media technologies, including social media sites such as Twitter and Facebook, as well as blogs, empower the "unvoiced" to challenge dominant media representations of sporting events by, principally, providing coverage to unpopular and unsavoury event images, such as human rights violations and displacement. For Miah and Jones, these technologies provide a valuable opportunity to produce and promote important media messages that would otherwise have been marginalised by mainstream media sources, such as giving voice to women within sport (Antunovic and Hardin, 2013) and youth in conflict zones (Thorpe and Ahmed, 2013). However, although new media technologies may have the potential to democratise media messages about sports events, current research suggests that this potential is rarely realised, as even new media forms remain largely controlled and dominated by corporate powers and elites (Dart, 2009; Millington and Darnell, 2012). In this collection, Irak's chapter develops these themes through an analysis of the reaction of fan blog – Papazın Çayırı – to match-fixing allegations affecting Turkish football clubs, particularly Fenerbahçe. Irak argues that the blog "represented a discourse of politicised fandom" (p. 126), and gave fans an opportunity to voice their opinions and concerns about the match-fixing scandal affecting "their" football club, but that ultimately this "did not lead to a fans' democracy, and rather served the inner nation status quo" (p. 126). Although Irak argues that the Papazın Çayırı blog "lacked the revolutionary approach that would democratise the 'micro-nation'" (p. 126) of Fenerbahçe, he points to recent political developments in Turkey which suggest that a paradigm shift may be taking place in which football fans use social media to come together under the banner of sport to challenge hegemonic political values and thus "maintain open communication of resistance" (Norman, 2012: 16).

## Identities

As Dashper and Fletcher (2013) note in their own research exploring gender, sexuality and class in equestrian sport, and "race" and ethnicity in cricket, for example, sport is heavily implicated in the (re)production of inequalities, but it may also offer opportunities for challenge, and possibly transformation (Dashper, 2012a, 2012b; Fletcher, 2011; Fletcher and Spracklen, 2013). However, although that potential is there, the reality of achieving this is limited. As a number of the contributions to this book illustrate, the role of sport cannot be considered in isolation from wider social structures and discourses: sport is a representation of these social relations.

Sports events have frequently been associated with expressions of national identity (Porter and Smith, 2004). Sports events often act as a focus for nationalist sentiments, providing citizens with opportunities to come together in a visible, collective expression of "who we are", in opposition to an equally important, but denigrated "who we are not" (Vaczi, 2013; Whigham, 2013). Such expressions of collective identity and togetherness are relatively rare in modern societies, and so sports events can be powerful symbols of nationhood and unity in people's otherwise fragmented lives. Whilst such symbolic expressions of nationalism can sometimes spill over into xenophobia, intolerance and violence towards opposing fans (Millward, 2009), or can act as a catalyst for conflict regarding ideas of "nation" (O'Bonsawin, 2010), for citizens no longer resident in their home country the power of sports events to link with ideas of "home" and belonging may take on extra significance in the diaspora (Fletcher, 2012). In this volume Frances Harkin explores the importance of Gaelic sports for the Irish diaspora in London. Central to her argument in Chapter 8 is the relationship between "Irishness" and sport in London's Irish diaspora and the different meanings and roles attributed to the Gaelic Athletic Association (GAA) and its events by Irish emigrants and their descendants. She utilises Brah's (1996) conceptualisation of "diaspora space" to argue that participation in Gaelic sports can reflect different or hybrid identities amongst the Irish diaspora. Harkin's interviews with first and second generation Irish immigrants illustrate how

> the GAA has become a bridgehead connecting their place of origin with their destination, providing a sense of continuation to their life prior to emigrating. It has also become a cultural symbol for many London-born second- and third-generation Irish, with GAA sporting events providing a means to connect with their heritage and the homeland of their parents.
>
> (p. 142)

In Chapter 9, Harpreet Bains takes up these issues relating to the heightened importance of sport for diasporic communities in her consideration of kabbadi. Bains' research participants, as with those in Harkin's study, see their connections with a sports event (in this case kabbadi), as part of their ethnic identity and thus link sport with an idea of "home". However, Bains' research focuses on British South Asian women and it is their *non*-involvement in kabbadi that forms an important part of their identities as Punjabi women, in the diaspora in the UK. Unlike much existing research into gender and sport, for Bains, kabbadi "is an arena where patriarchal relations are negotiated and maintained but, unlike many other sporting spaces ... it is not a contested site for women where they struggle for representation" (p. 155). She critiques dominant conceptions of the non-participation of British South Asian women within sport that portray them as oppressed by both their religion and culture and argues that non-participation, rather than reflecting their marginalisation, signals that they have "some autonomy within the patriarchal relations that exist in their everyday realities" (p. 155).

Events such as the Olympic Games have generally been used to promote the identity(ies) of host cities and regions (Roche, 2008). Roche suggests that nations will often use events to mark a new stage in their development (discussed further below). For example, he suggests that the Sydney Olympics opening ceremony (2000) was an attempt to mark a new stage in Australia's national narrative by symbolising its commitment to challenging racism and promoting multiculturalism. Roche also suggests that, at times, events can be used to express identities and aspirations of stateless "nations", which exist within multinational states. He cites the Olympics in Montreal 1976 and Barcelona 1992 as examples, as local populations appropriated event spaces in an attempt to express their respective Quebec and Catalan sub-nationalist identities, in addition to the Canadian and Spanish national identities of the host nations.

This use of events to express sub-nationalist identities is articulated by Jim O'Brien in Chapter 10 where he examines the ways in which football clubs are implicated in political struggles about nationhood in the Basque country. O'Brien traces the rivalry between Athletic Bilbao and Real Sociedad, against the backdrop of wider Spanish history from Republic, through Civil War, Francoist centralism and transition to democracy. For O'Brien, the Basque derby illustrates how sporting events can "serve as metaphors for cultural and political values" (p. 160) and become "the site of alternative nationalism" (p. 165), in this case around the highly contested notion of "what it is to be 'Basque'" (p. 160). Football in Spain – and particularly within the Basque country and Catalonia – is a clear illustration of how sports events can become a focus for wider political tensions and disputes over nationhood (see also Vaczi, 2013). O'Brien argues that "[t]radition and local rivalry transcends both changes within football itself and the implications of globalisation and identity" (p. 171). In such ways, sports events can be seen as part of wider narratives about identity, nationhood, belonging and citizenship.

Much research to date on the links between sports events and identities has focused on mega sports events, such as the Olympic Games (e.g. Silver *et al.*, 2012), or regular, culturally prominent events such as football matches (e.g. Whigham, 2013). Smaller niche events can be equally significant in terms of regional and local identity. In Chapter 11, Andrew Bradley introduces the unusual and highly localised event of cheese rolling, practiced in Gloucestershire in the UK. Bradley argues that local events, like cheese rolling, are "an important part of how people relate to their local area, how local traditions are passed from one generation to the next, and how distinctiveness of an individual place is preserved" (p. 174). Through an analysis of comments submitted to the local newspaper website, Bradley considers how the local community responded when "their" event, with a long history stretching back centuries, was passed into the hands of an event management company who sought to alter, (re)organise and commercialise this local event. This is an example of what Rojek (2013: 152) calls "event appropriation", which, drawing on Thompson (1991), he describes as "the seizure of folk traditions and/or collective gatherings which were originated by the people in the name *of* 'the people'". Bradley's case study illustrates how local communities can feel aggrieved when "their" event is taken over by outside parties and (re)packaged and (re)created for commercial interests, which is seen as "a clear threat to local ownership and the event's connection to its locality and the local community's identities" (p. 181).

## Mega-events

Sporting mega-events, including the summer and winter Olympic and Paralympic Games, and the FIFA (Fédération Internationale de Football Association) Football World Cup (male), are the staple of the majority of sports events research. The characteristics of mega-events are well rehearsed and well critiqued. According to Roche's (2000: 1) commonly cited definition, mega-events are "large-scale cultural (including commercial and sporting) events, which have a dramatic character, mass popular appeal and international significance". For Roche (2008: 286), mega-events are short-term events, which have significant long-term pre- and post-event impacts on the host nation across a range of dimensions of national society, particularly cultural, but also political and economic. According to Hayes and Karamichas (2012: 2) mega-events are not simply sporting or cultural phenomena:

> They are also political and economic events, characterized by the generation and projection of symbolic meanings – most obviously over the nature of statehood, economic power and collective cultural identity – and by social conflict, especially over land use, and over the extent and contours of public spending commitments.

For Hayes and Karamichas (2012: 249), sports mega-events are worth researching because they are "peculiar, recurrent, time-space compressions where global norms and the ideological operations that sustain them are made visible and identifiable". Similarly, Horne (2012) writes that they are "important elements in the orientation of national to international and global society". Naturally, it is not only mega-events that are important. Whilst smaller-scale events are unable to make comparable levels of "impact" and may not, strictly speaking, lead to "legacies", they remain rooted in local, national and global ideologies pertaining to power and privilege and thus should not be overlooked in analyses.

The vast majority of sports mega-event research has focused on the concepts of "impact" and "legacy". It is not our intention to critique these concepts here – this has been done more than adequately by a number of scholars (see, for example, Preuss, 2007). It is generally accepted that event impacts and legacies can be both positive and negative. As discussed above, positive impacts and legacies are thought to include social and economic benefits to host communities, enhanced community identity and image, regeneration and place (re)development, increased community cohesion and well-being, and a heightened sense of national identity, whilst negative impacts and legacies are thought to include institutional corruption, labour exploitation and other human rights violations, displacement and marginalisation, gentrification and terrorism. It is not possible to interrogate the efficacy of these assumptions here. Instead we focus on the ideas of development, regeneration and (post-)westernisation as these are the focus of the chapters in this volume.

Debate is on-going as to what benefit(s) the staging or hosting of an international sporting event can actually bring to a country or a city, especially one in the "emerging" world. The general consensus is that hosting sports mega-events will bring about much needed social improvement, or regeneration, within the host city/country. Cornelissen (2012: 78), for example, argues that sporting events are increasingly "seen as opportunities to project or 'show-case' [a country's] achieved levels of modernity to the outside world", whilst Darnell (2012: 105) argues that, "sports mega-events … are used to showcase successful development, particularly for states struggling for legitimacy within competitive globalisation". This concept of development may also extend to nation-building (see Dowse's Chapter 13 in this volume).

However, whilst mega-events present opportunities for development, crucially, the ways in which rights to host are contested, how they are allocated and subsequently, how they are expected to be delivered, are judged according to western standards. For Hayes and Karamichas (2012: 6), such western-centrism raises the question of homogenisation and cultural standardisation, or "rather the projection of a western, liberal model of social relations on local host communities". This point is taken up by a number of contributors to this volume.

For example, in Chapter 12 which examines sports mega-events and Islam, Karl Russell, Noëlle O'Connor, Katherine Dashper and Thomas Fletcher begin to consider some of the issues and challenges associated with hosting sports mega-events in non-secular Islamic countries, an area they contend requires greater academic focus. This chapter is a timely introduction to some of the issues and complexities associated with hosting major international sports events outside of the traditional power block of the western world. They argue that due to the imperatives of global sport and the desire to attract new audiences and investors, there is a need to expand sporting events into hitherto uncharted territories. They suggest that "recent global changes, such as shifting economic power, have seen a trend towards many 'emerging' regions outside of the western world hosting, and/or actively seeking to host, international sporting events" (p. 189). In so doing, the previously assumed hegemony of the developed west over the developing east, has been called into question. They draw upon the concept of post-westernisation (Rumford, 2007) to articulate the possibility that the power of the west in defining the standards for hosting mega-sporting events may be shifting to (or at least, being challenged by) a "new East". For Russell *et al.* staging international sporting events in different social and cultural contexts, such as those offered by non-secular Islamic states, may expose conflicts between the Christian-based ethics and values that underpin the ethos of most sports events, and the Islamic values of host nations. They identify a number of contemporary issues – namely gender segregation, dress codes and female modesty, and dietary rules (including alcohol consumption) – which present particular challenges when international sporting events are hosted and staged within non-secular Islamic countries. They argue that these are effectively "non-issues" in the west, but require a certain amount of cultural sensitivity when events take place outside of western contexts.

There is a subtle tension here between the prerogatives of global sport and local identities, which needs to be extrapolated. For Palmer (2013: 114) the contemporary pattern of hosting sports mega-events in BRIC (Brazil, Russia, India, China) and developing countries poses a number of unique challenges; one of these relates to whether these countries can successfully stage a mega-event without falling foul to "First World perceptions that they may be punching above their weight". Palmer draws on evidence surrounding the 2010 Commonwealth Games held in New Delhi and the 2014 Football World Cup and 2016 Summer

Olympics, to be held in Rio de Janeiro. For Palmer, the perceived inadequacies of New Delhi's preparations "resulted in India, and by extension, other BRIC and developing nations, losing the symbolic capital that helps secure public confidence that they are as capable as cities in the Global North to host a first-order mega-event" (Palmer, 2013: 116). For many BRIC/developing nations however, it is not simply a matter of demonstrating they are "as good as" those nations/cities in the developed world. Palmer suggests that, increasingly, there is a perception that the main challenge facing these hosts is leveraging their new status as an economic power not only to match, but to *outdo* nations/cities from the Global North. Crucially, in their pursuit of this marker of their arrival, many over-spend, are unable to deliver facilities on time, and/or produce substandard outcomes.

Reflecting specifically on South Africa's experience of hosting the 2010 Football World Cup, in Chapter 13 Suzanne Dowse argues that this pattern is as much the responsibility of the governing body as it is the host nation/city. She suggests that, for events held in developing contexts, the terms and conditions imposed by sports governing bodies, FIFA included, are often unrealistic and unobtainable and, effectively, setting the hosts up to fail, or at least, fall short of external expectations. More broadly, Dowse stresses how, "as historically mega-events have predominantly been hosted by developed and industrialised economies, the existing body of research may be unsuitable for informing decision-making and discussions about hosting opportunities in developing contexts" (p. 205). Indeed, crucial to globalisation is the manner in which social relations become "disembedded" from their local constituents. Palmer (2013) argues that a central feature of global sports events policy is the westernisation of cultural mores and values in non-western host cities. The 2010 Football World Cup acts as a case in point. Dowse argues that throughout South Africa's journey to host the event, the imperative to satisfy FIFA's various contractual demands regarding financing and infrastructure, amongst many others, "all but ensured the subordination of national interests to those of the event" (pp. 209–210). The subordination of national interests to accommodate mega-event prerogatives is significant because the rhetoric surrounding sports mega-events is that the event will act as a catalyst for much needed social improvements. Given these potential conflicts of interest, Dowse advocates for research to more effectively examine an event's realistic potential for national and international development. She acknowledges that "national unity was not expected as a result of a single event. Consequently, the FWC had to be considered as part of a policy process, rather than an independently effective intervention" (p. 213). In viewing an event as part of a country's wider policy process, she argues there is evidence that mega-events can be utilised for domestic and foreign policy processes.

Similarly, in Chapter 14 on the London 2012 Olympics, Iain Lindsay critiques London's Olympic hosting ambition via a case study of the lived realities of people residing in Newham, one of London's four Olympic boroughs. According to Lindsay, Newham's Olympic legacy was often portrayed as a panacea to its economic, social and political issues. This revolved around the consideration that Olympic hosting would provide a regenerative juncture for a "better" Newham. Lindsay argues that the mediatised narrative of East London's metamorphosis from deprived post-industrial wasteland to utopian Olympic city was in stark contrast to the lived realities of local communities. He contends that "development" was an integral part of London 2012 from Olympic bid to beyond the Games, but a specific definition of what this would entail, and exactly who would benefit, was never fully realised. Lindsay problematises Newham's regenerative framework, suggesting that: (1) it was based upon an assumption that all shared the same opinion of what constituted a "better life"; (2) it assumed that all living in the area had the ability to take advantage of the opportunities presented. Therefore, according to Lindsay, the "reality" of London 2012 Olympic delivery was far from utopian. Rather than following a people-focused agenda of space development, the narrative instead resembled one of gentrification and reclamation. He argues that "during the post-Games period, less affluent and/or minority (multi)ethnic communities who bordered the space of the Olympic Park were likely to become subject to increased regulation, surveillance, policing techniques and displacement to ensure the area was suitable for the habitation of the future [more affluent] populace" (p. 225). Consequently, for Lindsay, it is imperative to look critically beyond the macro-perspective to truly evaluate the reality of Olympic and other mega-event hosting.

The concluding chapter in this collection picks up on many of the issues and complexities raised in these contributions and returns to our earlier critique of the state of play of (sports) events as an academic field. In so doing we acknowledge continuing gaps and persisting debates within the field, and make some suggestions for future research directions.

## Notes

1 See Karl Spracklen's (2012) special issue of the *Journal of Policy Research in Tourism, Leisure and Events* on the unintended consequences of the Olympic and Paralympic Games for further discussion.
2 Thomas and Bowdin (2012: 105) argue that such is the ambivalence regarding the academic credibility of the field of events "there is a disincentive to publish in event management journals as these are generally not rated highly by the various league tables". Accordingly, Thomas and Bowdin (2012) believe this restricts the field's development.

## References

Abercrombie, N. and Longhurst, B. (1998) *Audiences*. London: Sage.

Antunovic, D. and Hardin, M. (2013) Women and the blogosphere: Exploring feminist approaches to sport. *International Review for the Sociology of Sport*. DOI: 10.1177/1012690213493106.

Blain, N. (2002) Beyond "media culture": Sports as dispersed symbolic activity. *Sport in Society*, 5(3): 228–254.

Bourdieu, P. (1988) Program for a sociology of sport. *Sociology of Sport Journal,* 5(2): 153–161.

Boyle, R. and Haynes, R. (2009) *Power play: Sport, media and popular culture*. Second edition. Edinburgh: Edinburgh University Press.

Brah, A. (1996) *Cartographies of diaspora: Contesting identities.* London: Routledge.

Carrington, B. (2012) *Race, sport and politics: The sporting black diaspora.* London: Sage.

Castells, M. (1996) *The rise of the network society, volume I.* Massachusetts: Blackwell.

COHRE (2007) *Fair play and housing rights: Mega-events, Olympic Games and housing rights.* Geneva: The Centre on Housing Rights and Evictions.

Cornelissen, S. (2012) A delicate balance: Major sports events and development. In R. Levermore and A. Beacon (eds). *Sport and International Development.* Basingstoke: Palgrave Macmillan, 76–97.

Crawford, G. (2004) *Consuming sport.* London: Routledge.

Crawford, G. (2009) Consuming sport, consuming beer: Sport fans, scene and everyday life. In L.A. Wenner and S.J. Jackson (eds). *Sport, beer, and gender: Promotional culture and contemporary social life.* New York: Peter Lang Publishing, 279–298.

Darnell, S. (2012) *Sport for development and peace: A critical sociology.* London: Bloomsbury.

Dart, J. (2009) Blogging the 2006 FIFA World Cup Finals. *Sociology of Sport Journal*, 26: 107–126.

Dashper, K. (2012a) "Dressage is full of queens!" Masculinity and sexuality within equestrian sport. *Sociology*, 46(6): 1109–1124.

Dashper, K. (2012b) Together, yet still not equal? Sex integration in equestrian sport. *Asia-Pacific Journal of Health, Sport and Physical Education*, 3(3): 213–225.

Dashper, K. and Fletcher, T. (2013) Introduction: Diversity, equity and inclusion in sport and leisure. *Sport in Society*, 16(10): 1227–1232.

Dixon, K. (2013) The football fan and the pub: An enduring relationship. *International Review for the Sociology of Sport.* [Online first] DOI: 10.1177/1012690213501500.

Donnelly, P. and Donnelly, M. (2013) *The London 2012 Olympics: A gender equality audit.* Centre for Sport Policy Studies Research Report. Toronto: University of Toronto.

Fletcher, T. (2011) "Aye, but it were wasted on thee": "Yorkshireness", cricket, ethnic identities, and the "magical recovery of community". *Sociological Research Online.* 16(4): 5. Available from www.socresonline.org.uk/16/4/5.html.

Fletcher, T. (2012) "Who do 'they' cheer for?" Cricket, diaspora, hybridity and divided loyalties amongst British Asians. *International Review for the Sociology of Sport*, 47(5): 612–631.

Fletcher, T. and Dashper, K. (2013) "Bring on the dancing horses!": Ambivalent reporting of Dressage at London 2012. *Sociological Research Online.* 18(2): 17. Available from www.socresonline.org.uk/18/2/17.html.

Fletcher, T. and Spracklen, K. (2013) "Cricket, drinking and exclusion of British Muslims?" *Ethnic and Racial Studies.* DOI: 10.1080/01419870.2013.790983.

Frontline (2009) Human trafficking, sex work safety and the 2010 Games. [Online] Available from http://vancouver.ca/police/assets/pdf/reports-policies/report-human-trafficking-2010-games.pdf [accessed 20 December 2013].

Getz, D. (2007) *Event studies: Theory, research and policy for planned events.* Oxford: Elsevier.

Getz, D. (2009) Policy for sustainable and responsible festivals and events: Institutionalization of a new paradigm. *Journal of Policy Research in Tourism, Leisure and Events.* 1(1): 61–78.

Giulianotti, R. and Klauser, F. (2012) Sport mega-events and "terrorism": A critical analysis. *International review for the Sociology of Sport.* DOI: 0.1177/1012690211433454.

Gratton, C., Shibli, S. and Coleman, R. (2006) The economic impact of major sports events: A review of ten events in the UK. In J. Horne and W. Manzenreiter (eds). *Sports mega-events: Social scientific analyses of a global phenomenon.* Oxford: Blackwell, 41–58.

Hayes, G. and Karamichas, J. (eds) (2012) *Olympic Games, mega-events and civil societies: Globalization, environment and resistance.* Basingstoke: Palgrave.

Horne, J. (2005) Sport and the mass media in Japan. *Sociology of Sport Journal,* 22(4): 415–432.

Horne, J. (2007) The four 'knowns' of sports mega-events. *Leisure Studies,* 26(1): 81–96.

Horne, J. (2012) The four 'Cs' of sports mega-events: Capitalism, connection, citizenship and contradictions. In G. Hayes and J. Karamichas (eds). *Olympic Games, mega-events and civil societies: Globalization, environment and resistance.* Basingstoke: Palgrave, 31–45.

Horne, J. and Manzenreiter, W. (eds) (2006) *Sports mega-events: Social scientific analyses of a global phenomenon.* Oxford: Blackwell.

Jago, L. (2012) Endnote. In R. Shipway and A. Fyall (eds). *International sports events.* London: Routledge, 221–223.

Jennings, A. (2011) Investigating corruption in corporate sport: The IOC and FIFA. *International Review for the Sociology of Sport,* 46(4): 387–398.

Kellner, D. (2003) *Media spectacle.* New York: Routledge.

Lenskyj, H. (2008) *Olympic industry resistance: Challenging Olympic power and propaganda.* Albany: State University of New York Press.

Matheson, C. and Finkel, R. (2013) Sex trafficking and the Vancouver Winter Olympic Games: Perceptions and preventative measures. *Tourism Management.* 36: 612–628.

McGillivray, D. (2013) Digital cultures, acceleration and mega sporting event narratives. *Leisure Studies.* DOI: 10.1080/02614367.2013.841747.

Miah, A. and Jones, J. (2012) The Olympic movement's new media revolution: Monetization, open media and intellectual property. In S. Wagg and H. Lenskyj (eds). *Handbook of Olympic studies.* Basingstoke: Palgrave, 274–288.

Miller, T. (1999) Televisualisation. *Journal of Sport and Social Issues,* 23(2): 123–125.

Millington, R. and Darnell, S.C. (2012) Constructing and contesting the Olympics online: The internet, Rio 2016 and the politics of Brazilian development. *International Review for the Sociology of Sport.* DOI: 10.1177/1012690212455374.

Millward, P. (2009) Glasgow Rangers supporters in the city of Manchester: The degeneration of a "fan party" into a "hooligan riot". *International Review for the Sociology of Sport,* 44(4): 381–398.

Nauright, J. and Ramfjord, J. (2010) Who owns England's game? American professional sporting influences and foreign ownership in the Premier League. *Soccer and Society,* 11(4): 428–441.

Norman, S. (2012) Saturday night's alright for tweeting: Cultural citizenship, collective discussion and the new media consumption/production of *Hockey Day* in Canada. *Sociology of Sport Journal,* 29: 306–324.

O'Bonsawin, C.M. (2010). "No Olympics on stolen native land": Contesting Olympic narratives and asserting indigenous rights within the discourse of the 2010 Vancouver Games. *Sport in Society,* 13(1): 143–156.

Palmer, C. (2013) *Global sports policy.* London: Sage.

Porter, D. and Smith, A. (eds) (2004) *Sport and national identity in the post-war world.* London: Routledge.

Postman, N. (1993) *Technopoly: The surrender of culture to technology.* New York: Vintage Books.

Preuss, H. (2007) The conceptualisation and measurement of mega sport event legacies. *Journal of Sport and Tourism*, 12(3–4): 207–227.

Richards, G. and de Brito, M. (2013) Conclusions: The future of events as a social phenomenon. In G. Richards, M. de Brito and L. Wilks (eds) *Exploring the social impacts of events*. London: Routledge, 219–235.

Richards, G., de Brito, M. and Wilks, L. (eds) (2013) *Exploring the social impacts of events*. London: Routledge.

Roche, M. (2000) *Mega-events and modernity*. London: Routledge.

Roche, M. (2008) Putting the London 2012 Olympics into perspective: The challenge of understanding mega-events. *Twenty-First Century Society*, 3(3): 285–290.

Rojek, C. (2012) Global Event Management: A critique. *Leisure Studies*, DOI: 10.1080/02614367.2012.716077.

Rojek, C. (2013) *Event power: How global events manipulate and manage*. London: Sage.

Rowe, D. (2009) Media and sport: The cultural dynamics of global games. *Sociology Compass*, 3/4: 543–558.

Rowe, D. and Gilmour, C. (2010) Sport, media and consumption in Asia: A merchandised milieu. *American Behavioral Scientist*, 53(10): 1530–1548.

Rumford, C. (2007) More than a game: Globalization and the post-Westernization of world cricket. *Global Networks*, 7(2): 202–214.

Sharpley, R. and Stone, P. (2011) Socio-cultural impacts of events. In S. Page and J. Connell (eds). *Routledge Handbook of Events*. London: Routledge, 347–361.

Silver, J.J., Meletis, Z.A. and Vadi, P. (2012) Complex context: Aboriginal participation in hosting the Vancouver 2010 Winter Olympic and Paralympic Games. *Leisure Studies*, 31(3): 291–308.

Spracklen, K. (ed.) (2012) Special issue: The unintended policy consequences of the Olympics and Paralympics. *Journal of Policy Research in Tourism, Leisure and Events*, 4(2).

Sugden, J. and Tomlinson, A. (eds) (2012) *Watching the Olympics: Politics, power and representation*. London: Routledge.

Thomas, R. and Bowdin, G. (2012) Events management research: State of the art. *Event Management*, 16(2): 103–106.

Thompson, E.P. (1991) *Customs in common*. London: Penguin.

Thorpe, H. and Ahmed, N. (2013) Youth, action sports and political agency in the Middle East: Lessons from a grassroots parkour group in Gaza. *International Review for the Sociology of Sport*. DOI: 10.1177/1012690213490521.

Vaczi, M. (2013) "The Spanish fury": A political geography of soccer in Spain. *International Review for the Sociology of Sport*. [Online first] DOI: 10.1177/1012690213478940.

Watt, P. (2013) "It's not for us": Regeneration, the 2012 Olympics and the gentrification of East London. *City*, 17(1): 99–118.

Weed, M. (2007) The pub as a virtual football fandom venue: An alternative to "Being there?" *Soccer and Society*, 8(2/3): 399–414.

Wenner, L.A. (ed.) (1998) *MediaSport*. London: Routledge.

Whigham, S. (2013) "Anyone but England?" Exploring anti-English sentiment as part of Scottish national identity in sport. *International Review for the Sociology of Sport*. [Online first] DOI: 10.1177/1012690212454359.

Wilks, L. (2013) Introduction. In G. Richards, M. de Brito and L. Wilks (eds). *Exploring the social impacts of events*. London: Routledge, 1–11.

# Part I

# Inventing, packaging and consuming sport

# 1 Connecting events to advertising

## Narrative strategies and dirty logics in Super Bowl commercials

*Lawrence A. Wenner*

## Introduction

The primacy of the Super Bowl as a sporting, cultural and consumer event in the United States is hard to miss. The 2012 Super Bowl, seen on 75 per cent of television sets with over 111 million domestic viewers, was the highest rated broadcast in U.S. history. Super Bowl broadcasts have regularly garnered over 100 million U.S. viewers, with only one other television programme, 1983's *M\*A\*S\*H* finale, exceeding that threshold (Bauder, 2012). The popularity of the Super Bowl with marketers and consumers alike has conspired, at a rate of US\$3.8 million for 30 seconds (Jordan, 2013), to make its broadcast the most expensive advertising purchase in U.S. television.

The magnitude of 'Super Bowl Sunday' celebrations has seemingly put the day's activities on par with those marking Christmas, Thanksgiving and New Year's Day. The day's "communal rituals" (Turner, 1997: 62) have made it "the busiest pizza day of the year" (Bradbury, 2013: para. 2), and it trails only Thanksgiving in overall food consumption. The routinisation of gustatory and other party rituals has caused one broadcast commentator to characterise Super Bowl Sunday as "an unannounced American holiday" (as cited in Wenner, 1989: 166). But, with its two weeks of what Buell (1980) and others have called 'superhype' that includes six-plus hours of 'pre-game' programming (for a game Real (1975) notes has less than ten minutes of actual football action) and prime-time 'interactive countdown specials', such as CBS's 2013 *Super Bowl's Greatest Commercials* where the 'fan community' votes for 'their favorite Super Bowl commercial' (Haiken, 2013), the event has become a spectacle that is anything but 'unannounced'.

The integration of and the preoccupation with consumption, from food to beverage to the commercials themselves, has led many critics to question the legitimacy of making something so clearly manufactured into both a cultural and 'nationalised' high holy day. For example, Real (2013) suggests such 'colonisation' of the Super Bowl has made it archetypal of the blurring of commodity and spectacle in everyday life. As noted by Debord (2004[1967]: 29): "It is not just that the relationship to commodities is plain to see – commodities are now all that there is to see; the world we see is the world of the commodity".

Debord's concerns over labour in spectacle are also easily seen, both in sporting performance in the service of entertainment, but more tellingly in terms of the viewer's labour, with our attention being bought by advertisers. The Super Bowl is at once both 'spectacle squared' and 'spectacle divided'. Not only is the game event a spectacle fuelled by entertainment and advertising, but its stakes as a ritualised and critical 'media event' (Dayan and Katz, 1992) in marketing has created a 'game within the game' seen as the 'Super Bowl of Advertising'. Ironically, in keeping with Debord's concerns, more people (39 per cent) cite the commercials than the game itself (28 per cent) as their "favorite thing about the Super Bowl" (Garibian, 2013). The resultant 'commercial celebration' (McAllister, 1999) may be viewed as 'end stage spectacle' because the spectacle is not just a vehicle upon which commodification catches a ride, but rather a spectacle that is comprised of the commercials themselves.

Driven by such concerns, this chapter examines the workings of commercial colonisation in the context of the Super Bowl. More specifically, this study explores how the Super Bowl as a constructed cultural and nationalised sporting mega-event transacts with Super Bowl and/or football referential advertising in the game's broadcast.

## Approaching the Super Bowl event to commercial connection

Two theoretical strains – those of consumer culture theory and dirt theory – frame this inquiry. Taken together, their lenses provide critical tools to deconstruct the event-to-commercial dynamic featured in advertising narratives.

### *Consumer culture theory*

Given the increasing roles that advertising and promotional culture play in both sport spectacle and everyday sport events, consumer culture theory (CCT) seems a tailor-made lens to focus understanding of today's media-driven sport marketplace. In digesting 20 years of work defining the core disposition of CCT, Arnould and Thompson (2005: 868, 875) note that:

> CCT is not a unified, grand theory, nor does it aspire to such nomothetic claims. Rather, it refers to a family of theoretical perspectives that address the dynamic relationships between consumer actions, the marketplace, and cultural meanings.... Consumer culture theorists read popular culture texts (advertisements, television programs, films) as lifestyle and identity instructions that convey unadulterated marketplace ideologies (i.e., look like this, act like this, want these things, aspire to this kind of lifestyles) and idealized consumer types.... By decoding and deconstructing these mass-mediated marketplace ideologies, consumer culture theorists reveal the ways in which capitalist cultural production systems invite consumers to covet certain identity and lifestyle ideals.

Indeed, many (Crawford, 2004; Horne, 2006) argue that understanding the increasing 'hypercommodification' of sport demands using a consumer culture lens. Such scholars, driven by Bauman's (2007) observation that in an era of 'consumer sociality' we act within an obligatory 'market-mediated mode of life', pose that our identities relative to sport must necessarily be studied in the context of consumption. One context where the shaping of identities is particularly 'inescapable' is in sport-referential advertising. Here, advertisers rely on the construction of 'imagined communities' (Anderson, 1983) ripe with 'identity instructions' (Arnould and Thompson, 2005) to fashion a transference from sport to consumption. No theory is more appropriate to study the way sporting logics may be re-appropriated in advertising narratives than dirt theory.

### *Dirt theory*

Evolving over 20 years and over a dozen studies (see Wenner, 2013b) on sport and promotional culture, and increasingly seen in other quarters of media studies (see Wolkowitz, 2007; West, 2011), an emergent 'dirt theory of narrative ethics' (Wenner, 2007, 2009) has special resonance in interrogating the strategies, reading dynamics and ethical problematics of advertising.

Anchored in the work of anthropologist and linguist Mary Douglas (1966: 35), dirt is simply "matter out of place". While the connotation of Douglas' 'dirt' did not equate to inherent deviousness, it spoke of and to the omnipresent dangers in strategically importing meaning from one place, where it may belong, to another where it may be problematic or tainting. Advertisers and others who employ persuasive communication strategies do this routinely. Indeed, a foundational strategy in advertising (and a necessity in a way in all communication) is the effective use of familiar associations to help explain a new communication. The point is reinforced broadly in communication and cultural theory, from simple recognition of associative strategies (Waide, 1987) to Hall's (1980) processes of 'articulation' to McCracken's (1990) assessment of 'meaning transfer' and 'displacement'.

For Douglas (1966), dirt set in communication is essential in transcending boundaries. Developing the concept, Leach (1976) notes that power is located in dirt because dirt, through contagion, brings meaning and creates change as it crosses boundaries. By importing old logics to new stories, dirt employs 'cultural borrowing' (Wenner, 1991: 392) to bring familiar understandings, impose restraints and pollute meaning. Further, because the "power of dirt ascends with its cultural primacy" (Wenner, 1991: 392), the 'cultural leaks' of sport become more important when we consider sport-referential media narratives. Indeed, when we note 'sport's appeal' or claim sport provides a special setting for marketing products, we recognise the power of sport's dirt. Of course, in analysing sport-referential narratives, we need to assess communicative dirt stemming from much more than sport. Dirty meanings that are ported from old to new settings to manufacture strategic connections can be diverse. Depending on the focus of study, 'out of place' meanings about gender, race, family, class, community and consumption (amongst others) may be concerns of the narrative.

Uniquely fit for the critical interrogation of the Super Bowl event-to-commercial pathway focus of this study, dirt theory analysis foremost 'follows the dirt'. In assessing Super Bowl commercials that port select understandings of (1) the Super Bowl event, (2) football's place in culture and (3) the nature of our fanship and other identities in relation to the Super Bowl and football, one must consider how communicative meaning 'out of place' may fashion 'dirtied' sensibilities and influence reading and interpretation. Of dirt, we need to ask: what are its origins and character? Where does it land? How is importation negotiated? How do entailments shape meaning? As dirt moves, what distortions and fallacies are embraced or masked? Such concerns frame consideration of reading dynamics and how dirt transacts with characterisations of both readers and 'preferred' assertions about the Super Bowl and football, and the ethical propriety of those transactions.

## Deconstructing Super Bowl dirtied commercial narratives

Diverse products and services advertise during the Super Bowl. Most ads are for general circulation and do not feature Super Bowl or football specific references. This study focuses on ads deemed 'dirty' by their attempt to connect the event (and/or football) to that being sold to assess whether such strategies raise problematic issues. These ads come from a large universe of Super Bowl commercials catalogued at the two websites dedicated to their archiving: superbowl-ads.com and superbowl-commercials.org.[1] Here, an examination of all Super Bowl commercials archived since 2000 yielded nearly 100 commercials featuring substantive Super Bowl and/or football-referenced narratives. Three ad variants were categorised, based on the 'dirty connection' being emphasised: (1) Super Bowl hero dirt; (2) Super Bowl event dirt; and (3) Super Bowl commercial dirt. The analysis of illustrative examples within each category now follows.

## Super Bowl hero dirt

Narratives in this category rely on former star players who, while notable for heroic Super Bowl performances, also developed post-playing-days media personae as advertising pitchmen and/or broadcast commentators. While most of these hero-anchored narratives feature both White and Black former players, 'imagining' the star White quarterback is dominant. Not only were all featured quarterbacks White, but, with one exception, a Black defensive star–White offensive star casting schism was observed. Even noting the limited sample, that the universe of Super Bowl hero narratives may be driven by de facto segregated casting decisions – with Black heroes 'normed' for defensive prowess and White heroes 'normed' for offense prowess – is problematic, as it risks reinforcing long-held stereotypic attributes of 'smart' and 'strategic' White versus 'brutish' and 'reactive' Black athletes (Leonard and King, 2012). Throughout, the White and blond 'All-American boy' motif was seemingly unshakeable, with former Denver Bronco quarterback John Elway cast as a 'Superman' landing from space to 'save the day' for rattled Black players in NBC's 'Football Promo' for a network drama, with former Green Bay Packer quarterback Brett Favre parodied for the length of his heroic valorisation in Hyundai's '2020' MVP commercial, and a 'stain' on a sweatshirt with the likeness of former San Francisco 49er quarterback Joe Montana seen as a miracle 'stigmata' by a Black man in Tide's 'Miracle Stain' commercial.

The intricacies of such narratives may be seen in two extended examples. The first, 2013 Sketchers "Relaxed Fit" commercial, also features friendly serial product endorser, Joe Montana, in his fifties but still the archetypal blond 'All-American boy', valorised as 'The Comeback Kid', ambling down a city street handling a football as he directly addresses the reader: "Being an ex-quarterback I know the importance of staying cool and relaxed", to frame his pitch for a comfortable Sketchers' casual shoe. Mid-pitch, Montana's football is stripped away by a running young man who gleefully mocks Montana by name only to be blindsided by a bone-crunching hit from a sweatshirt-clad Black man who grabs back the football. We see the Black man, revealed as former Montana teammate and star defensive back Ronnie Lott, smile and casually say, "here you go Joe", as he tosses the football back to Montana. Montana, rather than thanking or even acknowledging Lott, looks directly into the camera as he shrugs with a smile to the reader, "Ronnie always has got my back", as the commercial segues to a close shot of the shoe and the announcer touts its virtues of comfort. Importantly, it is the White quarterback Montana who makes the dirtied connection with the reader. Only Montana is privileged to speak to the audience directly. Lott's role is to support and 'save' Montana and to return the ball, and symbolically 'the power' of being an unblemished commercial spokesman, to Montana. Thus, the dirt that is spread about in connecting the Super Bowl to this 'super shoe' is dependent on an intriguing narrative of 'comfort'. The narrative assumes that the reader is comfortable with the White quarterback's entitlements to speak directly to them and that his 'friendliness' will be well received. Further, the reading position assumes trust in Montana and his 'smarts' to make a case for the shoe's virtues. As well, there is assumed comfort with the Black player's supportive role, one that 'naturally' restores order by force and enables the White star to continue in his similarly 'natural' dominant role which, in this instance is not football leadership, but in making connections to the consumer. That the narrative also implies that it is natural for there to be no acknowledgement of the value of the Black man's services and that the Black man is not privileged to address the audience directly, is only icing on this dirty cake.

Second, this dynamic is echoed in 2012 through Bridgestone's tongue-in-cheek "Performance Football" commercial featuring two 'former greats': White quarterback Troy Aikman and Black defensive back Deon Sanders – both known for their Super Bowl exploits. At Bridgestone tyre's 'research center', a blonde woman reporter begins her interview with a lab-coat clad White male 'scientist' holding a football: "So this performance football is another way Bridgestone is bringing its tire technologies to the world of sports". As we see a football constructed of tyre treads, the scientist notes that Aikman and Sanders are helping to 'test out' their 'polymer technology', as we see lab technicians at computers monitoring action on a football practice field. Of Aikman, another archetypal blond 'All-American boy', the scientist effuses, "Troy seems to like the control", as Aikman is seen gleeful of the zigzag trajectory of the polymer football. The next shot features Sanders who, after observing this, angrily charges one of the technicians with arms in the air exclaiming, "Hey, that ain't right, man" while the narrating scientist comparatively notes "Deon not so much". As Sanders reacts further he is mocked by a White male technician absurdly riding an 'air horse' while taunting Sanders, "Giddy-up now Deon", with an implication that Sanders needs to physically rise to the challenge of the new technology that Aikman is keen on. Playing to that, the coda features narration over the brand's logo that exhorts, "at Bridgestone, our passion knows no bounds", presumably in contrast to Sanders' objections. While this narrative is clearly farce, there is an explicit use of Super Bowl heroes to endorse the level of testing given to Bridgestone products. Yet even in farce, the reader confronts 'naturalised' assertions that facilitate this connection: (1) the White male scientist as authority; (2) the White athlete as smart in quickly adapting to the new technology; (3) the Black athlete as not 'smart enough' to adapt; and (4) that the Black athlete needs to 'work harder' to adapt. Thus, in fashioning its 'dirty connection' between Super Bowl heroes and their product, Bridgestone relies on 'dirtied' racial stereotypes, while the farce likely tempers reader resistance.

## Super Bowl event dirt

While commercials featuring Super Bowl 'event dirt' are varied, all speak to the cultural importance of the Super Bowl as a cultural high holy day. Here, the meaning of going to a game and understandings of what the game connotes are key thematic features. Still, there are tensions in some of the dirty understandings relied upon in fashioning narratives that connect the Super Bowl event-to-commercial.

The lengths to which 'characterised' fans as textual surrogates will go to get Super Bowl tickets is told in 2013's Bud Light "Journey" commercial, featuring singer Stevie Wonder playing the role of a Louisiana Voodoo 'priest' ('Louisiana Voodoo', 2013). The spot opens with a 20-something White man (as textual surrogate) reverently entering the New Orleans Superdome where the Super Bowl will be played. In what we find out is a ritual gathering for the 'priest' to implement a 'spell', the man clandestinely gathers a player's sweat sock, another player's hair brush (with strands of hair) and a handful of grass from the football field. To music connoting a caper, he disappears into the dark and enters an old cemetery. Here he is congratulated on his 'heist' by a beautiful female accomplice having a Bud Light at a festive Super Bowl party at the graveyard. The man continues through Mardi Gras-style partying in the New Orleans streets until he arrives at a bar, where the bartender greets him with a Bud Light and nods him knowingly into a hidden back room. Entering through a mysterious hallway lit with a myriad of candles, he creaks open a door to find the 'priest' on a throne. The 'priest' is revealed as Wonder, whose portrayal here appears to be 'modelled' (Shahzad, 2013) after Baron Samedi, head of the Guédé family of Loa of Haitian Voodoo and known for the practice of 'black magic' (see Baron Samedi, 2013). Wonder is wearing dark sunglasses and dressed in a religiously regal white tuxedo with tails and top hat. We see Wonder's fingers begin to snap as the volume on his funkadelic hit 'Superstition' comes up. Wonder queries, "You ready for a little Mojo?" to the White man, who puts down his ritual gatherings. Wonder promptly ignites the gatherings and the Voodoo spirits magically transport the White man to mid-field seats at the start of the 2013 Super Bowl. As he awkwardly holds up the Voodoo doll that got him there, he looks quizzically at another young White man in the seat beside him who holds his own doll as proof of a similar voyage. Superimposed titles commenting, "It's Only Weird If It Doesn't Work" frame the two men, followed by Wonder, as 'priest', laughing at what he has done, and closing with a close-up of two bottles of opened Bud Light and an announcer's summation: "For fans who do whatever it takes. Here we go".

The dirty connections here are complex. Foremost, this is an ad that builds from event-to-commercial by relying on themes associated with the New Orleans setting of the Super Bowl. The narrative builds too on it being a given that attending a Super Bowl is a young man's dream. Indeed, at the 'mecca' of the stadium, the 'holy' nature of the event comes into play, with the White man gathering 'sacraments' and then bringing them to Wonder as Voodoo priest. While the White man is cast as a familiar slacker and loser (Messner and Montez de Oca, 2005), so too is Wonder's casting as a Black man blessed with 'magical' abilities that come with the luck of being born rather than earned. The reader's position is characterised as comfortable in receiving both. Further, the reader's interrogation of the grand stereotyping of 'Black Voodoo' is likely blunted by the pleasurable surprise of the familiar Stevie Wonder and his 'Superstition': both highly valued cultural artifacts that mesh nicely with this narrative positioning of the worth of the Super Bowl.

Another strain in the Super Bowl 'event dirt' genre connects understandings about 'cultural moments' marked by the Super Bowl to the situation of their products. A prime example of this is the 'halftime' analogy in Chrysler's 2012 "It's Halftime in America" commercial, featuring movie star and rugged hero icon, Clint Eastwood. With Super Bowl 2012 30-second commercial prices set at US$3.5 million, this two-minute ad was notable for both cost and duration (ESPN, 2012). The ad opens with a silhouetted Eastwood walking down a shadowy urban street, stating an immediate event-to-commercial connection: "It's halftime. Both the teams are in their locker rooms discussing what they can do to win this game in the second half". Over a montage of everyday Americans in despair or preparing for work in modest homes, Eastwood makes the secondary connection: "It's halftime in America too. People are out of work and they're hurting. And they're all wondering what they're going to do to make a comeback. And we're all scared because this isn't a game". Transitioning to Chrysler's story, Eastwood notes, "The people of Detroit know a little something about this; they almost lost everything", as we see decayed streets and antiquated factories over somber music. The tide turns as the middle of Eastwood's narrative focuses on the 'American spirit' with themes of 'pulling together' and 'fighting again' over visuals of determined solidarity. Building on an 'imagined' American 'never say die' spirit, Eastwood's casting, as 'coach' of America's 'team' down at the half, has him giving a pep talk reliant on game analogies: "All that matters now is what's ahead. How do we come from behind? How do we come together? And how do we win?" Eastwood's answer that "it can be done" is seen in Chrysler's 'new' cars. Eastwood closes by growling: "The world's going to hear the roar of our (American) engines. Yeah, it's halftime America, and the second half is about to begin". With a somber music fade, titling with the "Imported From Detroit" tagline, the ad closes with a reveal of the Chrysler brand logos.

Chrysler took some considerable risks with this ad. It knew that one team would likely be 'down at the half', but not what the offset, if any, would be. It took a risk too with a 'downer' ad reminding the intended viewer of economic hard times. Yet, in very explicit ways, this ad is a 'direct connect' to the game, shown at halftime and building on its logic that the game is never over for those with will. It draws on the Super Bowl as a big game to point to another that 'isn't a game'. While it is difficult to judge the success of Chrysler's tactics, the dirty usages are clear enough. Assumed is that the 'imagined viewer' will shift gears from the 'celebration' of the Super Bowl to the 'realities' of gutting out hard times in America's present real challenges. Still, the posed leap does not raise overt ethical improprieties as the core values reified 'pulling together' and a 'determined spirit' are hard to fault. Yet the ad is of two minds concerning its key analogy. On the one hand, it provides a reminder that one's economic life 'isn't a game', but in the end life's goals are posed in sporting terms: 'How do we win?'

## Super Bowl commercial dirt

The final category of Super Bowl dirtied commercials draws on 'dirt', not from the game as an event, but rather cultural recognition of the alternative 'Super Bowl of Advertising' being played. These ads are self-reflexive in their awareness of the Super Bowl as 'commercial celebration' and seated in cultural knowledge of what Super Bowl commercials have been and should be.

One way to speak to what Super Bowl commercials *should be* is to speak to what they *should not be*. This tactic drove LifeMinders' 2000 "Worst commercial on the Super Bowl" ad. By calling attention to itself as intentionally inept in meeting the Super Bowl commercial standard, this narrative led to the most profitable month for the LifeMinders.com website (Woods, 2000). The commercial opens on a cheap looking title graphic pronouncing "This is the worst commercial on the Super Bowl". That the titling looks to have been produced with a worn ribbon on a manual typewriter and is accompanied by an impossibly awful piano rendition of 'Chopsticks' provides reinforcement. Still, later title cards 'introduce' LifeMinders.com by explaining: "We send highly personalised e-mails on topics you ask for free". Additional title cards promise "no junk", that they are "information experts (geeks)" and claim "over 7.5 million members". Before closing on a final title card, with the site's web address, comes the self-reflexively obvious, and presumably funny, title card: "But we don't know diddley about making ads". Imported here as 'dirt' is the general cultural knowledge that Super Bowl ads are very expensive to buy and generally produced on big budgets with an eye on making a splash. By going against this grain, LifeMinders.com 'characterises' that the reader knows this and will appreciate the irony of turning this logic upside down. At the very least, it is known that this will be noticed. That the spot did more than this is confirmed by the ad's producer, who observed that the impact of this commercial was that it 'crashed' the servers with all the additional web traffic (LaMonica, 2011).

While it is unusual to aim to be the 'worst' Super Bowl commercial, much effort goes into being recognised as one of the 'best'. This has accelerated (1) as purchase prices have skyrocketed, (2) with the institutionalisation of special programming such as CBS's 2013 *Super Bowl's Greatest Commercials* and (3) because popular Super Bowl ads will gain additional eyeballs and increased shelf life via the Internet. There is wide recognition (and critique) that the 'keys' to 'Adbowl' success have resulted in a 'stupidity sweepstakes', with reliance on 'frat-boy' humour, sexy women and cute animals (Elliott, 2004). In self-reflexive ironic comment on this formula, FedeEx's 2005 "Finish on Top" commercial considers what advertisers must do to win the Adbowl. Featuring actor Burt Reynolds as 'Dancing Burt' in humorous pairing with a dancing bear, the spot was introduced by an onscreen FedEx spokesman saying "FedEx is determined to have the best commercial in the Super Bowl". Speaking directly to the viewer, with the implication that the characterised viewer at home has good knowledge of Super Bowl commercials (thus bringing Super Bowl commercial dirt to the reading), he goes on to explain that, after studying recent commercials, they "believe there are 10 items needed to finish on top" of the ad derby. In the spot, the following items are seen at the bottom of the screen throughout the vignette: (1) celebrity; (2) animal; (3) dancing animal; (4) cute kid; (5) groin kick; (6) talking animal; (7) attractive females; (8) product message (optional); (9) famous pop song; and (10) bonus ending. All the while we see Reynolds hamming it up with a dancing and talking grizzly bear who, although he kicks Reynolds in the groin, apologises for it and closes the spot in the 'bonus ending' by saying: "I loved you in 'Smokey and the Bandit'". Along the way, a cute kid and two sexy football cheerleaders comment on the bear's talking and dancing, and Reynolds sneaks in the 'optional' product message about FedEx's services as the company's logo is seen over a familiar song.

In total, the spot is an exercise in the Super Bowl viewer's own self-reflexivity; it calls on intertextual knowledge and gains power from cultural dirt about the Super Bowl's ad climate. While the spot speaks directly to that cultural knowledge, the fact that it relies on a reminder of how silly and formulaic successful appeals can be raises questions about its success. One ad industry insider dismissed the ad's strategy by saying, "I don't think people like to be reminded how vulnerable we are to advertising" (Warchol, 2005: E1). Indeed, audience self-reflexivity – here embracing not only knowledge and appreciation of such pandering strategies, but recognition of complicity with them – is central to understanding the ad. Ironically, that the FedEx ad featured the seeming redundancy of animals, talking animals and dancing animals, signals an implicit assumption of the reader's willingness to be co-opted through such strategies.

Self-reflexivity is at play in other commercials that pay homage to, repurpose and remake 'classic' Super Bowl ads. Motorola's 2011 "Empower the People" Xoom tablet ad jabbed at Apple's iPad by referencing knowledge of that company's iconic '1984' commercial which was famously shown only once. Other self-reflexive efforts, such as Coke Zero's 2009's "Mean Troy" commercial adopt the *modus operandi* of Hollywood by 'remaking' the 1980 Coca-Cola "Mean Joe Greene" ad. Worthy of note is that both the 'original' and the 'remake' provide further evidence for a casting schism drawn on racial lines as seen in Super Bowl hero dirt commercials. Here, the two Super Bowl heroes, Black defensive tackle Joe Greene featured in the original and strong safety Troy Polamalu, of Samoan descent, seen in the remake, were both all-pro defensive stars for the Pittsburgh Steelers. Thus, the 'dirt' used here has a lineage. The popular original, often referred to by its catchphrase, "Hey Kid, Catch!" was a Clio award winner, expanded into a TV movie, and still tops lists of 'best' Super Bowl commercials ('Hey Kid, Catch', 2013). In it, a young White boy follows an injured Greene, who is limping down a field tunnel to the locker room. The boy timidly asks an initially impatient 'Mr. Greene' whether he needs help. The boy persists, gathering nerve, to tell Greene "I think you're the best ever". Greene disgustedly shrugs "Yeah, sure" to the compliment. Undeterred, the boy thrusts a bottle towards Greene, asking "Want my Coke?" After declining out of courtesy, Greene relents, guzzling the Coke and smiling as a Motown version of the brand's musical tagline "Have a Coke and smile, make me feel good" sets the mood. Realising that he has ignored the boy for his pleasures, Greene hails the disappointed departing boy. Saying, "Hey Kid, Catch!" Greene tosses his game jersey to the 'wowed' boy. All are smiling at the end.

The remake for Coke Zero mirrors the original, with a young White boy following a limping Polamalu and asking whether he needs help, offering his Coke Zero and eventually extending the bottle to the player. At the point where Coca Cola's old 'smile' music theme comes up, two men appear, stopping the theme music and interrupting the boy's hand-off of the bottle. One explains, "We're Coke's brand managers", while the other grabs the bottle and angrily asserts: "Coke Zero's stole our taste, they are NOT stealing our commercial". As the brand managers attempt to escape with the bottle, Polamalu charges down the tunnel, tackling one, and grabbing the boy's Coke Zero bottle and drinks it. The 'dirty' twist ending has Polamalu ripping off the downed brand manager's shirt, and with his, "Hey Kid, Catch!" line, tossing it to the boy. The fairly faithful importation of 'Mean Joe Greene' to 'Mean Troy' likely gains a toehold with readers for being a 'dirt-squared' strategy. It offers a cultural mechanism for older or more savvy readers who bring understandings of 'Mean Joe Greene' to contextualise this for newer readers. Here the circuit of commodification not only relies on a long shelf life and the cultural memory of individual audience members, but 'strategic cultural lingering' that has been manufactured by endless lists and special programming focused on 'all-time great' Super Bowl commercials. To retain the 'aura' of authenticity, much dirt from the original remains intact. Imported into both narratives are cultural understandings of the sports hero and the importance that they 'naturally' play in the lives of young boys. These remain necessarily unquestioned in the constructed reading position. What significantly changes in the remake is a self-reflexive nod to the competitive commercialism that now surrounds both the Super Bowl and everyday life. That the notion of 'brand managers' could be broadly understood, be read reliably, and with context to their dispositions and tendencies, is a mark of how dirty understandings of commodification have infiltrated basic commercial narratives. More intriguing is that Coke Zero uses those dirty understandings to demonise its own brand managers in the course of advancing the brands' commodification. So at once, they are the 'bad guys' in commodification, but they are also the 'good guys' in that the tale they tell brings a 'Hollywood ending' to the narrative they have constructed in service of their brand.

## Conclusions

The analyses here tell us much about how understandings of a sporting event, in this instance, the Super Bowl, may be selectively ported to commercial narratives that seek to fashion an event-to-advertising connection and reap the rewards of mutual benefice from this. Using tactics from consumer culture theory and a dirt theory of narrative ethics to deconstruct and interrogate Super Bowl dirtied narratives, this chapter has focused on the 'Super Bowl *of* Advertising' to deconstruct the more narrow use of the 'Super Bowl *in* Advertising' to understand the event-to-advertising pathway through sport. As such, it provides distinct case examples of how Bauman's (2007) notion of 'consumer sociality' is 'imagined' in narratives that both *feature* and are *featured in* the Super Bowl, America's most important sporting and television spectacle. In examining how consumer 'identity instructions' were shaped in this context, three narrative variants, based on the nature of the 'dirty connection' that was emphasised, were found: (1) Super Bowl hero dirt; (2) Super Bowl event dirt; and (3) Super Bowl commercial dirt. Therefore, while the range of products seeking to tell their story, to 'seal their sell', in combination with another inferred by the Super Bowl is considerable, the 'dirty connections' seen in the three categories relied more on 'old saws' than new ideas.

Here, the Super Bowl hero dirt category was glaring in its casting segregation that, almost without exception, lined up White offensive players on one side and Black defensive players on the other. In servicing a 'comfortable' reading position, the Black man's portrayal does not come off well. Collectively, the Black man is not allowed to speak directly to the viewer, typed for aggressive physical skills, prone to anger, mocked, shown to be the fool, 'naturally' shown in service to the White quarterback, and looks to the White quarterback to 'save the day'. In contrast, the seeming perpetual line-up of archetypal White blond 'All-American boy' quarterbacks are cheerful and friendly, speak comfortably and directly to 'imagined' readers, are quick to adapt to change, and maintain calm when they are, as expected, called upon for heroic action. Indeed, the character-ised reader's position assumes the 'inevitability' of this, and the stereotype's power is such that it can be seen, even in jest, as 'holy' and worthy of being worshipped by Blacks and Whites alike. The 'dirty' central tendencies here are hard to miss. What is disappointing is that the dirty importations that are relied upon in fashioning this genre of event-to-advertising connection are seemingly universal and unwavering. Not one example of the Super Bowl sport hero genre commercial could be found that was not reliant on the stereotype of the arche-typal White blond 'All-American boy' quarterback. In this day and age, such dirty constancy seems to make this type of Super Bowl referenced narrative par-ticularly retrograde.

In comparison, the 'dirty logics' that are imported into Super Bowl event dirt commercials are more benign. Still, the dirt that infuses 'imaginings' of 'con-sumer sociality' in relation to the Super Bowl relies on some old saws. Here are Stevie Wonder's 'Voodoo priest' and Clint Eastwood's 'coach' inspiring an America 'losing the game' at halftime. Both rely on dirty importations in their attempt to 'seal their sell' in the Super Bowl. Wonder's characterisation brings dirty associations with 'Black Voodoo' and wizards to the fore. Black 'power' is linked to 'magic' as Wonder's characterisation reinforces the notion that Black men's 'special' abilities stem from birth rather than hard work. Eastwood's 'coach' also speaks to the notion of work and, in this regard, invokes Debord's (2004[1967]) observations about labour in the service of spectacle. The reader for Eastwood's 'pep talk' is not only engaged in labour by virtue of consuming this narrative, but, by virtue of the characterisation that has been put forward, has been recruited as labour on Eastwood's team. At least two 'teams' that East-wood 'imagines' are put into play. One is a team of consumers, for which East-wood would like us to join the 'home' (that is American) team by buying Chrysler products. The second 'team' that Eastwood recruits us for is a team of workers, on which Eastwood would like us to 'pull together' by working harder and smarter, and although it is not mentioned, certainly 'cheaper' as the point made here is 'to win'. The essential 'dirtiness' in all this comes from a common conflation from nation and patriotism to corporation, and their priorities with consumption and production on terms that suit them best. Here, Eastwood ports dirty logics about an 'imagined' American spirit and patriotic pride in this to what is best for Chrysler which, of course, now is largely owned by Italy's Fiat.

Finally, the last category of ads featuring Super Bowl commercial dirt speaks to Debord's (2004[1967]) observation about the 'colonisation' of commodities necessarily becoming a key feature of spectacle. Indeed, the evidence that points clearly to the existence of a genre of advertising narratives that is so boldly self-referential and self-reflexive is perhaps the most compelling finding of this chapter. That the 'event-to-advertising' connection that was the object of study here has managed to double back on itself, such that advertising *in* the event has become such a constituent feature *of* the event that it has become a key feature in advertising, is a sobering realisation. It is hard to imagine a 'dirtier' state of affairs. Reified by this are Bauman's (2007) observation that we are now in an age of 'consumer sociality' driven by a 'market-mediated mode of life' and Debord's (2004[1967]: 29) realisation that "commodities are now all that there is to see". Indeed, the cultural frame of reference is such that standards for Super Bowl commercials are so well understood that narratives parodying 'how to' and 'how not to' do them are themselves embraced as part of a larger 'commercial celebration'. Finally, mirroring a longstanding Hollywood tendency, we have reached a point where 'classic original' Super Bowl commercials are culturally important enough to be 'remade', seemingly robbing from the past to be celebrated afresh in portraying the future.

In sum, the findings here suggest the contours of the 'game within the game' of the Super Bowl, known as the 'Adbowl', may be changing in ways that consumer culture theorists need take stock of. Certainly a select study such as this can only provide a small snapshot of the central tendencies at play in connecting sporting events to advertising. Still, the lessons here add to a growing body of work (see Wenner, 2013a) that examine commodified narratives that invoke sport. If we are to understand the cultural shadow of how sport and its logics permeate culture, an essential part of that agenda will have to be focused on how sport is re-appropriated in other settings. Understanding how select stories of sport may feature in the 'story of advertising' may be most important in this agenda. As Gerbner (cited in Morgan, 2002) was fond of saying, those people who tell most of the stories most of the time control a culture. Certainly, in today's increasingly 'hypercommodified' world, advertising tells most of the stories.

## Note

1 Rather than listing a unique URL reference for each commercial analysed, readers may access these commercials by year at either http://superbowl-ads.com/article_archive/ or www.superbowl-commercials.org/. They are also widely available by year, title, and subject at www.youtube.com/.

## References

Anderson, B. (1983) *Imagined communities*. London: Verso.

Arnould, E.J. and Thompson, C.J. (2005) Consumer culture theory (CCT): Twenty years of research. *Journal of Consumer Research*, 31: 868–882.

Baron Samedi (2013) *Baron Samedi* [online] Available from http://en.wikipedia.org/wiki/Baron_Samedi [accessed 11 November 2013].

Bauder, D. (2012) Super Bowl ratings record: Giants-Patriots game is highest-rated TV show in US history. *The Huffington Post* [online] Available from www.huffingtonpost.com/2012/02/06/super-bowl-ratings-record-tv-giants-patriots_n_1258107.html [accessed 6 February 2012].

Bauman, Z. (2007) *Consuming life.* Cambridge: Polity.

Bradbury, S. (2013) Pigskin pig out: Super Bowl Sunday second-biggest food day (behind Thanksgiving). *Timesfreepress.com* [online] Available from www.timesfreepress.com/news/2013/feb/02/pigskin-pig-out-Super-Bowl-Sunday-second-biggest [accessed 2 February 2013].

Buell, J. (1980) Superhype. *Progressive,* 44: 66.

Crawford, G. (2004) *Consuming sport: Fans, sport, and culture.* London: Routledge.

Dayan, D. and Katz, E. (1992) *Media events: The live broadcasting of history.* Cambridge, MA: Harvard University Press.

Debord, G. (2004[1967]) *The society of the spectacle* (translated into English by D. Nicholson-Smith). New York, NY: Zone Books.

Douglas, M. (1966) *Purity and danger: An analysis of the concepts of pollution and taboo.* London: Routledge.

Elliott, S. (2004) Class and taste take a beating as the Adbowl dissolves into the "stupidity sweepstakes". *New York Times* [online] Available from www.nytimes.com/2004/02/03/business/media-business-advertising-class-taste-take-beating-adbowl-dissolves-into.html [accessed 3 February 2013].

ESPN (2012) Super Bowl ads cost average of $3.5M. *ESPN NFL* [online] Available from http://espn.go.com/nfl/playoffs/2011/story/_/id/7544243/super-bowl-2012-commercials-cost-average-35m [accessed 4 November 2013].

Garibian, L. (2013) Super Bowl ads more popular than game action. *Marketing Profs* [online] Available from www.marketingprofs.com/charts/2013/9990/super-bowl-ads-more-popular-than-game-action [accessed 3 February 2013].

Haiken, B. (2013) "Super Bowl's Greatest Commercials 2013": An interactive countdown special hosted by Boomer Esiason and Aisha Tyler. *CBS Press Express* [online] Available from www.timesfreepress.com/news/2013/feb/02/pigskin-pig-out-Super-Bowl-Sunday-second-biggest [accessed 30 January 2013].

Hall, S. (1980) Race, articulation and societies structured in dominance. In UNESCO (ed.) *Sociological theories: Race and colonialism.* Paris, France: UNESCO: 305–345.

Hey kid, catch! (2013) *Hey kid, catch!* [online] Available from http://en.wikipedia.org/wiki/Hey_Kid,_Catch! [accessed 4 November 2013].

Horne, J. (2006) *Sport in consumer culture.* New York: Palgrave Macmillan.

Jordan, M. (2013) *Super Bowl ad prices rise: Worth the cost?* [online] Available from www.cbsnews.com/8301–500395_162–57566873/super-bowl-ad-prices-rise-worth-the-cost [accessed 4 November 2013].

LaMonica, M. (2011) *Super Bowl commercial for Lifeminders.com* [online] Available from www.youtube.com/watch?v=JEeYF3Pqils [accessed 3 February 2013].

Leach, E. (1976) *Culture and communication.* Cambridge, UK: Cambridge University Press.

Leonard, D.J. and King, C.R (eds) (2012) *Commodified and criminalized: New racism and African Americans in contemporary sports.* Lantham, MD: Rowman & Littlefield.

Louisiana Voodoo (2013) *Louisiana Voodoo* [online] Available from http://en.wikipedia.org/wiki/Louisiana_Voodoo [accessed 4 November 2013].

McAllister, M.P. (1999) Super Bowl advertising as commercial celebration. *The Communication Review.* 3: 403–428.

McCracken, G. (1990) *Culture and consumption.* Bloomington, IN: Indiana University Press.

Messner, M.A and Montez de Oca, J. (2005) The male consumer as loser: Beer and liquor ads in mega sports media events. *Signs,* 30: 1879–1909.

Morgan, M. (ed.) (2002) *Against the mainstream: The selected works of George Gerber.* New York: Peter Lang.

Real, M. (1975) Super Bowl: Mythic spectacle. *Journal of Communication.* 25: 31–43.

Real, M. (2013) Reflections on communication and sport: On spectacle and mega-events. *Communication and Sport,* 1: 30–42.

Shahzad, S. (2013) *Bud Light recruits Stevie Wonder for 2013 Super Bowl commercial* [online] Available from http://thefw.com/bud-light-stevie-wonder-2013-super-bowl-commercial [accessed 3 February 2013].

Turner, R. (1997) The ad game. *Newsweek:* 62–63.

Waide, J. (1987) Making of self and world in advertising. *Journal of Business Ethics,* 6: 73–79.

Warchol, G. (2005) This year's Super Bowl commercials rated 'D' for dull. *Salt Lake Tribune:* E1.

Wenner, L.A. (1989) The Super Bowl pregame show: Cultural fantasies and political subtext. In L.A. Wenner (ed.) *Media, sports, and society.* Newbury Park, CA: Sage: 157–179.

Wenner, L.A. (1991) One part alcohol, one part sport, one part dirt, stir gently: Beer commercials and television sports. In L.R. Van de Berg and L.A. Wenner (eds) *Television criticism: Approaches and applications.* New York: Longman: 388–407.

Wenner, L.A. (2007) Towards a dirty theory of narrative ethics: Prolegomenon on media, sport and commodity value. *International Journal of Media and Cultural Politics,* 3: 111–129.

Wenner, L.A. (2009) The unbearable dirtiness of being: On the commodification of mediasport and the need for ethical criticism. *Journal of Sports Media,* 4(1): 85–94.

Wenner, L.A. (2013a) The mediasport interpellation: Gender, fanship, and consumer culture. *Sociology of Sport Journal,* 30: 83–103.

Wenner, L.A. (2013b) Reflections on communication and sport: On reading sport and narrative ethics. *Communication and Sport,* 1: 188–199.

West, A. (2011) Reality television and the power of dirt: Metaphor and matter. *Screen.* 52: 63–77.

Wolkowitz, C. (2007) Linguistic leakiness or really dirty? Dirt in social theory. In B. Campkin and R. Cox (eds) *Dirt: New geographies of cleanliness and contamination,* London: B. Tauris: 15–24.

Woods, B. (2000) "Worst" commercial makes best month for LifeMinders.com. *Cyber Security and Information Systems Information Analysis Center* [online] Available from https://sw.thecsiac.com/techs/abstract/328638#.UZ06EYKs0eM [accessed 1 February 2013].

# 2 Football fandom in late modernity

## Alternative spaces and places of consumption[1]

*Mark Turner*

## Introduction

This chapter explores the way(s) in which modern English football is currently invented and packaged as a technologised media spectacle, and how this spectacle is consumed by fans present at the event itself and those watching it via alternative media platforms, such as television and the internet. As a result the chapter will pose critical questions of what it now means to experience the football event 'live', whether physically or virtually.[2]

Drawing on live performance cultural theorists from theatre and popular music such as Auslander (2008), in addition to Redhead's (1997, 2004a, 2004b, 2006, 2007, 2008) discussion of Jean Baudrillard and Paul Virilio, the chapter aims to critique the status of live football performance in a mass-media-dominated culture, and considers whether the encroachment of sports media technology(ies) on the live event itself has facilitated an ever increasing 'middle classing' of football.

In exploring Redhead's (2004a) discussion of Paul Virilio, and in particular his concept of 'city of the instant' within the context of the live football event, the chapter will examine how the culture of watching sport in late modernity is speeding up at an ever increasing rate. Interestingly, the modern football spectacle is now not only experienced 'physically' by those at the stadium, but also by millions of viewers absent from it who are watching the event as it happens, live, via satellite television and the internet, such as online streams and the iPhone's 'Sky Go' app. Interestingly, new online social media spaces and places such as internet message board forums and the micro blogging site Twitter offer supporters virtual ways of interacting with other supporters which are no longer dependent on physical presence at the live event. In some cases, this now takes place before, after and even during the live spectacle.

Taking the specific case of the pub as a virtual football fandom venue (Weed, 2007) the discussion will then critically consider how this acts as the "optimal sporting experience in late modernity" (Bale, 1998: 275), whereby this culture may have reproduced and recovered a somewhat dying traditional working-class community who continue to be, in some cases, priced out of Premier League football in particular. Pub spectatorship then produces a parody of the live spectacle and thus, according to Redhead (2007), leaves those absent from the stadium to be 'always right' as it is they, through their active television viewing presence, who help sustain the event economically. The chapter will explore this in more depth later. It begins by briefly conceptualising the changing nature of football fandom in late modernity.

## Conceptualising the changing nature of football fandom in late modernity

According to Sandvoss (2005: 8) fandom is "the regular, emotionally involved consumption of a given popular narrative or text". In the case of football, then, this popular narrative would centre on the formation of a football club's identity which might include, for example, regular engagement with its fixtures. Hills (2002) takes this further by noting how being a football fan is not just a label or category, rather it is also tied to individual and group identities and social performances: it becomes a way of life.

Drawing on the work of Taylor (1992), King (1998) and Giulianotti (2002), who specifically make distinctions between what might be termed 'traditional' fans and 'new' fans, both Crawford (2004) and Williams (2000) critique the discourse of authenticity "which sees the celebration of one form of fan culture and the rejection of all that is seen as new or consumerist" (Crawford, 2009: 78). Whilst Crawford's reading of Sandvoss (2003), in particular the notion that it is not space or place which captures fandom best, but rather the regularity of consumption and engagement, does offer a telling contribution to the sociology of football fandom, it is also important to appreciate the changing nature of fan participation as a result of various social, cultural and political processes.

Giulianotti's (2002) taxonomy of football fans is still important in recognising the differences between those 'hot' fans who hold a traditional identification with locality and 'cool' fans who hold a more detached consumer orientated identification with simulation spaces. Whilst Giulianotti (2002: 39) is right to consider how the cool "flaneur's social practices are increasingly orientated toward consumption", he does to some extent underplay the potential of virtual spaces and places to reconcile the changing social, cultural and political dynamic of 'traditional' fandom. Giulianotti (2002: 39) suggested that the "cool/consumer seeks relatively thin forms of social solidarity with other fans" and thus the "flaneur is definitively low in genuine collective affect". However, in reconciling Guilianotti's production of "ideal type taxonomical sets" (Wagg *et al.*, 2009: 79) with Crawford's more fluid social performativity, this chapter seeks to explore the paradox of hot and cold, or participatory and passive, in an increasingly complex mediatisation of modern football.

As Wagg *et al.* (2009: 80) note, Crawford raises an important question of whether it is "because of contemporary sports' commodified nature, rather than despite it, that sport functions as a particularly dynamic space for the reinterpretation or reimagining of identity and belonging". In the case of football fandom, then, the virtual spaces and places and media technology which are more akin to the cool flaneur offer potential for 'traditional' fans (in the sense of wanting a more participatory experience in person and often at the event) to reinterpret or renegotiate that collective participation in the face of rapid commercialisation.

As English football and its "largely male, fandom of the terraces becomes ever threatened by smaller all-seater stadia, steeply rising admission prices and the embourgeoisement of the sport" (Redhead, 1997: 30), at the same time "live sport venues themselves are becoming increasingly mediated environments" (Crawford, 2004: 32). In tandem with this, an alternative pub culture emerges which, according to Redhead (1997), facilitates 'traditional fandom' as being an integral expression of 'post-fandom'. Before examining this culture in more depth, the chapter will now explore how the modern football event has undergone a rapid accelerated cultural and technological change, particularly over the last 25 years.

## The acceleration of the 'technological' football viewer

From the early development of football through to the modern era of the 1960s and up to the early 1990s, there remained a strong hard proletarian masculine identity on the terraces at football stadia, which often developed into social sporting communities. This 'terrace culture' and the 'obsessive fan' became the dominant focus over the 'ordinary supporter' or developing 'casual television viewer' (Redhead, 1997: 29). Both Whannel (2002) and Boyle and Haynes (2000) explore the development of early live football broadcasting and highlight programmes and the construction of audiences and identities within this process.

Whilst this chapter is not primarily concerned with the historical development of the modern live mediatised football event per se, it is important to set the context for what has perhaps been one of the most critically important developments in football and popular culture since the football league was established in 1888; that is the formation in 1992 of the English Premier League and its relationship with the Rupert Murdoch-owned BSkyB satellite broadcasting service (Emery and Weed, 2006). Furthermore, the establishment of the Premier League and revamping of the European Cup as the Champions League also increased the spectacularisation of football, where new, more affluent customers were attracted. Consequently, admission prices to attend the live event rose, which led to many less affluent supporters being excluded (Whannel, 2002). According to Freeman "football was seen by BSkyB as the hook by which people on lower incomes could be persuaded to sign up to a satellite TV subscription" (cited in Weed, 2007: 401). This period then laid the foundation for an accelerated change in the way in which people experienced the live football spectacle.

For example, the traditional 3 p.m. Saturday afternoon kick-off would eventually make way for a series of alternative times to coincide with Sky Sports' marketing and programming. One extreme example of this critical change was an 11.15 a.m. Sunday kick-off between Manchester City and Everton in 2005. To date this is still the earliest kick-off in the Premiership League's history, and is representative of the way in which the modern football consumer has, to some extent, lost control of the event experience. It is also important to recognise a further significant change within English football during the 1990s in relation to the development of modern stadia after the Hillsborough tragedy: that of 'sanitisation'. The sanitisation of football grounds through the introduction of all seating stadia brought about as a result of the Taylor Report (1990) set the context for the increasing neoliberal marketisation of English football and coincided with the formation of the Premier League. Examples of other specific changes through the prism of various globalisation processes included the migration of coaching and playing talent from all over the world into the English game, the increase and multiple choice of 'on demand' live televised games, and the development of neoliberal policies and free market hegemony which expanded the game both globally and economically (Giulianotti, 2005).

As Redhead (2004b: 28), discussing Paul Virilio's work as a theorist of 'accelerated culture', notes, the era of twenty-first-century modernity and the 'age of the accelerator' might be best described as 'accelerated modernity' or 'accelerated culture'. Virilio's (2012) work explores the way in which modern contemporary society is shaped by an ever-increasing demand for speed. Whilst Virilio brings a high modernist stance in comparison to other theorisations of modernity such as Beck's (2006) 'second modernity', Bauman's (2000) 'liquid modernity' or Castells' (2000) conceptualisation of the global network society, it is nonetheless still appropriate here in considering 'twenty-first-century modernity' as the 'age of the accelerator' (Redhead, 2004a: 48). It is the study and analysis of 'dromology' which Virilio (2006) defined as the 'logic of speed', and the way in which "popular culture is increasingly characterised by the speed with which its products become outdated or by the speed with which the underground becomes overground" (Redhead, 2004a: 50) which helps us understand rapid changes in technology and the subsequent technological, consumption of modern football.

In applying this further, technology – whether it is in the form of instant action replays, 'trending' football dialogue on Twitter, or the global streaming of Premier League football matches on personal laptops – demonstrates how the modern football event has undergone a rapid accelerated cultural change. Thus, to understand the phenomenon of mass-media-dominated culture, and these changes in spectatorship communities and experiences, we must recognise this acceleration before exploring its relationship to the spaces and places in which football fans are interacting: this is an integral component of post-fandom.

## 'Post-fandom'

Since the proliferation of BSkyB and the Premier League in 1992 the experience for many supporters at the live event has changed significantly. Redhead describes these changes through a conceptualisation of 'post-fandom'. Post-fandom represents a distinction between the 'direct' experience of the live spectacle and the "experience of the game being always mediated" (Redhead, 1997: 30). What has literally taken place at the event during this acceleration of modernity is the shrinking of the differences between original and modern notions of live spectatorship, and the live mediatised version on television.

Redhead (1997) suggested that there is now a similarity between watching instant replays on giant video screens at the live event and watching these replays on television. As a result, there has also been a shrinking of the differences between the 'passive' and 'participatory' actions of spectators. Often during terrace culture, fans would congregate to specific areas of the stand to obtain a better view of a particular goal. Since the development of all seating stadia however, the participatory has now become intertwined with the passive, where spectators from different stands are able to see the whole pitch and event perfectly from similar angles and become part of the 'post-tourist' culture of 'gazing' at the event itself (Urry, 1990), principally through the viewing of action replays.

These changes have also produced a more cinematic consumer experience than that of the previous terrace culture. Arguably, the stadium has become an 'extension of the living room', thus leading to the development of an 'armchair fan culture' (Urry, 1990) through the constant supply of food and drink and the cost and style of the experience. The mediatisation of the live event has a further relationship with the live event itself, whereby spectators at the match, for example, "are not only seeing performances that resemble mediatised ones as closely as possible, but are apparently modelling their responses to the live event on those expected of them by television" (Auslander, 2008: 25).

Redhead has also offered a fascinating insight into the application of Paul Virilio's politics of speed to the study of the live event, and has perhaps captured this accelerated change most accurately. As he notes, "spectators at a Premiership match today constantly watch from an inert sedentary position in an accelerated, and accelerating, spectacle flash by in a blur" (Redhead, 2007: 13). Furthermore, in discussing the relationship between the live event experience and the mediatised representation of it, he suggests that the "way the spectator watching the game live at the stadium, actually sees the speeding spectacle, is conditioned by decades of watching such matches live on television, sofa surfing in the sedentary comfort of the armchair, an example of Virilio's pathological fixedness or polar inertia" (Redhead, 2007: 234)

What we witness here then, is not only a shrinking of the differences between the 'passive' and the 'participatory' at the live event, but also a paradoxical relationship between the live stadium event and the mediatised live. Furthermore, as we are "born into post-fandom" and the "fragmentary, self-conscious, reflexive, mediated and artistic become more pervasive", so too does the "self-conscious" experience of the mediated live event (Redhead, 1997: 29), an issue to which this chapter now turns.

## The compulsion of proximity to others

The traditional experience of watching the modern live football event at the stadium was more than just a 'viewing' or 'spectating' of the live spectacle. It was often a proletarian pilgrimage to a magical space, whereby a local and shared community experience could take place (Giulianotti, 1999). It is important to recognise here that this community primarily centred on the physical attendance and participation of fans at the stadium.

Weed (2007) discusses the nature of the live spectating experience by drawing on the concept of the 'leisure pursuit of being there'. What is interesting to note here is the idea that, whilst experiencing football live at the stadium is of course concerned with the immediate excitement of witnessing the event unfold in 'real time', this 'live presence' also plays an important role in being able to 're-call' and 're-tell' the experience after the event. It is also interesting to consider a parallel with the field of theatre and music. For example, Auslander (2008: 66) discusses the 'socio-cultural' value attached to live presence where being able to "say one saw a particular musician, actor or gig 'live'", enables one to perhaps gain social prestige within a social circle of friends or colleagues.

MacCannell's (1996) idea of 'returning' is a further significant part of the live event experience and that the 'being there' at the football stadium to see the drama unfold is one of the features which makes it distinct from not being there, or perhaps witnessing it live on television or recorded at a later time. This idea is also discussed within the context of television and space, where to watch an event live at a distance and not in person at the stadium, for example on television, prevents an individual from standing as a witness to history because they lack privileged, raw, authentic proximity to facts (Peters, 2001).

Furthermore, Boden and Molotch (1994) have suggested that the excitement of witnessing the live event itself holds a further important feature, that being the compulsion of proximity, where to fully experience the event unfold live, spectators are required to be in the company of others. This thus authenticates the experience through the shared belief that others are also experiencing similar emotions at the same time.

This idea of spectating at the live event itself is also, for many supporters, an actual physical bodily experience where they believe that, not only are they potentially able to influence a result (Whannel 2002), but the actual 'living' of the event and being able to 're-tell' and 're-call' it is heightened by the very fact that the experience is physical, not virtual. The live football stadium spectacle becomes then a dramatic theatre whereby the sporting audience's participation becomes both physical and psychological. All of these ideas are problematised via the increasingly mediated format of live football (and sport generally) events as they potentially threaten the authenticity, which perhaps comes from experiencing the event in a physical capacity.

However, before exploring the penetration of media technology at the football stadium it is also important to briefly consider how the modern football spectacle is packaged. The acceleration of live modernity, specifically after 1992, has also had a significant impact on the experience of the live mediatised event. The operation of the sports media, such as Sky Sports and the Rupert Murdoch press (News Corps) in particular, has placed the live event onto a larger platform than ever before.

Blackshaw and Crabbe (2004) have discussed how the English Premier League acts as the ultimate sporting soap opera, where narratives are constructed and characters created in order to heighten the experience and consumption of the live mediatised event. What we are often witnessing when consuming this live football event shown on Sky's 'Super Sunday' programme, for example, is the final climactic chapter of a story already created and narrated throughout the week prior to the event taking place. Whether it is a boxing analogy such as the clash of 'Ronaldo vs. Messi' or the script of a 'club in crisis', the experience and consumption of the live event itself is often understood within this narrative context. What often occurs during this scripting of the live mediatised event is the idea of the football spectacle being packaged in a way that "draws the attention of the audience to the emotional entanglement surrounding the narrative and characters rather than the actual match contest itself" (Barthes, 1957, cited in Blackshaw and Crabbe, 2004: 123).

Thus, the Premier League becomes a soap opera in which the story and commentary "satisfy the audience's insatiable demand to be titillated by the intricate details of a celebrity life style, which often concerns deviancy" (Blackshaw and Crabbe, 2004: 123), an example of which might be the latest 'Tweet' sent by the controversial player Joey Barton on the micro blogging social media site, Twitter. The chapter now turns to explore how, through the penetration of media technology, this liveness is often experienced in a hyperreal fashion.

## The penetration of media technology and hyperreality

The relationship between the live event and the mediatised live also raises the question of realism. Giulianotti (2004) discusses Baudrillard's notion of hyperreality and the role the media plays in the confusion and simulation of reality. The mediatised live event, according to Baudrillard, attempts to reproduce the 'realism' of the live event itself in simulated form, before the actual live event can materialise. This accelerated culture takes on a virtual life where the entire live experience of the event is reformulated and simulated by multiple camera angles.

There is increasing evidence of growing hyperrealism within the passive experience of modern football stadia where, in some cases, actual crowd participation and atmosphere have been simulated. This was evident at Highbury, the home of Arsenal Football Club, during rebuilding work in the early 1990s, where a simulated crowd was erected behind the goal (Redhead, 1997). Furthermore, during the 2006/2007 season at Manchester City's (currently, 'Etihad') stadium, the author personally experienced a simulated crowd noise being broadcast around the North Stand, producing a hyperreal atmosphere which was done to combat the perceived lack of 'real' singing amongst passive supporters.

As the acceleration of live modernity continues, according to Giulianotti, Baudrillard "anticipated the day when football matches will be played before empty stadiums where spectators decide to watch the match on TV at home, consuming the hyperrealism of pornographic sporting information in a virtual experience of directorial technological control" (Giulianotti, 2004: 234). In a sense then, the mediated live almost becomes a 'third order of simulacra' (Baudrillard 1994), replacing the original real live event itself, and simulating an almost 'realer than real' world in which the event is situated.

Perhaps the most telling contribution of Baudrillard (1994) to the discussion of the live event and the mediatised live is his idea of an event, in his case 'the Gulf War', becoming so virtualised and hyperreal that it can be said to have not taken place. What is suggested here is the idea that we can only understand the live event to have taken place through our understanding of the context in which it is transmitted in 'real time' rather than packaged as a scripted media event. As the football live event is packaged and organised around "commercials and television deadlines", the event becomes less about the clash between the players, and more about the "surgical execution of pre-programmed, simulated game strategies" (Giulianotti, 2004: 235). This virtual mediatised live provides a "pornography of sport" in which television interaction, numerous choice of angles and audio systems produce a "visual excess of reality that no spectator live at the event enjoys" (Giulianotti, 2005: 185). However, even for the most passive people at the event itself, within accelerated 'live' modernity it has become a televised, rather than an actual, participatory experience through the introduction of large screens within the stadium (Crawford, 2004; Redhead, 2007).

## Changing spaces and places: live internet streaming

As the differences between the *passive* and *participatory* and the *physical* and the *visual* shrink, so too does the difference between geography and technology where, in a sense, the live mediatised technological event has displaced the distinctiveness of the geographical live physical presence of space and place (Redhead, 1997). Whilst Virilio (2006) was specifically concerned with speed, military technology and modernity, and the relationship between new communication technologies such as satellite, digital and the idea of the global accident, Redhead has provided a cautionary application of his ideas to the analysis of sport and media events. He notes, "Virilio has been calling the virtual territory created by this broadcasting of a live event, the 'city of the instant' for over twenty years" (Redhead, 2007: 234). For Virilio, new sports communication technology(ies), such as Sky Sports and the internet and its "instantaneous digital mediation of sport symbolises the high tech potency of the white-dominated West's military-industrial complexes" (Giulianotti, 2005: 177). What we witness in the age of the accelerator is Virilio's 'dromocratic condition' where the speeding up of technologies have tended to abolish time and distance (Redhead, 2006). The live sporting conflict then becomes a 'war at the speed of light', not only taking place live at the stadium itself within a local geographical space, but, more importantly, 'occurring everywhere globally at the same time' (Redhead, 2006). A good example of this would be a Premier League or Champions League match whereby the traditional geographical understanding of the spectacle, for example, Old Trafford in Manchester, makes way for a more postmodern global 'city of the instant' space, which is consumed live by millions of people all over the world, via different sports channels and internet websites.

According to Virilio, this accelerated culture has produced a power shift from those present at the live event in person to those millions of people around the world who are watching it virtually at the same time. Virilio maintains that 'those absent from the stadium are always right' because they disqualify the presence of those participants live at the event and 'impose their power' by the very fact that it is they, the television and internet audience, who produce the live event (Redhead, 2007). These viewers do so because they are the ultimate consumers, inherent within the logic of neoliberal modern football.

As a result of these technological advancements, a recent global internet spectator subculture has emerged online, which is also an example of what Bale (1998) refers to as virtual fandom culture. Various internet websites provide free streams via worldwide Asian, American and European sport channels of live matches from a variety of European leagues, including the English Premier League and European Champions League, to audiences worldwide simultaneously (Birmingham and David, 2011). The main attraction of this particular live experience is that the websites not only provide actual mediatised live games shown on television, for example, Sky Sports, but also non-mediatised games.

In a thought provoking paper on the potential parallels between live football streaming and the advent in file sharing in popular music, Birmingham and David (2011) pose critical questions regarding the future consequences of live football streaming on the internet. Whilst they acknowledge "live streaming is unlikely to reduce willingness to pay for actual live attendance, it is likely to depress the revenues generated from broadcast (mediated access)" (Birmingham and David, 2011: 76). They do recognise, however, that clubs will need to pay more attention to retaining core fans' loyalty whilst noting that if both subscription-based television access and event ticket prices continue to rise, "even greater numbers of traditional fans will be unable to follow their team live through legitimate channels, encouraging illegal broadcasts from foreign channels in pubs or illegal streams broadcast over the internet" (Birmingham and David: 2011: 76). The chapter now turns to explore this pub spectatorship culture.

## The performative culture of pub spectatorship

A recent cultural phenomenon has developed which, perhaps, reveals a further interesting relationship between the passive and the participatory, and the 'real' and 'hyperreal'. This phenomenon is what Weed (2007) has referred to as the culture of pub spectatorship, where fans have begun to recognise the pub, not only as a place to socialise before the match, but as an actual virtual football fandom venue itself, which offers an alternative to being at the venue in person. According to market research by Mintel and Keynote, "more people (9.1 million) watched live sport on television in a pub or a bar than paid to watch live sport at an event (8.7 million)" (cited in Weed, 2013: 289). Whilst it is important to recognise the various nuanced contexts out of which this data emerged, such as the research period and sports identified, it still does offer a preliminary, albeit tentative, account of the increasing importance placed on alternative mediatised spaces and places.

As noted earlier, Redhead was quick to recognise the early development of this culture when he suggested that "one significant response to the Sky takeover of English football in the early 1990s has been for fans to congregate in large numbers across the country in bars, which have Sky TV at times of live matches, and that this 'pub culture' has in effect replaced the yesteryear participatory terrace culture" (Redhead, 1997: 30). The encroachment of media technology(ies) on the game has produced an opportunity for working-class supporters to now, in some cases at least, watch the game for free, and allow them to construct and re-imagine a community and social experience, which according to Readhead (1997), has been lost in the post-1990 period.

During traditional open 'terrace culture', fans were able to choose where they watched the game, which some believed to have been vital to the creation of atmosphere at the live event, and whilst the sanitised new stadium experience may have destroyed this traditional atmosphere (Weed, 2007), fans are now able to choose from a number of pub venues at which to watch a particular game. As Brimson (1998: 166) acknowledges, "it is cheaper and easier to simply go down the pub and watch the game while having a few beers, where in most cases it will be with the same group of geezers and so the atmosphere will be as good if not better than at the actual game". What is interesting to note here is whilst this culture has developed out of necessity, whereby a lack of access to "live televised matches at home and at the event" has meant supporters having to look elsewhere, the "culture of pub supporting experience has now developed into an activity that is attractive in its own right" (Weed, 2007: 403). More importantly, the pub venue now often streams English football matches from European channels, thus democratising spectatorship by providing fans with the option of watching a match live that may not be shown on TV at all.

As a result, the 'culture of pub spectatorship' reveals some of the key features identified by Weed (2007: 401) as being integral to the live event experience, such as the 'shared proletarian communal experience' and 'collective enjoyment' inherent within Giulianotti's (2002) 'traditional' fandom, which have, in some cases, decreased as a result of the embourgeoisement of Premier League football (Redhead, 1997). This is particularly evident due to the development of smaller all seater stadia and ticket price increases. Furthermore, it is the need for proximity – not to the actual live event itself, but to other people sharing that event – which, according to Weed (2007), makes this a collective experience.

The significance of this 'virtual fandom site' is that the pub becomes a space for symbolic protest in which some fans are able to reclaim the community taken away from them by the bourgeois authorities. As supporters attend the pub as a virtual alternative to being present at the live event, they socially construct an imagined community (Anderson, 2006), that in some cases allows for socialisation processes with other fans whom they have never met before. Equally, these fans are also aware that they are part of a broader imagined community of fellow supporters who are attending other pubs across the country. Perhaps this sporting space's relationship to 'traditional' fandom in terms of collective presence and experience, whilst now heavily reliant on modern technology in terms of screening the event, supports Crawford's (2004) idea of late-modern football being a source of deep identity construction, whilst also providing an opportunity for social performance. Whether one sees fans as opposed to consumers or fans *as* consumers (Crawford, 2004), ultimately all fans are now technologised.

## Conclusions

This chapter has discussed the live football event and its relationship with post-fandom culture and the hyperreal simulated style of the mediatised live. By understanding this accelerated culture and the growing influence of global media communications and technologies, we are able to recognise the way(s) in which the experience of the live event at the stadium and the hyperreal mediatised live have become so mixed up and intertwined that, in many ways, they now cannot be understood independent of each other. The chapter has demonstrated different ways in which the mediatised form is often modelled on the live form, but eventually usurps the live form's position in the cultural economy, and thus the live form begins to replicate the mediatised live (Auslander, 2008). In recognising this paradoxical relationship the chapter has provided a tentative exploration of 'pub spectatorship culture' that experiences both the virtual, almost simulacra of the mediatised live, whilst retaining and recovering some of the participatory and shared community experiences of the traditional live event itself. Whilst Birmingham and David (2011: 78) are right to note that the consequences of live streaming still remain uncertain, they do suggest that

> if increased prices for live attendance invert traditional patterns of attendance relative to socio-economic demographics then many traditional fans are likely to turn to live streaming (whether at home or the pub) as a means of following teams they are priced out of paying to see.

It is within these alternative spaces and places which future studies of football fandom should now focus.

## Notes

1 This is an amended and updated chapter of a journal article previously published as "Modern 'live' football: moving from the panopticon gaze to the performative, virtual and carnivalesque" in *Sport in Society* (Turner 2013). The author would like to thank Taylor and Francis and the editors for their permission to re-use parts of the original narrative.

2 The term 'live' is used throughout this chapter and is placed in inverted commas within the title to highlight the problematic nature of the term in relation to what is considered 'live' at a sports event which requires physical presence and a 'live' version of that event consumed via various media platforms.

# References

Anderson, B. (2006) *Imagined Communities: Reflections on the origin and spread of nationalism.* London: Verso.

Auslander, P. (2008) *Liveness: Performance in a mediatized culture,* 2nd edition. London: Routledge.

Bale, J. (1998) Virtual fandoms: Futurescapes of football. In A. Brown (ed.) *Fanatics! Power, identity and fandom in football.* London: Routledge, 265–278.

Baudrillard, J. (1994) *Simulacra and simulation. The body in theory: Histories of cultural Materialism.* Michigan: University of Michigan Press.

Bauman, Z. (2000) *Liquid modernity.* Cambridge: Polity Press.

Beck, U. (2006) *The cosmopolitan vision* (translated into English by Ciaran Cronin). Cambridge: Polity Press.

Birmingham, J. and David, M. (2011) Live-streaming: will football fans continue to be more law abiding than music fans? *Sport in Society,* 14(1): 69–80.

Blackshaw, T. and Crabbe, T. (2004) *New perspectives on sport and "deviance": Consumption, performativity and social control.* London: Routledge.

Boden, D. and Moltotch, H.L. (1994) The compulsion of proximity. In D. Boden and R. Friedland (eds) *Now here: Space, time and modernity.* Berkeley, CA: University of California Press, 257–286.

Boyle, R. and Haynes, R. (2000) *Power play: Sport, the media and popular culture.* Essex: Pearson Education.

Brimson, D. (1998) *The geezers guide to football: A lifetime of lads and lager.* London: Mainstream Publishing.

Castells, M. (2000) *The rise of the network society,* 2nd edition. New Jersey: Wiley-Blackwell.

Crawford, G. (2004) *Consuming sport: Sport, fans and culture.* London: Routledge.

Crawford, G. (2009) Fans. In G. Crawford and T. Blackshaw (eds) *The SAGE dictionary of leisure studies.* London: Sage, 77–78.

Emery, R. and Weed, M.E. (2006) Fighting for survival? The financial management of football clubs outside the top flight in England. *Managing Leisure,* 111(1): 1–21.

Giulianotti, R. (1999) *Football: A sociology of the global game.* Cambridge: Polity Press.

Giulianotti, R. (2002) Supporters, followers, fans and flaneurs: A taxonomy of spectator identities in football. *Journal of Sport and Social Issues,* 26(1): 25–46.

Giulianotti, R. (ed.) (2004) *Sport and modern social theorists.* Basingstoke: Palgrave Macmillan.

Giulianotti, R. (2005) *Sport: A critical sociology.* Cambridge: Polity Press.

Hills, M. (2002) *Fan cultures.* London: Routledge.

King, A. (1998) *The end of the terraces.* Leicester: Leicester University Press.

MacCannell, D. (1996) *Tourist or traveller?* London: BBC Education.

Peters, J. (2001) Witnessing. *Media, Culture and Society,* 23(6): 707–723.

Redhead, S. (1997) *Post-fandom and the millennial blues.* London: Routledge.

Redhead, S. (2004a) *Paul Virilio: Theorist for an accelerated culture.* Edinburgh: Edinburgh University Press.

Redhead, S. (ed.) (2004b) *The Paul Virilio reader.* Edinburgh: Edinburgh University Press.

Redhead, S. (2006) The art of the accident: Paul Virilio and accelerated modernity. *Fast Capitalism,* 2.1.

Redhead, S. (2007) Those absent from the stadium are always right. *Journal of Sport and Social Issues.* 31(3): 226–241.

Redhead, S. (ed.) (2008) *The Jean Baudrillard reader*. Edinburgh: Edinburgh University Press.

Sandvoss, C. (2003) *A game of two halves: Football, television and globalization*. London: Routledge.

Sandvoss, C. (2005) *Fans: The mirror of consumption*. Cambridge: Polity.

Taylor, I. (1992) *Football and its fans*. Leicester: Leicester University Press.

Turner, M. (2013) Modern 'live' football: moving from the panopticon gaze to the performative, virtual and carnivalesque. *Sport in Society*, 16(1): 85–93.

Urry, J. (1990) *The tourist gaze*. London: Sage.

Virilio, P. (2006) *Speed and politics*. Cambridge, MA: MIT Press.

Virilio, P. (2012) *The great accelerator*. Cambridge: Polity.

Wagg, S., Brick, C., Wheaton, B. and Caudwell, J. (2009) *Key concepts in Sport Studies*. London: Sage.

Weed, M. (2007) The pub as a virtual football fandom venue: An alternative to "being there"? *Soccer and Society*, 8(2/3): 399–414.

Weed, M. (2013) Exploring the sport spectator experience: Virtual football spectatorship in the pub. In D. Martinez and P.B. Mukharji (eds) *Football: From England to the World*. London: Routledge, 23–31.

Whannel, G. (2002) *Media sport stars: Masculinities and moralities*. London: Routledge.

Williams, J. (2000) The changing face of football: A case of national regulation? In S. Hamil, J. Michie, C. Oughton and S. Warby (eds) *Football in the digital age: Whose game is it anyway?* London: Mainstream, 94–106.

# 3 Debating with fists

## Professional wrestling: sport, spectacle and violent drama

*Daniel Schulze*

### The world of wrestling revisited

When Roland Barthes wrote his influential essay 'The world of wrestling' in 1957, analysing professional wrestling as culture and even comparing it to the classical tragedies of Molière seemed tantamount to blasphemy. Today, wrestling is firmly accepted as part of popular culture and no longer needs defending (Sammond, 2005a). This chapter seeks to illuminate the changes professional wrestling has undergone since Barthes' essay, critiquing both its terms of content and cultural context. A discussion of Barthes' interpretation of wrestling will be followed by a short historical overview of the development of the wrestling industry. Subsequently, the current spectacle of wrestling, its storylines and consumers, will be investigated with a specific focus on the live events. Third, wrestling's place in contemporary culture will be discussed.

### Barthes' conception of wrestling

The type of professional wrestling Barthes knew was very much a local business. Promoters staged their matches with amateur or semi-professionals in second rate, run-down halls (Barthes, 1976). For Barthes, professional wrestling has nothing (or very little) to do with sport and is, rather, conceived within the realms of theatre. It is a spectacle of a base nature that is, however, intelligible to all strata of society.

Intelligibility of the event (according to Barthes) is created through a simplification of signs. The audience is never in need of interpretation or reflection because all matches follow a clear dichotomy of hero versus villain. Even before the match begins, this dichotomy is visible in the body of the wrestlers. An overweight, hairy, sagging body will immediately denote a villain whereas a polished, muscular body is the signifier for a hero. Interestingly, these signs are not merely perceived through paradigms of semiotic interpretation; rather they are felt on a visceral level. As Barthes (1976: 17) remarks: "the passionate condemnation [of the villain] from the crowd no longer stems from its judgment, but instead from the very depths of its humours". While the body of the villain may cause nausea, the beautiful body of the hero will elicit passionate affection. The simplified sign in this context works on a visceral, not an intellectual level. That is why wrestling is so appealing to a broad range of spectators and that is also how it gains its immediacy. In the binary opposition of hero and villain, the drama of human emotions is played out through the match. For Barthes (1976: 18), wrestling is:

> a real Human Comedy, where the most socially-inspired nuances of passion (conceit, rightfulness, refined cruelty, a sense of 'paying one's debts') always felicitously find the clearest sign which can receive them, express them and triumphantly carry them to the confines of the hall.

This comedy is built on the climactic rhythm of "Suffering, defeat, and justice" (Barthes, 1976: 19). Audiences are active agents in the match; they scream, shout, cheer and ridicule. They accompany the athletes on their climactic journey which ultimately leads to a cathartic experience. By the end of a match, justice (literally and figuratively) is restored, the world is ordered again and good (rightly) triumphs over evil. This is the ultimate purpose of wrestling: it portrays the moral concept of justice. Within this paradigm, the whole world is reduced to the opposition of good and evil, which leads to "a perfect intelligibility of reality ... an ideal understanding of things" (Barthes, 1976: 25). While the real world may be complex and tinted in all shades of grey, wrestling reduces this confusion in an almost nostalgic move to a simple binary: good and evil.

Barthes is very clear on the fact that wrestling is a spectacle of make-believe. The audience does not wish for actual suffering but "enjoys the perfection of an iconography. It is not true that wrestling is a sadistic spectacle: it is only an intelligible spectacle" (Barthes, 1976: 20). This intelligible spectacle will then deliver a cathartic experience and also, time and again, confirm the mentality that good must eventually triumph over evil. For Barthes, this mentality is especially strong in the United States because "in America wrestling represents a sort of mythological fight between Good and Evil (of a quasi political nature, the 'bad' wrestler always being supposed to be a Red)" (Barthes, 1976: 23).

## After Barthes – a short history of professional wrestling

The type of wrestling that Barthes describes is virtually non-existent today. As Oliva and Calleja (2009: 6) point out, Barthes investigates single/discrete matches, but the possibilities of television and storytelling have altered this 'game' with overarching, soap-opera-like storylines that grow ever more complex. Today, small leagues which stage shows in smaller venues have become rare (albeit not extinct). Wrestling has become a multi-million dollar industry, dominated by one big player: World Wrestling Entertainment (WWE, formerly known as World Wrestling Federation (WWF)).

Up until the 1980s, a number of regional leagues and wrestling associations existed in the United States. They worked according to a territory system and – by code of honour – respected other promotions' territories (Beekman, 2006). However, with the advent of the media and television age one league grew in ambition, stepping into the territory of other franchises by buying up competitors and driving others out of business (Pratten, 2003). This league was WWE (then WWF), which now holds a virtual monopoly over the industry, with no national or international competitors to speak of (Beekman, 2006). The only two other promotions that have a nationwide exposure are Total Non Stop Action Wrestling (TNA) and Ring of Honor (ROH). However, neither threatens WWE's market position (MacFarlane, 2012). As the WWE is the biggest and also internationally most successful franchise, it will be the main subject of the following analysis, simply due to its broad visibility and market share.[1]

Up until the 1970s, professional wrestling – even on television – was a traditional affair; similar to the form seen in the Olympics. Stage names were uncommon and matches generally lasted not much longer than five minutes (Pratten, 2003). This changed in the 1980s due to the emergence of WWF. WWF led to the proliferation of flamboyant personas, entrance music, managers and storylines that have become ever more important. Wrestling now incorporates much of the "glitz and glitter" of Hollywood (Pratten, 2003: 32).

Before this transformation, wrestling promoters had been keen on maintaining 'kayfabe', i.e. the illusion that professional wrestling was a legitimate sport and not scripted (de Garis, 2005). Today, WWE consciously refers to its product as 'sports entertainment', emphasising the entertainment factor and not claiming sporting legitimacy. Arguably this is out of necessity rather than choice, as the ever more elaborate storylines and matches (often with comic effects) could not seriously be sold as legitimate sport. But, more fundamentally, Vince McMahon, owner and CEO of WWE, wanted to avoid regulations by, and fee payments to, the State Athletics Commission and thus decided to dispel any claims to legitimate sporting competition (Beekman, 2006).

The transition from sport to entertainment has also become evident in the transformation of wrestlers' bodies. Whereas in the mid-twentieth century the Johnny Weissmuller type (in very good shape but still average-build) was prevalent and seen as the cultural ideal, in the 1980s the muscle-packed superhero, akin to Rambo, for instance, became the norm (Oppliger, 2004). This trend of ever larger athletes has continued into the present day, to the extent that, "[t]he size of wrestlers has increased to the point where some are so muscular they are incapable of putting their arms down or having distinct necks between their heads and shoulders" (Oppliger, 2004: 162). There is agreement among scholars and fans alike that with the increased size of wrestlers and a greater emphasis on the 'show', the athletic performance itself has also transformed, becoming more elaborate and violent. Today, matches

> are longer and a great deal more spectacular. The wrestlers are often very large but also agile, some are most acrobatic. The moves of the amateur sport tend to be ignored, as they are often static and uninteresting except to the purist. Thus the style became less technical and more entertaining.
>
> (Pratten, 2003: 33)

When the WWE began to take control of the market, small and independent leagues – which were struggling to draw audiences away from the big competitor – began staging ever more dangerous and violent matches. The now defunct independent league, Extreme Championship Wrestling (ECW), which was later bought by and incorporated into WWE, began staging matches that not only involved tables, ladders and chairs as weapons and objects to fall on/through, but also introduced weapons such as barbed wire, forks or baseball bats into the shows (Oppliger, 2004). After the buyout of ECW, hardcore wrestling also found its way into 'mainstream' wrestling, when WWE introduced a 'hardcore' branch of events. One of the most infamous hardcore matches to take place in the WWE is the match of 'Mankind' against 'The Undertaker', in which 'Mankind' first fell from a five meter steel cage, crashing into a table, then again crashed from the same structure through the ring mat and finally smiled into the camera with a face bloodied from thumb tacks (Oppliger, 2004: 78). Violent matches such as this have been heavily criticised, not least by wrestlers themselves. Bret 'The Hitman' Hart, a retired wrestler and former WWE champion, remarked that wrestling used to be an elaborate, sporting performance while "[n] ow it's all about hurting each other for stupid reasons" (Hackett, 2006: 123). Today, it seems, the crowd does not simply want the image of passion (Barthes, 1976), but wants to see actual blood and suffering.

Professional wrestling has changed well beyond the obvious physicality and brutality of the events. Where Barthes could find a moral clarity in the struggle between good and evil, wrestling today is much more ambiguous in this respect. Wrestlers frequently do not adhere to such a clear dichotomy. Furthermore, characters like 'Stone Cold' Steve Austin or 'The Rock' prove that anti-heroes who misbehave publicly, drink beer and insult fellow wrestlers or the crowd, are often much more loved by audiences than the genuine, 'flawless' hero. As Pratten (2003: 41–42) argues, "previously, good prevailed over evil, so wrestling could be presented as a representation of traditional values. Now, however, critics can complain that anti-social behaviour is being supported and even encouraged". In the twenty-first century, the clear binary of good and evil which Barthes had in mind (e.g. communism vs. democracy) is simply not sufficient to appeal to the corporation's diverse audience(s). De Garis (2005: 205–206) sees this as a symptom of wider social changes:

> In today's wrestling scene the good/bad guy dichotomy has been replaced with a more rudimentary strong/weak dichotomy. [...] In the absence of a framework of sportsmanship that predominated wrestling for so long, it is no longer moral weaknesses or moral turpitude that is vilified; it is simply physical weakness. The sense of justice in Barthes' terms is based on a 'might makes right' ideology rather than some kind of traditional moral framework.

The moral framework of wrestling is thus reduced to a brutal economy of physical power where "the good and noble characters are now despised" (Oppliger, 2004: 91).

## Virtual WWE monopoly

The success of professional wrestling as a highly profitable, global entertainment industry goes hand in hand with the development of the home leisure industry in the form of on-demand television, video games and online media. In the UK, in the early 2000s, wrestling attracted larger television audiences than English Premier League football (apart from matches involving Manchester United) (Pratten, 2003). In the US, WWE's Monday night *Raw* is the longest running programme in the history of US television (Oliva and Calleja, 2009). This success is partly due to the entrepreneurial talent of Vince McMahon but also to television stations' eagerness to attract more viewers in the coveted and marketable group of males aged 18 to 49 (WWE, 2009a). In the late 1990s, a number of television stations in the US lost those male viewers, especially in professional sports programmes such as Monday night football or professional basketball where figures declined sharply (Battema and Sewell, 2005). Professional wrestling in the style of WWE proved to be just the right thing to regain this audience segment because, in contrast to 'real' sports, it could account for two and half hours of dramatic (scripted) entertainment (Schwartz, 2003).

Today, WWE has a fairly consistent turnover of nearly half a billion dollars each year (WWE, 2011: 26). Its bread and butter business continues to be pay-per-view events, such as *Wrestlemania*, which make the biggest contribution to its bottom line (WWE, 2011). As Migliore (1993) remarks, the WWE also branches out into popular culture with cameo appearances of wrestlers in popular television shows, 67 million fans on Facebook and 25 million followers on Twitter (WWE, 2012: 4). The WWE has also launched attempts to break into other media such as film and digital content, but those account for less than 10 per cent of overall revenues (WWE, 2011: 26), whereas licensing and merchandising make significant contributions to its earnings. The WWE thus sees itself as an entertainment company, and it is telling that in its self-description as 'sports entertainment' – as de Garis points out – the words 'professional wrestling' are nowhere to be found; this leads him to the conclusion that "[t]he WWF's definition of itself represents a shift in business models, away from a sports-based, live events business and more toward a television show" (de Garis, 2005: 194). Vince McMahon, owner and frequent storyline performer (as evil chairman Mr McMahon) has stated that his foremost competitors are not other wrestling leagues – because there are virtually none – but Hollywood (Oppliger, 2004). Thus, the WWE is a television entertainment company whose main lines of business are not sports events but television pay-per-views, DVD sales, as well as merchandising and licensing. While the live events are the core product (in 2009 the attendance at WWE's *Wrestlemania* event even superseded Super Bowl live attendance), their turnover is fairly minor in comparison to DVD sales, licensing and pay-per-views (WWE 2009b).

## The 'show'

It seems obvious that in a wrestling broadcast the actual matches should be the main element of the show. A detailed study of wrestling broadcasts by Woo and Kim suggests, however, that the matches only account for a relatively small portion of the overall programme, while ringside conflicts and backstage footage make up the majority of broadcast minutes (cited in Pawlowski, 2006). Specifically, Woo and Kim found that more than 28 per cent of an average WWE show consists of advertising. Of the remaining 72 per cent, actual matches only account for about 30 per cent of the time, while the remaining 70 per cent is filled with storyline content, ringside conflicts etc. (cited in Pawlowski, 2006: 350). Thus the 'sport' is, apparently, a minor matter, while advertising time and the soap opera-style stories account for the majority of the programme.

Two examples may illustrate the soap opera character of WWE storylines. In 2005 a storyline was built around wrestlers 'Eddie Guerrero' and 'Rey Mysterio' involving Mysterio's son, Dominik. For weeks, in television shows, Guerrero threatened Rey Mysterio by announcing that he would reveal a secret about Dominik. Eventually, Guerrero claimed to be Dominik's biological father and, accompanied by his 'lawyer', demanded custody. The question of custody was then resolved at the *Summer Slam* event where both wrestlers fought over custody for Dominik. The child watched the match ringside and eventually intervened, helping Mysterio to 'win' custody (Best of WWE Vol. 1). While there is still an element of good and evil present (Mysterio was clearly the audience's favourite), it becomes evident that wrestling here is more like a soap opera, focusing on thinly dramatised stories of social relations, rather than actual sporting contests.

Another example involved the above-mentioned 'Mankind'. Mankind was frequently portrayed as a deranged character, wearing a leather mask and carrying around a white sports sock ('Mr Socko') with a face painted on that served him as a hand-puppet and conversation partner. The WWE claimed that he had been severely neglected as a child, locked up in a furnace room with only Mr Socko as a friend. Therefore, he was constantly in search of an affectionate father figure, which he found both in Vince McMahon – eventually calling him Dad – and later on in Dwayne Johnson ('The Rock') (Ford, 2007b). In this storyline, which spanned a number of years, all the matches that Mankind fought were part of his quest for affection, friends and a father figure. Again, there is a binary of good and evil because sympathies of the audience were clearly with 'Mankind' and not McMahon or Johnson, who both abused 'Mankind's' affection. The mythological fight of Good and Evil, which Barthes ([1957] 1976) saw in wrestling, here becomes an almost vulgar, melodramatic narrative. For Barthes, the match itself was meaningful because it conveyed moral concepts. Today, storylines are necessary in order to give matches context and make them meaningful. It is only through the storylines that a framework of justice is established.

## Participation and audiences

In a live event, the relationship between wrestler and crowd is reciprocal and fans do play a highly active part in the construction of the event. In this sense, fans are also performers. As Ford (2007a: 30) argues, "without audience participation, the text of a professional wrestling performance cannot be completed". Professional wrestling thus stands in the tradition of both the Roman arena, where gladiators fought to the acclaim of the crowd, and Renaissance drama, where audiences could directly voice their opinions and sentiments about the performance or even participate in it (Schulze, 2013). In this sense, it brings back a tradition of theatre that was both participatory and inclusive.

Wrestling matches are not a matter of quiet spectating; rather, audiences *experience* a wrestling match with their whole bodies, and they externalise their emotions immediately by booing, heckling or cheering. "In effect the crowd tells the wrestler the story it wants to hear. It is up to the wrestler to listen and react" (de Garis, 2005: 206). The crowd thus shapes the pace and action of a match. Performers will normally be very attentive to the crowd and make sure they have them excited. A match only works if the audience are literally on their feet, cheering, shouting or waving their fists at the wrestlers.

Another important factor in this equation is the fans' chance of influencing the stories. The "attraction for the fans is the level of participation. Fans report that they love the fact that they are made to feel like they matter" (Oppliger, 2004: 146). Unlike in films or 'real' sports, they can influence the storyline by booing, cheering, supporting or withholding support. Wrestling promoters will normally react very quickly to the fans' opinions (Jenkins IV, 2005a). A wrestler who was planned to be a *heel* (villain) may easily become a *face* (hero), if the fans love him or vice versa. As Pratten (2003: 40) articulates:

> Dwayne Johnson (The Rock) was introduced as a pleasant young man. The crowds did not like this presentation and barracked him. He responded by showing increasing arrogance, which supporters loved, and so this angle was developed. Fans began to respond to him as though he was the traditional hero. Once again, an anti-hero had been created.

Wrestling audiences – at least at live events – are empowered to contribute to the story that is constructed before their eyes in two ways. First, they help generate the necessary atmosphere (in wrestling terms, *heat*) at a match, which is crucial to the performance. Second, they can alter the show in the medium-term through their reaction and turn a *face* to *heel* (or vice versa), or boost/curb the career of a performer.[2]

## Wrestling and culture

If for Barthes wrestling was almost a morality play that conveyed truths and confirmed mentalities (e.g. 'it is good to be noble and just'), what is the place of this 'soap opera-cum-violence' in today's culture? Sammond (2005b) argues that the

WWE's success in the late 1990s and early 2000s must be attributed to the decline of the American family as the central unit of social organisation and consumption. This decline, he claims, began subtly in the 1960s and 1970s and found its peak in the late 1980s and early 1990s. The rise of television shows that displayed dysfunctional families (such as *Married ... with Children*, *The Simpsons* or *Roseanne*) can be seen as cases in point. The healthy and happy family which, according to Sammond (2005b), in the 1950s and 1960s was the centre of American society, had eroded, providing fertile ground for the WWE's version of dysfunctionality. Vince McMahon, who frequently uses his own family to display betrayal, hate or assault within storylines, can be seen as an *example par excellence* of a culture of the new millennium. For example, WWE's *Smackdown!* was consciously designed as a counterpoint to clean, family-friendly entertainment (Sammond 2005b). Its gratuitous display of violence, misbehaviour and exaggerated sexuality fly in the face of traditional values. Sammond (2005b) proposes that it must be viewed as an expression of a culture of prolonged adolescence. *Smackdown!* is one of the highest rated US shows among male teenagers (Pawlowski, 2006), which suggests that wrestling serves teenagers' need for rebellion. A good example is the WWE's team 'D-Generation X', composed of wrestlers 'Shawn Michaels' and 'Triple H', and former member, X-Pac (Best of WWE Vol. 6). They frequently assaulted other wrestlers, harassed female audience members, appeared drunk on stage and generally behaved however they wanted. In turn they did not face any consequences, rather they became champions and one of the most popular collaborations in the show's history (Pratten, 2003).

Oppliger (2004: 144) argues that, "[w]restling with its lack of consequences and comical features, is a celebration of the perpetual adolescent", enabling the fans to "indulge in the Peter Pan syndrome of never having to grow up and take responsibilities". For fans, attending a wrestling event is a matter of becoming absorbed in "a crowd's triumphant foolishness" (Hackett 2006: 19). Fans who physically experience the event take part in a puerile exercise of misbehaviour. This can lead to catharsis in a Barthesian sense but may also be regarded as an expression of a wider phenomenon. Accordingly, wrestling is a "fantasy of 'adolescent' impropriety" (Sammond, 2005b: 135), which counters the traditional values displayed on prime-time-television in the preceding decades. Such tendencies, however, are not only recognisable in professional wrestling but are apparent in many branches of the entertainment industry. Shows such as *Jackass* or *South Park* are cases in point. Wrestling's development of anti-social behaviour and the glorification of anti-heroes must then be understood in the social context of teenage and adolescent culture of the past two decades. Oppliger (2004) characterises this 'mook' culture as one that indulges in happy violence and bathroom humour. She also points out that, in many other areas of media production, this form of behaviour is much more exaggerated: "video games are more graphic, sitcoms are bolder with sexual jokes, shock jock radio exploits women, and television talk shows cash in on class exploitation" (Oppliger, 2004: 160). As teenagers and young adolescents are its core demographic, wrestling has adapted to this bawdy, careless 'mook' culture.

## Criticism

Naturally, wrestling has been criticised for a number of these aspects, the most prominent being its use of violence as means of resolving conflicts. It is interesting to note that the WWE is under attack from both the left (violence, misogyny, homophobia, etc.) and the right (moral relativism, violence, etc.) (Sammond, 2005a). Professional wrestling today still presents a conservative and exaggerated image of masculinity, which "ultimately glorifies the most antisocial characteristics of traditional masculinity for its primarily young, male audience" (Pawlowski, 2006: 349). From 'Stone Cold' Steve Austin, one of the most popular and successful performers in WWE, viewers can learn that it is acceptable to 'flip off' (swear using hand gestures) your boss on a regular basis and then slam him head first onto the floor. The only justification needed are phrases like "I don't give a damn!" or "Because Stone Cold said so" (Pratten, 2003: 40).

But it is not only aggressive behaviour that viewers are exposed to. The status of women in professional wrestling is also highly ambivalent. While the scope of this chapter does not allow for a detailed discussion, I do offer a broad overview of the position of women in the industry.[3] Ring 'girls' have been part of wrestling's fixtures and fittings for decades. They are almost always scantily clad and conform to a mainstream beauty ideal. It is interesting that they are usually adjacent to a man and are only ever addressed in terms of their first name, while men are addressed with their full name. In other words, they are never complete without their man (Migliore, 1993). They are not subjects, but more often than not, objects of male desire, lust or jealousy, and men frequently treat 'their women' as though they were objects to be traded or sold (Oppliger, 2004). Such objectification of women also becomes evident in their relationship with the live audience who regularly subjugate their position by chanting for them to bring out their 'puppies' (breasts) (Oppliger, 2004: 131).

While female wrestling has existed for a number of decades, expectations over their physicality have changed. Traditionally, female wrestlers would be physically strong and muscular – both obvious prerequisites for being a wrestler. More contemporaneously, however, demands over their bodies have changed. Women in WWE's Diva Wrestling (the clue is in the name) almost uniformly conform to the male-gaze beauty ideal. They wear very revealing costumes, frequently appear just in bras and 'panties' and generally miss no opportunity to show their oversized breasts to the camera. This "hyperfeminine" (Oppliger, 2004: 130) version of wrestling is consciously designed to attract male fans. Their actual contribution, as sports people, to the event, is minor. Matches are never as spectacular as male ones and female wrestling will normally only appear once in a show.

Following Brian Pronger (1990), most sports events can be understood as arenas for defining and playing out gender in heteronormative ways. Professional wrestling is no exception. While women have to display hyperfeminine qualities, men need to show an exaggerated form of hypermasculinity. Such pronounced forms of masculinity become necessary due to the nature of professional wrestling. As Oppliger (2004) points out, two sweaty men in spandex pants grappling with each other will easily lead to homoerotic associations. To counter this impression, wrestlers will exaggerate their heterosexuality, for instance by engaging in 'school yard' homophobia in the form of name calling. The 'Beverly Brothers' are a case in point. They had a very effeminate look and consequently were regularly greeted by fans with chants of "faggot, faggot".[4] Another example is 'Goldust', a wrestler who came to the ring in a golden full body suit, golden make-up and wig. His special move was to kiss his opponents, which often stunned them in such a way that he was able to defeat them instantly. However, he was also regularly beaten up by 'straight' wrestlers who punished his purported homosexuality (Oppliger, 2004). Pronger (1990) suspects that a large percentage of wrestling fans are to some degree conscious of an homoerotic tension, and that some fans attend for that very reason. Currently there is no study on homosexuality and professional wrestling, and it is clear that, in the shows of the WWE, homoeroticism or homosexuality are never in any way shown as equal or openly practised.[5] Goldust today has turned from evil gay *heel* into a beloved *face*. He has dropped the homoerotic behaviour and manoeuvres, but still wears his wig and costume. A homoerotic tension is present, therefore, but only on a subtle level. It is dealt with, but only ever in a negative way, while the values of heterosexual, sportive competition and homosocial (but not homoerotic) bonding are glorified.

## Wrestling and contemporary society

Consequently, it must be asked whether professional wrestling is subversive or conservative in essence? Evidently, there is a problem with pinning down wrestling on either side of the fence. What is apparent is its great and steady popularity. As it speaks to broad audiences, it seems logical that it embodies both conservatism and subversion, but above all, it reflects current debates and anxieties of a society. According to Hackett (2006: 74):

> [T]here was a kind of genius to professional wrestling, so perfectly did it dramatize the preoccupations and pathologies of society. Through speech, song, and dance, pro wrestling spoke to matters of broad and compelling interest. It performed art's function: it said the right things at the right time in the right way to the right people.

Through its very physicality and legibility, wrestling can bring to the stage issues to be debated in society that cannot be debated in other forums. For instance, the wrestlers' bodies emanate that they are rebels against middle class, corporate lifestyles; their tattoos, piercings, flamboyant accessories and lewd behaviour seem to signify a certain rebellion against these values. At the same time, however, they are fitted into a highly corporate discourse of professional wrestling, so that they become both subject of rebellion and corporate object (Sammond, 2005a). Wrestling brings together these dichotomies without ever resolving, or even wanting, to resolve them. According to Sammond (2005a: 3) "[Wrestling] is about bodies marked by race, ethnicity, gender, class and sexuality, operating in a democratic capitalist national culture that lacks a robust language for speaking about concrete, lived experience". Wrestling, then, is democratic and elitist at the same time; it debates issues (or provides a stage for these issues to be aired) but does not answer them in any definitive way. It may, however, provide information about current sensitivities and anxieties in society. It is

> a hotly contested site for working out social, cultural, political and economic ideals and desires. While wrestlers grapple with each other, the signs that fit so uneasily across their straining bodies ... represent an unequal and uneasy negotiation of social meanings, a struggle to name what proper and just social relations are in a capitalist mass society.
>
> (Sammond, 2005a: 15)

For the majority of fans, wrestling is one of the few places to voice their concerns and to participate in public discourse. The wrestling ring is the locus where topics such as homosociality, family relations or the status of working-class men in a society characterised by an ever-accelerating information economy, can be debated. This is the reason why conservatives fear the subversive power of professional wrestling, and liberals condemn its conservatism.

Finally, wrestling's sheer physicality, the spectacle of brutality and excess, also serves another function in relation to the audience. As previously argued, over the past three decades, wrestling has grown much more violent, risky and brutal (Jenkins IV 2005b). Audiences apparently delight in the violence displayed, almost according to the rule 'the bloodier the better' (Oppliger, 2004), which raises the question as to why brutality seems to be so sought after by audiences. It can be argued that professional wrestling constitutes a civilised form of anger outlet (Schulze, 2013). The need of audiences for violent spectacles arises out of a society that is deemed very safe, where conflict and physical brutality play no role at all in most people's lives. While the media may revel in spiralling crime rates, and an ever more risk-laden society (Beck, 1992), in everyday life, risk is largely absent. At the same time, as Konrad Lorenz (1966) argues, humans are not much different from other primates (and other animals for that matter), in that they possess a certain degree of natural aggression. These instinctual urges can, in a postmodern society, no longer be tolerated, and so they are tamed, and other ways of dealing with them have to be found. Norbert Elias (1978: 202–203) has commented on this phenomenon:

> And this is very characteristic of the kind of transformation through which the civilization of the affects takes place. For example, belligerence and aggression find socially permitted expression in sporting contests. And they are expressed especially in 'spectating' (e.g., boxing matches), in the imaginary identification with a small number of combatants to whom moderate and precisely regulated scope is granted for the release of such affects.

The primitive structure of a wrestling match enables the spectator to connect with his/her instinctual urges while, at the same time, it never challenges the monopoly on legitimate violence. Wrestling has a pacifying function for society. While moral clarity may have vanished from professional wrestling, the cathartic moment that Barthes (1976) describes still very much exists. It is, however, not just a discharge of negative emotion but rather a renewed contact with brutality and violence that has been marginalised in contemporary society(ies).

## Conclusions

In Barthes' time, each match formed a discrete and complete unit that displayed a concept of moral clarity (i.e. good triumphs over evil). While a binary of good/evil still exists today, this dichotomy alone will no longer carry the event. Storylines are needed to build tension for each match, often evolving over many weeks or months. Matches are no longer structured around the concepts of good against evil; instead they revolve around specific (soap opera) issues, be it a staged battle for custody over a child, or the struggle to find a father figure. Wrestling events such as *Raw* or *Smackdown!* are certainly more spectacular than Barthes could/would have envisioned. They frequently involve music, pyrotechnics, guest-star appearances and other show effects (Pratten, 2003). Within this show, the audience's responses are, however, still as visceral as Barthes describes them. Audiences are able to experience cathartic moments, to influence the story they see, and they are crucial, through their physical responses, to the construction of the event. They cheer their heroes who do not necessarily fit into a good/evil dichotomy, but are still part of a strong/weak binary, that follows a 'might makes right' ideology (de Garis, 2005). The moral framework and concept of justice that Barthes saw has thus given way to an ideology of survival of the fittest where the only thing that matters is strength, not moral rectitude. The WWE itself, and Vince McMahon at the head, have shown how ruthlessness and brutal strength can transform a local business into a global monopoly. WWE enjoys global success and so the concept of brutality and survival of the fittest is a mentality of worldwide currency. Within this discourse, professional wrestling delights in pushing the boundaries of what is socially acceptable and in good taste, while at the same time displaying very conservative, heteronormative values (Sammond, 2005b). The values on display are often highly problematic with regards to their influence on young viewers, who make up the majority of fans. Specifically, the use of violence, homophobia, as well as misogyny and anti-social behaviour, constitute dubious role models. Wrestling thus provides a good target for both conservative and liberal criticism. As argued by Jenkins III (2005a: 302):

> For some wrestling is dangerous because it is so ruthlessly patriarchal and reactionary; for others, because it embodies moral relativism. For some it is a symptom for a world without gatekeepers and for others, the dangers of media concentration. For most, it is frightening because it crosses class boundaries.

In the same way that society has become much more morally ambiguous and diverse since the 1950s, wrestling has become less easy to pin down. It is an arena where many current issues and anxieties within a society are articulated, discussed and debated. In this respect, it can be both conservative (e.g. maintaining misogyny) or liberal (e.g. promoting youthful rebellion). Indeed, these aspects run side by side without ever really being resolved. Thus, it could be argued that professional wrestling is a paradox: it is conservative subversion.

## Notes

1 For a good description of the independent circuit in the United States, see Hackett (2006), Beekman (2006) and de Garis (2005).
2 For a detailed discussion of fan involvement at wrestling events, see Ford (2007a).
3 For an in-depth discussion of professional wrestling and gender issues, see Oppliger (2004) and Salmon and Clerk (2005).
4 It is interesting to note that 'faggot' is the general word of disapproval for any wrestler who underperforms, simply loses a match or is in some other way not liked (cf. Hackett 2006).
5 Pronger proffers that all sports have the inherent potential to threaten heteronormative sexuality (1999). For a discussion of sports, homsociality and homosexuality see Pronger (1990). Very recently (August 2013), WWE 'Superstar' Darren Young became the first active professional wrestler to announce that he was gay (cf. Rogers, 2013). While the initial responses from WWE and fellow wrestlers were all positive, it remains to be seen how his career develops from now on. It is certain that his case will prove fruitful for further research regarding wrestling and homosexuality.

## References

Barthes, R. ([1957] 1976) *Mythologies*. London: Vintage.
Battema, D. and Sewell, P. (2005) Trading in masculinity: Muscles, money, and market discourse in the WWF. In Sammond, N. (ed.) *Steel chair to the head: The pleasure and pain of professional wrestling*. Durham (NC): Duke University Press, 260–295.
Beck, U. (1992) *Risk society: Towards a new modernity*. London: Sage.
Beekman, S. (2006) *Ringside: A history of professional wrestling in America*. Westport (CT): Praeger.
Best of WWE: Vol. 1 (2009) *Rey Mysterio* [DVD] WWE. Silver Vision.
Best of WWE: Vol. 6 (2009) *New and Improved DX* [DVD] WWE. Silver Vision.
de Garis, L. (2005) The "logic" of professional wrestling. In Sammond, N. (ed.) *Steel chair to the head: The pleasure and pain of professional wrestling*. Durham (NC): Duke University Press, 192–212.
Elias, N. (1978) *The civilizing process: Sociogenetic and psychogenetic investigations. Vol 1: The history of manners*. Oxford: Blackwell.
Ford, S. (2007a) Pinning down fan involvement: An examination of multiple modes of engagement for professional wrestling fans. *Material of the MIT Programme in Comparative Media Studies* (2007). [Online] Available from http://ocw.mit.edu/courses/comparative-media-studies/cms-997-topics-in-comparative-media-american-pro-wrestling-spring-2007/readings/ford_role_playing.pdf [accessed 26 August 2013].

Ford, S. (2007b) Mick Foley: Pro wrestling and the contradictions of contemporary American heros. *Futures of Entertainment* [Online] Available from www.convergence-culture.org/weblog/2007/07/mick_foley_pro_wrestling_and_t_3.php [accessed 26 August 2013].

Hackett, T. (2006) *Slaphappy: Pride, prejudice and professional wrestling.* New York: HarperCollins.

*Hell in a Cell: The Greatest Hell in a Cell Matches of all Time* (2008) [DVD] WWE. WWE Home Video.

Jenkins, H. III. (2005a) Afterword, part I: Wrestling with theory, grappling with politics. In Sammond, N. (ed.) *Steel chair to the head: The pleasure and pain of professional wrestling.* Durham (NC): Duke University Press, 295–316.

Jenkins, H. IV. (2005b) Afterword, part II: Growing up and growing more risqué. In Sammond, N. (ed.) *Steel chair to the head: The pleasure and pain of professional wrestling.* Durham (NC): Duke University Press, 317–342.

Lorenz, K. (1966) *On aggression* (Translated by M. Latzke). London: Methuen.

MacFarlane, K. (2012) A sport, a tradition, a religion, a joke: The need for a poetics of in-ring storytelling and a reclamation of professional wrestling as global art. *Asiatic.* 6: 136–155.

Migliore, S. (1993) Professional wrestling: Moral commentary through ritual metaphor. *Journal of Ritual Studies,* 7(1): 65–84.

Oliva, C. and Calleja, G. (2009) Fake rules, real fiction: Professional wrestling and video-games. *The Proceedings of DIGRA 2009 Brunel University UK.* [Online] Available from www.digra.org/dl/db/09287.48172.pdf [accessed 26 August 2013].

Oppliger, P.A. (2004) *Wrestling and hypermasculinity.* Jefferson (NC): McFarland.

Pawlowski, C. (2006) Images of stereotypically masculine power in professional wrestling. In Wright, W. and Kaplan, S. (eds) *The image of power: Selected papers – 2006 Conference – Society for the interdisciplinary study of social imagery.* Pueblo (CO): Society for the Interdisciplinary Study of Social Imagery, 349–353.

Pratten, J.D. (2003) Professional wrestling: Multi-million pound soap opera of sports entertainment. *Management Research News,* 26(5): 32–43.

Pronger, B. (1990) *The arena of masculinity: Sports, homosexuality, and the meaning of sex.* London: St. Martin's Press.

Pronger, B. (1999) Fear and trembling: Homophobia in men's sport. In White, P. and Young, K. (eds) *Sport and gender in Canada.* Oxford: Oxford University Press, 182–196.

Rogers, K. (2013) Darren Young: American WWE star comes out as gay. *Guardian Online.* [Online] Available from www.theguardian.com/sport/2013/aug/15/darren-young-wwe-wrestler-comes-out [accessed 5 September 2013].

Salmon, C. and Clerk, S. (2005) "Ladies love wrestling too": Female wrestling fans online. In Sammond, N. (ed.) *Steel chair to the head: The pleasure and pain of professional wrestling.* Durham (NC): Duke University Press, 167–191.

Sammond, N. (2005a) Introduction. In Sammond, N. (ed.) *Steel chair to the head: The pleasure and pain of professional wrestling.* Durham (NC): Duke University Press, 1–22.

Sammond, N. (2005b) Squaring the family circle: WWF Smackdown assaults the social body. In Sammond, N. (ed.) *Steel chair to the head: The pleasure and pain of professional wrestling.* Durham (NC): Duke University Press, 132–166.

Schulze, D. (2013) Blood, guts and suffering: The body as communicative agent in professional wrestling and performance art. *Journal of Contemporary Drama in English,* 1(1): 113–125.

Schwartz, D.G. (2003) Carnival entertainment: The carnival origins of professional wrestling and casino gambling. *Popular Culture Review*, 2(14): 5–14.

WWE (World Wrestling Entertainment Inc.) (2009a) *Research: US Statistics*. [Online] Available from http://adsales.wwe.com/research [accessed 26 August 2013].

WWE (World Wrestling Entertainment Inc.) (2009b) *Press release: Wrestlemania record sellout* [Online] Available from http://corporate.wwe.com/news/2009/2009_04_05.jsp [accessed 26 August 2013].

WWE (World Wrestling Entertainment Inc.) (2011) *2011 Annual report* [Online] Available from http://ir.corporate.wwe.com/FinancialDocs.aspx?iid=4121687 [accessed 26 August 2013].

WWE (World Wrestling Entertainment Inc.) (2012) *First quarter 2012* [Online] Available from http://ir.corporate.wwe.com/corporateprofile.aspx?iid=4121687 [accessed 26 August 2013].

# 4 A glamorous and high-tech global spectacle of speed

## Formula One motor racing as mediated, global and corporate spectacle

*Damion Sturm*

## Introduction

Formula One is viewed as the pinnacle of motor racing (if not all motorsport), with many of the world's best drivers racing expensive, sophisticated and high-tech machines at circuits around the globe. This generates widespread media and audience interest, as well as substantial funding from large transnational corporations who adorn the cars and drivers with their sponsors' logos. This chapter focuses on Formula One's sporting spectacle, illuminating the mediated, global and commercial dimensions that constitute and permeate Formula One's projection of a glamorous and high-tech global spectacle of speed. I begin the chapter by exploring Formula One's media representations and technologies, with a focus on how televised coverage makes the racing engaging for its audience. Formula One's global spectacle is then interrogated, introducing Ritzer's (2004, 2006) theories of the 'grobal' and 'glocal' in relation to Formula One's imposition of a standardised global spectacle and its contested redeployment by and for branding localities. Finally, the Formula One corporate spectacle is developed, mapping the influence of transnational corporate sponsors who commercialise, brand and sell Formula One as a commodity spectacle.

## Formula One as media event and media spectacle

For many scholars, contemporary mediated sport is recognised for its various 'complexities' and interconnections, being discussed through terms such as the 'media sports cultural complex' (Rowe, 2004), the 'global media-sport complex' (Maguire, 1999), or in relation to the interdependence of sport, media, culture, commerce and politics (Whannel, 1992, 2008; Horne, 2006; Boyle and Haynes, 2009). Formula One's commercialism, innovative mediation, prestige and popular global status make it a prime example of such interrelationships in contemporary sport. Formula One is clearly also a major sporting event, currently comprising an annual series of 19 races at venues around the world. Whether this also constitutes a 'mega-event' is unclear. Roche (2000: 1) asserts that "'mega-events' are large-scale cultural (including commercial and sporting) events which have a dramatic character, mass popular appeal and international significance". Formula One would appear to fit these criteria through its sheer scale, global exposure, elite positioning, vast commercial and corporate interests, and the mass media attention that it garners. Nevertheless, the label 'mega-event' is often only applied exclusively to the Olympic Games or Football World Cup (Roche, 2000, 2002; Rowe, 2004; Hayes and Karamichas, 2012) while, inexplicably, Formula One is rarely discussed (see Boyle and Haynes, 2009; Fleming and Sturm, 2011; Sturm, 2011; Silk and Manley, 2012).

Intriguingly, Formula One remains largely inaccessible (and not always comprehensible) due to its commercial apparatuses and layers of technological sophistication (Noble and Hughes, 2004; Fleming and Sturm, 2011). To compensate, Formula One has been transformed into a media event that reproduces and projects itself as an exemplar of Kellner's (2003, 2010) 'spectacular and seductive' global media spectacle, a concept returned to shortly. The sport's historical context is important in this regard. Since its inception in 1950 through until the 1980s, Formula One essentially operated as an ad hoc and disjointed series of races with fluctuating team and grid numbers at every race. In the early 1980s, Bernie Ecclestone, president of the Formula One Constructors Association, sensed the commercial possibilities of the sport and, in particular, the influential role that televised coverage could play. Hotten (1999: 29) suggests that "Ecclestone's masterstroke was to promise circuit owners a full grid of teams; teams had to commit themselves to a full season of racing. This pleased the crowds, it pleased the sponsors, and it pleased the television stations". Not only did Ecclestone streamline the sport, he also re-packaged Formula One as an event *for* the media by negotiating lucrative worldwide television rights that currently are valued at US$600 million per year (Saward, 2013). Ecclestone's Formula One Management (FOM) can be directly credited with transforming the sport into a premier global spectacle, with races telecast to over 500 million viewers across 185 countries (Baldwin, 2013).

According to Kellner (2003, 2010), spectacles, images and commodities are fundamental aspects of our contemporary mediated and consumerist culture. The specific range and display of media spectacles is multifaceted but, broadly speaking, they comprise the spectacular, seductive and sensationalised representation of events. Kellner is drawing upon and reworking the earlier ideas of Debord (1994) who theorised media spectacles in relation to commodification. More specifically, for Debord, society was "organized around the production and consumption of images, commodities and staged events" (cited in Kellner, 2003: 2) with the commodity-spectacle integral and dominant. However, for Kellner, this monolithic, abstract and deterministic focus (e.g. spectacles as pre-packaged commodities) fails to reflect or understand the diversity of contemporary spectacles. Kellner (2010: 76) surmises:

> By spectacle, I mean media constructs that are out of the ordinary and outside of habitual daily routine which become special media spectacles. They involve an aesthetic dimension and are often dramatic.... They are

highly public social events, often taking a ritualistic form to celebrate society's highest values ... media spectacles are increasingly commercialized, vulgar, glitz, and ... important arenas of political contestation.

Moreover, he suggests that there has also been a significant temporal and cultural shift from media events to media spectacles. Previously, Dayan and Katz (1992) traced media events as a recurrent series of 'contests, conquests and coronations' (inclusive of sport). Kellner asserts that media events now are a form of media spectacle, whereby dazzling representations and excessive displays, in combination with the convergence of media, technologies, entertainment and commercialisation, serve to amplify the projection and circulation of images. Sport's integration with and transformation through the spectacle is evident. Collectively, lavish and spectacular displays of technology, commerce, celebrity and identities envelope and re-place sport events as spectacle. Formula One is an excellent case in point.

Representationally, Formula One is constructed as a glamorous and high-tech global spectacle of speed. Indeed, it can be asserted that the sport is premised on a mix of speed, expense and the exotic, with 'glamour' often the short-hand distillation. For example, Noble and Hughes (2004: 25) infer that Formula One's glamour relates to "impossibly fast cars driven by brave and handsome young men of all nationalities in a variety of exotic backdrops throughout the world, with beautiful women looking on adoringly". Such clichéd assumptions are continually evoked and redistributed via the Formula One spectacle. Hence, they emphasise the expense and technical sophistication of the cars and embellish Formula One's array of global locations (such as the 'spectacular' sights and sites of city-based circuits in Monaco and Singapore), while Formula One promotes an expensive, consumerist, jet-setting lifestyle. The male drivers are, conceivably, an embodiment of the sport's glamour too through their globe-trotting displays of masculine bravado and apparently luxurious lifestyles. In turn, problematically, the relatively few women in Formula One often function as adornments or trophies for the men and their cars. Regrettably, the perpetuation of such sexist stereotypes reifies Formula One's glamorous spectacle, with Turner (2004: 205) suggesting "it is the ultimate male fantasist's sport: fast cars, expensive kit, global jet-setting and beautiful women with spray-on smiles".

The prioritisation of creating a media spectacle does, however, have its limits. Indeed, due to the over-reliance on sophisticated technology and simulations that model and predict all aspects of racing, Formula One potentially risks providing a 'non-event' (Baudrillard, 2002; Fleming and Sturm, 2011). Specifically, all the teams have high-tech computers, machine and wind simulators back in the factories, as well as advanced driver training simulators that are extensively used prior to arriving at the event. Fortunately, a concerted effort has been made to enhance the racing spectacle, with recent regulatory and technological refinements making the sport less predictable, less processional and arguably less monotonous than earlier eras. Conversely, Pirelli's rapidly degrading tyres and the Drag Reduction System (DRS) – an aerodynamic device which assists with overtaking – potentially makes the current races too artificial and mere entertainment (Cary, 2013; Hughes and Noble, 2013).[1]

Outside of the racing, scandalous spectacles also emerge, such as Nelson Piquet Jnr. deliberately crashing at Singapore in 2008 to help his teammate win, or the farcical 2005 United States Grand Prix where only six cars actually participated due to Michelin's unsafe tyres. Staging recent races in Bahrain, despite its oppressive political regime, has also been controversial. The continued use of team orders to manipulate race results remains divisive, most infamously with Ferrari ordering Rubens Barrichello to let his teammate Michael Schumacher win only metres from the line in Austria 2002 or, more recently, Sebastian Vettel flouting team orders and passing team mate, and race leader, Mark Webber at Malaysia in 2013. Finally, the spectre of death looms; there have been no fatalities since 1994 but annual big crashes provide spectacles of destruction and carnage. Combining sophisticated machines, high-speed racing and both humanistic and consumerist ambitions, Formula One crystallises around its mediated projection as a glamorous and high-tech global spectacle of speed.

## Formula One's mediated spectacle

Formula One relies on pervasive and widespread mediation to affectively redirect its complex commercial apparatuses and technological dynamics as an engaging spectacle (Baudrillard, 2002; Fleming and Sturm, 2011). Surprisingly though, given the high-tech focus and sophistication of its cars, as well as the increasing prevalence of digital media, Formula One is still overwhelmingly reliant on traditional broadcast media forms for its global circulation and consumption. Like many other contemporary sports, it is the global television rights (estimated at US$600 million annually) that are fundamental for Formula One's revenue streams (Hayes and Karamichas, 2012; Saward, 2013). Therefore, understanding how sport is re-presented and transformed by television is essential, with notions of actuality, realism, anchorage, immediacy and liveness coming to the fore.

Productions aim for actuality and a "transparency effect" (Whannel, 1992: 37) when re-presenting sport. Nevertheless, television sport does not simply 'occur', nor present the 'reality' of sport. Rather, sport is circumscribed by its moulding, adaption and reinscription for the televisual format through a range of constructed and selective processes, including framing, editing and narrativisation. Such a reinscription also aims for a sense of viewer omnipotence through the liveness and immediacy of the event, conveying to viewers that they are receiving coverage in real time, live and direct from whichever global locality it is being staged from (Whannel, 1992; Boyle and Haynes, 2009).

Additionally, while the unpredictability of sport complements the demands of television, there is often a contradictory climate of seeking to entertain as well as inform viewers. Whannel (1992: 94) observes that, "entertainment values organise visual images according to the need to highlight pleasure points – action, stars, drama – attempting to construct an entertaining assemblage capable of winning and holding an audience". Such pleasure points are further emphasised and embellished by the anchoring role of commentators who effectively position, inform and entertain the audience during the telecast. The former voice of Formula One, Murray Walker, exemplified this, providing a mixture of encyclopaedic knowledge, banalities, over-excitement and error-ridden comments that were in equal parts compelling and frustrating for his large viewing audience between 1949 and 2001.

Collectively, these processes are essential elements for the representation and transformation of televised sport. Additionally, Formula One's highly advanced broadcasting techniques and technologies serve to re-create its televisual 'screen of speed' (Baudrillard, 2002). Representationally, an array of camera placements and positions are used to frame the racing from trackside (traditional cameras and wall-mounted), above (helicopters and cranes), below (cameras embedded in the track) and on the cars themselves. Overall, approximately 20–30 cameras are used to film most circuits, excluding the two or more on-board cameras (OBC) mounted on every car. Moreover, the rapid interchanging of perspectives adds to Formula One's spectacle of speed. There are continual intercuts from trackside cameras to cameras on the cars and even interchanges from varying individual driver OBCs when battling on track, interspersed with salient replays. This combination of camera work and editing produces a highly mobilised fluidity to an event notoriously difficult to frame given the high speeds and geographically diverse terrain (Whannel, 1992).

Complementing this highly mobilised fluidity is the deployment of technological innovations, particularly the sustained OBC footage. These afford degrees of Kellner's (2010: 77) "interactive spectacle", providing viewers with intriguing pseudo-racing perspectives and a 'dazzling' array of visual information to relay the driving experience. With all cars carrying on-board cameras and footage continually framed and intercut from this point-of-view, viewers are restricted to an illusory shared racer's perspective. Therefore, in a visual, temporal and spatial sense, viewers share the racer's experience and see only what he sees, getting a visceral, spatial and technologically embodied racing spectacle.

Finally, by combining sophisticated technologies with innovative camera placements, a continual flow of on-screen textual information, and expert commentary from ex-drivers, the slickly produced Formula One televisual broadcast (often in high definition) transforms the sometimes predictable sport into a glamorous and high-tech global spectacle of speed. The Formula One broadcast arguably has the ability to fascinate, allure and interpellate its viewers into the visual and visceral Formula One driving experience, while its illusory amplification of such intensities and affective impulses further furnishes and underscores its significance as a global media spectacle.

Seemingly confirming this spectacular status, the claimed viewing figures for the sport are phenomenal, albeit excessive, with Formula One telecasts building a cumulative global audience that surpassed 50 billion annually during the 1990s and 2000s. As with all sport viewing statistics, such figures are overstated 'guesstimates', and unreliable (Rowe, 2004), with Hotten (1999: 200) observing that these include "every time an item on Formula One appears on television, no matter how short". Recent measurements seem more realistic, with the viewing figures sitting above 500 million (across 185 territories in 2012), although steadily declining from the approximate 600 million viewers in 2008 (Baldwin, 2013). While the accuracy of such figures is debatable, Formula One's estimated 500 million viewers annually remains a significant audience within global televised sport.[2]

Presently steeped in the 'traditional' broadcast model, Formula One remains myopic in its vision for future media possibilities (F1 Broadcasting Blog, 2012). Formula One Management (FOM) attempts to control other forms of social media by rigorously policing and forcibly removing copyrighted Formula One-related clips online (e.g. YouTube). Arguably, such an approach will remain problematic, if not futile, in an increasingly digitalised media age. Additionally the official *Formula1.com* site tends towards self-promotional and sponsor-intensive content, although its 'live timing' service can be an invaluable tool to audiences. This provides a numeric and instantaneous representation of all pertinent Grand Prix data (e.g. lap times, sector times) during each session, allowing for an enhanced analysis of each driver's performance (Sturm, 2011).

While *Formula1.com* is seemingly the obvious site for future 'official' global live visual streaming, such transformations may still be some way off. Strategically, Formula One's media coverage is firmly interlocked with, and legally restricted to, FOM's 63 global televisual broadcasts and broadcast partners (Mann, 2013). Recent 'pay TV' providers – Sky Italia and UK's Sky Sports (both since 2012), and France's Canal+ (since 2013) – annually spend £30–60 million for the Formula One broadcasting rights, and have established their own live streaming capability (Allen, 2013). Nevertheless, as Mann (2013) notes, "under current arrangements, the rights to broadcast races online reside with F1's national broadcast partners who are responsible for ensuring that the action cannot be accessed outside their home territory for fear of impacting viewing figures" (for further discussion of the free to air vs. pay TV debate, see Chapter 6 in this volume).

Finally, in many respects, the durability of lucrative broadcasting rights explains why digital media and Formula One's 'gadget cultures' complement, replicate or provide new tools for accessing the existing televisual content rather than replacing it. Summarising these trends, Fleming and Sturm (2011: 169) observe that,

New applications facilitate sending race updates to mobile phones, provide 'live timing' on the internet (plotting of cars on the circuit) or, trackside, spectators holding 'kangaroo TV' handsets to view a combination of televised footage and live timing while having the track in front of them, and offering more personalized control (they can focus on only one driver for the entire race if they so wish). There are also increasingly sophisticated simulators and video game versions, as well as an array of inventive television graphics (g-force monitors) or camera placements (especially point-of-view shots mounted on the cars) but, by and large, Formula One gadgetry for consumers is either replicating or reproducing the television footage through applications and across platforms.

Hence, the contemporary Formula One audience is reliant upon, and imbricated in, the sport's mediated terrain. Most of the digital screens and technologies serve and reinforce the dominance of the televised spectacle; even live attendees rely on the large screen displays, broadcast coverage and/or the personalised handsets to interpret or 'experience' the event. Elsewhere, the Formula One audience is globally diffuse and reliant on mediations to follow the sport. The broader audience allegedly comprises Formula One's traditional European racing territories, although other localities are also well represented in terms of either race attendance or televisual viewing (Australia, Brazil, Canada and Japan), while China significantly impacts upon the annual viewing figures (Baldwin, 2013).

Furthermore, the assumed audience is purported to be primarily male, middle-aged and arguably somewhat affluent to afford the expensive Formula One merchandise (Noble and Hughes, 2004; Fleming and Sturm, 2011). In fact, Formula One's overt commodification often necessitates audiences adopting consumerist behaviours to demonstrate their fandom. While online and digital mediations may allow forms of audience participation and fan connectivity, the sport retains its commercial imperative of essentially 'selling' Formula One fandom through the branded merchandise (Sturm, 2011; Sturm and McKinney, 2013). The sport also strives to appeal to fans, invested audiences and a perceived younger gaming generation by recreating the inaccessible Formula One driving experience through video game simulations (on home gaming consoles, networked online and as computer-based 'virtual' simulations). These games provide a technologically immersive, embodied and engaging experience for players as, through first-person driving perspectives and innovative technologies, many of these games or simulators afford sophisticated levels of realism as Formula One sensory spectacles. While televised viewing and gaming may heighten audience participant-performance experiences (Sturm, 2011), these are further diffused across various networked, online, gaming and mobile technologies, with audiences creating, producing and disseminating Formula One-inspired debate, intrigue and mediations. Collectively these mediated aspects unravel and demystify Formula One's commercial and technical apparatuses, while furnishing affective audience engagements with the seductive Formula One media spectacle.

## Formula One as global spectacle

The projection of Formula One as a glamorous and high-tech global spectacle of speed reveals an intriguing interplay between FOM's arguably monolithic conceptualisation of the sport as a globalised (or more accurately westernised) spectacle, juxtaposed against partial appropriations by glocal cities that use Grand Prix racing as a self-promotional marketing tool. Formula One certainly has a 'global' quality, comprising a range of team and driver nationalities, race localities and integrates transnational corporations as sponsors. Conceptually, globalisation reflects the altering relationship between the local and global, an interrelationship that exposes contradictions between a perhaps *mythical* shared sense of the nation on the one hand, and more fluid notions of global citizenship, processes and connectedness on the other hand (Maguire, 1999; Urry, 2003; Whannel, 2008). As Rowe (2013: 22) summarises, globalisation is generally agreed to involve "a greater interconnectedness across time and space, and that of necessity its advancement involves breaking down boundaries between institutions, people, and practices that are concentrated in nation-states". Formula One affords paradoxical evocations of nationalism, drawing on articulations of the nation-state in relation to teams and/or drivers (represented via national symbols and imagery) while positioning itself as a global sport through its mediated, commercial and geographical spread. Force India seems to be a pointed example as, despite the team's nationalistic name, it is essentially 'British' in terms of its technical staff and location in Silverstone, Northamptonshire (the site for the British Grand Prix). The drivers are Scottish and German, and there are few Indian nationals in the team.

Conceptually, the term globalisation is debated and regularly refined, with Roche (2002) identifying a paradigmatic shift from 'basic' to more 'complex' forms. For example, Roche notes distinctive shifts around initial theories that considered globalisation to be techno-economically determined, a process of standardisation and that predominantly impacted on the national-level. In turn, recent revisions have argued for greater degrees of agency, fluidity and disruption. Hence 'complex globalisation' counters that the processes are less obvious or overtly determining, are not applied universally, and that globalisation impacts in varying temporal and spatial ways on and within the nation. Before beginning to map such 'complexities' in relation to Formula One, a quick overview of some of the sport's characteristics can usefully be detailed.

Despite its global aspirations, localities and projections, Formula One still largely reflects its European origins. For example, most of the teams are based either in Britain (McLaren, Williams, Lotus, Red Bull, Force India, Mercedes, Caterham and Marussia) or another European locality (Ferrari and Toro Rosso in Italy, and Sauber in Switzerland). Furthermore, 16 of the 22 drivers in 2013 are also European, including 12 from Britain, France and Germany (four each), while four South Americans and two Australians complete the grid. As a counterpoint, Formula One has also reflected an increasing global presence as European events are steadily replaced on the calendar (for example, 11 of 17 races were in Europe in 2000). Currently, the 12 non-European localities, particularly the six races across Asia, book-end the seven European events in 2013. Furthermore, with new venues provisionally approved in Russia, Mexico and New Jersey for 2014, the sport continues to strive for global expansion beyond its European origins.

Nevertheless, while Formula One serves as an obvious contemporary example of global sport, it seemingly still remains rooted in an older model of globalisation. In particular, Formula One projects a standardised and universalised spectacle of Grand Prix racing to the world, while primarily imposing itself on the host localities through a set of Eurocentric and westernised expectations. In this regard Formula One reproduces Roche's (2002) articulation of 'basic globalisation', albeit with the cautionary reminder that "in different locations, different contexts, different circumstances, the nature and configuration of the globalization process will vary" (Robins, 1997: 23). Although the final section of this chapter specifically considers Formula One as a corporate spectacle, the significant commercial orientations and implications that Formula One's globalising process has for both the FOM and for the regions will be traced here. Specifically, the concepts of the 'grobal' and the 'glocal' are now introduced to tease out the impositions, the localised variations and the possibilities for negotiating, adapting and reconfiguring the Formula One 'global brand' within the local–global nexus.

Formula One arguably reproduces a version of cultural imperialism, whereby the host nations have Formula One's homogenous global commodity spectacle imposed upon them, seemingly with little regard for the specifics of the country or culture. The terms 'grobal' and 'grobalisation' are pertinent to illuminate this process (Ritzer, 2004; Andrews and Ritzer, 2007). Grobalisation is defined as "the imperialistic ambitions of nations, corporations, organizations and the like and their desire, indeed need, to impose themselves on various geographical areas and realize their own regional and global economic aspirations and presence" (Ritzer, 2006: 338). The grobal seemingly encapsulates much of how Formula One operates, with the FOM (and its transnational sponsors) eager to tap into wealthy and populous regions, specifically to capitalise on potential revenue streams through signing up new host nations and broadcasting rights (or to furnish new sponsor markets). Indirectly, this also allows Formula One to further 'globalise' the series and possibly generate larger potential fan/audience bases but, ultimately, it is about harnessing global capital, securing global partners and disseminating the Formula One commodity spectacle.

Arguably, the pronounced focus on new markets in Asia and the Middle East have made the transposing of Formula One's homogenous global commodity spectacle most apparent (see Chapter 12 in this volume). Grobally ambitious, FOM can be conceived as imposing a stylised template for how Formula One will both operate as an event and be presented as spectacle. So, for example, with the circuits, although localised symbolism or features are often incorporated into the construction of new race venues (see below), they are predominantly designed by Herman Tilke, himself sometimes accused of reproducing 'carbon-copy' tracks (Smith, 2012). Additionally, FOM streamlines all aspects of the event to keep Formula One to some degree formulaic and, contentiously, Eurocentric. Thus, English is the first language used in all communications, while race start times differ in the distinctive localities primarily to accommodate the European televisual audience. As a result, many localities face increased pressure to align with the European time zone and requests for night races in Australia and Asia remain persistent (Tomazin, 2012). In turn, since 2007, the FOM have solely controlled the production and dissemination of race telecasts through a 'world feed' that, arguably, protects the global Formula One brand being projected.

Finally, although unique elements persist within each of the host nations, a degree of sameness and 'stylised exoticism' envelopes Formula One's commodity spectacle. For example, Silk and Manley (2012: 475) infer that while existing differences are incorporated within sporting spectacles in Asia, most often these are reduced to a "stylized global exotic", a "surface aesthetic" and "mere symbolic novelty" to make it "palatable for a global audience". Hence iconic and localised symbols are drawn upon as 'seductive images' and as representations of the 'other', albeit in often clichéd and superficial ways. Within Formula One, for example, the Malaysian track has lotus-leaf inspired grandstands or China's circuit is designed in the form of the 'Shang' symbol, but little sense of diverse cultural heritages or contexts are provided beyond these spectacular surfaces.

This applies to more overt identificatory tools, such as the iconic landscapes at city-based circuits in Monaco and Singapore, the 'localised' architectural designs or features at circuits in Abu Dhabi, Turkey and India, or venues producing individuated trophies symbolic of the host region. Unfortunately and regrettably, these techniques are also undercut by the stereotypical 'glamorous' projection of localised beauty as an 'exotic' prize, with attentive young females applauding the winning drivers in the host nation's (sexualised) attire. Hence, while such aspects may 'place' the event in a different locale, Formula One's glamorous and high-tech global spectacle of speed can be viewed as essentially a standardised grobal imposition reflecting the commercial interests of FOM.

Of course, there will always be local variations, nuances and anomalies, as well as a broader duality of both homogenisation and heterogenisation at play within the glocal (Whannel, 2008; Giulianotti and Robertson, 2012). For example, Ritzer (2006: 337) defines glocalisation as "the interpenetration of the global and the local, resulting in unique outcomes in different geographic areas". This grobal and glocal interplay is significant as, in fact, many localities share Formula One's 'grobalising' vision. That is, some localities conceive of sport as a prominent global platform, as a means to establish their global cultural currency, for instilling civic pride, boosting tourism and, particularly, as a pertinent global/corporate spectacle through which projections of their cities, nations and global aspirations can manifest (Giulianotti and Robertson, 2012; Hayes and Karamichas, 2012; Silk and Manley, 2012). Formula One itself relies upon seductive images to market its commodity spectacle. Equally, host locations redeploy Formula One's global brand as glocally marketable images of 'global' cities and desirable destinations.

In the case of Singapore, Silk and Manley (2012) suggest that the city-state has intentionally constructed a 'spectacle of speed' that is glamorous and self-promotional. As Formula One's only night race, Singapore sells a "'unique' image of self for internal and external consumption" (Silk and Manley, 2012:

464), connoting vibrancy, entertainment, atmosphere and the 'exotic', while the racing backdrop affords a dazzling visual display. Silk and Manley (2012: 465) conclude, "the event offered unique signifiers palatable for global consumption—highly visible (or perhaps hyperreal) images of the material landscape—with skyscrapers, speed and roads as the epitome of symbolic corporate power and global cultural capital".

Alternatively, South Korea's creation of a track in Yeongam to promote the lesser known southern regions (far removed from the larger cities of Seoul and Busan) has struggled to attract its projected commercial interest, development or audiences. Therefore, strategically, South Korea's Formula One commodity spectacle has had questionable value for regional/global marketing, boosting tourism or for fulfilling FOM's commercial ambitions. Moreover, South Korea's perceived failure in relation to Singapore's success underscores Formula One's grobal equation of sports tourism with large cities and Eurocentric symbols of consumption. Thus, these globalising ambitions reveal an intriguing grobal/ glocal interrelationship colluding around the imposition, display and usage of Formula One as a global commodity spectacle.

## Formula One as corporate spectacle

Emblematic of Debord's (1994) commodity spectacle, Formula One provides a dazzling and spectacular display of sport as corporatised media spectacle through its extravagance and excess. Kellner (2003: 14) suggests that, within the society of the spectacle, "individuals are transfixed by the packaging, display, and consumption of commodities and the play of media events". With cars and drivers saturated in transnational corporate logos, races set against a materialistic backdrop of branded billboards (or at times through self-promotional city landscapes) and being staged as a major global media event, Formula One seems the perfect exemplar of the corporate commodity spectacle. Indeed, it could be asserted that, commercially, Formula One's glamorous and high-tech global spectacle of speed revolves around corporations, branding and exploiting Formula One's symbolic value.

Derived from its perceived elite positioning and high-tech emphasis, exorbitant funds are spent annually on the series, previously exceeding US$2 billion for all the teams during the 2000s (Henry, 2005). However, the sport has introduced continual 'cost-cutting' measures to curb such expenditure, enforced in part by the global economic recession and three high-profile manufacturers exiting the sport (Honda in 2008 and subsequently BMW and Toyota in 2009). The teams often operate as brands themselves, with Fleming and Sturm (2011: 170) noting "Ferrari *is* the F1 brand among brands" given its aura of history, success and broader mythical tapestries of personalities, performances and prestige. Of course, given the public inaccessibility to teams and technologies, such projections are redirected symbolically back into the hands (and onto the bodies) of its fans through the commodified merchandise as noted earlier.

Of the current teams, only Ferrari (1950), McLaren (1963) and Williams (1977) have long histories, with most being more recent and potentially ever-changing acquisitions. For example, Mercedes re-emerged in 2010 to evoke its previous successes in Formula One, acquiring an established team with a succession of owners to do so; Mercedes was originally Tyrell in 1968, British American Racing (BAR) from 1999, Honda from 2006 and Brawn in 2009. Alternatively, the iconic Lotus name, brand and/or trademark was purchased by a new or existing team (Team Lotus in 2010; Renault as Lotus F1 in 2012) in an instant attempt to procure 'aura' and symbolic Formula One status with, for example, Lotus F1 replicating the much admired black Lotus colour scheme of the 1970s and 1980s. Alternatively, other teams, such as Toyota, fail to project these prestigious elements, generating a bland corporate image with limited success, fan interest or 'charisma' and subsequently exit the sport (Fleming and Sturm, 2011).

The emergence of Red Bull Racing in 2005 further illustrates Formula One's overtly corporate spectacle. Red Bull can be viewed as a grobally ambitious company using the sport's global platform to promote and sell its product. As *F1 Racing* magazine asserts, "Red Bull aren't a racing team, they're a soft drinks company, and are in F1 only to increase sales through brand awareness" (Pitpass expose, 2007: 29). Thus, in its initial years, Red Bull Racing promulgated 'lifestyle' images as a high-energy, fun, hard-partying and 'rebellious' team. Ironically its recent years of success have seen a shift from such posturing to being symptomatic of Formula One's complicit corporate conservativism. Their Formula One operation evinces teams as branded commodities, with Red Bull reliant on Formula One's corporate spectacle to enable the spread of global capital and generate more potential revenue streams.

Clearly other grobally ambitious transnational companies also flock to the sport, primarily as major sponsors contributing vast sums to the teams' operating budgets. In return, the cars, team members and drivers are adorned with the sponsored logos which underpin Formula One's branded corporate spectacle. Not surprisingly, key players in the automobile industry have been involved, such as fuel, lubricant and tyre companies, while car manufacturers were pertinent investors and teams between 2006 and 2009 (currently only Ferrari and Mercedes are active). Previously tobacco companies had sustained Grand Prix racing for nearly 40 years (1968–2005), with their sponsored cars often resembling racing 'cigarette packets'. British American Tobacco took the radical step of founding its own team in 1998, using BAR as high speed billboards for their 'Lucky Strike' brand (Fleming and Sturm, 2011).

Aside from the automobile and tobacco industries, numerous transnational companies have also been involved in Formula One. Collectively, these recent sponsors tend to reflect masculine products and interests which evoke a 'jet-set', highly-mobile and consumerist lifestyle (e.g. primarily alcohol, airlines, electronics, fashion, finance, fragrances, grooming and jewellery). However, many of the teams remain desperate for further revenue with, for example, Brawn and Sauber forced to race as predominantly unbranded, white cars in 2009 and 2010 respectively. Given the over-reliance on corporate financing, the prominence of heavily funded drivers, who literally pay for their race seats, escalated in 2013.

In relation to driver selection and expectations, transnational corporations purchase a degree of influence through sponsorship (Turner, 2004), often favouring or financially supporting a particular driver, pending the team's final approval. Obviously high-profile drivers are preferred, yet sponsors also consider other global marketing imperatives. For example, Honda created a second team for Takuma Sato (Super Aguri between 2006–2008) to keep their Japanese driver on the grid after two disappointing seasons with BAR (Fleming and Sturm, 2011). Most recently, Sauber have tapped into the Telmex South American money of Carlos Slim by, in turn, fielding the Mexican drivers Sergio Perez (2011–2012) and then Esteban Gutierrez in 2013. Williams is also financed by South American money, receiving a reputed £46 million annually from the Venezuelan Government to run Pastor Maldonado (Crash.net, 2010), a move designed to raise the nation's profile through global sporting platforms (Wise, 2013). Collectively, these interrelationships expose the deeply ingrained commercial underpinnings to Formula One's corporate spectacle, with teams dependent on sponsorship (and sponsored drivers) for their operating costs and/ or potential survival within this brand-saturated sport.

## Conclusions

With Formula One operating simultaneously as a major sporting event, media event and media spectacle, this chapter has suggested that it effectively (and affectively) redirects its complex commercial apparatuses and technological dynamics as an engaging media spectacle for its global audiences. Specifically, Formula One projects a glamorous and high-tech global spectacle of speed that evokes elitism, the exotic and an aura of expensive sophistication, often directly associated with its technologies, localities or assumed luxurious jet-set lifestyle. Primarily, Formula One's overarching spectacle is disseminated through its innovative global telecasts that construct alluring representations of the sport as an accessible and engaging spectacle. In turn, the imposition of a globalising and grobalising commodity spectacle embellishes the scale and grandeur of this sporting event. Problematically, Formula One's ambitious global brand is essentially homogenous and Eurocentric, although the host nations often recast and utilise Formula One as a global platform for glocal self-promotion. Finally, the mechanisms of commercialisation are manifest in the practices of transnational sponsors who, through their prominently displayed logos, brand and commodify Formula One cars, drivers and fans as a consumptive corporate spectacle. Vexed, complex and contradictory, Formula One's projection of a glamorous and high-tech global spectacle of speed nonetheless constitutes a seductive and dazzling global media event and spectacle.

## Notes

1 Safety concerns with the degrading Pirelli tyres were dangerously exposed during the 2013 British Grand Prix, when five drivers experienced high-speed tyre failures (shredding tyres that exploded). Fortunately no drivers were injured, but the race was almost called off on safety grounds (Cary, 2013).

2 For example, Harris (2007) lists the Formula One Brazilian Grand Prix as fifth (83 million viewers) of the most watched televised sports 'events' of 2006, well clear of the sixth-placed NASCAR Daytona 500 race (20 million). The top four were the Football World Cup final (260 million), NFL Superbowl (98 million), Winter Olympics Opening Ceremony (87 million) and the Champions League final (86 million).

# References

Allen, J. (2013) *France follows UK and Italy to pay TV model for F1 coverage*. Available at www.jamesallenonf1.com/2013/02/france-follows-uk-and-italy-to-pay-tv-model-for-f1-coverage [accessed 20 July 2013].

Andrews, D.L. and Ritzer, G. (2007) The grobal in the sporting glocal. In Giulianotti, R. and Robertson, R. (eds) *Globalization and sport*. Oxford: Blackwell, 28–45.

Baldwin, A. (2013) *Formula One viewing figures down in 2012*. Available at http://uk.reuters.com/article/2013/02/18/uk-motor-racing-television-idUKBRE91H0B020130218 [accessed 16 April 2013].

Baudrillard, J. (2002[2000]). *Screened out* (Translated by C. Turner). New York: Verso.

Boyle, R. and Haynes, R. (2009) *Power play: sport, the media and popular culture.* Second edition. Essex: Longman.

Cary, T. (2013) *British Grand Prix 2013: drivers threaten to boycott German Grand Prix after dangerous tyre explosions.* Available at www.telegraph.co.uk/sport/motorsport/formulaone/10151649/British-Grand-Prix-2013-Drivers-threaten-to-boycott-German-Grand-Prix-after-dangerous-tyre-explosions.html [accessed 20 July 2013].

Crash.net (2010) *Government backing for Maldonado.* Available at www.crash.net/f1/news/165457/1/maldonado_secures_government_backing.html [accessed 23 June 2013].

Dayan, D. and Katz, E. (1992) *Media events: the live broadcasting of history.* Cambridge: Harvard University.

Debord, G. (1994[1967]) *The society of the spectacle* (Translated by D. Nicholson-Smith). New York: Zone.

Fleming, D. and Sturm, D. (2011) *Media, masculinities and the machine: F1, Transformers and fantasizing technology at its limits.* New York: Continuum.

*F1 Broadcasting Blog* (2012) Available at http://f1broadcasting.wordpress.com/2012/10/18/why-formula-one-management-needs-a-kick-up-the-backside [accessed 20 July 2013].

Giulianotti, R. and Robertson, R. (2012) Glocalization and sport in Asia: diverse perspectives and future possibilities. *Sociology of Sport Journal*, 29: 433–454.

Harris, N. (2007). *Why Fifa's claim of one billion TV viewers was a quarter right* Available from www.independent.co.uk/sport/football/news-and-comment/why-fifas-claim-of-one-billion-tv-viewers-was-a-quarter-right-438302.html [accessed 17 June 2013].

Hayes, G. and Karamichas, J. (eds) (2012) *Olympic games, mega-events and civil societies: globalization, environment, resistance.* New York: Palgrave Macmillan.

Henry, A. (2005) Counting the cost. *F1 Racing.* Australian edition, 46–53.

Horne, J. (2006) *Sport in consumer society.* London: Palgrave Macmillan.

Hotten, R. (1999) *Formula One: the business of winning. The people, money and profits that power the world's richest sport.* London: Orion Business.

Hughes, M. and Noble, J. (2013) Formula One's tyre debate. *Autosport*, 2 May, 14–22.

Kellner, D. (2003) *Media spectacle.* New York: Routledge.

Kellner, D. (2010) Media spectacle and media events: some critical reflections. In Couldry, N., Hepp, A. and Krotz, F. (eds) *Media events in a global age.* New York: Routledge, 76–91.

Maguire, J. (1999) *Global sport: identities, societies, civilizations.* Cambridge: Polity.

Mann, C. (2013) *F1 considers online streaming.* Available at http://advanced-television. com/2013/05/28/f1-considers-online-streaming [accessed 20 July 2013].

Noble, J. and Hughes, M. (2004) *Formula One racing for dummies: an insider's guide to Formula One.* Chichester: John Wiley & Sons.

Pitpass Expose (2007) *F1 Racing.* Australian edition, 28–29.

Ritzer, G. (2004) *The globalization of nothing.* Thousand Oaks: Pine Forge.

Ritzer, G. (2006) Globalization and McDonaldization: does it all amount to … nothing? In Ritzer, G. (ed.) *McDonaldization: the reader.* Second edition. Thousand Oaks: Pine Forge, 335–348.

Robins, K. (1997) What in the world is going on? In Du Gay, P. (ed.) *Productions of culture/cultures of production.* London: Sage, 11–45.

Roche, M. (2000) *Mega-events and modernity: Olympics and expos in the growth of global culture.* London: Routledge.

Roche, M. (2002) Olympic and sport mega-events as media-events: reflections on the globalisation paradigm. *Sixth International Symposium for Olympic Research,* 1–12.

Rowe, D. (2004) *Sport, culture and the media: the unruly trinity.* Second edition. Maidenhead: Open University.

Rowe, D. (2013) Reflections on communication and sport: on nation and globalization. *Communication and Sport,* 1: 18–29.

Saward, J. (2013) *Some ruminations on TV rights.* Available at http://joesaward.wordpress.com/2013/01/07/some-ruminations-on-tv-rights [accessed 16 April 2013].

Silk, M. and Manley, A. (2012) Globalization, urbanization and sporting spectacle in Pacific Asia: places, peoples and pastness. *Sociology of Sport Journal,* 29: 455–484.

Smith, S.C. (2012) *How safety has killed great racetrack design.* Available at www. caranddriver.com/features/how-safety-has-killed-great-racetrack-design-feature [accessed 18 June 2013].

Sturm, D. (2011) Masculinities, affect and the (re)place(ment) of stardom in Formula One fan leisure practices. *Annals of Leisure Research,* 14(2–3): 224–241.

Sturm, D. and McKinney, A. (2013) Affective hyper-consumption and immaterial labors of love: theorizing sport fandom in the age of new media. *Participations,* 10(1): 357–362.

Tomazin, F. (2012) *Coalition slams brakes on GP night race option.* Available at www. theage.com.au/victoria/coalition-slams-brakes-on-gp-night-race-option-20121020–27yje.html [accessed 23 June 2013].

Turner, B. (2004) *The pits: the real world of Formula One.* London: Atlantic.

Urry, J. (2003) *Global complexity.* Cambridge: Polity.

Whannel, G. (1992) *Fields in vision: television sport and cultural transformation.* London: Routledge.

Whannel, G. (2008) *Culture, politics and sport: blowing the whistle, revisited.* London: Routledge.

Wise, M. (2013) *Pastor Maldonado isn't sure whether he will continue to receive Venezuelan state backing.* Available at www1.skysports.com/formula-1/news/12476/8566306/Pastor-Maldonado-isn-t-sure-whether-he-will-continue-to-receive-Venezuelan-state-backing [accessed 23 June 2013].

# Part II
# Media and 'mediatisation'

# 5 Broadcasting from a neutral corner?

## An analysis of the mainstream media's representation of women's boxing at the London 2012 Olympic Games

*Rebecca Finkel*

## Introduction

Women's boxing was included in the Summer Olympic Games for the first time at the London 2012 Olympics. This chapter critically analyses mainstream media representations of women's boxing at the London 2012 Olympics in newspapers and TV broadcasts, and seeks to examine how female competitors were represented in terms of the linkages between gender and athleticism in the traditionally masculine space of the boxing ring (Mennessen, 2000). It also explores to what extent this representation reinforces or challenges male-dominated narratives in sports participation and related discourses (Theberge, 1997). For example, prior to the Games, there had been debates about whether women boxers would be made to wear skirts, thus emphasising the production and performance of femininity (Choi, 2000). Female boxers can be seen to go against the prevailing trend in the mainstream media of portraying women as 'victims' of violence or as hyper-sexualised 'objects' (Levy, 2005). It has been argued that there has been a normalisation and systematic representation of physical and sexualised violence against women in the mainstream media (Pacheco and Hurtado, 2001). However, many female boxers maintain that the sport can promote self-esteem through physical strength and positive expressions of power. Part of the legacy agenda(s) for the London 2012 Olympics was to provide an international platform to encourage more women to become involved in sport. This can be achieved not only through medal success, but also positive media representations of female athletes' abilities to act as positive role models. As Woodward (2013: 3) argues, as a result of the London 2012 Olympics, "it became possible to think seriously, rationally and routinely about women boxers and women engaging in pugilism competitively without introducing ideas about it being parodic, bizarre or sexualised".

Wide acceptance of women's boxing as a serious sport is a recent phenomenon Undoubtedly, the London 2012 Olympics played a big part in changing the perceptions of the sport on the international stage for mass audiences. Jarvie (1991) suggests certain dominant groups define 'what sport is' or 'what sport should be like' and how it is actually experienced by various groups within various cultural contexts. Perceptions of female athletes, especially those who participate in violent sport, are socially constructed within culture and through cultural discourses (Lenskyj, 2003), which can often be disapproving because it is suggested that female athletes in violent sports challenge heteronormative perceptions of how women 'should' act and what they 'should' look like (Messner, 2007). Research for this chapter involved document research methods, including content analysis of both mainstream newspapers and televised broadcast coverage of female boxers and women's boxing matches at the London 2012 Olympics. It is argued that the London 2012 Olympics have been successful in improving the collectively recognised legitimacy of women's boxing and providing an arena for the global consumption of women's violent sport, where issues of power and representation are tested and contested through a gendered mediated lens.

## Female athletes and the London 2012 Olympics

The role of women in sport is arguably one of the most important issues in the Olympic Movement right now (Jowell, 2009). The London 2012 Olympics were heralded as the most gender equal to date, and yet it has been recognised that more still needs to be done in this area (Donnelly and Donnelly, 2013). At the Opening Ceremony of the London 2012 Olympics, IOC president Jacques Rogge said that the Games signified "a major boost for gender equality" (Beech, 2012). To put this statement into perspective, a few of the main gender-related 'milestones' at the London 2012 Olympics were as follows:

- More women (269) were on the USA team than men (261);
- Russia's team also had a female majority;
- 45 per cent of 10,800 London athletes were women, which is a new record;
- Saudi Arabia sent (two) women athletes for the first time, which meant every participating nation now has women competing;
- A pregnant athlete participated: Nur Suryani Mohamed Taibi, a shooter, also became the first woman to represent Malaysia;
- Women featured strongly in media coverage and Olympic-related promotion, such as billboards and advertisements;
- Addition of women's boxing, meaning that women now compete in all summer Olympic events.

(Beech, 2012)

It is also worth noting that 29 of Britain's 65 medals – and 11 of the 29 gold medals – were won by women. This means that British women would be seventh in the gold medal table if they competed as their own country. Women from the USA team also outperformed their male counterparts – they won 27 of the USA's 41 gold medals, and 54 of their 95 total medals (Moorhouse, 2012).

One of the important agenda items directed from the UK government for the London 2012 Olympics was a youth sports participation legacy. The London 2012 Olympics promised to 'inspire a generation'. This theme was visualised in the Opening Ceremonies and reinforced in media discourses throughout the duration of the Games. Moreover, motivating young people – including and, perhaps especially, girls – to participate in sport at a grassroots level was a key legacy goal (Lindner, 2012). The language used by the UK government and media was cognisant with this agenda. For example, athletes became 'sporting heroes' and, thus, 'role models'. Tessa Jowell (2009), British Shadow Minister for the Olympics said:

> Women watch the Olympics more than any other sporting event; this makes it even more important to me to pursue equal representation in the Olympic Games. Women, like men, need to have strong sporting role models to look up to.

Although the inclusion of women's boxing in the London 2012 Olympics meant that all summer Olympic sports that are open to men are now also open to women, Donnelly and Donnelly (2013) found that gender-based structural and rule differences still exist in sports at large, and on the Olympic programme. This observation applies to women's boxing; for example, there were only 36 female boxers at the Games compared to 250 men, and the weight categories were condensed into three divisions, compared to ten for the men. This was the fewest in any Olympic combat sport (Bearak, 2012). Bearak (2012) suggested that women's boxing was set up in this manner because the IOC only allow a certain number of athletes to participate, which limited the number of female boxers who could be included in the programme. There were additional disparities, including the fact that men fight three rounds of three minutes each, whereas the women fight four rounds of two minutes. As women's boxing is the newest sport on the Olympic programme there may have been some apprehension about its reception and support, which may be why it was designed on a smaller scale than men's boxing (Degun, 2012a). For example, some countries, such as Cuba and Afghanistan, did not send female boxers to the London 2012 Olympics due to negative or perhaps ambivalent feelings towards the inclusion of women's boxing. Indeed, in the case of Afghanistan, there were concerns over 'safety' for female boxers (Baker, 2012).

Other controversies, such as whether or not the women boxers would be required to wear skirts (Degun, 2012b), overshadowed the athletic performances of female boxers in the run-up to the London 2012 Olympics. This ambivalence towards female competitors is evident in relation to other combat sports in which women participate. For example, in spite of its gender equality PR strategy, during the London 2012 Olympics the *Independent* newspaper ran an opinion piece asking: "Is women fighting each other violently a perfectly wholesome spectator sport?" (Brown, 2012). The piece did not discuss the pros and cons of violent sport per se; instead, it was questioning if it is morally acceptable for women to participate in violent sport. Thus, despite the rhetoric of progress and equality, and improvements in women's sporting participation, there are still individuals and collectives who are uncomfortable with the idea of women beating each other up in the name of sport.

## Socio-cultural constructions of women's boxing

Lindner (2012: 464) argues that "sports represent a context in which traditional notions of gender and gender relations are enforced". This includes 'gendering' different types of sport in order to maintain the binary status quo between what is perceived to be masculine and feminine. Messner (2007) suggests that, from a young age, females are encouraged to pursue 'gender-appropriate' sport(s) in order to be socially accepted. Women who engage in sports traditionally conceived to be masculine, including most combat sports, are often maligned by having their gender and sexuality called into question based on their perceived inappropriate embodiments of femininity, such as having a muscular body (Weaving, 2012). Butler (1990) argues that gender is performative; it is not something we are born with and 'have' or 'are', but rather something we must continually perform, in conscious and subconscious ways. Butler (1998) regards women's sport as a "special case" that may offer environments in which what it means to be a socially accepted (female) gendered body can be challenged and reworked. Traditionally, boxing has been seen as a masculine sport. This is due in no small part to its use of force and aggression, which are perceived and widely accepted to be male attributes in the vast majority of societies. Women competing in boxing competitions challenge the taken-for-granted associations between boxing, physical strength (and violence) and masculinity and thus threaten to "blur already destabilised gender boundaries" (Lindner, 2012: 466). As Woodward (2013: 3) argues, "Possibilities of re-thinking gendered identifications within sport ... might also disrupt some of the performance of hegemonic masculinity".

Additionally, Weaving (2012: 88) argues that

> persistent reinforcement of traditional gender binaries creates the expectation that women be less physically aggressive than males, which explains why boxing heightens the struggle and tension regarding women's bodies and physical capabilities ... Boxing is at odds with the traditional sense of femininity.

Mennessen (2000) supports this by stating that women boxers challenge the existing gender order, though Sekules (2012) views this challenge as a form of culturally constructed patriarchy. She argues that

> it is because it used to be a man's world and, somewhere deep in their psyches, the men who controlled society didn't like the idea of their mother in a fight.... To see that symbol temporarily engaged in violence – even if it's controlled and deliberate and contained – that terrifies men.

Consequently, women are seen to need protection from the violence, aggression and physicality that boxing embraces and embodies. The 'fantasy' of masculinity offered by boxing excludes women based on the archaic notion that they need to be safeguarded against such expressions of (violent) masculinity (Woodward, 2007). This view has been reinforced by British male boxer and 2004 Olympic silver medallist, Amir Khan, who initially disapproved of women's boxing because of the difficulty he felt watching women get hurt. He said: "Deep down I think women shouldn't fight. That's my opinion. When you get hit it can be very painful. Women can get knocked out" (cited in Lindner, 2012: 464). Khan's discomfort with the fact that women can (and will) get "knocked out" reinforces the hegemonic perception of the male as protector and the female as victim in need of saving. In reality, of course, it is a rational assumption that female athletes are aware of such risks and have taken them into account when deciding to pursue the sport, as do male boxers.

These culturally constructed preconceptions of violence as the antithesis of femininity have followed women into, and often chased them out of, the boxing ring for centuries (Woodward, 2007). As with female athletes in other sports, women boxers have often been represented in ways that emphasise their femininity and heterosexual attractiveness, and thus begin to reconcile the perceived incompatibility between femaleness, femininity and participation in combat sports. For example, Mia St John – a commercially successful boxer – has posed for *Playboy* (Heiskanen, 2012). Myths – such as the suggestion that premenstrual syndrome made women too 'unstable' to box, or that boxing destroys fertility and can cause breast cancer – were thought to be formulated in an attempt to keep women away from boxing (Topping, 2012). Relegated to the periphery, women's boxing was seen as a side-show spectacle in the nineteenth and twentieth centuries. It was comparable to a circus act, and watched mainly out of morbid curiosity (Smith, 2008). This history of marginalisation of women athletes in boxing has led to perceptions of boxing as "a bastion of embodied, heroic masculinity", and the accompanying resistance to having women participants projects "an anxiety about masculinity, which is very fragile in spite of the bluster" (Topping 2012).

## Media representations of women's boxing at the London 2012 Olympics

The media's relationship with female athletes remains contentious. Many scholars have analysed inequality in representation (Fletcher and Dashper, 2013; Gee and Leberman, 2011; Jones, 2011) in both the amount of coverage and also type of coverage of marginalised groups, including women. Jowell (2009), for instance, highlights the discrimination of women in popular media representation by stating "There is more than 50 times as much coverage in the media for men's sport than women's, with just two percent of articles and one percent of images devoted to elite female athletes and women's sport". A study by Nieland and Horkey (2011) also found gender bias in the reporting of sports news: 90 per cent of sports writers are male, and 85 per cent of content covers male sports. 'Gendering' in sport can often be reinforced through media coverage; not to mention the frequent sexualisation and trivialisation of female sport and athletes

(Donnelly and Donnelly, 2013). To put this into perspective, in a moment of reflection on the industry in which it operates, the *Toronto Star* (2012) reported:

> Women's events continue to get less coverage, making it impossible for most female athletes to get the attention and sponsorship deals their male counterparts can swing. They must constantly fight attempts to drive up interest in women's sport the cheap way – by sexing it up.

## Research methods

The aim of the research for this chapter was to evaluate the mainstream media's coverage of women's boxing in order to examine how the sport was represented given the historic systemic sexism within the sport, and the general context of media bias that continues to surround women's sport, at all levels. As Fletcher and Dashper (2013: 17) argue, "Media analyses of coverage of sports events thus remains an important tool in exploring social attitudes, both within and beyond sport". The data for this chapter are based on a content analysis of mainstream articles from mainly British (e.g. the *Guardian*, the *Daily Mail*), Irish (e.g. the *Irish Times*), American (e.g. the *New York Times, US Today*) and Indian (e.g. *The Times of India*) broadsheet and tabloid newspapers. The main reason for this focus was that the majority of the 'top' female boxers competing at the Games represented these countries. Searches were carried out using Google Alerts and LexisNexis, using search terms as 'women's Olympic boxing' and 'women's boxing London Olympics'. These searches took place from one month before, during and one month after the women's boxing events. The broadcasts by the British Broadcasting Corporation (BBC) of the women's boxing events were also analysed, as the BBC were the 'official' UK broadcasters of the Games. The articles were coded, and thematic analysis was employed (Braun and Clarke, 2006).

## Media narratives concerning women's boxing

The vast majority of newspaper articles that were focused on women's boxing told of the sexist discourses dominating boxing's past. The many 'myths' surrounding women's boxing (as discussed above), as well as the sport's exclusion from participation on the international sporting stage legitimately in its own right, were staple inclusions for many publications. This included multiple retellings in the British press of how women's boxing was banned in Britain until 1996. Similarly, the American press told how USA Boxing, the amateur governing body, had a males-only policy until 1993. The sport has only recently established itself on the world stage. The first Women's World Amateur Boxing Championship was held in the United States in 2001. A quotation from Cuba coach, Pedro Roque, which was circulated by the Associated Press was commonly used to illustrate the narrative of contention surrounding women's boxing. In explaining why Cuba was not sending female boxers to the Games, Roque said that women should be "showing off their beautiful faces, not getting punched in the face" (Patel, 2012). Another frequently cited quotation was from manager and promoter, Frank Maloney, who was most famous for being the manager of male boxer Lennox Lewis, in which he described the first British women's amateur boxing match as "a freak show" (Patel, 2012).

A demarcation from those 'old fashioned' attitudes and the 'reality' of the London 2012 Olympics was made clear in all the media reports. Such direct sexist remarks were used as a foil for the more progressive attitudes positioned at the heart of the London 2012 Olympics (Jowell, 2009). The way the media reported these narratives was to draw a line demarcating what was past and what was now and, moreover, what the future of Olympic sport might be. This fits into the overall media narrative of the London 2012 Olympics as the 'gender equality' Games (Beech, 2012). The majority of accounts systematically dismissed the sexist world of boxing as something belonging in the past, and instead focused attention on the sporting legitimacy of women's boxing. The BBC broadcast (August 5, 2012) of the first women's boxing events stated: "The gender barrier has now come crashing down with the inclusion of women's boxing into the Olympic Games, and women can compete with men on equal footing.... Women can set about creating their own Olympic legacy". Throughout the sources analysed there was an emphasis on 'skill', 'inspiration', 'athleticism', and sport as a 'progressive cultural force'. Indeed, these terms were recurring, appearing in international sources over a hundred times. The overwhelming message from the media reports analysed was: naysayers, those who do not think women should be boxing, are outdated and wrong.

The collective consensus from American and British media accounts of the International Amateur Boxing Association's (AIBA) recommendation for female boxers to wear skirts in competition, which the organisation claimed could help viewers better distinguish them from male boxers, was overwhelmingly dismissed as backward and archaic (van Ingen and Kovacs, 2012). This has echoes with attempts by promoters in the twentieth century to overtly 'feminise' women boxers by, amongst other things, encouraging/forcing them to wear make up in the ring and pose for men's magazines, including *Playboy*; generally to assert their femininity – as opposed to the assigned masculine traits of violence, aggression and athleticism. This serves to uphold the status quo of culturally constructed gender ideas (Hargeaves, 1997). However, the idea of trying to bring women's sports more in line with ideas of socially accepted femininity is not new, nor is it exclusive to combat sports. According to former England cricketer Ebony Rainford-Brent, for example, "sexing up women's sport is key to attracting new female spectators and participants" (BBC 2012). Yet, AIBA's skirt recommendation did not fit in with the gender-equal Games narrative, and it was heavily criticised in the press. A number of reports suggested AIBA's skirt recommendation was less about helping viewers differentiate between male and female competitors and more about attracting male viewers through the sexualisation of female boxers. As one opinion piece published in *US News and World Report*, whose ideas were reproduced in multiple media outlets, stated:

It was to diminish female sportswomen and sexualize their competitions to attract male viewers—who, the boxing association presumes, don't really think of women as actual athletes and just want to watch their breasts and behinds bop up and down in a ring or an arena.

(Milligan 2012)

As Milligan suggests, the sexualisation of female athletes reinforces patriarchal oppression (Woodward, 2013) by degrading women's contributions to sport. Moreover, in so doing, it also insults men in assuming they would only be interested in women's sport at a base, sexual level. Although 'feminisation' – meaning making female athletes act or appear more in keeping with socially constructed ideals of what is 'feminine' – features heavily in the boxing literature (Lindner, 2012; Woodward, 2007, 2013), it was not a dominant theme emerging from this research. Indeed, in breaking a trend, the photographic images accompanying newspaper articles analysed were of the athletes either boxing in regulation uniforms, standing near a boxing ring in workout clothes, or close-ups in their Olympic team uniforms. There were no glamour shots, no overt make-up or revealing clothing, no culturally constructed feminised poses, such as looking coy, blowing kisses or jutting out hips and breasts. Thus, unlike in other sports at the London 2012 Olympics, the media did not sexually exploit or objectify women boxers. On the contrary, they largely emphasised their athleticism and talent; both in writing and via visual representation. Woodward's (2013: 8) research confirms this finding; she states that "There were no attempts to sexualise or infantilise the women boxers and their events.... Commentary was conducted in the language of boxing and its techniques". Indeed, the media appeared to be rather in awe of the female boxers for their determination to pursue a sport despite its masculine image, sexist history and scant monetary reward.

A related theme that emerged from the content analysis is the idea that the women boxers need to 'stymie' sexist actions against them, 'fight' for their place in the international boxing arena and 'strive' to prove their legitimacy and worth by 'punching above their weight' (Milligan, 2012). Indeed, verbs of struggle and of overcoming obstacles put in place by the patriarchal worlds of sport and boxing were prevalent throughout the content analysed. Many of the women boxers themselves also overcame personal obstacles, which were explored in media content as part of in-depth pieces about athletes' lives. Personal struggles with poverty, abuse and employment instability emerged as part of the wider women's boxing Olympic narrative. This had the effect of making the debut of the sport on the Olympic stage more dramatic and meaningful, as a few of the boxers' more 'challenging' histories were reported, meaning that audiences were aware of the journey they had taken, and what they had put at stake to get to the Games.

An example of this is Nicola Adams, the British Gold medallist, who was profiled extensively in the British media. Her various jobs were reported, including her role as an extra on the British soap opera, *Coronation Street*. There was one quote from Adams that was reproduced on a number of occasions in a variety of sources. It told of her struggle to get to the Games: "I was really close to giving up, it's hard to be able to train full time and earn enough money to live as well". Hers was a tale of sacrifice, with a conclusion in Olympic victory, which demonstrates rewards for not giving up. Although this became a celebratory narrative, it also highlights the lack of resources, funding and sponsorship available for women boxers to train effectively and be taken seriously in an economic sense, and is part of the wider discourses of women's sports and financial inequality (Donnelly and Donnelly, 2013); neither of which were interrogated in the sources analysed.

Due to her success at the Games, Adams is now considered a role model for aspiring women athletes, and boxers in particular. Indeed, as part of the wider London 2012 Olympics media narrative of gender equality, there was an emphasis on athletes as role models for young people, especially young girls (Woodward, 2013). Women's boxing fits into this well due to the 'sad' back stories of many of the athletes and, like other Olympic athletes, their perseverance and dedication to the sport. As the BBC television broadcast (August 5, 2012) said about American boxer, Quanitta "Queen" Underwood, who had been sexually abused as a child, "She is a beacon of hope that youngsters can overcome difficult beginnings to go on to become significant individuals in the world". The language of this broadcast conveys an epic journey, which fits into the UK government agenda for the London 2012 Olympics of creating 'sporting heroes' who are 'role models' from the Games. In an attempt to identify the Games' 'impact' on participation in sport and physical activity, many media outlets from the UK cited statistics, including participation rates and boxing club attendance, which showed the rise in interest in boxing among women and girls in the past five years. As the *Guardian* reported about Irish gold-medal winner Katie Taylor, "Taylor has since been a trailblazer for women's boxing both in Ireland and around the world. Half of the 60 young fighters who train at her gym every week are female" (McDonald, 2012). The athlete-as-role-model pieces were predictably more prevalent following gold-medal performances. For example, following victories for Irish, American and British boxers, pieces about gold-medallist women boxers being celebrated in schools, home towns and local boxing clubs dominated much of the coverage. A good example of this is Claressa Shields, the USA gold-medal winner, who is from a deprived area in Flint, Michigan. The local newspaper, *The Detroit Free Press*, reported:

> Flint was once a great city and like Detroit will become a great one again, however it will take time. Claressa has given our community hope and inspiration when it has been needed the most. She may help define Flint for the future, especially our younger generation: Work hard, stay focused, never give up, follow your dreams and good things will happen.
>
> (Barnas, 2012)

This was presented as the 'heroic' legacy of the new Olympic sport (Woodward, 2013).

Interestingly, throughout the sources analysed, there was still the need for confirmation from a (sporting) man that women boxers are dedicated athletes, who deliver high-quality boxing performances, and deserve their place in the Olympic arena. On this basis, it can be argued that these women are still not viewed as 'boxers' but 'women boxers'. As a consequence, even in spite of Olympic-related equality rhetoric, these women are still operating within male frameworks and to male standards. For example, during a BBC broadcast (8 August 2012), Amir Khan was interviewed and asked if he thought Irish boxer, Katie Taylor, who also carried the flag for the entire Irish Olympic delegation during the opening ceremonies, could beat a man in the boxing ring. He agreed she probably could and said: "I think she's one of the best fighters I've seen – especially a woman". He most likely meant this to be complimentary; however, by bringing up gender, he positioned the female boxer as an 'Other', and set her apart from the assumed default perspective: that being a 'fighter' means being a man. In so doing this sets the 'extraordinary' aspect of her performance in relation to her gender, not her skill as a fighter. Such comments reinforce the hierarchy of the boxing world, that is, the position of men is routinely and unequivocally hegemonic.

There were a number of key words used to describe women's boxing which occurred time after time in the sources analysed. These were: 'historic', 'inspirational', 'significant', 'trailblazing' and 'pioneering'. These terms emphasise the newness of the sport in the context of the Olympics, and reinforce meaning tied to the aforementioned narratives of overcoming obstacles, and becoming role models. In terms of the boxing itself, there was an emphasis on skill, strategy, footwork, punch combinations, speed and scoring points – the technical side of the sport – not knockouts, violence or blood. The consensus was that women's boxing had more to do with technique and style; 'speed, grace and aggression' was a phrase used regularly (and uncritically) throughout the data. This distinguished it from men's boxing, where the emphasis generally focuses on power and force, ostensibly 'male' and 'manly' virtues (cf. Billings *et al.*, 2010). The women themselves were described most as 'bubbly', 'smiling', 'cheerful', 'diminutive' and 'amiable'. This can be seen to feminise the women boxers indirectly by tying them to overly feminine descriptions linked to hegemonic imaginings of women as eager to please, pleasant and caring (Lindner, 2012). Moreover, both the print media and the boxers themselves referred to female athletes as 'girls', thereby infantilising and trivialising their participation. Notably though, the term 'girls' was not used in any BBC broadcasts. This may be attributed to the fact that there had been some controversy over its use given that male athletes were never referred to as 'boys' (Bacon, 2012). After the events, the words most used by writers, spectators, and practically everyone involved in women's boxing were 'momentous', 'joy' and 'surprise'. The overlying message was that the female boxers had proven sceptics wrong and, on an international stage, did the sport proud. Irish gold medallist, Katie Taylor, who was also a media and crowd favourite, was profiled internationally. The media picked up on one key statement that she made and used it over and over to articulate the strides women boxers were making: "People didn't really realise the standard of women's boxing. I think we're shocking the world here this week, they can't believe the standard and it's opening their eyes to women's boxing" (Halpin, 2012). A BBC broadcast (9 August 2012) managed to epitomise the dominant feeling at the time in the following passage: "These pioneering, trailblazing boxers can be sure that they've laid solid foundations and now future generations can take inspiration from their exploits and work toward fulfilling their own Olympic dreams in the roped arena of the Olympic boxing ring".

The media emphasised the atmosphere of the women's boxing events during the London 2012 Olympics, which seemed to give further legitimacy to women's boxing. Words most used to describe the spectators in the media were 'packed', 'loud', 'noise', 'chanting, clapping, stomping', 'fans making presence felt', 'standing ovation'. The fact that women's boxing was evidently very well received by spectators demonstrates that women's boxing was not a 'side show'; rather, it was core to overall sporting action. The BBC broadcast (9 August 2012) captured the moment by stating, "The atmosphere is more tantamount to a rock concert than a boxing ring" and "There is the pomp and pageantry of a party". This can be situated in the legitimacy arguments made for the sport, including Woodward's (2013: 3) assertion that, due to the legacy of the London 2012 Olympics, "women's boxing can be taken seriously".

The overwhelming opinion of the media following the culmination of female boxing events was that the future for women's boxing looks bright. A BBC broadcast (9 August 2012) stated: "What an advertisement for women's boxing.... Everyone will want to join their local gyms". It is simplistic to assume that the success of women's boxing in this context will automatically result in increased participation in the sport. There are a whole host of structural issues constraining women's participation, which remain firmly rooted in the sport at all levels. Although there have been reports of an increase in the number of women joining gyms immediately after the London 2012 Olympics (Woodward, 2013), it is uncertain if participation rates have actually increased in any sustainable way, and/or if more women have started boxing seriously. However, regardless of the reality, there is now the perception that women's boxing has contributed towards London 2012's legacy plans (Degun, 2012a) by enabling women to try boxing without embarrassment or marginalisation. IOC President, Jacques Rogge's, comment that he was "thrilled the competition removed any doubt of the sport's Olympic worthiness" was featured in many press reports. Similarly, a BBC broadcast (9 August 2012) stated that the women boxers will "join the boxing immortals", which situates these women with the historic male heroes of the sport, such as Muhammad Ali and Sugar Ray Leonard.

## Conclusions

The increasingly fluid relationships between sport, power and culture can be understood through media representations because these highlight dominant and emerging narratives. As Briggs and Cobley (1998: 277) argue, "Media representations contribute to shared systems of belief and are related to the power relations of our cultures". Interestingly, female athletes in a violent sport, with strong ties to constructed masculinity, can be seen to have fared better in their media representations than those in non-contact sports, such as women's beach volleyball, where there was strong criticism for overly sexualising and objectifying female athletes (Sailors *et al.*, 2012), and gymnastics, where media coverage appeared to focus more on athletes' hair styles than their technical skills (Bacon, 2012). The media's representation of women's boxing highlighted personal and professional triumph, and helped to legitimise the sport by not tolerating direct sexism, and by focusing attention on narratives of determination, peak performance and spectator excitement. However, it should be noted that this representation still exists within the male-dominated framework of the mainstream media, where male sports receive more coverage and are hegemonic; the standard to which women's sports are compared and measured (Billings *et al.*, 2010).

The main themes of gender equality, performance of gender, and sport influencing social change came through in the mainstream media reports of women's boxing. From a cultural perspective, it is not to be assumed that the association of boxing and masculinity has been seriously challenged by the London 2012 Olympics alone; however, it could be argued that some space has opened for the inclusion of positive female narratives in association with the sport. Media representations of women's boxing at the London 2012 Olympics, just like the inclusion of women's boxing in the Games themselves, has set about an incremental shift in how the sport is viewed, and has altered the meanings associated with women's participation in combat sports. Further research in the field could focus on a comparison between media representations of women's boxing or, indeed, women's sport in general, at upcoming sporting events, such as any similarities and differences with reporting at different mega and smaller sports events. Comparisons between representation in mainstream and social media could also contribute to knowledge in media and gender studies. A long-term analysis charting the changes in media representation would be able to show the historical nuances in cultural constructions of women's combat sports. Finally, once the furore surrounding women's boxing and the Olympics has died down, and when women's boxing is no longer 'new' and considered 'historic', it would be beneficial to examine its treatment by the media to see whether it continues to push boundaries in perceptions of women's participation in violent sport or fades back into obscurity.

## References

Bacon, J. (2012) "Girl Games" still grappled with gendered language, commentary. *Gender Report.* [Online] Available from http://genderreport.com/2012/08/12/girl-games-still-grappled-with-gendered-language-commentary [accessed 2 January 2014].

Baker, A. (2012) Rahimi's TKO: Afghan woman boxer's Olympic invite rescinded amid safety concerns. *Time.* [Online] Available from http://olympics.time.com/2012/07/19/rahimis-tko-afghan-woman-boxers-olympic-invite-rescinded-amid-safety-concerns [accessed 2 January 2014].

BBC (2012) Sexing up key to boosting profile of women's sport – Rainford-Brent. [Online] Available from www.bbc.co.uk/sport/0/cricket/19878249 [accessed 2 January 2014].

Barnas, J. (2012) Flint goes crazy over Olympic gold medal boxer Claressa Shields. *Detroit Free Press.* [Online] Available from www.freep.com/article/20120810/ NEWS01/308100088 [accessed 2 January 2014].

Bearak, B. (2012) Women finally get their chance to be contenders in Olympic boxing. *New York Times.* [Online] Available from www.nytimes.com/2012/08/06/sports/olympics/ women-participate-in-olympic-boxing-for-first-time.html [accessed 2 January 2014].

Beech, H. (2012) The Year of the Woman: The London Olympics strike early for gender equality. *Time.* [Online] Available from http://olympics.time.com/2012/07/29/the-year-of-the-woman-the-london-olympics-strikes-early-for-gender-equality [accessed 2 January 2014].

Billings, A., Angelini, J. and Duke, A. (2010) Gendered profiles of Olympic history: Sportscaster dialogue in the 2008 Beijing Olympics. *Journal of Broadcasting and Electronic Media,* 54(1): 9–23.

Briggs, A. and Cobley, P. (1998) Introduction to "in the media". In Briggs, A. and Cobley, P. (eds) *The media: An introduction.* Harlow: Longman, 277–282.

Brown, A. (2012) Women's judo: It's disturbing to watch these girls beat each other up. *Independent.* [Online] Available from http://blogs.telegraph.co.uk/news/andrewmcf-brown/100174361/womens-judo-its-disturbing-to-watch-these-girls-beat-each-other-up [accessed 2 January 2014].

Butler, J. (1990) *Gender trouble: Feminism and the subversion of identity.* London: Routledge.

Butler, J. (1998) Athletic genders: Hyperbolic instance and/or the overcoming of sexual binarism. *Stanford Humanities Review,* 6.2. [Online] Available from www.stanford. edu.group/SHR/6–2/butler.html [accessed 8 February 2010].

Braun, V. and Clarke, V. (2006) Using thematic analysis in psychology. *Qualitative Research in Psychology,* 3(2): 77–101.

Choi, P. (2000) *Femininity and the physically active woman.* London: Routledge.

Degun, T. (2012a) Big 2013 ahead for AIBA and boxing. *Inside the Games.* [Online] Available from www.insidethegames.biz/blogs/1012239-tom-degun-big-2013-ahead-for-aiba-and-boxing [accessed 2 January 2014].

Degun, T. (2012b) Women's boxing skirts issue remains unclear for now. *Inside the Games.* [Online] Available from www.insidethegames.biz/sports/summer/ boxing/15610-exclusive-womens-boxing-skirts-issue-remains-unclear-for-now [accessed 2 January 2014].

Donnelly, P. and Donnelly, M. (2013) *The London 2012 Olympics: A gender equality audit.* Centre for Sport Policy Studies Research Report. Toronto: University of Toronto.

Fletcher, T. and Dashper, K. (2013) "Bring on the dancing horses!": Ambivalence and class obsession within British media reports of the dressage at London 2012. *Sociological Research Online,* 18(2): 17.

Gee, B. and Leberman, S. (2011) Sports media decision making in France: How they choose what we get to see and read. *International Journal of Sport Communication,* 4(3): 321–343.

Halpin, P. (2012) Boxing-Olympics-World champ Taylor delights high-decibel Irish. *Reuters.* [Online] Available from http://mobile.reuters.com/article/olympicsNews/ idUSL6E8J6A0L20120806?irpc=914 [accessed 14 January 2014].

Hargreaves, J. (1997) Boxing and related activities: Introducing images and meanings. *Body and Society*, 3: 33–49.

Heiskanen, B. (2012) *The urban geography of boxing: Race, class, and gender in the ring*. London: Routledge.

Jarvie, G. (ed.) (1991) *Sport, racism and ethnicity*. London: Routledge.

Jones, A. (2011) Visual and verbal gender cues in the televised coverage of the 2010 Winter Olympics. *The International Journal of Interdisciplinary Social Sciences*, 6(2): 199–216.

Jowell, T. (2009) London 2012: A chance to nurture strong female role models. [Online] Available from www.internationalwomensday.com/article.asp?m=11&e=88#.Ul0L-2SQQpPo [accessed 2 January 2014].

Lenskyj, H. (2003) *Out on the field: Gender, sport and sexualities*. Toronto: Women's Press.

Levy, A. (2005) *Female chauvinist pigs*. New York: Simon and Schuster.

Lindner, K. (2012) Women's Boxing at the 2012 Olympics: Gender trouble? *Feminist Media Studies*, 12(3): 464–467.

McDonald, H. (2012) Katie Taylor's hometown fans cheer on Ireland's Olympic gold medal hope. *Guardian*. [Online] Available from www.theguardian.com/sport/2012/aug/08/katie-taylor-olympics-boxing-bray [accessed 2 January 2014].

Mennessen, C. (2000) "Hard" women and "soft" women: The social construction of identities among female boxers. *International Review for the Sociology of Sport*, 35: 21–33.

Messner, M. (2007) Out of play: Critical essays on gender and sport. Albany, NY: State University of New York Press.

Milligan, S. (2012) Female athletes still not taken seriously. US News and World Report. [Online] Available from www.usnews.com/opinion/blogs/susan-milligan/2012/07/30/female-olympic-athletes-still-not-taken-seriously [accessed 2 January 2014].

Moorhouse, A. (2012) Girl power! The success of female athletes at the Games. *Huffington Post*. [Online] Available from www.huffingtonpost.co.uk/adrian-moorhouse/girl-power-female-athletes-olympics_b_1840490.html [accessed 2 January 2014].

Nieland, J. and Horky, T. (2011) *International sports press survey*. Copenhagen: Play the Game.

Pacheco, S. and Hurtado, A. (2001) Media stereotypes. In Worrell, J. (ed.) *Encyclopaedia of women and gender: Sex similarities and differences and the impact of society on gender*. London: Academic Press.

Patel, I. (2012) London 2012 Olympics: The joy of women's boxing. *Guardian*. [Online] Available from www.theguardian.com/commentisfree/2012/aug/09/london-2012-joy-womens-boxing [accessed 14 January 2014].

Sailors, P., Teetzil, S. and Weaving, C. (2012) No net gain: A critique of media representations of women's Olympic beach volleyball. *Feminist Media Studies*, 12(3): 468–472.

Sekules, K. (2012) *The boxer's heart: A woman fighting*. New York: Overlook Publishing.

Smith, J. (2008) Female boxers: "Sideshow freaks?" In Hickie, T.V., Healey, D., Scutt, J. and Hughes, A. (eds) *Essays in sport and the law*. Melbourne: Australian Society of Sports History, 177–190.

Theberge, N. (1997) "It's part of the game": Physicality and the production of gender in women's hockey. *Gender and Society*, 11: 69–87.

Topping, A. (2012) Women boxers take on "bastion of masculinity" in first ever Olympic bouts. *Guardian*. [Online] Available from www.theguardian.com/sport/2012/aug/03/women-boxers-first-olympic-bouts [accessed 2 January 2014].

*Toronto Star* (2012) London Olympics: Faster, higher, stronger and more women than ever before. [Online] Available from www.thestar.com/opinion/editorials/2012/07/26/london_olympics_faster_higher_stronger_and_ more_women_than_ever_before.html [accessed 3 November 2013].

van Ingen, C. and Kovacs, N. (2012) Subverting the skirt: Female boxers' "troubling" uniforms. *Feminist Media Studies*, 12(3): 460–463.

Weaving, C. (2012) Babes boxing in skirts: A critique of the proposed AIBA uniform rule. In Forsyth, J. and Heine, M. (eds) *Problems, possibilities, promising practices: Critical dialogues on the Olympic and Paralympic Games*. Eleventh International Symposium for Olympic Research. International Centre for Olympic Studies. London, Ontario: Western University Canada, 88–93.

Woodward, K. (2007) *Boxing, masculinity and identity: The "I" of the tiger*. London: Routledge.

Woodward, K. (2013) Legacies of 2012: Putting women's boxing into discourse. *Contemporary Social Science: Journal of the Academy of Social Sciences*, DOI: 10.1080/21582041.2013.838295.

# 6 Sport, broadcasting and cultural citizenship in Singapore

*Donna Wong*

## Introduction

The study of media and sport is still relatively new and has only developed within the past three decades (Bernstein and Blain, 2002; Rowe, 2011). Despite the rich seam of academic enquiry in media sport in recent years, there has been relatively little discussion on media sport development in Asia. Given that Asia has been identified as *the* primary growth area for global media sport (Rowe, 2011), the relative dearth of research in the growing field of media sport studies in Asia must be addressed. This chapter answers scholars' calls (Horne, 2005; Rowe, 2011) for more research on contemporary Asian societies to broaden the narrow Anglo-American focus predominating in existing media sport studies. With Singapore establishing itself as Asia's global media city and sports hub, this chapter focuses on the trajectory and development of the relationship between media and sport in Singapore.

Singapore is an island city-state with a population of a mere five million, yet has established itself as regional headquarters for a host of global broadcasters such as ESPN Star Sports, Discovery, HBO, MTV, Sony Pictures Entertainment, NBC Universal and CNBC. As one of the prime targets for the expansionary strategies for global (Western) sports commodities, there is an increasing presence of transnational broadcasters in Singapore. This chapter considers how an understanding of media sport development in Singapore, as an exemplar of a cosmopolitan, urbanised Asian city-state, helps provide an additional account for its comparison with existing discourse on the development of media sport in advanced capitalist Asian countries.

In light of this, the chapter commences with a sketch of the development of media broadcasting in Singapore. It considers the institutional context within which mediated sport is produced in Singapore, shedding light on the underlying political economy that steers that development. It then continues with an outline of sport development in Singapore, sketching the contemporary 'sportscape' against the backdrop of globalisation. It illustrates how the development of new transmission technologies brought in new players in the sport broadcasting industry. It then proceeds to outline the major issues in the development of media sport in Singapore. Finally, it considers the implications of this development for the viewing rights of citizens.

## Broadcasting development

Introduced by the government to keep people off the streets following a period of communal unrest in the 1960s (Katz and Wedell, 1978), the first free-to-air (FTA) terrestrial television broadcasting was introduced in 1963 by *Television Singapura*. Full-colour transmission arrived in Singapore with its first live satellite telecast of the World Cup Football Finals on 7 July 1974. To promote greater operational efficiency, broadcasting was corporatised in 1979 and renamed the *Singapore Broadcasting Corporation* (SBC), with the government retaining control over the policy of the Corporation. In 1994, in a move to restructure the broadcasting industry to deal with a more competitive global environment, SBC was replaced by the *Singapore International Media*, a privatised entity that controls all broadcasting enterprises in Singapore. The *Television Corporation of Singapore* (TCS) was set up to manage its television broadcasting arm. In 2001, after yet another corporate restructuring exercise, the *Singapore International Media* become the *Media Corporation of Singapore*. TCS was renamed *MediaCorp*[1] where it currently fulfils the role of the national public service broadcaster (PSB).

In spite of its stated objective of becoming a world financial centre and broadcasting hub, regionally and internationally (which requires access to real time news to remain competitive), private ownership of satellite dishes is banned in Singapore. The ban is justified on the ground that it potentially threatens the social stability of Singapore via foreign influence (Ang and Lee, 2002). The contradiction between Singapore's economic objective and political stance was exemplified during the 1991 Gulf War, when the lack of access to real-time news made it difficult for financial institutions to make critical decisions on stock market activities in a timely fashion. The delay in access to news on the breakout of the Gulf War resulted in financial losses in Singapore (Lovestock and Schoenfeld, 1995). The government has since, in 2003, granted financial institutions permission to install satellite dishes, which extended to hotels and selected educational institutions, as part of its media deregulation. In view of the lessons learnt from the delayed access to information during the 1991 Gulf War, cable television was subsequently introduced to provide wire service stories. The *Singapore Cable Vision* (SCV) was launched in 1995 as Singapore's first pay-TV service. The SCV was renamed Starhub Cable Vision[2] when Starhub, one of the major telecommunication companies based in Singapore, acquired the SCV in 2002. Although its major direct shareholders are foreign media companies – ST Telemedia, Qtel (Qatar Telecom) and NTT Communications Corporation – it remained indirectly controlled by the government-owned Temasek Holdings.

In addition to the restructuring of the broadcasting industry, the introduction of competition through the creation of several competing companies has been the other major development in Singapore's media sector in recent years. The move to first deregulate local media was carried out in 2001 by introducing a second FTA broadcaster to end its monopolistic broadcast structure. However, the exercise to inject competition was a futile attempt as Singapore's local market was too small to accommodate two media players as viable economic operations. In a multi-cultural society, the requirement to have a media mix of programmes for all cultures in Singapore proved to be financially challenging. The resources required to produce programmes in four languages has the potential to cripple a media corporation. To stem financial losses, *MediaCorp* regained its monopoly on broadcasting in 2004. This rationalises and reaffirms that "the good old monopolistic setup was more 'realistic' for Singapore media", as declared by its Minster for Information and Communications (Leo and Lee, 2004: 207).

Under the encouragement of media deregulation, telecommunication companies, which had not previously been involved in broadcasting, began to enter the market – as in the case of *Starhub* (see above) and *SingTel* (another long-established major telecommunications provider in Singapore). *SingTel* started offering its broadband customers Video-on-Demand content via broadband streaming in 2005. It furthered its reach by launching *mioTV*, a subscription-based internet-TV in 2007. The proliferation of broadcast players has provided consumers with a suite of international channels of news, entertainment and sports to choose from. With a sketch of media development in Singapore already provided, the next section moves on to consider the ways in which the popularity of sports events has been tied in to the emergence and development of new media technology. Through an overview of the developing relationship between sport and media, it provides a framework within which to understand the development of sport broadcasting in Singapore.

## Sport broadcasting

### *Sports in Singapore*

Sport in Singapore has been characterised as amateurish, with, until relatively recently, the nation's sports scene being virtually non-existent (Wong, 2012). This is attributable to the historical development of its socio-political climate. Economic success has always been at the forefront of the nation's developmental policy. Under the state's highly interventionist and pragmatic leadership, its citizens have focused on economic productivity. Since its early years of independence, economy-based values and extrinsic goals were given precedence over the promotion of all other cultural practices, including sport. This was exacerbated by the argument by its (then) Prime Minister Lee Kuan Yew that financial expenditure in creating a sporting infrastructure may only benefit a minority of the population. As a result, sport did not feature highly in the culture of its citizens. The focus on economic survival in Singapore was to have deep-rooted consequences for its fledgling sports culture. The significance of this inclination towards materialism has resulted in the indifferent attitude of Singaporeans to sport (and participation in it). The prioritisation of time and space for the pursuit of sport has, for a long time, remained of relatively low importance. The indifference towards sport has inevitably impacted on the reception of mediated sport. For example, in 2000, the audience for TV sports in Singapore constituted only about 52 per cent of the population, as reflected in its National Sports Participation Survey (compared to UK's 73 per cent in 2003 – see Mintel, 2003). The figure dropped further to 43 per cent of the population in 2005 (SSC, 2006).

Having successfully addressed the economic progress of the country, the government turned to redress the imbalance in its cultural progress at the turn of the millennium, through campaigns to promote public awareness, support and participation in sport. This phase of sport development coincided with the accelerated growth of its media industry as explicated earlier. During the same period, the increasing professionalisation and commercialisation witnessed the expansion of sport from its once highly localised origins into an increasingly internationalised, mediatised cultural form that diffuses across the globe (Rowe, 2011). Like other commodities, sport has sought to branch out from saturated domestic markets in the West and to expand into new territories, targeting the Asia-Pacific region specifically as it represents the most populous and fastest-growing media sports market in the world (Gilmour and Rowe, 2012).

### The early days of sport broadcasting

Having identified media markets as one of its economic growth strategies at the beginning of the twenty-first century, the Singapore government started the deregulation of its broadcast industry to encourage competition. The competition for viewers brought about the first FTA sport channel, *SportCity*, in January 2000. It was modelled on other pay-TV sports channels with the intention of competing for viewers who were yet to subscribe to pay-TV, through providing coverage and highlights of national and international sports events. *SportsCity's* debut was an addition to three existing pay-TV sports channels: then, ESPN, Star Sports and the Football Channel offered by the SCV (*The Straits Times*, 2000). By 2001, the media war between the two local FTA broadcasters had intensified. In a bid to capture a larger share of audience over its competitor, *SportsCity* was renamed *CityTV* to provide more than just sports programmes (Tan, 2001). In this move sports broadcasts were cutback and replaced with Chinese entertainment programmes. Despite the revamping strategy to rescue viewership, *CityTV* was subsequently shut down in 2002. Although the global financial crisis around the same period was cited as one of the reasons for the cessation of the channel, a lack of viewership was the defining cause (*The Straits Times*, 2002). The global economic recession in the early 2000s not only impacted on advertising revenue, it also resulted in a cutback of broadcast rights to live matches and games. In place of live broadcasts of popular football leagues and world-class sporting tournaments, audiences in Singapore were only provided with match highlights and broadcasts of local sports action. The dwindling viewership ultimately led to the cessation of Singapore's first FTA sports channel.

## Contemporary development

The recognition of the significance of sport as a potential means for highlighting the nation's international status at the turn of the century indirectly accelerated the development of sport broadcasting in Singapore. The growing presence of international sports broadcasting was encouraged by Singapore's open policy to international media, deregulation, commercialisation and breaking up of staid public broadcast regimes. During this period, intensive economic development in Singapore led to increased affluence and leisure time among its people. Increases in disposable incomes and purchasing power stimulated the rise of consumerism, which provided the opportunity for the inception of Western-influenced lifestyle modes. These transformations were particularly conducive to the development of media sports culture, which witnessed the rising popularity of Western professional sports, in particular, football (soccer).

As shown in Table 6.1, football is the nation's favourite sports television programme.[3] The new culture of consumption which was rapidly developing across the Asia-Pacific region created perfect conditions for the promotion of Western professional football, particularly the English Premier League (EPL), which started actively pursuing broadcast rights and image-based marketing beyond its home-base in the UK around the same time (Gilmour and Rowe, 2012). The Asia-Pacific region was targeted as a key market from the 1990s due to its populousness and was then the fastest-growing media sports market in the world. Unlike other Western cultural programmes (e.g. soap operas), sports content traverses cultural and linguistic barriers, which enables a relatively easy penetration of the vast Asia-Pacific market. At the same time, the disappointing performances and quality of the local football league have led to the defection of local football supporters to European football (see Davidson, 2010 for further discussion). This was exacerbated by the reduction of public-sector broadcasting

*Table 6.1* Top ten spectator sports on TV in Singapore

| Sports | Year 2001 | | Year 2005 | |
|---|---|---|---|---|
| | Rate (%) | Rank | Rate (%) | Rank |
| Football | 33.1 | 1 | 31.6 | 1 |
| Basketball | 8.9 | 2 | 5.6 | 4 |
| Badminton | 8.2 | 3 | 5.8 | 3 |
| Tennis | 7.5 | 4 | 5.9 | 2 |
| Swimming | 6.1 | 5 | 4.9 | 5 |
| Wrestling | 5.0 | 6 | 3.8 | 7 |
| Motor Racing | 4.9 | 7 | 3.3 | 8 |
| Table Tennis | 3.9 | 8 | 1.2 | 10 |
| Golf | 2.7 | 9 | 4.8 | 6 |
| Athletics | 2.4 | 10 | – | – |
| Billiard/Snooker/Pool | – | – | 1.8 | 9 |

Source: Singapore Sports Council (2001, 2006).

budgets for sports as discussed earlier. Demands for football on TV were consequently met by the significant increase of international sports transmissions brought in by pay-TV providers (i.e. *Starhub* and *SingTel)*. Western sports programmes, especially UK and European football competitions (e.g. the EPL, the UEFA Champions League and the UEFA Europa League) and, to a lesser extent American NBA basketball, slowly became staple products of the commercialised leisure economy in Singapore.

## Threats to cultural citizenship

### *Cultural citizenship*

While the deregulation of media broadcast services and the emergence of a cable system brought about unprecedented access to international sports events in Singapore, it also implied increased competition for international sports transmission on FTA from pay-TV networks. Since its setup in 1995, Singapore's pay-TV market has been monopolised by *Starhub*. With the entry of a second pay-TV provider – *mioTV* in 2007 (see earlier discussion) – there has been a steady increase in the uptake of pay-TV in Singapore (Paul Budde Communication, 2008). Although the introduction of competition (i.e. *mioTV*) in 2007 has resulted in an initial broadening of content and consumption options, the expanded viewing opportunities have actually challenged the 'viewing rights' of citizens. For example, it brings into question issues of equality in citizens' access to sporting events of national cultural significance, which has been increasingly siphoned off to pay-TV platforms. Whilst historically access to these sporting events was free, access to them is now largely restricted to those with the ability to pay.

Similar to the trajectory of sport television development in Europe, sport television provision has initially been undertaken by the national FTA broadcaster in Singapore. Thereafter, it gradually followed the global path of consumption capitalism. Television sport has now become the most prized content for the attraction of subscription revenue. With the intensification of competition in Singapore's pay-TV market, broadcasts of popular sports have been used as a lead offering to secure market share by both *Starhub* and *SingTel*. This development has witnessed the shift in the general public's media access to sporting events from FTA television to pay-TV platforms within the last decade. In 2000, the UEFA European Championships was on FTA with TCS (the nation's PSB), which reportedly paid £144,000 for its exclusive rights. With the intense competition and bidding war between pay-TV operators, the national PSB could no longer afford to compete for premium sports content. For the subsequent European Championships in 2004, only eight out of a total of 31 matches were broadcasted FTA by *MediaCorp*, with *Starhub* securing broadcast rights to all the matches (*Starhub*, 2003). Over the course of the next decade, coverage provided by the PSB for the FIFA World Cup was reduced to four key matches, with pay-TV operators securing exclusive broadcasting rights. Although there is still other sports content on FTA television, broadcasts are currently limited to smaller scale, less popular and/or regional events where rights are cheaper to acquire. Viewers without pay-TV are now left with effectively no access to some of the most popular global sports events.

The issue of mediated access to significant sporting events was perhaps not a critical matter a few decades ago when television ownership was limited and broadcasts of sports events did not reach the majority of households. More contemporaneously, however, it has grown in importance as access to television in domestic households is close to universal, turning into a feature of daily domestic facility. Television is an essential element of any current conception of sport, and television sport is a key component of any consideration of the rights pertaining to contemporary cultural citizenship. Cultural citizenship, as suggested by Rowe (2011), entails the universal right to mediated sporting festivals of nation, irrespective of their class position or personal financial circumstances. The cultural rights of all citizens includes having access "to the most important sports presented in the best possible way – 'live-to-air' – shown where possible in prime time and presented in a critically informative and incisive manner, and not reserved only for those watching on a subscription or per-view basis" (Rowe, 2004: 387). The notions of access to, and equity in, television sport are thus significant constituents of citizenship and civil liberty (Rowe, 2004). Under such circumstances, it brings into question what has been done by the regulator to protect sports television on public airwaves in the name of national interest. This is discussed further in the next section where we explore the pay-TV industry and the regulatory development in Singapore.

### *Starhub vs. SingTel*

Until 2006, broadcast rights in Singapore for popular international sports events, particularly the EPL, were held by the pan-regional Asian broadcaster, *ESPN Star Sports*, with which *Starhub* had an exclusive deal. In 2006, *Starhub* managed to secure exclusive broadcast rights to the EPL for three seasons from 2007 to 2010 with a bid that was several times higher than the amount paid by the incumbent *ESPN Star Sports* for previous rights (Harris, 2010). This move saw a rise in its cable TV subscription base the following year (Paul Budde Communication, 2008). The rising popularity of the EPL also saw the rise of its sports package from S$8 per month in 2001 to S$15 per month in 2004 and, following *Starhub*'s acquisition of the EPL rights in 2006 (Png, 2008), this figure rose again in 2007 to S$25 per month.[4]

In 2007 competition from the second pay-TV provider – *SingTel*'s *mioTV* – resulted in an intense rights bidding war. Securing popular (sport) content is the key driver to attract pay-TV subscriptions. In order to secure a critical market share, both the dominant operator (*Starhub*) and the challenger (*SingTel*) adopted an exclusive content strategy which inevitably resulted in a high degree of content fragmentation. *SingTel* managed to secure a number of content agreement rights, notably in 2008 for the exclusive broadcast rights of the UEFA Champions League and the UEFA Europa League for the period between 2009 and 2012 (UEFA,

2008). This was followed by its acquisition of the EPL (formerly with *Starhub*) in 2009 for the exclusive broadcast rights between 2010 and 2013. Currently, *SingTel* owns the rights to the UEFA Europa League (2012–2015), Formula One races and tennis competitions, such as Wimbledon and the Australian Open (SingTel, 2012). The advent of fierce competition between these two operators has also resulted in the migration of *ESPN Star Sports* from *Starhub* to *SingTel*. As a result of the exclusive carriage agreements between these pay-TV operators and content owners, sports fans wishing to gain access to popular content like the UEFA Champions League (available exclusively on *SingTel*) and the FIFA World Cup (coverage of all matches available only on *Starhub*) were required to subscribe to both *Starhub* and *SingTel*. The 'necessary evil' for dual subscriptions remains a highly charged area, bringing about increased inconvenience for the maintenance of set-top box from each provider and accompanying costs for consumers.

Predictably, the need to double subscribe infuriated consumers, especially fans and supporters, and was frequently debated in the press. Even with a subscription fee of S$150 (£75)[5] per month for the two pay-TV sports packages, coverage often excludes popular major sports events like the FIFA World Cup where viewers have to pay extra for access. The debates reached a tipping point when a joint bid by *SingTel* and *Starhub* almost failed to secure the broadcast rights to the FIFA World Cup 2010. It has been suggested that early negotiations between the FIFA and the operators broke down over rights fees (Shine, 2010), which had risen substantially since the previous FIFA World Cup. Broadcast rights were eventually secured when an agreement was reached between the parties a month before the official start of the games. The increased fee was passed on to the consumers, at the price of S$94 for the FIFA World Cup football package, in addition to the base charges of subscription. This was a four-fold increase compared to S$25 for the previous World Cup in 2006 (Tan, 2010), while their Malaysian counterparts were enjoying the same matches FTA over their PSB (*Radio Televisyen Malaysia*).[6] This sparked a call within Singapore to boycott the World Cup package. Such activism was deemed unusual for a nation with a docile demeanour (CNN, 2010). These developments have raised questions pertaining to the waning ability of PSB to compete with pay-TV operators for the broadcast rights to sporting events. The right to watch global sports mega media events like the FIFA World Cup for reasonable costs, or even without charge, has clearly become a highly contentious localised issue, which is now starting to gain momentum as a global issue (see Rowe and Scherer, 2013). It was within this context that the Singapore government initiated a public consultation exercise on the availability of premium sport content on FTA TV platforms, explored further in the next section.

## *Regulating the media industry in Singapore*

The Media Development Authority (MDA) was established in 2003 to standardise regulations for different media platforms in Singapore in the era of media convergence, where a Code of Practice for Market Conduct was released. The code highlighted MDA's objectives to: first, enable and maintain fair market conduct and effective competition in Singapore's media industry; second, ensure the availability of a comprehensive range of quality media services in Singapore; and third, safeguard public interest (MDA, 2013). In view of fulfilling these objectives, an anti-siphoning scheme was introduced in the same year to ensure viewers in Singapore were given the opportunity to access programmes of public interest and national significance on FTA TV platforms. This scheme ensured that rights to (particularly sports) programmes that are of national interest and importance will not be siphoned off to pay-TV operators, and are available for FTA broadcasters to acquire and broadcast for the entire nation's access. Similar to the UK and Australia, the scheme involves a tiered-list which classifies the programmes into two categories – A and B:

I    Category A programmes: Subscription TV Licensees cannot acquire exclusive 'live' or 'delayed' rights to broadcast all or part of the programme;[7]
II   Category B programmes: Subscription TV Licensees can acquire exclusive 'live' rights, but not exclusive 'delayed' rights to broadcast all or part of the programme.

(MDA, 2013)

Following a series of deregulatory developments in the late 1990s, television markets in Singapore became increasingly market-oriented. The number of dual subscription (for pay-TV) households continues to grow as consumers attempt to gain access to combinations of popular content from both operators. By 2010, it had reached 15 per cent of the market and is predicted to increase to 25 per cent by 2020 (Jenna *et al.*, 2012). While on the surface the growth and latent demand in the pay-TV market appears to be positive for the mediascape in Singapore, public interests and viewing rights of its citizens remain in question. The lack of regulatory intervention not only brought about increased inconvenience and costs for consumers, pay-TV operators were devoting their resources to secure exclusive content in order to safeguard their respective market share. Research indicates that pay-TV operators in Singapore spent a higher proportion of revenue on content than their peers in Australia, New Zealand, the UK and the US (Jenna *et al.*, 2012). This implies lower profit margins for the operators. As reflected in their joint public statement in their bid for FIFA World Cup 2010, *Starhub* and *SingTel* have "sacrificed all World Cup margins while keeping the price affordable for consumers" (SingTel, 2009).

Left to the device of market forces, the impact of deregulatory measures was forcefully felt as the media market in Singapore started to stagnate shortly after its implementation. It failed to deliver the full consumer benefits associated with a competitive market in terms of the pay-TV operators' ability to improve its services (e.g. lower subscription fee) and offerings to consumers (e.g. variety in content). Any further content innovation by the operators was limited as resources were restricted to securing rights to premium sports content. The MDA eventually conceded that an intervention was deemed necessary to protect and promote consumer interests and, more importantly, to ensure the sustainability of its media industry. It was within this context that the MDA introduced the Cross-Carriage Measure in 2010. Under the Cross-Carriage Measure, exclusive content is decoupled where pay-TV operators which have acquired content rights have to ensure that the exclusive content is made available to consumers across both pay-TV platforms. Although the exclusive rights remain with the pay-TV operator (i.e. the successful bidder), the content would have to be provided in an unabridged form and available at the same price and with the same terms and conditions to any subscriber. The Cross-Carriage Measure was officially implemented in August 2011 (MDA, 2011). With the content being decoupled, it is envisioned that there would be improved access to popular sports content for consumers by eliminating the need for dual subscription. Consumers would also be able to choose freely between operators. Overall, the measure could potentially lead to improvements in programme access for consumers with wider content availability. Moreover, with a broader basis for competition between the pay-TV operators, consumer prices could remain under control.

Since its implementation in 2011, the effects of the measure have been unfolding. The measure was first exercised for the broadcast of the UEFA Euro 2012 football championships, where *Starhub* had obtained exclusive broadcast rights, with the 64 matches cross-carried on *SingTel's mio TV* platform (Saad, 2013). The measure was put to a test again in 2013 as *SingTel* renewed its deal with the EPL on a non-exclusive basis for a further three seasons from 2013, with the intention of circumventing MDA's cross-carriage rule. With a non-exclusive deal, *StarHub* was left to negotiate its own terms for an EPL deal. This was stalled by the rebate clause between *SingTel* and Football Association Premier League (which manages the league's broadcast agreements) (Lim, 2013).[8] It resulted in an intervention by the MDA in April 2013 which invoked the Cross-Carriage Measure where *SingTel* had to allow *StarHub* to cross-carry the EPL (*The Straits Times*, 2013). When *SingTel*'s appeal to overturn the MDA measure was rejected in July 2013, *SingTel* doubled the subscription price for its existing offering of premium sports content, citing the need to subsidise *Starhub* customers as the main reason (Tham, 2013).[9]

Despite the noble intention to decouple content and safeguard public interest, the price hike to popular sports content became an unintended consequence. Although the MDA reiterated its commitment not to intervene in the prerogative of pay-TV operators in their service provision, these episodes exposed some shortcomings. The fact that Singapore is a small market with only two pay-TV operators needs to be carefully considered by the MDA. Special clauses may be required to go with its regulation to ensure public interest is adequately protected, and that effective competition is supported for its media industry. In view of recent development within its media market, it necessitated an update on its existing regulatory framework. A joint consultation between the MDA and the Singapore Sports Council[10] was launched in late 2012 to review its anti-siphoning list to ensure that the list remained relevant to market developments and within the public's interest (MDA, 2012). The revised anti-siphoning list was gazetted in January 2013 (see Table 6.2).

*Table 6.2* Singapore's media development authority anti-siphoning list as at 2013

| Status | Programme | Changes |
| --- | --- | --- |
| Existing events in Category A | Asian Games Commonwealth Games Southeast Asian Games (SEA Games) Summer Olympic Games Singapore League (Football S-League) | Maintained on list Removed from list |
| New events in Category A | Fédération Internationale de Football Association (FIFA) World Cup (Key matches – opening, semi-finals and finals) and matches involving Team Singapore, including qualifiers Formula One (F1) Singapore | New inclusion |
| New events in Category B | ASEAN Football Federation (AFF) Suzuki Cup Malaysia Cup (matches involving Singapore Club team/s) Summer Paralympic Games Summer Youth Olympic Games | New inclusion |

Note
Adapted from Media Development Authority (2013: 1–2).

With strong team participation from Singapore, coverage of the Asian Games, Commonwealth Games, SEA Games and the (Summer) Olympic Games has remained protected within the list since the anti-siphoning scheme was introduced in 2003. This, in a way, fulfils the 'promise' of public service television to deliver programmes representative of a 'common culture' (Williams, 1989). To align itself with an agenda of distributive justice reflective of public interests, the new list was expanded to include key matches (opening, semi-finals and finals) and all matches involving the Singapore team at the FIFA World Cup. On the one hand, the key consideration involved the strong sentiment expressed by the public that the FIFA World Cup is a sporting event of national significance that should be made available on FTA TV. It can be argued that the event can help to further establish and promote local leagues and interest in the sport itself, thereby possibly impacting on football culture in Singapore. On the other hand, the regulator has to carefully avoid potential losses to pay-TV operators arising from the acquisition of broadcast rights to premium sports content (e.g. FIFA World Cup). This may adversely affect the ability of pay-TV operators to provide a commercially viable service. A decision was thus undertaken to protect only key matches, following a common practice in most European countries under the European Audiovisual Media Services Directive.

As the first night race of the F1 World Championships, F1 Singapore was added to the Category A list for the first time. It was considered by the local government as a major international sporting event of national significance with mass appeal (MDA, 2012). It can be suggested that its availability on FTA television would instil a sense of pride among citizens in Singapore as a host city of a world-class sporting event. Along with the revision, coverage for its domestic football league (S-League) was dropped from the protected list with its dwindling viewership in recent years. S-League matches are currently available on pay-TV platforms, with selected delayed broadcasts on FTA TV. To increase opportunities for public viewers without pay-TV to watch events of 'public interest and national signifi-cance' featuring world-class sporting events, Category B events were introduced to the list for the first time since the scheme had been put in place. The AFF Suzuki Cup[11] and the Malaysia Cup[12] are events that garnered much public interest with viewers resonating with clubs representing Singapore. With Singapore hosting the inaugural Youth Olympic Games in 2010, the significance of the event saw the inclusion of the Summer Youth Olympic Games in the list, while the Summer Par-alympic Games featuring Singapore representatives is also included.

The implications that can be drawn from the revision of the anti-siphoning list are twofold: first, it revealed the rising significance of sports events as an important aspect of national popular culture. Brought about by the advent of transmission technology, mediated sports events have become an ever more prominent feature of contemporary households in Singapore. Second, TV sport could not be left safely to the commercial markets. Although any programme which meets the quali-fying criteria can be considered for inclusion into the anti-siphoning list, the current list comprises only sports events. By gazetting only sport events, the state's inter-vention is clearly a response to the threat to public access to quality FTA TV sport. This seems necessary to prevent the complete capture of (sporting) events for restricted access pay-TV platforms. This measure has meant that global sports mega-events, including the summer Olympic Games and the FIFA World Cup (to a lesser extent), sports events of significance (e.g. Youth Olympic Games) and longstanding importance (e.g. SEA Games) remain widely available to the public.

## Conclusions

The chapter has provided an overview of sport broadcast development in Singa-pore. It has looked at how the rapidly changing economic and political landscape changed the structures and relations surrounding mediated sports. With near uni-versal access to television and sport programming becoming a major social insti-tution, televised sport is said to have achieved the status of a public good or service, whereby all citizens can expect reasonable access to it (Rowe, 2004). Yet access to live telecast sports events on FTA are often not without challenge. Recent developments in Singapore reveal the nature of complications facing the regulator. As with most 'advanced' societies, there is the need to balance both public interest in enabling access to major sport events and commercial interests of pay-TV providers. Although the regulator in Singapore has designated a list of sports events for which exclusive rights could not be granted to pay-TV, the level of protection it offers over the public's right to watch sporting events is far from those tightly regulated broadcast markets like Australia (currently the most stringent in the world) and the UK. Nonetheless, there is a further role to play for the regulator in Singapore. As a public service, it is imperative for the state to find ways to enable public FTA broadcasters to improve their provision of sport, even if it means back-tracking on previous deregulation strategies. This is particularly relevant given the ever-increasing commodification of sport content within the broadcast sector. To ensure that all of its citizens are able to participate in, and have access to, televised sport, the government will have to continue to be vigilant and get involved in the defence, maintenance and extension of the rights of the cultural citizenship associated with broadcast sport, in recognition of the increased standing of sport events within public culture.

## Notes

1 MediaCorp is wholly owned by Temasek Holdings, a government-owned investment arm.
2 The acronym for Starhub Cable Vision remains as SCV.
3 The National Sports Participation Survey (NSPS) in Singapore is conducted every five to six years. The most recent survey was conducted in 2012 and results have yet to be released.
4 S$1=£0.52.
5 Average fee paid by consumers in other parts of South-East Asia like Malaysia, Hong Kong and Thailand is estimated at S$32 (£16) a month (Chen, 2012).
6 *Radio Televisyen Malaysia* has remained the official broadcaster in Malaysia for FIFA World Cup since 1974 (with the exception of 1982).
7 Asian Games, Commonwealth Games, Southeast Asian Games, Summer Olympic Games and the Singapore League were the only specific sporting events included in the list when it was introduced in 2003.
8 Rebates would be payable to *SingTel* if the Football Association Premier League sold the broadcast rights to another pay-TV provider, i.e. *StarHub*.
9 As explicated earlier, SingTel has been strategically subsidising its content to garner subscribers for its *mioTV* service. Their existing strategy with low profit margin carries the implication of extending the subsidised rate to Starhub customers under the Cross-Carriage Measure.
10 The Singapore Sports Council has been involved as the anti-siphoning list currently comprises only sports events.
11 The AFF Suzuki Cup was previously known as the Tiger Cup after its inception 1996. It is a biennial football tournament involving national football teams from SEA countries.
12 Although participating teams are predominantly from Malaysia, there was significant public interest in the matches since Singapore's renewed participation in the Malaysia Cup since 2012 after six years' absence.

## References

Ang, P.H. and Lee, B. (2002) Wiring an intelligent island: The internet in Singapore. In Rao, S. and Klopfenstein, B.C. (eds) *Cyberpath to development in Asia*. London: Praeger, 159–182.
Bernstein, A. and Blain, N. (2002) Sport and the media: The emergence of a major research field. *Culture, Sport, Society*, 5(3): 1–30.
Chen, M. (2012) Paying the price for sports on television. *The Straits Times* [Online], 16 June. Available at www.straitstimes.com/BreakingNews/Singapore/Story/STIStory_811898.html [accessed 11 July 2012].

CNN (2010) Singapore finally gets to watch World Cup 2010, but at what price? [Online] Available at http://travel.cnn.com/singapore/play/mrbrown-singapore-gets-world-cup-2010–538201 [accessed 10 January 2013].

Davidson, J. (2010) How Europe is killing Singaporean football. *CNN* [Online], 20 October. Available at http://travel.cnn.com/singapore/life/how-europe-killing-singaporean-football-045489 [accessed 10 January 2013].

Gilmour, C. and Rowe, D. (2012) Sport in Malaysia: National imperatives and western seductions. *Sociology of Sport Journal*, 29(4): 485–505.

Harris, N. (2010) Premier League nets £1.4bn TV rights bonanza. *Independent* [Online], 23 March. Available at: www.independent.co.uk/sport/football/premier-league/premier-league-nets-16314bn-tv-rights-bonanza-1925462.html [accessed 6 February 2013].

Horne, J. (2005) Sport and the mass media in Japan. *Sociology of Sport Journal*, 22(4): 415–432.

Jenna, R., Arena, D. and Lim, C. (2012) *Exclusive content cross-carriage obligation in Singapore: An innovation intervention that promises to create value for all stakeholders.* Singapore: Value Partners Management Consulting.

Katz, E. and Wedell, G. (1978) *Broadcasting in the Third World: Promise and performance.* London: Macmillan.

Leo, P. and Lee, T. (2004) The "new" Singapore: Mediating culture and creativity. *Continuum: Journal of Media and Cultural Studies*, 18(2): 205–218.

Lim, S.H. (2013) StarHub to broadcast EPL for next three seasons. *Asia One* [Online], 27 April. Available at http://news.asiaone.com/print/News/Latest%2BNews/Sports/Story/A1Story20130426–418485.html [accessed 28 April 2013].

Lovestock, P. and Schoenfeld, S. (1995) The broadcast media markets in Asia. In Ure, J. (ed.) *Telecommunication in Asia: Policy, planning and development.* Hong Kong: Hong Kong University, 147–191.

Media Development Authority (2011) Cross-carriage to be implemented from 1 August 2011. [Online], 1 July. Available at www.mda.gov.sg/NewsAndEvents/Press Release/2011/Pages/20110701.aspx [accessed 15 March 2013].

Media Development Authority (2012) *Proposed revisions to the anti-siphoning list and definition of delayed broadcast public consultation.* Singapore: Media Development Authority.

Media Development Authority (2013) Closing note to public consultation on revisions to the anti-siphoning list and definition of delayed broadcast. [Online], 11 January. Available at www.mda.gov.sg/Reports/ConsultationReports/Documents/Anti-Siphoning%20 Closing%20Note%20to%20Public%20Consultation%20(11%20Jan%202013).pdf [accessed 6 April 2013].

Mintel (2003) *Leisure intelligence: Spectator sports.* London: Mintel.

Paul Budde Communication (2008) *Singapore – broadcasting.* New South Wales, Australia: Paul Budde Communication.

Png, I. (2008) Case study – StarHub: English Premier League. *National University of Singapore* [Online] Available at www.comp.nus.edu.sg/~ipng/mecon/cases/StarHub.pdf [accessed 8 November 2012].

Rowe, D. (2004) Watching brief: Cultural citizenship and viewing rights. *Sport in Society*, 7(3): 385–402.

Rowe, D. (2011) *Global media sport: Flows, forms and futures.* London: Bloomsbury Academic.

Rowe, D. and Gilmour, C. (2010) Sport, media and consumption in Asia: A merchandised milieu. *American Behavioral Scientist*, 53(10): 1530–1548.

Rowe, D. and Scherer, J. (eds) (2013) *Sport, public broadcasting, and cultural citizenship: Signal lost?* London: Routledge.

Saad, I. (2013) SingNet to cross-carry Barclays Premier League on StarHub platform. *Channel News Asia* [Online], 24 April. Available at www.channelnewsasia.com/news/singapore/singnet-to-cross-carry/651448.html [accessed 1 May 2013].

Shine, O. (2010) Deadlock could drive World Cup online in Singapore. *Reuters* [Online], 29 January. Available at www.reuters.com/article/2010/01/29/us-soccer-world-rights-singapore-idUSTRE60S1V120100129 [accessed 13 December 2012].

Singapore Government (2013) *Media Development Authority of Singapore Act* (Chapter 172, No. 116). Singapore: Government Gazette.

Singapore Sports Council (2001) *National sports participation survey 2000.* Singapore: Singapore Sports Council.

Singapore Sports Council (2006) *National sports participation survey 2005.* Singapore: Singapore Sports Council.

SingTel (2009) News release. [Online], 15 December. Available at http://info.singtel.com/node/6704 [accessed 6 April 2013].

SingTel (2012) SingTel mioTV reinforces commitment to sports with new carriage deal with ESPN STAR Sports. [Online], 1 December. Available at http://info.singtel.com/node/12512 [accessed 1 February 2013].

Starhub (2003) StarHub and MediaCorp TV to bring the UEFA EURO 2004 to soccer fans in Singapore. [Online], 17 November. Available at www.starhub.com/content/corporate/newsroom/2003/11/17112003_starhubandmediacorptvtobringtheuefaeuro-2004tosoccerfansinsingapore.html [accessed 1 October 2012].

Starhub (2012) Starhub launches TV anywhere. [Online], 7 June. Available at www.starhub.com/content/corporate/newsroom/2012/06/starhub-launches-tv-anywhere.html [accessed 12 December 2012].

Tan, L. (2010) Football World Cup broadcast comes to Singapore (you all can start handing over the money now). *Singapore: Red Sports* [Online]. Available at www.redsports.sg/2010/05/07/world-cup-broadcast [accessed 10 January 2013].

Tan, T. (2001) MediaCorp puts listing on hold. *The Straits Times.* 15 May, p. 1.

Tham, I. (2013) Prices to watch EPL shoots up after SingTel loses appeal. *Asia One* [Online], 29 July. Available at http://news.asiaone.com/news/singapore/prices-watch-epl-shoots-after-singtel-loses-appeal [accessed 6 August 2013].

*The Straits Times* (1999) Even the most sporty will be glued to couch. *Life!* 29 October, p. 5.

*The Straits Times* (2000) Fuzz over tuning in to SportsCity. *Life!* 1 February, p. 2.

*The Straits Times* (2002) MediaCorp TV to shut down City TV channel. *Hom.* 11 January, p. H2.

*The Straits Times* (2013) MCI rejects SingTel's application for stay on cross-carriage ruling. [Online], 6 June. Available at www.straitstimes.com/breaking-news/singapore/story/mci-rejects-singtels-appeal-stay-cross-carriage-ruling-20130606 [accessed on 18 June 2013].

UEFA (2008) Singtel win Singapore rights. [Online], 20 March. Available at www.uefa.com/uefa/events/tv/news/newsid=674237.html [accessed 2 February 2013].

Williams, R. (1989) *Resources of hope: Culture, democracy, socialism.* London: Verso.

Wong, D. (2012) "No manual available": The creation of a Youth Olympic legacy – A case study of Singapore 2010 Youth Olympic Games. In Fyall, A. and Shipway, R. (eds) *International sport events: Impacts, experiences and identities.* London: Routledge, 55–68.

# 7 Turkish football, match-fixing and the fan's media

## A case study of Fenerbahçe fans

*Dağhan Irak*

## Introduction

Football was imported to Turkey by British merchants in the 1890s and has since become the most popular sport in the country (Irak, 2013: 30–31). While football is popular nationwide, the leading football clubs are predominantly concentrated in the city of Istanbul. Nearly 95 per cent of football enthusiasts throughout Turkey support either Fenerbahçe, Galatasaray or Beşiktaş – known as the 'three giants' of Turkish football (En fazla taraftarı, 2012). These three clubs owe their popularity to their historical position as Turkey's semi-official 'national team'. Throughout the 1910s, for example, these clubs represented rising Turkish nationalism and ethnic rivalries against Greek and Armenian teams, and later against occupation forces in the late Ottoman period (Gökaçtı, 2008: 70–73). These teams have subsequently managed to preserve their symbolic status in the modern era of football.

The popularity and historical significance of the 'three giants', combined with their centrality to Turkish nationalism and politics, means that any off-the-pitch 'controversies' involving these clubs (and Trabzonspor to a lesser extent) become wider political issues in Turkey. In 2011, for example, a police operation against match-fixing was initiated, targeting Fenerbahçe, the league champion of the previous season, and also featuring Beşiktaş and Trabzonspor to a lesser extent. Through an examination of fan blogs this chapter provides a critical account of the events surrounding the match-fixing scandal. According to a police investigation during the 2010/11 Turkish Super League season, 19 matches involving champions Fenerbahçe were fixed. League runner-up, Trabzonspor, and cup winner, Beşiktaş, were also implicated in the scandal as attempting to manipulate the outcome of games. Despite these serious allegations, the evidence base was low. Nevertheless, there were a number of conspiracy theories in circulation.

This chapter aims to analyse the Fenerbahçe fans' reactions to match-fixing through their use of fan media; principally the blog Papazın Çayırı. In doing this I also critique fans' perceptions of conventional media, the government, the judicial system, police, other teams, the Fenerbahçe Board and their imprisoned President, Aziz Yıldırım, the principal actor in the match-fixing operation. The aim is to understand the political nature of these reactions, and to articulate whether these responses create a fans' democracy, which gives fans a share in the daily running of the football environment in Turkey. Arguably, due to their level of popularity amongst fans, the 'three giants' may appropriately be considered as 'micro-nations', possessing their own identities. Thus, it is important to know if the fans were primarily interested in defending their own group interests (such as more affordable ticket prices or better police treatment at the stadia) in their clubs, or in reaffirming their allegiance to the powerful ruling elite of the clubs.

## Football stands, democratisation and politicisation

Since the 1970s, as football began to be aired extensively on television, football stands have gradually become more visible and audible. Football stands became a channel of fan expression, related or unrelated to football. The political feud between Spanish, Argentinian and English fans about the Falklands/Malvinas crisis during the 1982 World Cup in Spain, for example, was a textbook case of how football stadiums could be used to convey political messages (Williams *et al.*, 1984). Sandvoss (2003: 50–51) states that fandom is a part of 'everyday politics' and writes "the everyday discourses and actions of football fans suggest that fandom is political in both its content and its implications, even though negotiated outside the traditional spheres of political discourse." In his work about Lebanese football fans, Moroy (2000) confirms Sandvoss' view, claiming that the politicisation of football stands creates a 'liberated' space for the fans to express their political views. It can be said that football stands, as rather autonomous places, provide fans with an environment to express themselves. However, as McLean and Wainwright (2009: 68) argue, the hegemonic football culture – which is dominated by media, club owners and politicians – may easily block and manipulate the 'free speech' atmosphere of the stands.

In Turkey, as football has been dominated by a number of powerful individuals since the very beginning, the politicisation of football stands has been controlled and sanitised by dominant groups. Prior to the 1980 coup d'état, people had rarely considered the significance of football stands as spaces for mobilised political action. According to Bostancıoğlu (1993: 242–244), in Turkey, left-wing politics discarded football as the 'opium of masses' while, as Bora (1993: 231–237) argues, the right-wing perceived the rivalries of football as a "disturbance against the national unity". Therefore, the junta of the 1980 coup, which aimed to depoliticise the masses in order to impose its own crafted ideology, considered football as an ideal, harmless and apolitical social gathering. The junta government and the following Özal government invested highly in football, often subsidising bigger clubs. Football was also used as a distraction from Turkey's isolation from the Western world. Turkish football clubs started to excel in European cups in the 1990s, and these successes triggered a 'pop-nationalism' wave in football stands. This wave reflected Turkey's liminal position in relation to Europe, both seeking involvement, and reinforcing Turkish distinctiveness (and separatism). This was in line with the official ideology of Turkey, which is, at the same time, nationalistic yet also pro-Western.

In the 2010s, under the stewardship of the Islamo-conservative Justice and Development Party, Turkey's football stands have witnessed a new politicisation trend. This trend's harbinger was the upper-middle class: urban football fans with higher education who were uncomfortable with the government's interventions in secular lifestyles. The Gezi Park protests of June 2013, which also involved these fan groups, is a good indicator of such discontent (returned to later). The match-fixing investigation examined in this chapter has also been at the forefront of the politicisation of Turkish football stands.

## New media = instant democratisation?

Since the introduction of Web 2.0 in 1999, many scholars have discussed the role of this new technology, as both a media tool and a tool for political protest. Gibson (2009) claims that web-enabled citizen-campaigning may revitalise and empower de-politicised citizens. Similarly, Birdsall (2007) proposes that the Web 2.0 development can be seen as part of a larger human rights movement, which could enhance people's right to communicate. Coleman (2005: 280) notes that the internet has "the capacity of ordinary people to enter, shape and govern it to a greater extent than with any previous communication medium". Mounir Bensalah (2012: 24), in his work on the role of the internet during the Arab Spring, states that the "the individuals' personal revolts [on social networks] helped developing communities who share, associate, contemplate and react."

While it is generally accepted that new media technologies enable 'ordinary' users to produce content, and that this may, to some extent, have a democratising effect, all aforementioned assessments seem to be based on an assumption that accepts that citizens have the means to be engaged in democratic processes. However, while access to the internet and bourgeoning new-media literacy of people in Turkey varies, the differences between citizens on these aspects could lead to pre-existing socio-economic inequalities being reinforced and exacerbated, particularly as the content of new media would be dominated by those who are more able to use them. For instance, the lack of a Turkish-language interface on social networking tools such as Twitter has, for years, excluded Turkish people from accessing and using them. The use of Twitter in Turkey remains well below that of Facebook for instance, but when a Turkish interface was introduced in April 2011 (five years after its global emergence) it was dominated by two main groups: Turkish users with higher levels of education and professional media institutions.

Furthermore, the instant democratising effect popularly attributed to new media tools needs to be discussed on a socio-political level. What needs to be analysed is the extent to which this effect could function in case an anti-democratic, but populist power manufactures consent in society. As Rızvanoğlu and Gidişoğlu (2011: 84) underline, studying nationalism in the

Turkish context is critical as it has been the predominant and hegemonic ideology in Turkish political culture. Furthermore, Bora and Canefe (2002) demonstrate that nationalism, which was employed to justify the new republic in the days of its emergence, later converted itself to a hegemonic ideology, which glorified populism that served right-wing governments and juntas in different eras and combined with Islam and economic liberalism after the pro-American coup in 1980. Özkırımlı (2002: 710) states that popular nationalism in daily life, to which sports contribute, reproduces nationalism better than the 'official' channels could manage. Therefore, it should be questioned whether new media tools democratise masses or reproduce 'official' tendencies in societies where hegemonic ideologies prevail. Popular football culture, which "has been a stronghold of hegemonic-social practices where nationalistic discourse is reproduced" (Erdoğan, 1993), and its associated products on the internet, is a fruitful research area in Turkey, where the voters of all major parties define themselves as 'nationalists' ('Halkın yarısı Atatürkçü', 2010). As Turkish media is one of the locomotives of nationalistic discourse, fans' media should be analysed to question if and how they adopt a similar nationalistic discourse about their clubs.

## Method

In order to analyse Fenerbahçe fans' reactions via social media during the match-fixing scandal, a popular fans' blog which covered the events in detail was chosen. This chapter focuses on the coverage of the blog, Papazın Çayırı (the Priest's Meadow, the former name of the terrain where Fenerbahçe Stadium is located) (see http://papazincayiri.blogspot.com), which has been online since April 2008. The founder of the blog, Gürman Timurhan (also known as *aethewulf* on Twitter and popular *EkşiSözlük* forums) was known for his critical stance against the government and against the Fenerbahçe administration, even before the match-fixing scandal became public. Timurhan was also a keynote speaker in the fans' 'Great Fenerbahçe' rally in December 2011, after the investigation had started. Papazın Çayırı has no ties with the official media of Fenerbahçe and it is contributed to by dozens of bloggers, all of whom are Fenerbahçe fans. Due to its popularity and overt critical stance, Papazın Çayırı is representative of non-official fans' media. The data used in this chapter were collected via qualitative analysis of blog content archived under the label '3 Temmuz' ('July 3', the day the investigation started). I was particularly interested in obtaining data regarding the blog's stance towards the government, wider politics, the justice system, media, rival clubs, 'home' fans, Fenerbahçe's administration and club President Aziz Yıldırım.

The research contains qualitative content analysis of Papazın Çayırı's interpretation of the match-fixing operation. Within the analysis, I show how these sources perceived various actors (such as other clubs' fans, government, judicial system and Turkish Football Federation) in the operation, and how they interpreted their actions.

## The match-fixing operation

Match-fixing has been a recurring theme in Turkish football over the last two decades. In this period, various rumours about the existence of match-fixing were circulated in the press, although any investigation started by the Turkish Football Federation (TFF) about elite division teams were quickly dismissed by legal sections of the Federation.

On 31 March 2011 Parliament passed Law No. 6222, which aimed to regulate illegal acts in sports. This law was supported by major sports clubs and meant that match-fixing attempts could be more rigorously investigated by state attorneys. Therefore, match-fixing cases entered into court jurisdiction, which was a departure from existing policy.

On 3 July 2011, three months after Law No. 6222 was passed, Turkish police started early-morning raids on many sports officials' residences. Amongst those implicated in the raids was Fenerbahçe President Aziz Yıldırım, who was taken into police custody. According to police, 19 matches involving Super League clubs in the 2010/11 season had had their outcomes fixed. Images of Aziz Yıldırım were leaked to the press by police sources, along with pieces of evidence and telephone transcripts, which reinforced the allegations. This not only constituted a violation of the defendants' personal rights, but also threatened the secrecy and credibility of the investigation.

In May 2012, the TFF announced the results of its own investigation. It concluded that no individual clubs would be punished for match-fixing. Instead, only minor penalties would be given to certain club officials. Following these decisions the TFF amended its regulations' Article 58, removing the responsibility from the clubs and instead targeting any penalties at individuals. This was in light of the fact that, as recently as three days previous, Fenerbahçe withdrew its case from the Court of Arbitration for Sports (CAS) demanding €45 million in compensation. They explained their actions as being in the 'national interest' (see CAS davasını, 2012). In December 2012, the court gave its verdict and sentenced Aziz Yıldırım to a six-year prison sentence and US$1 million pecuniary punishment (the penalties for match-fixing in Law No. 6222 were also alleviated by a parliamentary motion in December 2011).

## The conventional Turkish media and its political context

The decade-long Justice and Development Party (AKP) government period dramatically changed the face of Turkish media, particularly in terms of ownership and freedom of expression. The Doğan Group, which once owned a substantial part of Turkish media (Barış, 2008), for example, was forced to downsize due to heavy tax penalties imposed by the government (Sözeri and Kurban, 2012); while another major actor, Merkez Medya, was taken over by the pro-government Turkuaz Group, with a state auction bid in 2007. The other prominent media actors of today, Ciner Group, Çukurova Group and Doğuş Group, all have state connections in different sectors, while other holdings such as Koza

Group, Albayrak Group and Star Medya are openly pro-government. Meanwhile, at the time of writing, the flagship of the pro-Gülen media group, Zaman newspaper, is the only remaining newspaper selling more than a million copies per day (along with subscriptions) (see Tiraj, n.d). In fact, it sells as many as the total of its three closest competitors combined. In saying this, despite selling only around 50,000 copies, the Taraf newspaper was also very influential during the match-fixing affair because it published many of the leaked documents, including coup plot cases and, therefore, is perceived to be an important actor in the battle for hegemony between the military and the civil government (Elpeze Ergeç, 2012).

## Papazın Çayırı: the Fenerbahçe fans' voice?

The police operation into match-fixing was unprecedented, and the arrest of Aziz Yıldırım, a prominent figure in Turkish football, was quite shocking for many football enthusiasts, especially Fenerbahçe fans. The severity of the situation meant that is was necessary to establish a social discussion environment, where concerned members of football's community, including millions of football fans, could attempt to unravel what was going on. The conventional media failed to satisfy this need as it mainly concentrated on publishing leaked and ethically dubious documents about the ongoing operation. A number of sensational moves, such as publishing Aziz Yıldırım's 'mugshot' (Belli and Uludağ, 2011) or speculative headlines such as 'The State Attorney Scores the Goal' (Savcı Doksandan Çaktı, 2011) or '(Aziz Yıldırım), the Armed Gang Leader' (Silahlı Çete Reisi, 2011), showed the media's lack of social empathy on an incident of such a scale, and therefore failed to convey public opinion on this issue. This meant that the fans, and their personal narratives and opinions, were all the more important at this time.

The Papazın Çayırı blog sarcastically calls itself "an illegal publication"[1] and has been known for its critical stance against state elites, as well as the Fenerbahçe administration. It once suggested that the club's official statements "sound like military statements that negate the contra-guerilla" (blog post, Jitem'le İlgilenmiyoruz, 2011). The loudly critical and politically charged nature of the blog meant that it was an influential source of information throughout the match-fixing event. For example, the blog's former disputes with the club's Executive Board and President Aziz Yıldırım, gave the blog an air of credibility on the basis that the contributors were known to have no ties with the club's inner-politics.

## Papazın Çayırı's response to the match-fixing event

### *Attitudes towards the 'mainstream' media*

Among 126 articles published by Papazın Çayırı under the label 'July 3', the vast majority criticised the conventional media's coverage of the scandal.

Throughout the 13-month period where the Papazın Çayırı blog published posts about the event, not a single article with positive sentiments towards conventional media appeared. During the first week (3–9 July), for example, out of 12 articles published in the blog, 50 per cent contained negative sentiments towards the conventional media. Similarly, during the first month, out of 63 articles published, 43 (68 per cent) contained negative sentiments about the media coverage. Whilst the number of posts criticising the conventional media diminished as the situation lengthened, overall perception towards the media did not change. It should also be mentioned that media is the most recurring theme in this blog's posts about the scandal, as over 63 per cent of the total articles expressed some interest in the media. This clearly shows that the Papazın Çayırı blog saw conventional media as one of the primary actors in this operation; specifically, they believed the conventional media manipulated public opinion against the defendants.

Looking at the content, the language used about the media verifies this assumption. In its article entitled 'Lynching through media' (5 July 2011), the blog interprets the first days of the scandal as "the obnoxious hysteria of pro-government newspapers ... head[ing] to a defamation operation through media of which examples we already know" (blog post, Medya Yoluyla Linç, 2011). In this quotation, the media is portrayed as an apparatus of strong political power, which also controls the justice system. This perception overlaps with the aforementioned concerns about wider political influence within Turkish media.

One striking point about Papazın Çayırı's criticism of the media is that the blog publishes special features focused on rather impartial figures of the media who expressed their concerns about the corrupt football system and were critical of Aziz Yıldırım. These blog posts accuse these pundits of "being fake and two-faced" (blog post, Banu Hanım'ın Hayalkırıklıkları Üstüne, 2011), and "participating in the horrible lynching against Fenerbahçe" (blog post, Tekmili Birden Radikal Spor Servisine Sorular, 2012). The insistence of putting these writers in the same category with the pro-government columnists suggests that the blog employs an 'us' and 'them' logic and rejects anyone who does not accept their version of 'truth'. This kind of logic is inherent within nationalist discourse, as Joshua Searle-White (2001: 12) suggests, "along with the tendency to favour one's ingroup, [we] also tend to think in predictable ways about outgroups". In this case, the mainstream media is clearly seen as an outgroup and its more moderate members are included alongside the pro-government journalists. Meanwhile, the perception of bias which constant 'ingroup favouritism' might create was diluted by quoting a few 'sane' outsider voices. The perfect example of this practice is the article entitled 'The Last Stronghold: The Fenerbahçe Sports Club and Turkish Politics' by Hay Ethan Cohen Yanarocak. The blog announces this article by an introductory sentence: "I left it untranslated on purpose, so you can see an outsider's view without any mediation". The writer of this 'outsider article', completely in line with Papazın Çayırı's views, happens to be an Istanbul-born Turkish citizen who completed his Bachelor's studies in Turkey (see Hay Eytan Cohen Yanarocak, n.d). He is also an avid Fenerbahçe fan who decorates his Facebook profile with Fenerbahçe apparel. Thus he can hardly be considered to be an 'outsider' (implying impartiality) as the blog presented him to be.

## Attitudes towards the justice system

The justice system, or the lack of trust towards it, was also a very common theme in Papazın Çayırı's blog entries during the match-fixing scandal. The critical articles about the judiciary system start with the first detentions and accelerate again after the indictment towards the defendants, including Aziz Yıldırım, was announced in December 2011. The Papazın Çayırı blog criticised the justice system in two main ways. First, especially in the early articles (July-August 2011), the blog made several references to other big political cases, such as the Ergenekon coup attempt (blog post, Neden tedirginiz? 2011), and the journalist trials (blog post, Tutukluluk Kararları ve Şimdi Ne Olacak? 2011). They claimed that the match-fixing case was similarly politically motivated. Here it can be seen that the Papazın Çayırı blog unreservedly accepts that the justice system is controlled by the government, which is clearly a political statement. Similarly, there were a number of articles comparing the match-fixing defendants with anti-government defendants from other cases. There are similarities between these groups, such as the long duration of detentions, or the leakage of evidence. However, the defendants from other cases, who are mainly pro-opposition journalists, lawyers, students and former high-ranking military officials, come from very different social status than the defendants of the match-fixing case, who are mainly businessmen with very close ties to the government. Therefore the comparison between these groups reflects the political leanings of the blog.

## Attitudes towards the police

During the first days of the event, Papazın Çayırı published several articles criticising actions of the police. In fact, during the first month there were more posts criticising the police than the government or justice system; though this was likely due to the fact that the trials had not yet started. What Papazın Çayırı predominantly criticised during the first days of the scandal were the personal rights violations against the defendants, especially the club President Aziz Yıldırım. Papazın Çayırı claimed the police handled the operation in a way that incriminated the defendants and, in so doing, ensured that public opinion revolved around their culpability. In May 2012, criticism of the police by the blog was reheated after a major incident. In the final game of the championship playoff – Fenerbahçe vs. Galatasaray – the police used tear gas in the stadium against the fans in the stands, injuring small children. After the game hundreds of fans clashed with police in the Kadıköy area (where the club and its stadium are located), causing damage to police vehicles. In this period, the blog refocused on critical articles about police violence, linking this to other sections of Turkish society, for example the Gülen religious group (blog post, Yasama, Yürütme, Yargı, Cemaat, 2012).

*Attitudes towards other clubs*

Papazın Çayırı's perception of other clubs' administration and fans presents a very negative picture. Throughout the process, in addition to the media, rival teams are the other consistent target of criticism. On analysing the comments made about other teams' fans and administrations, there were conflicting views. Initially, the blog tries to preserve its fan-focused approach and attempts to relate to the other teams' fans. However, when the other teams' fans are critical of Fenerbahçe and Aziz Yıldırım, the blog's authors put those fans into the same category as their clubs' Boards, whom Papazın Çayırı sees cooperating with the 'coalition against Fenerbahçe'.

Fenerbahçe's inner-city rival, Galatasaray, appears to be one of the major culprits of the 'conspiracy'. Contributors perceived Galatasaray to be a 'state team', which consequently received support from the state and other influential bodies, in the hope that the club would dominate Turkish football. In a posting on 8 May 2012, entitled 'The Children of Other Worlds in the Same Era – Love and Hate', the perception of Galatasaray by the blog's author is described in the following terms: "Another aspect Galatasaray regained in this situation [the operation against Fenerbahçe] is their new status. Galatasaray, excluding any remaining bits of truth and becoming a persistent follower of punishment [against Fenerbahçe], advanced to become a part of a wide coalition of assault [against Fenerbahçe]" (blog post Aynı Çağda Başka Dünyaların Çocukları Sevgi – Nefret, 2012). The article, associating Fenerbahçe fans with 'love' and Galatasaray fans with 'hate', is a prime example of the club-nationalism which classifies different groups according to their identities: attributing 'good' and 'bad' characteristics to all the members of these groups. Accordingly, Fenerbahçe fans act out of love for their team, and Galatasaray fans act out of hate for Fenerbahçe. Defining all other groups according to their relationships with 'us' is a very popular theme in Turkish nationalism. "A Turk has no friend other than a Turk" (*Türk'ün Türkten Başka Dostu Yoktur*) is still the most popular answer when Turks are asked to define their relationships with 'Others' (Akgün *et al.*, 2011: 11). In this example, Fenerbahçe fans used a similar slogan: 'We suffice for ourselves' (*biz bize yeteriz.*).

Trabzonspor, the biggest provincial team, also received similar criticism, especially after Environment and Urban Affairs Minister, Erdoğan Bayraktar (Trabzon MP of the ruling-party), said they (implying the government or AKP) "work[ed] diligently to give the title to Trabzonspor" (see Konuştu, 2012). The blog developed a theory about Trabzonspor's affiliation with the government. It claimed that the government supported this club because of a previous incident. In 2004, Prime Minister Recep Tayyip Erdoğan (also a Fenerbahçe fan) criticised the punishment of visiting Fenerbahçe fans after a brawl with Trabzonspor fans. After this incident, AKP lost the local elections in Trabzon. According to the blog, after this incident the government started to favour Trabzonspor to regain popularity in the city and "AKP learned that the political power in Trabzon is connected to Trabzonspor" (blog post, Bordo Mavi Hükümet, 2012).

The 'ingroup favouritism' and 'outgroup defamation' in Turkish football fans' behaviours are neither exclusive to Fenerbahçe fans and/or to the Papazın Çayırı blog, nor did they first appear during the match-fixing event. While 'micro-nation' nationalism helps create 'ingroup' and 'outgroup' classifications, the common distrust, and the lack of transparency in Turkish football, pushes this mentality to a series of conspiracy theories. The match-fixing event not only aggravated the problems already apparent in Turkish football, but also deepened this type of self-centred scepticism among fans. Thus, Papazın Çayırı's tendency to manufacture 'us' against 'them' rhetoric can only be considered to be its result, rather than being its cause.

### Attitudes towards the Board, President, and players

Throughout the match-fixing event, the Papazın Çayırı blog mostly retained its critical approach towards the Fenerbahçe Board, which it has had since its inception. The blog mainly criticised the board for not being active against the operation, and not supporting the club President, Aziz Yıldırım. However, the blog's overt criticism of the Board was short-lived. After the Board initially challenged the TFF regulation change in January 2012, the interests of the blog and Board were realigned and the blog's posts reflected this.

During the event, Aziz Yıldırım was perceived quite positively in Papazın Çayırı postings. Over 13 months, the only criticism about Aziz Yıldırım was about his silence in the first two weeks. After that, despite his close ties with the state, he received no overt criticism in the blog. Whereas the blog's attitude to the Board and President was ambivalent, portrayal of the fans was wholly positive during this time. At the beginning of the scandal the blog separated the fans from the Board, saying:

> This club is great, not because you sign sponsorship deals and spare some of your valuable time spent in the plazas to Fenerbahçe, [but] because there are people who dare to face tear gas just to defend their club's rights.
>
> (blog post, Fenerbahçe Yönetimi Ne İş Yapar? 2011)

Players and technical staff were also included in the 'ingroup' that the blog praised: "what those who travel to Topuk Yaylası [club's training site] by buses cherish is not the championship title, Aziz Yıldırım or Şekip Mosturoğlu [board member]; it's the sweat of Fenerbahçe footballers through the season. No more, no less" (blog post, En Büyük Delilimiz Alınterimiz, 2011). This rhetoric was repeated on several occasions as the fans and players were perceived and portrayed as the main victims of the whole event.

## Conclusions

Throughout this event, the fans' media, which was led by Papazın Çayırı, helped the fans develop a political interpretation of their fandom. Most of the slogans used by Papazın Çayırı, such as 'Fenerbahçe halktır' (Fenerbahçe is people) and 'Haklıyız, kazanacağız' ('We're right, we'll prevail' (well-known lyrics by communist music ensemble, Grup Yorum)) were used in fans' rallies arranged in front of the Silivri prison and Çağlayan courthouse (these rallies were also promoted by Papazın Çayırı). Unlike other media outlets, including the semi-official blog, 12 Numara, Papazın Çayırı did not glorify club President Aziz Yıldırım, and remained critical of the club Board on several issues. Throughout the match-fixing event Papazın Çayırı decried injustice against Fenerbahçe and took a fan-centred approach. The blog's stance was visibly different to 'official' or 'semi-official' discourse(s), which glorified Aziz Yıldırım by using his images on official fan apparel, hanging posters of him in the stadium, and even producing paper facemasks out of his portrait. Papazın Çayırı was evidently an independent fan media source. As it was an independent and politically critical source of information, the blog can be compared to other independently produced blogs, for example those in Egypt, which were involved in the mass protests against Hosni Mubarak. As Eltantawy and Wiest (2011: 1207) underlined on the role of social media in the Egyptian revolution:

> social media technologies have been used especially in organizing and implementing collective activities, promoting a sense of community and collective identity among marginalized group members, creating less-confined political spaces, establishing connections with other social movements, and publicizing causes to gain support from the global community.

In another study on Egyptian social media, Khamis and Vaughn (2011) claim that "Social media can also serve as channels for expressing collective consciousness and national solidarity."

Despite being distant from the imprisoned President, and critical of the club Board, Papazın Çayırı also employed a nationalistic discourse, mainly based on the glorification of fans and the 'workers' (players and other staff) of the club. In the same way that Anderson (2006: 12) defines the nation as "an imagined political community and imagined as both inherently limited and sovereign", the blog conceives the Fenerbahçe 'nation' as "a deep, horizontal comradeship". The question, however, is whether it does that "regardless of the actual inequality and exploitation that may prevail", as Anderson (2006: 7) proposed. This research shows that Papazın Çayırı does not try to camouflage the class-based differences between fans and dominant groups within the club; however, through the match-fixing operation, it tactfully abstained from reminding anyone about them. It perceives the club as a 'micro-nation', where these differences are not a priority when it comes to a period of hardship. However, despite the blog's critical approach towards the club Board, and even club President at times, and the ever-present fan glorification among the articles examined, there was not a single post discussing how fans could join or influence the decision-making process and democratise the club. Even when the TFF changed the controversial Article 58 of its regulation, which saved clubs from receiving penalties for match-fixing, the blog did not encourage fans to become more active in democratic processes, despite its criticism of the TFF, clubs and the Fenerbahçe Board for 'staging a match-fixing of justice'.

It is visibly true that Papazın Çayırı represented a discourse of politicised fandom, though this did not lead to a fans' democracy, and rather served the inner-nation status quo, which had constantly pacified fans and reduced them to customers buying season tickets, TV subscriptions and other official consumables. Therefore, the Papazın Çayırı blog appeared as a political media, contesting the conventional media, justice system, government and police. However, it lacked the revolutionary approach that would democratise the 'micro-nation'. Therefore, while contributing to the democratic mobilisation gradually diminished by authoritarian policies in Turkey, the fans were unable to overcome wider inequalities and exploitation within their 'micro-nation'. This can only be explained by the blog's adherence to inner-club nationalism, despite heavily criticising the state ideology which favours nationalism over other ideologies. Conversely, complete adherence to the nation's imagined identity also explains why and how the traditional Turkish media failed to contribute to democratisation in the country. Papazın Çayırı mimicked a similar failure on another level of nationalism, despite succeeding in filling the traditional media's void in Turkish democratisation. To that end, it shows that even though the sports domain holds social characteristics that may trigger democratic mobilisation, its own set of dogmas inherited from Turkish political culture blocks it from democratising its own realm.

However, this is not to say that protests cannot prompt over-arching cultural changes. For example, the Gezi Park protests of June 2013 unified many Beşiktaş, Galatasaray and Fenerbahçe fans, of similar upbringing, around similar concerns. They mobilised under the banner 'Istanbul United'. It could be argued that such events represent a paradigm shift in contrast to the other events illustrated in this chapter. During the Gezi Park protests, urban, well-educated, modern football fans from different clubs (along with many other dissident groups, such as socialists, anarchists, LGBTs and even anti-capitalist Muslims) voiced their concerns about the government's autocratic agenda and, in so doing, created a supra-identity of football fans. These groups pursued their protests in stadia in the first weeks of the Turkish Super League, chanting "Taksim [the Square where Gezi protests took place] is everywhere, resistance is everywhere" in the 34th (license plate number of Istanbul) minute of games. Whilst these events would appear to contradict the dominant paradigm of Turkish football, it is too early to draw conclusions about their lasting significance. But, as these protests are very significant in the recent political history of Turkey, and football fans were ever-present in these events, their significance cannot be overlooked, and should be closely followed.

## Note

1 "Örgütsel yayın" (organisation's publication), a well-known expression used by Turkish police for illegal organisations' publications.

# References

Akgün, M., Gündoğar, S.S., Görgülü, A. and Aydın, E. (2011) *Türkiye'de dış politika algısı: TESEV dış politika programı*. İstanbul: TESEV.

Anderson, B.R. (2006) *Imagined communities: Reflections on the origin and spread of nationalism*. London: Verso.

Barış, R (2008) Turkish media landscape. In G. Terzis (ed.) *European media governance national and regional dimensions*. Bristol, UK: Intellect, 290–293.

Belli, E. and Uludağ, N. (2011) Yıldırım'ın Gözaltı Fotoğrafı. *Habertürk*, July 7: 1.

Bensalah, M. (2012) *Réseaux sociaux et Révolutions arabes?* Paris: Michalon.

Birdsall, W.F. (2007) Web 2.0 as a social movement. *Webology*, 4(2): 1–13.

Bora, T. (1993) Dur Tarih, Vur Türkiye. In T. Bora., W. Reiter and R. Horak (eds) *Futbol ve Kültürü*. Istanbul: Iletisim, 221–240.

Bora, T. and Canefe, N. (2002) Türkiye'de popülist milliyetçilik. In T. Bora (ed.) *Milliyetçilik*. İstanbul: İletişim Yayınları, 635–662.

Bostancıoğlu, A. (1993) Taraftar ve Solcu Olmak. In T. Bora., W. Reiter and R. Horak (eds) *Futbol ve Kültürü*. Istanbul: Iletisim, 241–250.

CAS davasını ülke menfaatleri adına geri çektik (2012) *Fenerbahçe Spor Kulübü Resmi Sitesi*. [Online] Available from www.fenerbahce.org/detay.asp?ContentID=29069 [accessed 23 April 2013].

Coleman, S. (2005) Blogs and the new politics of listening. *The Political Quarterly*, 76(2): 272–280.

Elpeze Ergeç, N. (2012) Usage of press as a hegemonic struggle field. *Observatorio*, 6(4): 235–245.

Eltantawy, N. and Wiest, J.B. (2011) Social media in the egyptian revolution: Reconsidering resource mobilization theory. *International Journal of Communication*, 5: 1207–1224.

En fazla taraftarı olan kulüp (2012) *Milliyet.com*. [Online] Available from http://skorer. milliyet.com.tr/en-fazla-taraftari-olan-kulup-/besiktas-galatasaray-fenerbahce-trabzonspor/detay/1597283/default.htm [accessed 29 April 2013].

Erdoğan, N. (1993) Popüler Futbol Kültürü ve Milliyetçilik. *Birikim*, 49 [Online] Availablefromwww.birikimdergisi.com/birikim/dergiyazi.aspx?did=1&dsid=47&dyid=1469 [accessed 29 April 2013].

Gibson, R. (2009) New media and the revitalisation of politics. *Representation*, 45(3): 289–299.

Gökaçtı, M.A. (2008) *"Bizim için oyna": Türkiye'de futbol ve siyaset*. Istanbul: İletişim Yayınları.

Halkın Yarısı Atatürkçü (2010) *Taraf*, January 27: 1.

Hay Eytan, C.Y. (n.d) Türkiye ile İlişkileri Kesmek İsrail'in Zararınadır. *Hastürk TV* [Online] Available from www.hasturktv.com/israilde_gundem/1126.htm [accessed 29 April 2013].

Irak, D. (2013) *Hükmen Yenik!: Türkiye'de ve İngiltere'de Futbolun Sosyo-Politiği*. Istanbul: Evrensel Basım Yayın.

Khamis, S. and Vaughn, K. (2011) Cyberactivism in the Egyptian revolution: How civic engagement and citizen journalism tilted the balance. *Arab Media and Society*, 13 [Online] Available from www.arabmediasociety.com/?article=769 [accessed 7 November 2013].

Konuştu, Ortalık Karıştı (2012) *Hürriyet*, January 10: 1.

McLean, R. and Wainwright, D.W. (2009) Social networks, football fans, fantasy and reality: How corporate and media interests are invading our lifeworld. *Journal of Information, Communication and Ethics in Society*, 7(1): 54–71.

Moroy, F. (2000) Le Sport Comme Adjuvant à L'action Politique. Le Cas du Hezbollah à Beyrouth. *Politix*, 13(50): 93–106.

Özkırımlı, U. (2002) Türkiye'de Gayriresmi ve Popüler Milliyetçilik. In T. Bora (ed.) *Milliyetçilik*. İstanbul: İletişim Yayınları, 706–718.

Rızvanoğlu, K. and Gidişoğlu, S. (2011) Nationalism on the internet: A discursive analysis of the Turkish case. *Bogazici Journal of Economics and Administrative Sciences*, 25(2): 83–107.

Sandvoss, C. (2003) *A game of two halves: Football, television, and globalisation.* London and New York: Routledge.

Savcı Doksandan Çaktı (2011) *Taraf*, July 4: 1.

Searle-White, J. (2001) *The psychology of nationalism*. New York: Palgrave.

Silahlı Çete Reisi (2011) *Taraf*, July 5: 1.

Sözeri, C. and Kurban, D. (2012) *İktidarın Çarkında Medya: Türkiye'de Medya Bağımsızlığı ve Özgürlüğü Önündeki Siyasi, Yasal ve Ekonomik Engeller*. Istanbul: TESEV.

Tiraj (n.d.) *Medyatava*. [Online] Available from www.medyatava.com/tiraj/07.04.2013 [accessed 20 April 2013].

Williams, J., Dunning, E. and Murphy, P. (1984) *Hooligans abroad: The behaviour and control of English fans in continental Europe*. London: Routledge.

# Part III
# Identities

# 8 The Gaelic Athletic Association and London's 'Irish' diaspora

*Frances Harkin*

## Introduction

A significant body of literature which seeks to consider the Irish diaspora experience through the medium of sport has emerged in recent years, with a particular focus upon the Gaelic Athletic Association (GAA) within the Irish diaspora.[1] Despite the strong historical links between Irish emigration and the city, the relationship between sport, 'Irishness' and the Irish diaspora in the context of London has received limited attention, with fleeting references within wider research concerning the Irish population in Britain (cf. Coogan 2000; Sorohan 2012). Stephen Moore has addressed this neglect through his historical study of the position of the GAA in nineteenth- and twentieth-century London, which considers the role it played in galvanising a sense of Irish nationalism amongst the Irish émigré (Moore 2010; Moore and Darby 2011).[2] By drawing upon ethnographic research conducted with members of London's Irish community, this chapter seeks to complement this existing research and contribute towards a greater understanding of the role that the GAA and its sporting events play for the Irish in London. Central to this chapter is the relationship between 'Irishness' and sport in London's Irish diaspora, and the different meanings and roles attributed to the GAA by Irish emigrants and their descendants. This analysis will conclude with an exploration of how participation in the GAA and its events can reflect different or hybrid identities for different members of London's Irish diaspora.

## The Gaelic Athletic Association in Ireland

The Gaelic Athletic Association (GAA) holds a prominent position in Irish society as an influential sporting and cultural institution. Since its inception in 1884, the GAA has grown to become one of Ireland's biggest sporting organisations, with a membership base in all 32 counties on the island of Ireland. Established amidst a wider Irish nationalist movement which sought to undermine British cultural and political hegemony in Ireland, the GAA emerged in response to the apparent need to revitalise and promote indigenous Irish sporting and cultural activities (Cronin 1999: 79). The primary function of the GAA is to promote and organise the playing of Gaelic games such as Gaelic football, Hurling, Handball and Rounders, as well as work with its sister organisations, the Ladies Gaelic Football Association and the Camogie Association, to promote Ladies Gaelic football and Camogie. The GAA is structured through a hierarchy of Provincial Councils, County Boards and unit clubs, with the President of the GAA and the Central Council overseeing the administration of the entire organisation. It defines itself as "a community based volunteer organisation" (Central Council of the Association 2009: 15) with grassroots members and unit clubs forming the foundations of the GAA. Local clubs field Gaelic football and Ladies Gaelic football teams, and Hurling and Camogie teams which play in their respective county championships and leagues. Gaelic football, Hurling and Camogie are all played with two teams of 15 players, on a rectangular playing field with goal posts similar to those used in rugby matches at each end. They are also played at different grades or levels according to age and ability, with 'Senior' and 'Minor' differentiating between adults and youth players under the age of 18 years, and 'Senior', 'Intermediate' and 'Junior' indicating different levels of ability.

Gaelic games are distinct in their style of play and are unique in that Gaelic games are largely played within the territorial confines of the island of Ireland and the Irish diaspora. The island of Ireland is divided into two political jurisdictions: the Republic of Ireland, and Northern Ireland which remains part of the United Kingdom. However, the GAA pre-dates the partition of the island of Ireland which occurred in 1921 and, as a result, continues to operate in both Northern Ireland and the Republic of Ireland. Each of the 32 counties on the island of Ireland has their own designated county ground where home games for the county's GAA teams are played. They also provide a focus for supporters, contributing towards a sense of belonging and identity, rooted in their county. The inter-county All-Ireland Championships are Ireland's most prominent sporting tournaments and are held during the summer months, concluding in September with highly anticipated finals held at Croke Park in Dublin. The All-Ireland Championships are a major feature in the Irish media during the summer months, with the finals, in particular, being high profile events. There are three main Irish broadcasters providing coverage of live GAA games and numerous television and radio shows presenting in-depth reportage of the build-up and post-analysis of matches. RTÉ is the national state broadcaster in Ireland and provides intensive radio and televised coverage of the All-Ireland Gaelic football and Hurling Championships. It shares its broadcasting rights with TV3, an independent Irish television channel. Coverage of the Ladies Gaelic football and Camogie All-Ireland Championships are provided by the independent Irish language channel TG4.

The All-Ireland Championships are played at different age levels, including Senior, Under-21 and Minor. The Provincial Championships, which constitute the early stages of the All-Ireland Gaelic football and Hurling Championships, see the counties in each of the four provinces on the island of Ireland compete against each other. London and New York also compete in the Senior All-Ireland

Gaelic football Championship as guests of the Connacht Provincial Council, and therefore compete in the Connacht Championship. As of 2013, London also competes in the Leinster Hurling Championship. The Provincial Champions progress to the latter stages of the All-Ireland Championship where they play the winners of the qualifiers, which see the remaining counties play-off against each other. In contrast to the Gaelic football and Hurling All-Ireland Championships, the Ladies Gaelic football and the Camogie All-Ireland Championships are organised according to ability with Junior, Intermediate and Senior Championships. Gaelic games are amateur sports and therefore players are not professional athletes and do not receive any substantial monetary reward for their involvement on club or county teams. The amateur status of Gaelic games is an integral feature of the GAA and is protected by Section 1.10 in the Official Guide for the GAA (Gaelic Athletic Association *Official guide, Part 1* 2012: 7). The overall importance of the GAA within Irish society is highlighted by Tom Humphries (1996: 3) who states that the GAA is a "national trust, an entity which we feel we hold in common ownership". This interpretation illustrates how the GAA is an effective vehicle for envisaging the 'imagined community' (Anderson, 1991) of the Irish nation, aiding the establishment and maintenance of a collective sense of belonging and identity, whilst also contributing towards the construction of more localised Irish county and community identities.

## Diaspora and 'diaspora space'

The discourse of diaspora is typically considered through the process of migration from a place of origin and the development of multiple communities of the dispersed population beyond the homeland (Safran 1991; Clifford 1994). Safran (1991: 83–84) provides a list of criteria for defining diaspora which includes the dispersal of a group of people from a place of origin; who retain links to this tangible location through collective myths and memories of the homeland; "believe they are not and perhaps cannot be fully accepted by their host country"; and retain aspirations to eventually return to their homeland; as well as a commitment to the maintenance of the homeland; an attachment which informs the collective identity of the diaspora group. The dispersal of people from their homeland is often seen as a temporary measure with the intention to eventually return, an aspiration which Brah (1996) refers to as a 'homing desire'. However, the process of migration is not always temporary, as long-term or permanent settled communities are often constructed and maintained in host societies. This contributes towards a dual attachment to both the place of origin and to the host society which is held simultaneously by members of a diaspora, creating multiple senses of belonging and 'home'.

The diaspora is largely associated with those who have been subject to the processes of migration and exile, reinforced through the privileging of the place of origin within the discourse of diaspora. However, as Gordon and Anderson (1999: 288) have illustrated, the term diaspora is conceptualised both as a reference to a particular group of people who have dispersed from a central point of departure, and "a certain kind of identity formation, the feeling of belonging to a community that transcends national boundaries". Consequently, Roger Brubaker (2005) suggests that the concept of diaspora should not be considered as a bounded entity, but rather as a stance, which provides for theorisation of diaspora as a collective group of people bound by commonalities. This latter imagining of diaspora is relevant to individuals not usually considered part of the dispersed population, such as those who identify with a diaspora through heritage or ancestry. A diaspora is a heterogeneous collective of different narratives of migration, as the migratory journeys undertaken by members of a diaspora and their experiences of their host societies are subjective, "each with its own history and particularities" (Brah 1996: 183). Therefore the formation of identity within a diaspora is also subjective, influenced by the roots (place of origin) of the diaspora community and the routes (experience of migration and host society) by which it was established and has been maintained. The interplay between diaspora groups such as the Irish diaspora and the indigenous population in the diaspora space that is London facilitates the negotiation of hybrid and fluid identities, which are infused with characteristics of wider society and lived experience of cosmopolitan London. The specific context of the diaspora space of London has contributed towards the emergence of hybrid and diasporic identities within London's Irish community.

## Methodology

The research here draws upon interviews and a survey conducted between July 2011 and August 2013 as part of a wider project. Participants were either members or supporters of the GAA in London and recruited via a number of methods, including social media platforms and Irish-orientated media such as the national Irish newspaper *The Irish Times* and their dedicated 'Generation Emigration' blog, as well as Irish community newspapers in Britain, *The Irish Post* and *The Irish World*. An outline of the research and a link to the online survey was sent to a number of GAA clubs in London which proved beneficial in terms of recruitment for survey responses and interview participants. A total of 70 surveys were completed by individuals currently living in London or who had previously lived in London, 42 of whom were Irish born and 28 of whom were second- or third-generation Irish and had been born in Britain. A total of 20 interviews were conducted with individuals who were involved with the GAA in London in some form as players, committee members or supporters. Eleven of these participants were Irish born, eight were second-generation Irish born in Britain and one did not identify themselves as Irish.

The survey was used as the first stage of data collection and was useful in terms of gathering knowledge which was used to structure the second stage in-depth interviews. Questions revolved around the respondent's level of participation in the GAA and their reasons for becoming involved on the island of Ireland (if applicable) and in London, their perception of the strengths and weaknesses of the GAA in London and an explicit reference to the role of the GAA and

Gaelic games in facilitating an expression of Irish identity in London. An interview guideline was used that enabled further analysis of the experience of living in London and of the GAA scene. Further ethnographic fieldwork in the form of participant observation was also deployed and proved useful as it enabled direct engagement with the London GAA scene and wider Irish community in London.

## The exiles: the Gaelic Athletic Association in London

The GAA was established in London in 1896[3] and has grown to become a prominent part of the Irish diaspora experience in London. This position is emphasised by Irene, a Gaelic footballer with the Parnell's GAA club who suggests that "the Irish community shrinks and grows over the years in London, and the GAA helps its sense of identity" (Survey 27). There were approximately 40 established GAA clubs in London in 2012, fielding Gaelic football, Hurling, Ladies Gaelic football and Camogie teams (London GAA, 2012). There are a higher number of Gaelic football teams in the city suggesting that there is greater support for and participation in Gaelic football in London than Hurling and Camogie. The London club Championships for each code are organised according to grade (Senior, Intermediate and Junior) and are the main focus for clubs. Clubs in each code also compete in their respective Leagues as well as a number of tournaments which provide further opportunities for competitive sporting events. Whilst clubs form the foundations of the GAA, county teams often remain the main focus for players and supporters alike, as inter-county competitions remain the highest competitive level within the GAA. The London County Board of the GAA, established in 1896, was officially recognised by the Central Council of the GAA and consequently granted permission to compete in the All-Ireland Championships (Moore and Darby 2011: 267).

During the twentieth century, the GAA in London became an invaluable source of social and welfare support for Irish emigrants, providing refuge and solace in an unfamiliar environment.[4] Contacts for employment and accommodation, as well as social connections were established and maintained within the network of individuals, groups and clubs involved with the London GAA scene:

> It [the GAA] provides a starting point for many people when they first arrive either through gaining them work and accommodation or by helping them meet new people and finding their feet in London.
>
> (Survey 24)

For Stephen McLaughlin, secretary of the Tir Chonaill Gaels GAA club, who arrived in 1988 with no knowledge of London, the Irish community, or the GAA scene, the social aspects of the GAA became a fundamental aspect of his early life in London. Stephen considers the GAA to be the focal point for himself and other young Irish emigrants in London, suggesting that "a lot of young people ... certainly wouldn't have survived without being involved with a GAA club" (Interview, January 2012). Attending GAA events as player or spectator facilitates communication between large numbers of Irish people in London, and can offset the sense of dislocation and isolation which may occur after arriving in a new environment.

The majority of interview and survey participants referred to the familiarity of the GAA and the desire to interact with other Irish people as their main reasons for playing Gaelic games in London. According to Brendan "if you're involved at home, you go and get involved over here ... it's often the first thing [emigrants] ask can I play a bit of football" (Interview, July 2011). This suggests aspirations to celebrate and express a sense of Irish identity are not necessarily the primary objective of engaging with Gaelic games in London. Instead, motivation for playing Gaelic football, Hurling or Camogie may be explained as simply providing an opportunity for physical sporting competition. Teams in the Senior grade are generally the most competitive and feature skilled Gaelic footballers, Hurlers and Camogie players. However, Gaelic games in London are not restricted to experienced players. Teams of varying abilities in Gaelic football, Hurling and Camogie are available, thereby encouraging people to play according to their abilities. This was highlighted by Marie, a second-generation Irish Gaelic footballer who referred to opportunities available for women to play:

> We have a Junior and a Senior [team] and for those that are capable that's useful as they can get their competitive games straight away, but those who haven't played for a while or wouldn't be as confident, they can come and start learning the skills again.
>
> (Interview, January 2012)

Whilst there was an emphasis upon the role of the GAA and Gaelic games in terms of being a social network and sporting activity, the relationship between Gaelic games and Irish identity did emerge in many of the survey and interview responses, including one which suggested the "GAA in London is more connected to identity than it is in the West of Ireland" (Survey 56). When explicitly asked to what extent involvement with the London GAA scene is related to an expression of Irish identity, the relationship between the GAA and 'Irishness' was emphasised by a number of individuals. For example, Sean said:

> It gives you the opportunity to express your 'Irishness', and you don't lose touch with home. Because if you're meeting thirty Irish lads every Tuesday and Thursday night, go training and then play matches, inevitably you'll spend a lot of your time with Irish people.
>
> (Interview, July 2011)

The displacement from 'home' can heighten an awareness of individual and national identities, an emotion which was apparent in a number of the responses given by interview participants. It was also suggested that their sense of 'Irishness' increased outside of Ireland, as summarised by Brendan: "A very good friend of mine ... when he went away he said you never realise you're Irish until you're actually away" (Interview, Brendan July 2011). The significance of the relationship between the GAA, 'Irishness' and 'home' was a common theme in the interview and survey responses, illustrating the extent to which Gaelic games and the construction and maintenance of an Irish identity within the Irish diaspora are rooted in the notion of 'home'.

The attachment to place is significant in the Irish diaspora as local, county and national identifications are employed as a means to negotiate and construct a sense of self beyond Irish territorial borders. Cronin *et al.* (2009: 293) illustrate how club and county jerseys have become a prominent symbol for Irish people as an expression of local and national identities. GAA jerseys have become particularly relevant in the Irish diaspora as emigrants and second- and third-generation Irish individuals use them to identify with the 'homeland' and more localised places of origin. During this research process I encountered a number of London-born second-generation Irish and indeed emigrants who do not actively participate in the GAA as players, but attend club and county matches in London whilst wearing GAA jerseys. The wearing of GAA jerseys by non-players is most visible during high profile inter-county Gaelic football matches at the Emerald GAA grounds located in Ruislip, West London, which is the headquarters of the GAA in London and a focal point for the Irish community in the city. Jerseys worn by the supporters of the visiting county team often outnumber those worn by London supporters, illustrating the strength of the attachment people hold with their home county. This was particularly evident during the first round of the Connacht Gaelic football Championship in 2011 between London and Mayo where the majority of spectators were wearing Mayo jerseys or another item of clothing associated with Mayo GAA. The visibility of GAA jerseys in the city are representative of a proud Irish community in London.

Gaelic games played at the Emerald GAA grounds in Ruislip have become a community event for many Irish individuals in London, enabling people to "meet first-, second-, third- and fourth-generation Irish people who may be spread out over the city but come together for games" (Survey 56). The scene during high profile inter-county matches are "reminiscent of match days in Ireland" (Interview, Mary July 2011), with the replication of rituals played out at matches there; most notably the singing of the Irish national anthem, *Amhrán na bhFiann*, prior to the match and the flying of the national flag. These are emblems of the Irish nation, and as such their use by the GAA reinforces the nationalist ethos of the Irish sporting organisation. The significance of these symbols within the GAA is illustrated in the Official Guide, in which Section 1.8 states that the Irish flag should be flown at GAA matches, and where "the National anthem precedes a game, teams shall stand to attention facing the Flag, in a respectful manner" (Gaelic Athletic Association *Official guide, Part 1*, 2012: 6). Hunter (2003) raises the question as to whether the use of visible symbols such as national anthems and flags strengthens national identity. However, as indicated by Mary, these symbols are considered by many to be a prominent expression of 'Irishness'; "they're part of our heritage" contributing towards a coherent sense of Irish identity in London (Interview, 2011). Thus, the GAA grounds at Ruislip must be viewed as more than literally spaces to play sport.

It has become a place where Irish people can come together to imagine themselves as a community in London as well as part of the Irish diaspora with a strong connection with the Irish nation.

## 'Maybe it's because I'm an Irish Londoner':[5] the Gaelic Athletic Association and second-generation Irish

Many within Ireland and the Irish diaspora consider the GAA abroad to be an Irish emigrant network acting as a bridgehead between their place of origin and destination. This perception is reinforced through the establishment and maintenance of GAA structures in locations which have experienced successive waves of Irish emigration. The displacement of the dispersed is often intended as a temporary measure with the intention of many being to return to the homeland; yet the process of migration often results in the formation of long-term or permanently settled diaspora communities which encompass emigrants and their children, who were born in the host society. Sorohan (2012) provides a detailed analysis of the development of a distinctive Irish community in London during the 1970s, focusing upon the experiences of London-born second- and third-generation Irish. He argues that this section of the Irish diaspora population provided the foundations for a coherent and assertive settled Irish community in London, which embraced a "dual sense of 'home'" and a sense of belonging to both Ireland and London (Sorohan 2012: 51). The GAA in London incorporates this dual belonging to Ireland and London, essentially becoming inclusive of the entire diaspora community in London, rather than Irish emigrants exclusively. This suggests the sense of 'Irishness' articulated through the GAA in London is not bound within the Irish nation state but is situated within the diaspora.

The dependence of the GAA abroad upon Irish emigration was officially recognised by the London County Board and British Provincial Council during the 1960s, and as a result, emphasis was placed upon developing clubs to incorporate and attract youth players (Provincial Council of Britain *Minute Book* 1964–1971: 26). Many of the clubs which continue to exist in London in 2013 are situated in areas to the north and west of London where large numbers of Irish emigrants settled and raised their young families in the second half of the twentieth century. These clubs rely heavily on the participation and support of these family members. Links between these clubs and local schools have developed in recent years, with coaches sponsored by the GAA introducing Gaelic games into a number of schools (Cronin *et al.* 2009: 374). Lloyd Colfer, Community Development Officer for the London GAA County Board, considers this to be an effective way to broaden the appeal of Gaelic games and introduce second- and third-generation Irish children to Gaelic games: "There are currently 35 schools involved and it has been very successful, and there are more schools looking to get involved" (Interview Lloyd Colfer, August 2013). The significance of second- and third-generation Irish children to the GAA in the city is summarised most effectively by Larry O'Leary, Chairman of Fr. Murphy's Ladies Gaelic football and Camogie club, and former Chairman of the London County Board:

You'll always get ups and downs in emigration and at the moment there's a lot coming over, but I think it's still good to have your second-generation people or as many of them as possible. They'll be there for a long time, whereas the others you have a roving population and you have a great team for two or three years and then they're all gone. With these [second-generation Irish] they'll be there for a long time and grow up in the club.

(Interview, January 2012)

There are a considerable number of second- and subsequent-generation Irish people living in London,[6] many of whom are, or have been involved with, Irish cultural activities such as Gaelic games, Irish music and dance (Sorohan 2012: 52). Many of the Irish parents of London-born children consider these Irish cultural forms to be an important means through which their children could potentially form a sense of Irish identity: "My daughters play Irish music, it's another form of your Irishness, it's very important. And you have all the sports Camogie and Hurling, and Gaelic football. It's all part of the Irish identity over here" (Interview Stephen, January 2012).

Playing Gaelic football, Hurling or Camogie, and representing the club on the playing field was considered by several second-generation Irish participants as an explicit way to express an Irish identity, demonstrating that "people from London can be Irish too" (Interview, Mary, July 2011). Other London-born second-generation Irish individuals saw Gaelic games primarily as a way to engage with, and develop a better understanding of Irish culture and their heritage. These sentiments were encapsulated within the survey responses given by a London-born second-generation Irishman:

Playing GAA in London proves to be one of the most important ways I am able to express my Irish identity in London. This involves even minor things such as socialising with Irish people and talking about Irish history or happenings. All this would not exist if I didn't play Gaelic in London.

(Survey 47)

Prevailing discourses regarding 'Irishness' within Irish and British societies highlight what are perceived to be differences between the Irish identity held by Irish emigrants and the London-born second- and third-generation Irish. This raises the question of what constitutes an authentic Irish identity, which in turn contributes towards tension within London's Irish population. The notion that emigrants' Irish identity and ability to play Gaelic games is more authentic as a result of being born and having lived in Ireland has influenced attitudes towards the second- and third-generation Irish in London. Various accounts, from second-generation Irish male players in particular, highlight the opposition from some emigrants on account of having been raised in London with an English accent:

As a London-born player it is believed that we have to work that bit harder to prove that we can play the game, it is as if you are judged initially on your accent. Often players coming over from Ireland don't understand how these 'English' lads can play their national game.

(Interview Ryan, May 2012)

Their English accent marks the London-born players out as different and has prevented some Irish-born individuals from accepting their sense of 'Irishness'.[7] Ryan, a second-generation Irishman indicated that this has manifested itself in verbal abuse towards London-born players from their opponents during GAA sporting events. This is reminiscent of the 'Plastic Paddy' term prevalent in London during the 1980s, which was used in a derogatory way to distinguish between the latest cohort of emigrants who considered themselves authentically Irish and the wider settled Irish community in London, which incorporated the London born second- and third-generation Irish.

## Negotiating Irish identities in London

The GAA and the sporting events it promotes and organises have become an important part of the Irish diaspora experience in London. Thus, it provides an invaluable tool for exploring the notions of identity and homeland. The composition of the sporting organisation in London reflects the heterogeneous nature of London's Irish population encompassing different cohorts of Irish emigrants and their descendants, the London-born second- and third-generation Irish, all of whom hold subjective interpretations of what constitutes an Irish identity. Prevailing discourses surrounding Irish identities have generally prescribed a fixed impression of what delineates an authentic Irish identity. Akenson (1997) suggests that this conceptualisation is rooted in the place of origin and the tangible connection an individual has with Ireland through being born or having lived there. The multifaceted nature of the Irish population in London has highlighted the complexities of Irish identity, particularly beyond Irish territorial confines, thereby contributing towards the growing debate surrounding the hybridity of identities in the diaspora (Anthias 1998, 2001). The sense of Irish identity expressed by the second-generation participants in this research does not correspond with the essentialist criteria described by Akenson (1997), and has raised questions regarding the validity of their 'Irishness'. In recognition of these differences, Ryan stated that the "English-born player can never fully enter into this shared sense of an exile identity" (Interview, May 2012). The GAA in London has made a concerted effort to develop the appeal of Gaelic games beyond the Irish émigré, as illustrated through the development of links between the GAA, clubs and local schools in London and the increased focus upon retaining second-generation Irish youth players to Senior level (Interview Lloyd Colfer, August 2013).

The concept of 'diaspora space' emphasises the reality of hybridised identities which are not fixed to the place of origin, challenging dominant discourses about authenticity and belonging. It becomes the "point at which the boundaries of inclusion and exclusion, of belonging and otherness, of 'us' and 'them' are contested" (Brah 1996: 209). Within the 'diaspora space' that is London, the notion of authenticity and a fixed identity are contested, facilitating the negotiation of hybrid and fluid identities which are infused with characteristics of the wider society in London. The interplay between diaspora groups such as the Irish diaspora and the host society provides for the reality of different or hybrid Irish identities which take into account the lived experience of 'Irishness' in London and are not fixed to the place of origin. This has contributed towards the emergence of a positive hybridised identity which contrasts with the essentialist and exclusivist interpretation of an Irish identity firmly rooted in Ireland. Hybrid identities, often claimed by the children of Irish emigrants, are entities which engage with the differences between the migrant and diaspora experiences. Whilst the 'London Irish' identity expresses a connection with the Irish nation, it is situated within the locational specificity of London. Therefore, the exiled identity and the 'London Irish' identity can both be considered different forms of a diasporic 'Irishness' which are not any less authentic than the 'Irishness' encapsulated by those still living at 'home'.

The formation of identity in the diaspora is subjective, influenced by the 'roots' of the diaspora community and the 'routes' by which it has been constructed and maintained (Clifford 1994). Engagement with the GAA through active participation as a player and member, or as a spectator and supporter provides different people who have different experiences of 'living Irish' in London with a means to embrace and celebrate an Irish identity which reflects the different modalities of their sense of self. Attending GAA events has enabled numerous second-generation Irish participants to develop a sense of belonging to the Irish community in London and a connection with their parent's roots in Ireland. For some, this has manifested in the emphasis placed upon London GAA county jerseys as a symbol of their 'London Irishness'. Martin, a second-generation Irish man recalls making a conscious decision to wear his London GAA county jersey when visiting family in Ireland, "to show them I'm Irish and I'm from London" (Interview, January 2013). The celebration of a 'London Irish' identity through London GAA county jerseys was very evident during the summer of 2013. The relative success of the London Gaelic footballers in the Connacht Championship galvanised a sense of pride in the jersey and the GAA in London and this was expressed through the increased visibility of London GAA jerseys during match day events, both at Ruislip and at MacHale Park in Castlebar for the Connacht Championship against Mayo. This was emphasised by Ronan, who is second-generation Irish and a member of the London Irish band Biblecode Sundays:

> The on-field success is extremely important to the London Irish people. The GAA represents something that is uniquely Irish here in London, and for a London team to be doing so well, it brings an immense sense of pride.
>
> (Interview, July 2013)

Many of those who have left Ireland and settled in London have established roots in the city through professional connections and personal circumstances such as starting a family, thereby interrupting the desire to physically return 'home', to Ireland. For many, London has become a home away from home, and the GAA, Niall argues, has played a significant part in generating feelings of attachment and belonging to London. He suggests that he "wouldn't have stayed here without the GAA, not as long as I have anyway" (Interview, March 2012). For Niall, who left Ireland over a decade ago and has two young London-born daughters, the social and sporting events organised through the GAA, both at local club and county level, have become a prominent part of his experience of living in London. Many of those who participated in this research indicated that their enjoyment of GAA events in London stems from their identification with the Irish subculture of the organisation, and their shared understanding of the symbols and roles attached to the GAA and Gaelic games. Attendance at sporting and social events organised by the GAA, through active participation as a player or as a spectator and supporter, provides different people with different experiences of 'living Irish' (Scully 2010) in London. The GAA in the city has generated an affiliation to London amongst Irish people, both Irish- and London-born, through London County teams and local clubs contributing towards the formation of a diaspora consciousness.

## Conclusions

The medium of sport provides an invaluable insight into the structure and dynamics of society, revealing the most salient features within that society (Sugden and Bairner 1993: 203). Central to this chapter has been the role of Gaelic games, quintessentially Irish cultural and sporting pastimes for members of the Irish diaspora in London, and the different modalities of Irish identity articulated through this medium. Sporting events organised by the GAA in London including club and inter-county matches have become an important part of the experience of 'living Irish' (Scully 2010) for many in London. Whilst high-profile inter-county Gaelic football matches attract large numbers of spectators to the GAA grounds in Ruislip, attendances at many club games and indeed inter-county Hurling and Ladies Gaelic football matches remain relatively low in comparison. This illustrates the prominence of Gaelic football in London. It also indicates that whilst the GAA is considered culturally important to the Irish diaspora, the core group of people for whom it holds particular significance are active players and the families who have been long associated with particular clubs over the generations, rather than every Irish person living in London. For many emigrants the GAA has become a bridgehead connecting their place of origin with their destination, providing a sense of continuation to their life prior to emigrating. It has also become a cultural symbol for many London-born second- and third-generation Irish, with GAA sporting events providing a means to connect with their heritage and the homeland of their parents, whilst also engaging with the locational specificity of their identity. As the dynamics of London's Irish population have changed, the role of the GAA and the interpretations of 'Irishness' articulated through the sporting medium of Gaelic games have also evolved.

# Notes

1 Space does not allow for discussion of the discourse surrounding the relationship between sport and the Irish diaspora; for further reference, see Bradley (1996, 2006, 2007), Darby (2009, 2010) and Darby and Hassan (2008).
2 Robert Mulhern (2011) and Pat Griffin (2011) have provided invaluable insights into the social impact of the Gaelic games in London, and the historical development of the GAA in London respectively.
3 A GAA outfit fully incorporated into the GAA in Ireland was established in London in 1896 and continues to operate in the present day. For further reference, see Moore (2010).
4 There are a number of other social and welfare support mechanisms for Irish emigrants in London, including the public house and Catholic Church. See Sorohan (2012) for a detailed analysis of these informal networks in twentieth-century London.
5 'Maybe it's because I'm an Irish Londoner' is the title of a song from London Irish band Biblecode Sundays.
6 It is difficult to quantify the second-generation Irish population in Britain, which may be due in part to the ambiguities surrounding ethnicity in the Census for England and Wales.
7 See Marcus Free's (2007) study of second-generation Irish supporters of the Republic of Ireland team which considers the ways in which sporting events are used to construct a national identity.

# References

Akenson, D.H. (1997) *The Irish diaspora: A primer.* Toronto: P.D. Meany.

Anderson, B. (1991) *Imagined communities: Reflections on the origins and spread of nationalism.* London: Verso.

Anthias, F. (1998) Evaluating 'diaspora': Beyond ethnicity? *Sociology*, 32(3): 557–580.

Anthias, F. (2001) New hybridities, old concepts: the limits of 'culture'. *Ethnic and Racial Studies*, 24(4): 619–641.

Bradley, J. (1996) Abstruse and obscure? Irish immigrant identity in modern Scotland. *Social Identities*, 2: 293–309.

Bradley, J. (2006) Sport and the contestation of ethnic identity: Football and Irishness in Scotland. *Journal of Migration Studies*, 32: 1189–1203.

Bradley, J. (2007) *The Gaelic Athletic Association and Irishness in Scotland.* Argyll: Argyll Publishing Group.

Brah, A. (1996) *Cartographies of diaspora: Contesting identities.* London: Routledge.

Brubaker, R. (2005) The 'diaspora' diaspora. *Ethnic and Racial Studies*, 28: 1–9.

Central Council of the Association (2009) *Gaelic Athletic Association: The official guide part 1.* Dublin: Gaelic Athletic Association.

Clifford, J. (1994) Diasporas. *Cultural Anthropology*, 9: 302–338.

Coogan, T.P. (2000) *Wherever green is worn: The story of the Irish diaspora.* London: Hutchinson.

Cronin, M. (1999) *Sport and nationalism in Ireland: Gaelic games, soccer and Irish identity since 1884.* Dublin: Four Courts Press.

Cronin, M., Duncan, M. and Rouse, P. (2009) *The GAA: A people's history.* Cork: Collins Press.

Darby, P. (2009) *Gaelic games, nationalism and the Irish diaspora in the United States.* Dublin: Dublin University Press.

Darby, P. (2010) Playing for Ireland in foreign fields: The Gaelic Athletic Association and Irish nationalism in America. *Irish Studies Review*, 18: 69–89.

Darby, P. and Hassan, D. (2008) *Emigrant players: Sport and the Irish Diaspora.* Abingdon: Routledge.

Free, M. (2007) Tales from the fifth green field: The psychodynamics of migration, masculinity and national identity among Republic of Ireland soccer supporters in England. *Sport and Society*, 10: 476–494.

Gaelic Athletic Association (2012) *Official guide part 1, containing the constitution and rules of the G.A.A., revised and corrected up to date, and published by authority of the Central Council.* [Online] Available from www.gaa.ie/content/documents/publications/official_guides/Official_Guide_2012_Part1.pdf [accessed 29 April 2013].

Gordon, E.T. and Anderson, M. (1999) The African diaspora: Toward an ethnography of diasporic identification. *The Journal of American Folklore*, 112: 282–296.

Griffin, P. (2011) *Gaelic hearts: The history of the Gaelic Athletic Association in London: 1896–1996.* London: London County Board Gaelic Athletic Association.

Hunter, J. (2003) Flying the flag: Identities, the nation and sport. *Identities*, 10: 409–425.

Humphries, T. (1996) *Green fields: Gaelic sport in Ireland.* London: Weidenfeld and Nicolson.

London GAA (2010) *Club secretaries.* [Online] Available from www.londongaa.org/contentPage/257461/club_secretaries_london [accessed 11 April 2012].

Moore, S. (2010) *Gaelic games and the Irish diaspora in London.* Unpublished PhD thesis, University of Ulster.

Moore, S. and Darby, P. (2011) Gaelic games, Irish nationalist politics and the Irish diaspora in London, 1895–1915. *Sport in History*, 31: 257–282.

Mulhern, R. (2011) *A very different county.* Great Britain: MPG Books Group.

Provincial Council of Britain (1964–1971) *Minutes Book 1964–1971.* GAA Library and Archive. Croke Park, Dublin.

Safran, W. (1991) Diasporas in modern societies: Myths of homeland and return. *Diaspora*, 1: 83–99.

Scully, M. (2010) *Discourses of authenticity and national identity among the Irish diaspora in England.* Unpublished PhD thesis, Open University.

Sorohan, S. (2012) *Irish London during the Troubles.* Dublin: Irish Academic Press.

Sugden, J. and Bairner, A. (1993) National identity and community relations and the sporting life in Northern Ireland. In Allison, L. (ed.) *The changing politics of sport.* Manchester: Manchester University Press, 90–117.

# 9 Kabbadi tournaments

## Patriarchal spaces and women's rejection of the masculine field

*Harpreet Bains*

## Introduction

Current literature on sport and South Asians in the UK has focused primarily on football (Bains and Patel, 1996; Johal, 2001; Burdsey, 2007; Ratna, 2010) and cricket (Burdsey, 2010; Fletcher, 2012; Fletcher and Spracklen, 2013). This chapter attempts to explore the neglected field of kabbadi and bring together discussion of British South Asians, patriarchy and masculinities. There is a need to critically explore sport as a patriarchal structure and its role in reinforcing patriarchal relations (Hall, 1996; Scraton and Flintoff, 2002) within the South Asian community in the UK. In this chapter, sport, as a reinforcement of patriarchal relations within the South Asian context, is specifically conceptualised and understood by exploring localised kabbadi tournaments in the UK. Further, the chapter explores how patriarchal structures and patriarchal relations within the sphere of kabbadi are contested and agreed.[1]

Kabbadi can be defined as a form of team wrestling, which incorporates tagging and running away from your opponent. It originates from the Punjab, India. The form of kabbadi played in the Punjab is called Amar, and both men and women play it locally and nationally. In India the game is often played on grass or a field and it involves two teams of six players each. The two teams dominate opposite halves of the field; "one player [raider] moves into the enemy territory alone, and has to touch an opposing player and return to his side" (McDonald, 1999: 352). The raider has to hold his/her breath and chant "kabbadi kabbadi kabbadi...". This has to be heard by the umpire, and cannot be broken. The defending or opposing team wait with interlocked arms/hands to tackle their opponent. Points are given if the 'raider' tags one of the opponents and returns to his/her half; if the opposing team stop the 'raider' from returning to his/her starting point they also get a point.

Kabbadi is a prominent sport in a number of East and South Asian countries. The significance of the sport across Asia is illustrated by it featuring in the Asian Games. The Punjab also hosted the Kabbadi World Cup in 2012. Basu (2004: 470) states that "in the sports history of contemporary India, kabbadi plays an important role". Indian immigrant communities have transmitted their enjoyment and passion for kabbadi to the UK. Johal (2002: 138), for example, states that "while the majority of Punjabi-Sikhs did not use leisure time as actively as some of the more sports-minded of their peers, there was an undeniable momentum in this diasporic group's desire for physical and sporting activity". Johal (2002) notes that the very first Sikh Games in the UK took place in 1965 and were supported by Shelby Gurdwara (Sikh place of worship). The gurdwara is not only a place for individual worship and religious congregation, it is an organisation that serves communities and importantly, it is "a centre for internal social activities" (Desai, 1963: 94). The gurdwara has played a role in supporting local kabbadi clubs financially and has assisted in the emergence of localised tournaments. Currently, every summer, competitive kabbadi tournaments take place in 14 different cities and towns all over England. There are 18 competitive clubs that are registered under the England Kabbadi Federation UK website.

Whilst both men and women play kabbadi nationally, the local tournaments in England are exclusively male and often take place in local parks. Spectators of these events are not only first-generation Punjabi males, but also second-generation and third-generation British born Punjabi men. Women are not involved in the game as either participants or spectators at local level: the localised kabbadi arena is specifically for men. In fact, it is a culturally forbidden space for women. This chapter argues that the practice of localised kabbadi is a way in which British Punjabi communities, both male and female, construct and maintain gender relations.

Many researchers and academics prefer to explore the differences between men and women, but have failed to explore the relations between them (Hargreaves, 1990; Pfister, 2010). However, Dashper's (2012) research into sex integration in equestrianism and Thorpe's (2005) exploration of gender and snowboarding do investigate the relations between men and women. Importantly, however, the focus for both Dashper (2012) and Thorpe (2005) is the analysis of a middle-class or affluent sport as well as the relations between white men and women. This chapter, on the other hand, attempts to add to the knowledge of sport and gender relations among ethnic minority groups. Further, "modern sport has always been a crucial cultural domain for constructing and reproducing dominant, heterosexual masculine identities. Sports institutions at elite and grass roots levels still typically harbour formal and informal restrictions on women's full participation" (Giulianotti, 2005: 80). This chapter will not attempt to explore the formal institutions of kabbadi, which construct and reproduce dominant masculine identities. It will, however, seek to understand the role of individuals, the family and British Punjabi community in establishing a male-dominated kabbadi field.

## A man's sport and a woman's *izzat* (honour)

Smart (1995) suggests 'patriarchal relations' imply a more fluid system than the concept of 'patriarchy'. Smart (1995: 130) summarises 'patriarchal relations' as "containing numerous contradictions and employing varying mechanisms and strategies in the exercise of power". The concept of patriarchal relations is used in this chapter because it permits women's negotiation of patriarchal spaces and allows for the concept of *izzat* (honour) to be applied.

Within the context of South Asian culture, patriarchy manifests itself mainly through the notion of *izzat*. *Izzat* constrains the behaviour and movement of South Asian women and is patriarchal in its application and character. *Izzat*, Ballard (1982: 185) claims, is "in its narrower sense ... a matter of male pride". *Izzat* affects the family as a group, and not just individuals. This is a marked difference to Western families, where responsibility and shame lies largely on the individual. Further, *izzat* "is 'upheld' or 'ruined' in social transactions, markedly those involving unmarried daughters" (Hall, 1995: 252). Consequently, a family's honour and reputation is dependent on its ability to control the behaviour of its women, which in turn maintains and ensures the family's status in the community (Rozario, 2005). Many women are constrained by the knowledge that they must not jeopardise the status and *izzat* of their family.

Nevertheless, in the case of South Asian families in the UK, the stereotype of South Asian women as oppressed creatures within the family unit who need rescuing from their degradation is misleading (Bhachu, 1991). Thus, it is important to note that for many ethnic minority women the family marks a sense of belonging and solidarity and remains an arena away from racism and discrimination experienced at the hands of the white community (hooks, 1984; Collins, 1991; Jackson, 2007; Bains, 2005). To add to the discussion, sport tournaments can be sites of oppression for women spectators. The experiences of oppression can also differ among white, black and South Asian women. However, for Indian women, the 'family' remains an important unit for social organisation; not only for first-generation women but also second-generation women. For example, Brah's (1979) study of South Asian and white fifteen-year-old girls and boys and their parents, found that women often stressed the importance of the 'family' but, by doing this, they did not necessarily accept as legitimate the hierarchal organisation of the household, or the exercise of male power. Similarly, in relation to kabbadi tournaments and women's spectatorship, the importance of the family, the implementation of male power and resistance of non-participation in a masculine field is explored in this chapter.

In relation to sport, Dworkin and Messner (2001) suggest that discourse surrounding women and sport is ethnocentric. Additionally, there is limited literature and research in sport from a black feminist perspective. British South Asian females remain largely absent in the research on sport (see as exceptions Verma and Darby, 1994; Walseth, 2006; Ratna, 2010). The limited literature suggests that 'looking after children' (Williams *et al.* 1996: 3) is the main barrier to exercise for South Asian women, and explains the lower use of exercise facilities among women in terms of their lack of knowledge and poor access to information (Carrington and McDonald, 2008). Johnson's (2000) research into barriers to physical activity among South Asian communities revealed that modesty was an important factor related to participation. More specifically, Johnson (2000: 59) states "modesty, whether a dislike of being in a mixed sex setting, or simply being in a place where other people bare their bodies, was a very clear disincentive among all Asian groups, irrespective of gender". Other factors that Johnson identified as possible barriers to entry for South Asian women are family and partner's disapproval, fear of going out alone and community pressures. Further, South Asian women are believed to be constrained from participating in sport because of religious practices and cultural norms (see Walseth, 2006). Additionally, Ratna (2010: 117) explores how British-Asian women "improvise and perform identities ... carve out spaces of belonging" in sport. The limited research on British Asian women focuses specifically on women's participation and access to sport. There are no comprehensive studies on spectatorship and British South Asian women and there is no previous research on kabaddi and women.

Thus, Birrell (1990: 193) states "we need to increase the awareness of issues in the lives of women of colour as they themselves articulate these issues". Although Birrell makes a claim of increasing awareness of women of 'colour', in sport there is little evidence, 23 years later, that this has happened, particularly in relation to British Indian women. Academics continue to portray ethnic minority women in sport as lacking a voice and knowledge, and explaining their minimal involvement in sport due to simplistic understandings of gender oppression, religious constraints and racism. This chapter goes some way towards beginning to redress this omission.

## Methodology

The study of feminism and feminist research produces knowledge from a feminist standpoint, which is sensitised to women's experiences and encounters of patriarchy (Olesen, 2000). Thus, from/through my standpoints as a woman researcher, who is British and a Punjabi, someone who engages with sport as well as being excluded from sport, I am sensitised to the experiences of the women I research (Bhopal, 2001).

Twenty unstructured interviews with British Punjabi women took place in the summer of 2011 in the south-east of England. Ten interviews were conducted with first-generation women and ten interviews were conducted with second-generation women. The interviews were conducted separately with a mother and a daughter living within the same household. First-generation women were born in India, settled in the UK and ran businesses with their husbands, or were retired. Second-generation women were all in professional occupations with the exception of one who was a student. Throughout this study pseudonyms have been used in place of the respondents' names. The interviews aimed to explore women's experiences and perceptions of kabbadi tournaments as well as their motivations for participation and non-participation alike. They were conducted adhering to what can be called the 'biographical method' or 'life history' method (Schwandt, 1997, cited in Tierney, 2000). Shorter life stories (see Plummer, 2001) were most suitable for this study as they gathered in-depth information on an individual's life which was specific to kabbadi.

## The masculine field of kabbadi

First- and second-generation British Punjabi women discussed their perceptions of kabbadi tournaments taking place in England and highlighted why they do not engage in the events. They discussed the barriers to entry to the kabbadi field and stated their preferences for how they spend their time. Both first- and second-generation women acknowledged that the kabbadi tournament is an exclusive space for men. For the respondents, the exclusive space for men is bound with activities such as consuming alcohol and fighting. Women suggested that, for men, the kabbadi tournament is a 'social event' or 'party' for male family members and friends to meet and socialise. The following respondents describe kabbadi tournaments. For example, Kalwinder believed that:

> All the men from the town get together in a park in the name of watching kabbadi, but what they actually do is drink. It is another excuse for them to drink with their friends. They take food and alcohol with them and share it with their friends. It is a party.... Everyone knows that women should not go, you know, they go to the tournament and we do our own thing.
>
> (Kalwinder, 62, business owner)

Similarly, Sarbjit suggested that the kabbadi tournament is an arena where socialising takes place between men. The event is a place where alcohol is consumed and, as a consequence, aggressive behaviour is played out:

> They have been doing this for a long time. My husband, my brothers, all the men. They like to go to the kabbadi and meet their friends and drink [laughs]. The women have fun on their side; we meet our friends and eat [laughs]. It is a social thing.... They [men] drink too much and eat too much and watch the kabbadi. With the drink there is fighting also ... that is what alcohol does. I do not like that. I worry about my husband when he goes.
>
> (Sarbjit, 59, shop owner)

As well as emphasising the consumption of alcohol and its relationship to drunken men at the event, Balbir additionally perceives the tournament as a 'party', and further illustrates women's contribution to the event:

> It is not a sport or game, it's a party with lots of drunk men. The ladies help them make food, they take the food and drink and enjoy with their relatives and friends. It is an enjoying activity.... [But] I do not like it. Men are drunk and say rude things.... The kabbadi players are big and scary, they are half naked. It is actually quite boring. It is not a place for me.
>
> (Balbir, 56, factory owner)

Continuing Balbir's reasoning, Palo stressed that she was not interested in kabbadi, and did not want to be involved:

Fighting, drinking, eating meat, fat naked men, it's stupid and boring. Let them have fun in the cold.

(Palo, 56, shop owner)

The above respondents associate the field of kabbadi with alcohol consumption, food and fighting. Consumption of alcohol and its relationship to the spectator experience is illustrated by Collins and Vamplew (2002: 69):

it is no exaggeration to suggest that, no matter what the sport or its level of popularity, the consumption of alcohol is almost an intrinsic part of the spectator experience. Indeed, it would be difficult to argue with the contention that for many spectators, the activity on the field of play is often secondary to the opportunity to drink.

Collins and Vamplew (2002) support the respondents' testimonies that men attend the kabbadi tournament to drink. Further, Bradley (2007: 154) exemplifies the relationship between drinking and sport among men, arguing that "men's leisure tends to revolve round sport, with drinking … as a popular sub-theme".

Within this study, Surinder further articulates the relationship between spectatorship, drinking and violence, and how each intersects to exclude women:

You see, it is part of our culture. I remember my dad and brothers being interested in the kabbadi players' muscles, their bodies and their tactics. But now in England it is something different. Today it is about aggression, fighting and drinking. The people that go to watch have more of an interest in the social aspect. It is not taken seriously. Maybe some people take it seriously, it is more about going for fun and meeting your friends and family. […] you know it is a safe environment for the men, away from any racism and black this and white this…. Not (safe) for the women, the men are there [laughs].

(Surinder, 68, retired teacher)

Many respondents stated that the kabbadi tournament is an arena where male family members and friends meet and socialise. Surinder suggests that kabbadi is 'part of our culture' and that it is 'a safe environment for men' away from racism. Carrington and McDonald (2001) and Fletcher (2011) support the claim that in a hostile society, ethnic minorities use sport as a tool for establishing and maintaining cultural identity (see also Burdsey, 2007). Additionally, meeting family and friends at the tournament coincides with it being a place for men where they share a sense of belonging and emotional attachment (Bradley, 2007). It is also a site of bonding for men, a place where they reassert their masculinities and ethnic identities. Interestingly, unlike men who use the kabbadi events as 'bonding sites', the women in the study have stated that kabbadi tournaments are not sites for women to share a sense of belonging or to reassert their social identities. The respondents reveal that they have a preference to engage in other social and leisure activities and, thus, reject the masculine fields of kabbadi tournaments.

## Women rejecting the masculine field of kabbadi

Research for this chapter reveals that complex traditional cultural norms impact women's participation in the field of kabbadi. Thus, the following respondents suggest that the reason why women do not attend kabbadi tournaments is because they disapprove of, or are uncomfortable around the men's behaviour. Rajinder for example, said:

> [...] it is not for women. Kabbadi tournaments are for men. I would not let my daughter go. They all get together in a park, drink and use bad language. It is not safe for women ... it's not a classy place.
>
> (Rajinder, 48, care worker)

Similarly, Kulvinder's narrative highlights patriarchal relations and *izzat* at play:

> Why do I want to see a bunch of naked men push and shove each other to cross the line? It's crap. It's boring. It's in a shit park ... anyway, it's a no go area for women. It's not that my dad or husband would ever say "you are not going", they are amazing and treat me as an equal, we are all the same. We all just know it's a no-go area.
>
> (Kulvinder, 35, banker)

Throughout this research many respondents made reference to kabbadi tournaments taking place in a 'park'. Bradley (2007) highlights that an event taking place in a public space is a limitation and restriction for some women. Although she is not speaking specifically about ethnic minorities, Bradley (2007: 153) suggests that "men's leisure has characteristically involved the outdoors" and for women certain spaces are "forbidden". Bradley's argument supports the issues highlighted by the respondents that the field(s) of kabbadi are restricted or forbidden arenas for women. The respondent's claim that "we all just know it's a no-go area" not only supports Bradley's argument of 'forbidden' spaces, but also adds to the discussion of socially negotiated patriarchal spaces. There are no religious practices or written guidelines which explicitly assert women should be excluded from the kabbadi tournament. However, there are socially situated conditions or barriers that forbid women entry into the space of kabbadi. The kabbadi field is normalised as a masculine arena and accepted as 'a no-go area' for many of the women interviewed. Further, Kulvinder's reference to 'naked men' being present within the field supports Johnson's (2000) claim that 'bare bodies' may be a disincentive for South Asian groups to participate in sport or leisure activities. More specifically, the notion of *izzat* plays an important role in the understanding of women being subjected to 'naked men' and it being a disincentive for women's participation into the field of kabbadi. Family honour and controlling female sexuality is implicit here and it is implemented by sanctions, restrictions, discipline and judgement(s) from men and elderly women. The judgements are clearly illustrated by Simi, who states "it would be frowned upon" if a woman was seen at the kabbadi tournament. She continues:

> It is a place for men, not women. It would be frowned upon if a woman went to the kabbadi tournament … but she is allowed to go. It is not as if women cannot attend … I would not say it is sexist or patriarchal because women do not want to go.
>
> (Simi, 35, lawyer)

"It would be frowned upon" is an illustration of *izzat* at play and "it is a place for men, not women" is an explicit negotiated understanding of patriarchal relations. Thus, the narratives of separatism and that kabbadi is 'a no-go area for women' implies codified patriarchal relations taking place. Clearly, there is an unwritten rule between men and women that the field of kabbadi is exclusively male. Women are conscious of the exclusion and follow the unwritten patriarchal relation. The women's narratives refer

> to the ways in which individuals live out their daily lives through practices that are synchronized with the actions of others around them, functioning to produce a social collective that is not ordered by rules per se but influenced by objective structures.
>
> (Coles, 2009: 34)

Relationships between women and men as well as the environments in which they interact form unwritten patriarchal relations, support notions of *izzat* and construct fields of participation and non-participation. The situated negotiations embedded within the frameworks of *izzat* and honour allow individuals to navigate through everyday realities with flexibility. Neelam, for instance, notes an acute awareness of the male gaze:

> It's [watching kabbadi] not for me or my daughter. It's a real masculine environment, men are drunk and aggressive. I don't put myself in these environments. You just wouldn't would you? Men staring at you and checking you out after a drink, it makes me cringe.
>
> (Neelam, 31, teacher)

Most of the respondents in this chapter made it clear that they do not want to participate as spectators at the kabbadi tournament. For the respondents, the field of the kabbadi tournament is a place where men drink and exude aggressive behaviour. Interestingly, their non-participation is a reaction to masculine culture. The respondents are critical and interpret the field as 'unsafe' and 'boring'. The narratives of kabbadi tournaments from the women in this research highlight a form of separatism between men and women: an acknowledgment and belief that the tournaments are spaces for men. The respondents clearly articulate what is an acceptable and safe environment for women and children, and consequently the kabbadi tournament is not an arena for women. It is important to note that, although patriarchal relations are at play, women are not contesting participation in the field of kabbadi; rather they are rejecting the masculine field and are choosing not to participate.

Simran further illustrates the reasons for her non-participation as a spectator at kabbadi tournaments:

> I am not really in to going to watch it [kabbadi], it's always raining and it's cold. I wouldn't mind going to check out the boys [laughs]. I am actually being serious. I think it would be a good place to meet sporty muscular men. My parents are always harassing me to get married, I should tell them that I am going to the kabbadi tournament to check out the boys [laughs]. I think my mum and dad would kill me if I went ... everyone knows that men drink there and there are fights.... I suppose my mum and dad want to protect me ... my dad and mum would kill me if I turned up with my mates. We'd be the only girls there ... it's a boring game anyway. I've seen the kabbadi players and they're not fit [laughs]. What's the point? ... I'll stick to [names clubs in London] the men in there are probably less desi [traditional] anyway [laughs].
>
> (Simran, 25, banker)

Simran is aware that if she engages as a spectator at the kabbadi tournament it will be interpreted or linked to an act of sexual deviance. Sexual deviance within the South Asian context is related to the concept of *izzat*, which is embedded within the field of kabbadi. Simran, and other women in this research, engage with patriarchal relations and embed the objective social reality of *izzat* in their decision making processes. Hall (1995) explains that *izzat* is either 'upheld' or 'ruined', thus within the context of kabbadi, the social transaction of a woman entering the field would ultimately ruin her family's *izzat*. Carroll (1985) states that women's infringement within sports echoes a 'matricidal culture' that questions male identity. Further, Giulianotti (2005: 87) explains that "strong patriarchal gender codes dissuade many women from sport participation". Consequently, Ratna (2010: 121) suggests that:

> in the spaces of sport and leisure, a closer examination of the praxis of British-Asians reveals that they negotiate their entry by using a fusion of different resources – drawn from both their religious beliefs and South Asian cultures as well as from other resources stemming from living in an increasingly globalised world – to move from outside to inside these spaces.

Thus, other current research and literature on South Asian females explores spaces that women are 'trying' to access, rather than spaces they do not want to participate in. It is important to note that women in this study are not interested in 'negotiating their entry' into kabbadi tournaments. Instead, they are protecting their children and themselves from the perceived harsh realities of 'fighting', 'drinking' and 'checking you out' by consciously not taking part.

## Women's social and cultural activities

Due to a masculine alcohol-fuelled field, combined with the awareness of *izzat*, the British Punjabi women in this research refrained from attending kabbadi events. For many, this is *not* an affliction; rather it provided them with the opportunity to pursue their own personal interests. Indeed, within this research it was common for the women to narrate what they prefer to do when their husbands attend kabbadi tournaments. Simi for example, summarises:

> [...] women would prefer to do other things. I cannot think of anything worse than going to a kabbadi tournament. If my husband said shall we go to the kabbadi, I would be really disappointed and we would probably have an argument [laughs].
>
> (Simi, 35, lawyer)

Similarly, Rajinder draws on gender divisions and highlights how the men and women in her household spend their leisure time:

> The boys enjoy it ... watching all the strong men fighting. We [daughters] hang out, have a girls' day and go shopping. They wouldn't want to go, stand in the cold and watch a boring sport.
>
> (Rajinder, 48, care worker)

Interestingly, throughout this research respondents have revealed that the practice of localised kabbadi tournaments is a way in which British Punjabi communities, both males and females, construct and maintain gender relations and notions of *izzat*. Women clearly reproduce cultural meanings of femininity and masculinity. For example, 'girls' day' and 'go shopping', 'housework' and 'watching all the strong men fighting' illustrate how they arrange and construct gender relations within their homes.

Surinder, for example, states that kabbadi spectatorship is not for women and demonstrates her preferences for other gendered activities:

> It is for young people and men, not for an old woman like me. I have better things to do. [...] I go to the gurdwara, see my friends and family, my daughter takes me to Green Street [shopping district].... It is a lot more fun.
>
> (Surinder, 68, retired reacher)

Similarly, Luckvir emphasises spending time with a female relative and friends rather than going to the kabbadi:

> It doesn't excite me. It doesn't do anything for me. Do you understand? I would rather read a book, go shopping or watch a film. I usually end up driving my mum around the town so she can see her friends. It's always nice to see them.
>
> (Luckvir, 26, health care professional)

The respondents state that they would not like to participate in or attend kabbadi tournaments. Many women suggest that they would 'prefer' to go shopping, spend time with other female friends and family and go to the gurdwara. The women spend time with their mother or daughter(s); this can be perceived as both a leisure restriction and an opportunity for the women (Henderson, 1991). However, for these women, the main arena for leisure to take place was the family and they expressed this as a positive opportunity. Further, Deem (1986: 7) suggests that 'safe' leisure activities of women means spending time with other female friends or relatives with "few or no men". Bradley (2007) develops the argument and explains that women's leisure is situated around 'interaction' rather than specific activities. Additionally, throughout the research, women assert and make a distinction between men and women's activities. Women make it clear that the behaviours and activities associated with kabbadi tournaments are conflicting with the notions of British Punjabi femininity. Women's narratives reproduce cultural meanings and descriptions of masculinities and femininities. These descriptions reinforce a gendered division of leisure and its consumption.

## Conclusions

There is an implicit understanding between men and women that kabbadi events are exclusively male. It is an arena where patriarchal relations are negotiated and maintained but, unlike many other sporting spaces (cf. Thorpe, 2005; Ratna, 2010; Dashper, 2012), it is not a contested site for women where they struggle for representation. Notions of *izzat*, understandings of femininity and rejection of a masculine field reinforce women's non-participation as participants and spectators. Thus, this chapter further informs discussions around spectatorship and adds to knowledge on the subject of non-participation of British Punjabi women at sporting events. Importantly, the data reveals that British Punjabi women have some autonomy within the patriarchal relations that exist in their everyday realities. The women in the study celebrate and mark out the differences between men and women and identify, as well as reinforce, cultural meanings of *izzat* in the context of kabbadi tournaments.

Further, Watson and Scraton (2001: 266) suggest that

> there is an "uneasy marriage" between leisure and sport studies and feminist work in gender studies and women's studies. This reflects the dominant perception that sport and leisure are "male" defined, dominated by a patriarchal discourse and peripheral to the key concerns of feminist praxis.

It is important to recognise that the field of sport is 'male defined', but it is also important to note that it is ethnocentric. Leisure and sport studies, and feminist work within it, is led by essentialist and static representations of 'South Asian culture' and 'South Asian women' who 'struggle' to participate within the field of sport because of 'modesty' (Johnson, 2000) and a lack of knowledge (Carrington and McDonald, 2008). Further, there is an assumption placed on British South Asian women that they need to be 'rescued' from oppressive practices or that they do not participate in sport because of 'religion' or 'culture' (Walseth, 2006). Theorists fail to acknowledge that women can, and do, negotiate their non-participation in sport. Feminists and scholars of sport studies cannot start with the assumption that limited participation is solely due to patriarchal relations. Consideration should be given to how community and individual everyday realities are formed and the various strategies that are employed by agents in their fields to negotiate and reject access to events.

The research reveals that both first- and second-generation women are critical of the kabbadi field and, based on cultural subjectivities, decide not to attend these events. The kabbadi field is a 'field of masculinity', which is perceived by the respondents as an arena where there are naked men and bad language, a space which is 'unsafe', alcohol fuelled and aggressive. Collins (1991) and hooks (1984) argue that, for many black women, the home is a site of resistance to oppression. To develop this analysis further, this chapter reveals that the reason why women do not want to participate in kabbadi events is due to being exposed to a masculine environment that they do not approve of, or want to be a part of. Thus, spending time with female family members and female friends is seen as a site of resistance to oppression, objectification and danger.

Additionally, it is important to note that the practice of localised kabbadi events is a way in which British Punjabi communities, both male and female, construct and maintain gender relations. Thus, consideration needs to be given to the fact there is an implicit acknowledgment between individuals and the community that it is a forbidden space for women. The exclusion of women as spectators in the field of kabbadi is negotiated and mutually agreed by both men and women. The implicit acknowledgment of the forbidden space is where intersections of *izzat* and protection play out. Consequently, women's non-participation as spectators in the field of kabbadi is partly directed by their awareness of *izzat*, and its implications for family honour, individual and familial identities. Therefore, the everyday realities of British Punjabi women consist of numerous overlapping fields of *izzat*, rejection of the masculine field and the pursuit of familial, social and cultural activities. It is these negotiated overlapping fields that reinforce non-participation of female spectators at kabbadi events.

## Note

1 Some remarks on the categories most used throughout this chapter are necessary. Discussions are restricted to the terms 'South Asian' and 'British Punjabi'. The expression 'South Asian' has been used "to apply exclusively to people of the Indian subcontinent and their descendants" (Khan, 1999: 1). The term 'British Punjabi' refers broadly to individuals who are British residents and who have an affiliation (either direct or by family membership) to the region of Punjab, India.

# References

Bains, H.K. (2005) *Individual and family expectations among first and second generation Sikh women in the UK: Aspirations, constraints and patriarchal practices.* Unpublished PhD thesis. University of Sheffield.

Bains, J. and Patel, R. (1996) *Asians can't play football.* Solihull: Asian Social Development Agency.

Ballard, R. (1982) South Asian families: Structure and process. In Fogarty, M.P. and Rapoport, R. (eds) *Families in Britain.* London: Routledge.

Basu, S. (2004) Bengali girls in sport: A socio-economic study of Kabaddi. *International Journal of the History of Sport*, 21(3–4): 467–477.

Bhachu, P. (1991) Culture, ethnicity and class among Punjabi Sikh Women in 1990s Britain. *New Community*, 17(3): 401–412.

Bhopal, K. (2001) Researching South Asian women: Issues of sameness and difference in the research process. *Journal of Gender Studies*, 10(3): 279–286.

Birrell, S. (1990) Women of color: Critical autobiography and sport. In Messner, M. and Sabo, D. (eds) *Sport, men and the gender order.* Champaign, IL: Human Kinetics, 185–199.

Bradley, H. (2007) *Gender.* Cambridge: Polity Press.

Brah, A. (1979) *Inter-generational and inter-ethnic perceptions: A comparative study of South Asian and English adolescents and their parents in Southhall, West London.* Unpublished PhD thesis, University of Bristol.

Burdsey, D. (2007) *British Asians and football: Culture, identity, exclusion.* New York: Routledge.

Burdsey, D. (2010) British Muslim experiences on English first-class cricket. *International Review for the Sociology of Sport*, 45(3): 315–334.

Carrington, B. and McDonald, I. (eds) (2001) *'Race', sport and British society*, London: Routledge.

Carrington, B. and McDonald, I. (2008) The politics of 'race' and sports policy in the United Kingdom. In Houlihan, B. (ed.) *Sport and society: A student introduction.* Second edition. London: Sage, 230–254.

Carroll, J. (1985) Sport: Virtue and grace. *Theory, Culture and Society*, 3(1): 91–98.

Coles, T. (2009) Negotiating the field of masculinity: The production and reproduction of multiple dominant masculinities. *Men and Masculinities*, 12(1): 30–44.

Collins, P.H. (1991) *Black feminist thought: Knowledge, consciousness, and the politics of empowerment.* London: Routledge.

Collins, T. and Vamplew, W. (2002) *Mud, sweat and beers: A cultural history of sport and alcohol.* Oxford: Berg.

Dashper, K. (2012) Together, yet still not equal? Sex integration in equestrian sport. *Asia-Pacific Journal of Health, Sport and Physical Education*, 3(3): 213–225.

Deem, R. (1986) *All work and no play.* Milton Keynes: Open University Press.

Desai, R. (1963) *Indian immigrants in Britain.* London: Oxford University Press.

Dworkin, S. and Messner, M. (2001) Just do … what? Sport, bodies, gender. In Scraton, S. and Flintoff, A. (eds) *Gender and sport: A reader.* London: Routledge, 17–29.

Fletcher, T. (2011) The making of English cricket cultures: Empire, globalization and (post) colonialism. *Sport in Society*, 14(1): 17–36.

Fletcher, T. (2012) All Yorkshiremen are from Yorkshire, but some are more "Yorkshire" than others: British Asians and the myths of Yorkshire cricket. *Sport in Society*, 15(2): 227–245.

Fletcher, T. and Spracklen, K. (2013) Cricket, drinking and exclusion of British Pakistani Muslims? *Ethnic and Racial Studies.* DOI: 10.1080/01419870.2013.790983.

Giulianotti, R. (2005) *Sport: A critical sociology.* Polity: Cambridge.

Hall, K. (1995) There's a time to act English and a time to act Indian: The politics of identity among British-Sikh teenagers. In Stephens, S. (ed.) *Children and the politics of culture.* Princeton: Princeton University Press, 170–193.

Hall, M.A. (1996) *Feminism and sporting bodies: Essays on theory and practice.* Champaign, IL: Human Kinetics.

Hargreaves, J.A. (1990) Gender on the sports agenda. *International Review for the Sociology of Sport*, 25(4): 287–305.

Henderson, K.A. (1991) The contribution of feminism to an understanding of leisure constraints. *Journal of Leisure Research*, 23(4): 363–377.

hooks, b. (1984) *Feminist theory: From margins to centre.* Boston: South End Press.

Jackson, S. (2007) Families, domesticity and intimacy. In Robinson, V. and Richardson, D. (eds) *Introducing women studies.* Second edition. Basingstoke: Macmillan, 125–143.

Johal, S. (2001) Playing their own game: A South Asian football experience. In Carrington, B. and McDonald, I. (eds) *"Race", sport and British Society.* New York: Routledge, 153–169.

Johal, S. (2002) *The sport of lions: The Punjabi-Sikh sporting experience.* Unpublished PhD thesis, University of Warwick.

Johnson, M.R.D. (2000) Perceptions of barriers to health and physical activity among Asian communities. *Sport Education and Society*, 5(1): 51–70.

Khan, S. (1999) *A glimpse through Purdah: Asian women – the myth and the reality.* Stoke-on-Trent: Trentham Books.

McDonald, I. (1999) "Physiological patriots?": The politics of physical culture and Hindu nationalism in India. *International Review for the Sociology of Sport*, 34(4): 343–358.

Olesen, V. (2000) Feminisms and qualitative research at and into the Millenium. In Denzin, N.K. and Lincoln, Y.S. (eds) *Handbook of qualitative research.* 2nd edition. London: Sage, 332–397.

Pfister, G. (2010) Women in sport: Gender relations and future perspectives. *Sport in Society*, 12(2): 234–248.

Plummer, K. (2001) *Documents of life 2: An invitation to a critical humanism.* Second edition. London: Sage.

Ratna, A. (2010) "Taking the power back!": The politics of British-Asian female football players. *Young: Nordic Journal of Youth Research*, 18(2): 117–132.

Rozario, S. (2005) *Building solidarity against patriarchy.* Rural Livelihoods Program. CARE Bangladesh, Dhaka.

Scraton, S. and Flintoff, A. (eds) (2002) *Gender and sport: A Reader.* London: Routledge.

Smart, C. (1995) *Legal regulation or male control? Law, crime and sexuality.* London: Sage.

Thorpe, H. (2005) Jibbing the gender order: Females in the snowboarding culture. *Sport in Society*, 8(1): 76–100.

Tierney, W.G. (2000) Undaunted courage: Life history and the postmodern challenge. In Denzin, N.K and Lincoln, Y.S. (eds) *Handbook of qualitative research.* Second edition. Thousand Oaks, California: Sage, 537–554.

Verma, G.K. and Darby, D.S. (1994) *Winners and losers: Ethnic minorities in sport and recreation.* London: Flamer Press.

Walseth, K. (2006) Young Muslim women and sport: The impact of identity work. *Leisure Studies*, 25(1): 75–94.

Watson, B. and Scraton, S. (2001) Confronting whiteness? Researching leisure lives of South Asian mothers. *Journal of Gender Studies*, 10(3): 265–277.

Williams, R., Bush, H., Anderson, A., Lean, M. and Bradby, H. (1996) *Dietary change in South Asian and Italian women in the West of Scotland: Final report to the ESRC.* Glasgow: MRC Medical Sociology Unit.

# 10 'Shades of Basqueness'

## Football, politics and ethnicity in the Basque Country

*Jim O'Brien*

### Introduction: Athletic Bilbao and Real Sociedad in the shaping of Basque identities

> It is perhaps the price that two clubs, so close in some ways, but so far apart in others, must pay.
>
> (Rivas, 2012:113)

The Basque derby between Athletic Bilbao and Real Sociedad is a seminal event in the Spanish sporting calendar. For over a century the rivalry between the two clubs has been about more than football. When the clubs meet, more is at stake for the fans than the spoils of victory or the despair of defeat. From the first clash in the 1909 Kings Cup final, history and politics are contested each time Athletic play Real, encompassing complex issues around 'Basqueness', ethnicity and identity. This chapter examines the ways in which these clubs have defined 'Shades of Basqueness' and the capacity of sporting events to serve as metaphors for cultural and political values. Both Athletic and Real have followed distinctive paths in defining what it is to be 'Basque'. This has shaped the historic rivalry for fans of these Basque neighbours. The occasionally hostile nature of this football derby has created and legitimised alternative interpretations of history because of the role sporting events play in framing folklore and memory (Billings, 2009).

From the medieval 'fueros'[1] to contemporary campaigns for independence, 'Basqueness' has been contested. Since football's introduction into the Basque Country in the late nineteenth century, it has been a metaphor for paradoxical debates about the nation within the nation, centre–regional tensions and stateless nationhood. Football's folkloric role within the Basque Country, both as one of the traditional heartbeats of the Spanish game and as a catalyst for the articulation of local and regional identities, provides insights into the historic and contemporary fusion of politics, social class and ethnicities at the root of constructions of Basqueness in the early twenty-first century. From the emergence of the historic communities and the PNV (Basque Nationalist Party)[2] in the 1890s, through the defining political contexts of twentieth-century Spain; embracing monarchy, republic, civil war, dictatorship and democracy, to the current crisis in Spanish statehood and national identity, the Basque Country's football has been an interlocking synthesis of cleavage, unity and rivalry in shifting definitions of what it is to be Basque. Many of these competing constructions of identity and ethnicity are expressed in the relationship between the region's two major clubs. If Basqueness itself is contested, the capacity of Athletic and Real to act as filters for 'Shades of Basqueness' is open to interpretation.

This chapter first considers football's emergence in the Basque Country. The formative years of both Athletic and Real embraced major political, economic and societal developments. Football became embedded in contested and shared notions of Basque ethnicity, in which divergent embodiments of Basqueness were located in factors shaping the identities of both clubs. The chapter then discusses the key aspects defining the Athletic–Real dichotomy: from the civil war of the 1930s, to the transition to democracy in the late 1970s. Throughout these periods Basqueness became articulated as a dissident expression of suppressed nationalist aspiration, obscuring many of the nuances underlying conflicting sentiments shaping identity in both clubs, to foster a sense of homogenous opposition to Francoist centralism. Finally, the chapter evaluates the relationship between football and the resurgent regionalism of the 1980s in the Spain of the autonomous communities, before considering evolving definitions of Basqueness as both clubs adapted to the game's globalisation, whilst continuing to be custodians of vaunted traditions of Basque ethnicity. Key questions emerge in this analysis. In the early twenty-first century, is football in the Basque Country still xenophobic in its ethnic purity, as Hanlon (2011) suggests? Where does the essence of Basqueness remain: with the high profile self-promotion of Athletic Bilbao, or the team from the other side of the tracks, Real Sociedad? Finally, what does the rivalry reveal about football and nationalism at a time of changing patterns of national and ethnic identities? (O'Brien, 2013; see also Woodworth, 2008).

## Football and the roots of Basque ethnicity

> Nationalism in the Basque Country, as in Catalonia, is as much an emotion, or an identity, as a set of political arguments.
>
> (Tremlett, 2012: 285)

Football's representations of contemporary constructions of Basque identity are rooted in the political and socio-economic changes of the late nineteenth century. Re-emergent regionalism and nationalism was at the core of the historic communities of the Basque Country, Catalonia and Galicia which defined centre-regional fissures in 1898 – the 'year of disaster'. Industrialisation and urbanisation in the Basque Country emphasised language, class cleavage and factionalism in challenging state authority following the end of the Spanish Empire (Junco and Shubert, 2000). Nationalism found a political voice with the foundation of the PNV by Sabino Arana in 1894 (Sainz, 2009). Football first carved its niche with the birth of Athletic Bilbao in 1898. The symbiosis between football, social class, politics and ethnicity was intertwined and critical issues underscoring Basque identity are reflected in the history of the game's development in the region. Two questions stand out: what is the Basque Country? and what is it to be 'Basque'? (Kurlansky, 2000).

The Basque Country is territorially contested. Loyalty to the values of 'La Patria Chica' (The Mother Country) based on locality, province and region were central to ethnic constructions of Basqueness (Vincent, 2010). When rivalries around football's growth in the region developed, they tapped into the political and societal changes of the 1890s, so that the game's nascent folklore embellished the rituals and symbols of emergent nationalism and its complex relationship with an imploding Spanish state. In the Basque Country of the late nineteenth century, the province was the articulation of a highly localised set of distinctive values based on 'race', language and fervent Catholicism (Payne, 1971). The Basque nation came to be defined as the three provinces of Vizcaya, Guipuzcoa and Alava, each with a strong degree of autonomy, but unified through a common bond of nationhood and opposition to the centralisation of Madrid. The position of Navarre, and the three French Basque provinces was, and remains, contentious in definitions of a stateless Basque nation. These internecine territorial debates found expression in the development of the Basque Country's football, and gave rise to one of the subsequent cornerstones of the Athletic Bilbao–Real Sociedad nexus, with each club claiming to be the embodiment of Basque ethnicity.

Jon Aridiano, Senior Sports Journalist with 'El Correo', believes that the Basque derby soon became an emotionally charged event around rival claims of identity (personal communication, Bilbao, 2010). Real, historically drawing its players from the province of Guipuzcoa, with San Sebastian at the core of a local–provincial axis, perceives itself to be more 'pure' in its Basqueness than the orthodoxy of Athletic's symbolic role in representing the Basque nation since the club's inception.

Spanish football developed gradually in the first two decades of the twentieth century. The Basque Country and Catalonia established the game's credentials as cultural and political counterpoints to Madrid as arenas of regional identity and nationalist aspirations (O'Brien, 2013; see also Goldblatt, 2008). Football was amateur and regional, rooted in locality in its embryonic growth. English influences and the pulse of modernity were pivotal in the early years of Athletic's genesis. The game's first backdrop of political and cultural Basqueness embellished locality and provincialism. In the game's pre-professional phase (1896–1928) a cluster of clubs, from Getxo (1909) to Real Irun (1915) emerged with Athletic and Real to express local contexts of Basque identity. The success of Basque football in this period, given profile by the participation of Athletic Bilbao as regional champions in the inaugural 1902 'King's Cup' (Burns, 2012), provided coherence in a volatile, uncertain period for the PNV and alternative manifestations of Basque nationalism until its electoral surge in the 1920s. The Basque Country's sense of linguistic, cultural and ethnic difference, and its distinctive juxtaposition of locality, province and nation, became established through the synthesis between football, politics and culture. For example, Mikel Olazabel, Head of Sports Broadcasting at ETB (Basque Regional Television), asserts that religious symbols such as San Mames and La Basilica[3] were used to bind the club with its supporters (personal communication, Bilbao, 2010).

The relationship between Athletic and Real soon became embroiled within Basque factionalism; most specifically in the ethos and application of the Cantera system (discussed below) governing both clubs. Its development defines the fluidity of the relationship between the clubs once they became the dominant expressions of Basqueness when the Spanish league became national and professional (1928). The fact that four clubs from the region were amongst the league's founder members demonstrates the potency of Basque football and is indicative of the game's wider role in cultural and political spheres, and in reflecting local and provincial manifestations of Basque regionalism. The cluster of clubs which had been significant in shaping the blueprint of Basque football subsequently slipped into the hinterland of the game at lower, regional levels, although clubs such as Alaves and more especially, Osasuna, remained vibrant expressions of their own specific provincial autonomy. The Cantera philosophy, based on the use of local players, is the seminal link defining the relationship between supporter, player, club and locality. It remains a key dynamic of inter-club rivalry.

Whilst early influences introducing football into the Basque Country were English – from the shipbuilders of Southampton playing ad hoc games in the early 1890s, to returning exchange students from Manchester – football soon became assimilated into the political and cultural changes impacting on the region (O'Brien, 2013; see also Riordan and Kruger, 2003). The vision of Basqueness emanating from the PNV reflected political schisms between rural conservative Catholic radicalism, which saw the Basque people as a separate 'race', urban moderates and the political left of Bilbao and San Sebastian. This rural–urban dichotomy was reinforced by cleavages between working-class Bilbao and the affluent middle-class of San Sebastian, which became the summer retreat of the Spanish Monarchy. Until 1918, the PNV was characterised by electoral weakness and divisions over the racial and ethnic values of Basque separatism and its relationship to the central Spanish state (O'Brien, 2013; see also Encarnacion, 2008). Football crystallised many of these influences, and though early teams of Athletic Bilbao contained many English players, home-grown talent was soon developed and prioritised. The club mirrored the political objectives of the PNV, which recognised the game's potential as a unifying cultural force. The first successes of the Basque clubs at a regional level and in the early King's Cups established the tactical approach of Athletic in particular: tough, direct, courageous and spirited. Indeed, the Basque diaspora expanded its influence when migrant workers set up Athletico Madrid (1905). When Real Socie dad was founded (1909), football's burgeoning strength in the region reinforced claims to separate nationhood. However, territorial and class divisions soon opened up between these two football identities (Crolley and Hand, 2006).

The first derbies (1909–1918) set the pattern of the relationship between the clubs. From criticism of Athletic by Real for fielding an all-English team (1911), to recorded incidents of objects being thrown onto the San Mames pitch (1915 and 1916), the matches were marred by sporadic outbreaks of crowd disturbance, pitch invasions and the formal break up of relations between Athletic and Real, culminating in the closure of Real's stadium (the Atocha) for a year following injury to a child during a clash between supporters during a 2–2 draw in 1918 (Rivas, 2012). This fierce rivalry was punctuated by attempts to foster more harmonious relations through playing a series of friendly games, establishing an engrained tradition of rivalry and fraternity between the clubs. The matches showed the sports event as a site for deeply rooted feelings of historic rivalry. These disputes were caused by tensions around alleged refereeing errors, rule breaking and non-sporting behaviour. They were also underpinned by questions of ethnicity and identity surrounding emergent Basque nationhood in the volatile politics of the period. In the turbulent 1920s and 1930s, when Spain lurched from monarchy to dictatorship, then from republic to civil war, football became central to Basque identity, particularly as manifest through the divergent strands of the Athletic versus Real rivalry.

The game itself witnessed significant changes. These mirrored implosions in the fabric of Spanish society. Two main developments reinforced the symbiosis between football, culture and Basque ethnicity: the Cantera and La Furia. The former, introduced by Athletic and Real (1912) to promote a Basque players only policy, indelibly fused football and Basqueness in the construction and legitimisation of ethnicity. It also contrasted the provincial interpretation of the Cantera adopted by Real until 1989 with the more expansive approach adopted by Athletic, in which Basqueness was passed on within the organic diasporic boundaries of the Basque nation, as well as through inculcation in the club's youth scheme. In a football context, it ensured continuity of tradition for both clubs, whilst limiting Real to a more restricted source of players. It suggested that issues pertaining to Basque identity would remain contested within football's lexicon in the pursuit and application of the Cantera as a sporting and political metaphor for carving distinctive ethnicity within the centre–regional axis. The national team's participation in the Antwerp Olympics (1920) created the cultural symbolism of La Furia. The heroic display of the team in winning the silver medal soon became embedded in the folklore of the Spanish game. As the team had a number of Basque Players and Paco Bru – a Basque – as coach, the courage, direct play and passion, especially in the match against Sweden, became identified with core Basque values in the expanding public and press profile of football (Paradinas, 2010). It played a key role in defining stereotypes around Basque identity, which were grafted onto perceptions of the Spanish national team to become La Furia Espanola (Spanish Fury). In the 1920s the fusion of the Cantera and La Furia gave Basque football its specific characteristics (Hanlon, 2011).

Basque football created many of the first stars of the Spanish game; a growing mass profile developed a synthesis between football, politics and identity. Moreno, later immortalised as 'El Piccichi',[4] who scored the first goal at San Mames (1913), Balauste, one of the 'Lions of Antwerp', Sota and Aguirre, all secured iconic status. They cemented the regional power base of Basque football, and became symbols of cultural opposition to the Primo de Rivera dictatorship in the 1920s. In doing so, the capacity of football to represent dissident identities threatened state hegemony for the first time. The PNV won its first significant electoral success in this decade. The founding of La Liga (The League) in 1928 anchored Basque football in a national context and paved the way for Athletic's next golden age, when the club won successive doubles (1930 and 1931) under the stewardship of English Manager, Mr Pentland.

The expanding sports pages of 'El Excelsior' gave these achievements a prominent press profile. Derby matches were hotly contested during football's first boom period, with huge crowds at both the Atocha and San Mames. Athletic generally held the upper hand, although Real secured a notable 3–2 success over their Basque rivals in April 1932, on the way to securing their first league title. The Cantera and La Furia reaped dividends on the field, and gave Basque football a national profile – although notably, both clubs subsequently became entangled in the period's turbulent politics. As the PNV lurched into political factionalism during the second republic (1931–1936) an autonomous Basque nation found a vibrant, if brief, foothold. Consequently, the synergy between Athletic Bilbao and political autonomy became more pronounced, whilst Real Sociedad became FC Donastia to shed its previous association with the monarchy. This made the link between Basque identity and football explicit. During the political uncertainties of the republic, La Liga was one of the few remaining national arenas into which sporting and cultural rivalries could be channelled (Duke and Crolley, 1996). The subsequent civil war (1936–1939) had profound implications for Basque politics, and the stability fashioned by football evaporated. The 1930s are significant for Basque football in that the uncertainty projected by the republic and the civil war, allied to the fact that the game was gradually becoming more politicised and international in focus, meant that the ideological perspective of a dislocated Basque nation moved into the orbit of international relations. This was certainly the case for Athletic Bilbao (personal communication with Mikel Olazabel, Bilbao, 2010). The period saw the club become a mouthpiece and symbol of Basque identity, further sharpening the divisions with Real Sociedad. Athletic's links with Paris, Moscow, Mexico and England reinforced the propagandist representation of a nation in exile (Payne, 1971). By the time the republic was defeated in 1939, football was established at the expense of traditional sports as the site of alternative nationalism. The role of Basque football changed dramatically during Franco's dictatorship.

## Athletic Bilbao and Real Sociedad: brothers in arms

Under Franco, the notion of a single Spanish identity and the promotion of its image were encouraged by football and the sport's role as the vehicle for frustrated nationalism was central.

(Crolley and Hand, 2006: 108)

If the uniqueness of Basqueness is most acutely expressed by language (Hooper, 2007), Euskara, the Basque language, was the central target of Francoist suppression in the post-civil war years. From the repression of the 1940s to the technocracy of the 1960s, the rationale underpinning the regime's hold on power was driven by Franco's belief in the existence of a unitary, centralised Catholic Spanish State in which any aspirations for separatism or regional autonomy were to be explicitly denied (O'Brien, 2013; see also Balfour, 2005). Football's boom period of the 1950s was a key component in this manufacture of a national consensus. Sport was governed and regulated under the apparatus of control from Madrid. This had implications for constructions of ethnicity in the historically dissident regions, particularly the Basque Country and Catalonia, in which football had been critical in expressing cultural values. Thus the regime both exploited football's potential as mass spectacle to distract from economic austerity and political suppression, whilst also denying it the capacity to be a catalyst for regional diversity or alternative nationhood (O'Brien, 2013; see also Vinolo, 2009). Under Franco, a subtle interplay emerged, in which the symbols, folklore and publicity around football were utilised to manufacture legitimacy, coherence and consensus within the parameters of contained rivalries in which the organisation of the game was rigidly centralised. This was important for the survival and subsequent development of the Basque Country's football.

In the immediate post-civil war period, Spain struggled both internally and externally for survival and legitimacy. Football in the Basque Country was quickly inculcated into the fabric of the unitary state. For Athletic Bilbao this meant an imposed change of name and identity to Athletico de Bilbao (1941). Such change was part of the wider process of the homogenisation of Spanish society. For both Athletic and Real their institutional and cultural autonomy was compromised by the appointment and monitoring of compliant presidents from Madrid, so that the power centre of the game shifted away from the regions to the centralised authoritarianism of Moscardi, El Caudillo's Minister of Sport. Due to the rigid control and repression of Madrid, the 1940s were dark days for Basque football as a focus for separate ethnic identity. Moreover, through the international profile generated by Spain's victory over England in the 1950 World Cup in Brazil, the only goal scored by the iconic Zarra, the latest talisman to emerge from Athletic Bilbao, the regime, and its strictly censored press, exploited the achievement for propaganda purposes, utilising the fabled Basque values of La Furia as quintessential elements of Franco's Spain (Crolley and Hand, 2006).

The qualities of courage, hard work and fierce pride were characterised as Spanish in the 'New Spain' which followed the national team's victory over the Soviet Union in the final of the European Nations Cup in Madrid in 1964 (Duke and Crolley, 1996). In spite of the appropriation of La Furia, and the fact that Spain played at San Mames several times during the regime, there was no support for the national team in the Basque Country, further highlighting the polarisation of football, politics and culture under Franco. In contrast, the success of Real Madrid in the 1950s pushed the club into an ambassadorial role in representing and legitimising Franco's Spain. Football in the Basque Country emerged as the clandestine protector of ethnic and cultural difference. Whilst the PNV and other sources of political opposition were circumscribed, the game's rivalries, generated at either San Mames or the Atocha, became the sole public space in which suppressed identities were allowed to be silently manifested (O'Brien, 2013; see also Giulianotti, 2000; Wagg, 1995).

Whilst all other demonstrations and displays of Basque nationalism were forbidden in the political and cultural spheres, the club colours and flags of Real and Athletic became substitutes for the Ikurruna (Basque Country Flag), and fans could speak Euskara in the stadium without fear of sanction. Football was the only public arena in which alternative ethnicities could be expressed beneath the surface of imposed, manufactured unity. Athletic's debut in the European Cup (1957) and their victory over the all-conquering Real Madrid side in the final of the renamed Generalisimo's Cup (1958) were seminal moments in which the team exhibited the qualities of La Furia. The match against Real Madrid, at the Bernabeu, was a folkloric sporting event, showing that aspirations of nationhood could never be fully suppressed (Rivas, 2012).

The interplay between football's political and cultural symbolism projected the club's traditions nationally and internationally. As Moltalban (2005: 64) commented, referring to the FC Barcelona and Real Madrid axis, the regime needed the "necessary enemies" that football generates. Football became the custodian of cultural heritage, expressed in the solidarity between fans of Athletic, Real and Barcelona in their enmity towards Real Madrid, the perceived manifestation of Francoism. The two major Basque clubs forged a kindred spirit through football's folkloric rituals whilst maintaining their respective traditions in framing Basque nationhood.

Ethnicity was protected through the organic links of the Cantera. The European successes of Athletic in reaching the UEFA Cup Final (1980) gave the club a more visible profile as the representation of a stateless Basque nation (Rivas, 2012). The narrow defeat against Italian giants Juventus redefined the values of La Furia for contemporary fans, the spectacle acting as a reminder of the club's traditions. The fusion between football and politics was emphasised by distinct phases of Basque nationalism and its relationship with the dictatorship from the 1940s to the 1960s. In the 1950s, the ideological ossification and impotence of the PNV (Conversi, 2000) was challenged with the gradual emergence of ETA[5] as the arena of violent resistance to Franco in the pursuit of Basque independence. Olazabel (Bilbao, 2010) notes that the relationship between football and the armed struggle was ambivalent; it was based on informal connections within the broad social compass of the clubs' support, without official endorsement from either Athletic or Real. In the 1960s and early 1970s, opposition to the regime evolved within a fracturing unitary state, so that the period prior to Franco's death in 1975, and the subsequent transition to democracy, was marked by a rise in ETA activity, peaking with the assassination of Franco's Prime Minister, Carrero Blanco, in 1973 (Ball, 2011).

Whilst political parties re-emerged as engines of democratic change, the nuances of Basque football became more political, though Athletic still retained its ethnically pure traditions (Olazabel, Bilbao, 2010). Moltalban (2005) asserts that football was crucial in maintaining national consensus from 1975 to 1982, when Spain hosted the World Cup and elected a socialist government (cited in Crolley and Hand, 2006). This was especially so in respect of the developing relationship between state, nation and identity. During the transition, football represented forces of continuity and change. Continuity was provided by the normalcy and cohesion of the traditional rivalries contained within La Liga, engendering a sense of order, whilst the politics of the period oscillated between mass protest, strikes, and a failed coup d'état (1981). Change was reflected through football's role in confronting old orthodoxies and maximising its potency as mass cultural spectacle, thereby paving the way for constitutional and political developments. Crucially, clubs started to assume functions of public responsibility as components of an emergent civic society.

In the Basque Country, this was most visibly expressed in the aftermath of Franco's death (1975), when the game introduced public use of Euskara again, with Athletic swiftly reverting to their traditional name and identity after years of subjugation. It also made dramatic breaks with the past. When the two distinctive 'Shades of Basqueness' met at the Atocha in December 1976, the occasion was celebrated by the ritual symbolism of the respective team captains, Iribar (Athletic) and Kortabarria (Real), unfurling the Ikurrina (Basque flag) whilst the Eusakido Ereserkia (Basque national anthem) played. This public display of nationhood became rooted in Basque football folklore, and demonstrated the power of the sporting spectacle to publically articulate cultural and political sentiments (Ball, 2011). Moreover, it reflected football's ability to unlock processes of change, and mirrored the contemporary evolution of Basque political sensibilities.

In the 1970s and 1980s splits occurred in the PNV to define alternative voices of Basque nationalism: from the emergence of Batasuna[6] to Basque solidarity and the growth of left-wing movements (Conversi, 2000). These developments ushered in the paradoxes and ambivalences of the constitutional settlement of 1978, revealing the pragmatism and underpinning the rubric of Spain's fledgling democracy. As the following section demonstrates, football in the Basque Country came to embrace many of these aspects in its synthesis with politics, culture and identity.[7]

## 'Shades of Basqueness': identity, tradition and change

> With home grown teams and supporters, there is no need for imports.
>
> (Club motto, Athletic Bilbao)

The celebrations of 'La Gabarra' marked Athletic's winning of the league and cup double (1984). The event defined the unifying power of the game as a public display of solidarity and nationalism at a time of economic recession.[8] It also illustrated the renaissance in football's capacity to express competing strands of ethnicity in the success of both Real and Athletic (Capistegui and Walton, 2001). From 1980 to 1984, the clubs shared four league titles; these achievements mirrored the shift towards a pluri-national Spain established by the autonomous communities in which the historic communities re-emerged from decades of centralised oppression. The Basque derbies of this period, with Welshman John Toshack as manager of Real, were high profile sporting events, illustrating the fierce rivalry of Spain's emergent nationalisms at club level. When Real overcame Athletic 2–1 (1982), for instance, the victory represented vindication of the club's distinctive Basque heritage. This process helped redefine centre–regional dynamics in respect of language, politics, history and cultural identity.

The democratisation of the media was crucial in giving a voice to Spain's regions. Football was critical as it acted as a set of competing rituals and symbols around the consensus of 'banal nationalism' (Billig 2004); a neutral set of folkloric traditions and mass populism binding nation, state and region together through the increased mediatisation and globalisation of La Liga. In the Basque Country, 'Shades of Basqueness' were gradually reframed within the political and cultural landscape of a more autonomous Spain. The region's football renaissance in the early and mid-1980s highlighted these developments. The respective interpretations of the Cantera based on either province or the wider diaspora of the Basque nation created a culturally distinctive ethnicity within football's lexicon. Tradition was central in preserving the link between locality, province, player, club and community. Competing constructs of identity, for the heart and soul of Basqueness, always lurked beneath the surface of kindred spirits of opposition and dissidence. In order to maintain its Basques-only policy, and to cement cultural hegemony, Athletic had frequently utilised its status as the bigger club to 'poach' players from Real Sociedad. According to Rivas (2012), the transfer of star player Exteberria from Real to Athletic (1995) soured relations between the clubs, and intensified the rivalry of the Basque derby.

In the more competitive political contexts of democratic Spain, marked by ETA's renunciation of their armed struggle in October 2011 (Tremlett, 2012), football evolved from the controls imposed under Franco. More fluid interpretations of ethnicity, a burgeoning media and changing patterns of global migration impacted on contested notions of Basque identity, thereby challenging traditional orthodoxies. These changes were most acutely felt by Real Sociedad, due to the narrow adherence to the province of Guipuzcoa as the root of its Cantera system. The club was struggling to compete by the late 1980s, leading to the momentous decision to abandon its Basques-only policy (1989) with the signature of John Aldridge from Liverpool. The practice began whereby Real affected uneasy compromises in signing non-Basque and non-Spanish players for the first time. These changes provided Athletic Bilbao with greater legitimacy as custodians of the Basque nation. This mirrored the generally stable governance of the PNV and its coalition patterns from the 1980s onwards. The shift in policy further opened up the rivalry between the two clubs. From Real's perspective, Athletic's greater wealth and status had forced the club into making this decision (Rivas, 2012).

The freedom of movement brought about by the Bosman Ruling,[9] coupled with the influx of foreign players into La Liga, linked economic, sporting and cultural aspects of globalisation to alter many of the traditional connections between football and identity in Spain (O'Brien, 2013; see also Niemann *et al.*, 2011). For Athletic Bilbao and Real Sociedad it has been difficult to maintain folkloric icons, myths and legends in the face of political, economic and cultural change. The Basque Country's football has responded to the combined impacts of regionalism, nationalism and globalisation with greater flexibility in preserving cultural heritage. However, it is difficult to see how either club can ever return to the halcyon days of the early 1980s; especially given the relegation of Real (2006/2007) and the struggles of Athletic the same season.

Clearly then, 'Shades of Basqueness' have been reframed depending on political and cultural contexts. Athletic Bilbao has adapted in order to retain the symbolism of the Cantera whilst remaining competitive. Olazabel (Bilbao, 2010) suggests that this has enabled the club to continue as an institutional and cultural phenomenon, with mass support in the Basque Country. This separatism accounts for the more muted response to the successes of Spain since 2008. Basque ethnicity has broadened to include Ramalho, the first black player to represent Bilbao (November 2011), a move which would have enflamed Sabino Arana in challenging the traditional racial stereotyping around the purity of Basque history and ethnicity.

Furthermore, patterns of immigration, migration and cultural assimilation have necessitated a degree of adaptation to ensure each club's survival. More recently for example, following relegation in 2007, Real reverted to a youth policy based on the provincial Cantera at the club's core. By 2011, with both clubs back in La Liga, football in the Basque Country continued to embellish competing local and regional dynamics around a distinctive set of ethnic identities, with club football central to the game's nexus. This constitutes a counterbalance to the dominance of Real Madrid and FC Barcelona, the evolution of La Furia to La Roja (Burns, 2012) and the global reach of the Champion's League.

## Conclusions

> Let everything seen by our eyes, spoken by our mouths, written by our hands, thought by our intelligence and felt by our hearts to be Basque.
>
> (Sabino Arana, in Vincent, 2010: 97)

In October 2012, Real played Athletic at the Anoeta Stadium in the Basque derby. For over 100 years the commonality underpinning rivalry between the two clubs has masked divisions around the appropriation of Basque identity. This recent clash demonstrated that the battle to secure supremacy in laying claim to ethnic legitimacy still smoulders beneath the surface, alongside lingering legacies of xenophobia (Burns, 2012). After a number of fallow years the stock of both clubs has risen recently, parallel to the rise of nationalist aspirations in the region as a whole. The match itself was a comfortable victory for

Real; but when Llorente, Athletic's talisman, came on as substitute, he was baited with jeers of 'Español' (Spanish) by the Sociedad fans. In the eyes of Real supporters, the player is not truly Basque, having been born in Pamplona and grown up in La Rioja before being incorporated into Athletic's youth system to frame his 'Basqueness'. This contrasted with a Real side containing a nucleus of players from Guipuzcoa, at the root of the club's traditional identity.

Such instances show that debates defining Basqueness through football are as contested as ever. The sporting rivalry generated by the spectacle of the Basque derby continues to resonate for fans of both clubs. Tradition and local rivalry transcends both changes within football itself and the implications of globalisation for ethnicity and identity. Given the globalised and media saturated nature of La Liga, spawning the FC Barcelona–Real Madrid duopoly, Athletic Bilbao and Real Sociedad are at a crossroads in trying to project and protect their respective traditions of Basque ethnicity whilst remaining competitive within the higher echelons of Spanish club football. This process of adaptation comes at a time when Spain, as a unified nation state, is experiencing its latest crisis of legitimacy in the wake of economic meltdown and resurgent claims for autonomy and independence in the Basque Country and Catalonia (Sutherland, 2012).

Tensions between tradition, divergent models of state and nation and opposing representations of ethnicity and identity, are at the core of football's role in underscoring current cultural and political issues. The future development of football in the Basque Country reflects these dilemmas. At the end of the 2012/2013 season what the club's fans call 'the cathedral' of San Mames, the first purpose-built football stadium in Spain, embedded in the iconography of Basque and Spanish football, was due to be replaced by the 'new' San Mames. Construction delays meant that, in a display of Basque fraternalism, Athletic played at the Anoeta until mid-September 2013 – another example of the paradoxical rivalry between the clubs. It remains to be seen if the revamped stadium will be able to capture the atmosphere of the original San Mames as a focal point of Basque nationhood, rooted in history and folklore (Duke and Crolley, 1996). Its construction gave rise to impassioned debate between traditionalists and modernisers amongst the club's members.

Similarly, the profile generated by the success of Real in qualifying for the 2013/2014 Champions League (the club's first appearance since 2003/2004) promotes a distinctive Basqueness, whilst being driven by the commercial impulse of the European game at its highest level. The capacity of both clubs to articulate 'Shades of Basqueness' will be shaped by changes both within and outside the game, as patterns of ethnicity become ever more complex and fluid. This raises the issue as to whether factors shaping the cultural identity of both clubs are inherited, imagined or manufactured within wider political and societal domains. It is doubtful whether they can ever recapture historic successes without compromising their respective traditions, or broadening their cultural spheres to retain the distinctive hue of the Cantera. Indeed, had Athletic been relegated in the 2006/2007 season, for the first time in their history, rather than surviving in the final match, their ability to compete at the top level without further compromising the Basques-only policy might have come under greater threat.

Both clubs have recovered from recent failures. They remain critical to the fashioning of Basque nationhood and ethnicity within the changing dynamics of football itself; a focal point of coherence and stability amidst political, economic and cultural chaos. The different 'Shades of Basqueness', as defined by Athletic and Real, demonstrate the power of football (and sport more generally) to engender sentiments of local and nationalist community and identity. Through the idealism of La Furia, the iconic status and rich heritage of its players, the alliances and rivalries fostered by the ritualistic traditions of the Basque derby, the unique facets of Basque football will continue to reflect contrasting aspects of nationalism and ethnicity in the communities fostered by its two most celebrated clubs.

## Notes

1 'Fueros' refers to the medieval customs of autonomy and self-rule. They are used in the Basque Country to legitimise historic and contemporary independence claims.
2 Partido Nacionalisto Vasco.
3 San Mames refers to an early Christian saint, thrown to lions by the Romans; La Basilica – The Cathedral of Our Lady of Begoña, patron saint of Bilbao. Athletic's players visit the site to mark the club's triumphs.
4 'El Piccichi', inauguarated in season 1953, is the trophy awarded to the top goal scorer in La Liga each season.
5 ETA – Euskadi Ta Askatasuna (Basque Homeland in Freedom) was founded in 1959.
6 Batasuna was founded by Henri Batasuna in 1978 as a Basque Nationalist Party. It was outlawed in 2003, and dissolved in 2013.
7 Articles 2 and 3 of the Spanish Constitution (1978) demonstrate the document's ambivalences and paradoxes.
8 'La Gabarra' is the barge which sailed down the River Nervion through Bilbao in May 1984, with players and officials of Athletic Bilbao on board.
9 The Bosman Ruling (1995) by the European Court of Justice allowed freedom of movement at end of contract for players without a transfer fee being paid (Article 39, EC treaty). It followed a dispute between Jean-Marc Bosman and the Belgian Football Association.

## References

Balfour, S. (ed.) (2005) *The politics of contemporary Spain*. London: Routledge.
Ball, P. (2011) *Morbo: The story of Spanish football*. London: WSC Books.
Billig, M. (2004) *Banal nationalism*. London: Sage.
Billings, A. (2009) *Communicating about sports media: Cultures collide*. Madrid: Aresta.
Burns, J. (2012) *La Roja: A journey through Spanish football*. London: Simon and Schuster.
Caspistegui, J. and Walton, J. (2001) *Guerras danzada futbol: identidades locales y regionales en Europa* (*Football's dancing wars: Regional and local identities in Europe*). Madrid: Eunsa.
Conversi, D. (2000) *The Basques, the Catalans and Spain: Alternate routes to nationalist mobilization*. Reno: University of Nevada Press.
Crolley, L. and Hand, D. (2006) *Football, Europe and the press*. London: Routledge.

Duke, V. and Crolley, L. (1996) *Storming the Bastille: Football, nationality and the state.* London: Longman.

Encarnacion, O. (2008) *Spanish politics: Democracy after dictatorship.* London: Polity Press.

Goldblatt, D. (2008) *The ball is round.* London: Riverhead.

Giulianotti, R. (2000) *Football: A sociology of the global game.* Cambridge: Polity Press.

Hanlon, T. (2011) *A Catalan dream: Football, artistry and political intrigue.* London: Peak Publishing.

Hooper, J. (2007) *The new Spaniards,* 2nd edition. London: Penguin.

Junco, J. and Shubert, A. (2000) *Spanish history since 1808.* London: Hodder Arnold.

Kurlansky, M. (2000) *The Basque history of the world.* London: Vintage.

Moltalban, M.V. (2005) *Futbol: una religion en busca de un dios (Football: A religion in search of a god).* Barcelona: Arena Abierta.

Niemann, A., Garcia, B. and Grant, W. (eds) (2011) *The transformation of European football.* Manchester: Manchester University Press.

O'Brien, J. (2013) "El Clasico" and the demise of tradition in Spanish club football: Perspectives on shifting patterns of cultural identity. *Soccer and Society,* 14(3): 315–330.

Paradinas, E. (2010) *La roja en la copa del mundo (The reds in the World Cup).* Madrid: T&B ediciones.

Payne, S. (1971) Catalan and Basque nationalism. *Journal of Contemporary History,* 6(1): 15–51.

Riordan, J. and Kruger, A. (2003) *European cultures in sport: Examining the nations and regions.* Intellect Books: Bristol.

Rivas, J. (2012) *Athletic: Paisajes, escenas y personajes (Athletic: Landscapes, scenes and people).* Rocabosillo: Barcelona.

Sainz, J.L. (2009) *El nacionalismo vasco: claves de su historia (Basque nationalism: Keys to its history).* Anaya: Barcelona.

Sutherland, C. (2012) *Nationalism in the twenty-first century: Challenges and responses.* New York: Palgrave Macmillan.

Tremlett, G. (2012) *Ghosts of Spain,* 2nd edition. London: Faber and Faber.

Vincent, M. (2010) *Spain 1833–2002.* Oxford: Oxford University Press.

Vinolo, V. (2009) *Los años 50 (The 1950s).* Madrid: La Esfera.

Wagg, S. (1995) *Giving the game away: Football, politics and culture on five continents.* Leicester: Leicester University Press.

Woodworth, P. (2008) *The Basque country: A cultural history.* Oxford: Oxford University Press.

# 11 Local identity and local events

## A case study of cheese rolling in Gloucestershire

*Andrew Bradley*

## Introduction

Events can play an important role in enhancing or preserving local culture and history. As such, they may have a significant role in how local people relate to the area in which they live and how local traditions are preserved and maintained (De Bres and Davis, 2001). Events have also become important from a financial standpoint and can be used to generate economic impacts and benefits for event organisers, local communities and businesses (Bradley and Hall, 2006; Bradley, 2011). However, tensions can be created between events that have long-standing traditions and associations with particular places, and the manipulation of these events for financial gain by external bodies, as some people may feel that the event has 'sold out' and moved away from its roots within local culture, thereby losing the coherency of its identity (Sharpley and Stone, 2011). These tensions are also reflected in local media sources as the media can play an important role in how people consume messages about their local area and its associated events, whilst also providing an outlet for people to articulate their concerns (Bradley, 2011). This chapter examines these issues through the use of a case study of the cheese rolling event in Brockworth on the outskirts of Gloucester, England. The chapter explores how local people reacted when, due to a variety of perceived problems with the event, a professional event management company was hired to become involved with the event.

## Events as a mechanism for preserving local culture, traditions and identity

Many communities produce a host of festivals and events that are distinctive to that area, and are targeted at local audiences for their social, fun or entertainment value (Bowdin *et al.*, 2011). The significance of these local events should not be understated because, as Derrett (2008: 107) notes, "the more one peels back the layers of interaction that occur within community festivals, the easier it is to appreciate how they nurture resilience through sharing the values, interests and traditions to the host community". These events, therefore, become an important part of how people relate to their local area, how local traditions are passed from one generation to the next and how the distinctiveness of an individual place is preserved.

Janiskee (1996) notes that some locally situated events have grown to become hallmark events, in that they become inextricably linked with a particular location, and attract a large number of visitors to a specific community. However, the influx of 'outsiders' during the time of certain events can cause tensions with local people who may perceive they are losing ownership of 'their' event. Traditionally, local events "are considered 'owned' by a community because they use volunteer services from the host community, employ public venues such as streets, parks and schools and are produced at the discretion of local government agencies or non-government agencies" (Janiskee, 1996: 404). From an event management perspective, however, there is a need for events to be planned and organised, and as an event grows in size and scale, there is an increasing need for professional event managers to be involved.

Events that are firmly rooted in local tradition(s) are often viewed as being in stark contrast to what Ferdinand and Kitchen (2012) refer to as 'placeless festivals', which are not associated with a particular place and are staged purely for commercial interests. Occasionally this involves transforming formerly meaningful celebrations into largely meaningless tourist spectacles (MacLeod, 2006). Van Aalst and Van Melik (2012) use the example of the North Sea Jazz Festival to demonstrate this 'placelessness', as the festival has recently been forced to move to another city. Their findings indicate that local governments often regard festivals as important urban showcases, although their survey data reveals that the direct links between the festival and the population of the new host city are weak. Events, therefore, can become 'placeless' (MacLeod, 2006), in that the location for the event becomes, simply, the arena in which the event takes place, rather than being symbolic of the event, local lore and traditions. Thus, according to Sharpley and Stone (2011: 355), "for local communities this may mean a loss of identity".

Sharpley and Stone (2011) conceptualise the difference between events that are firmly rooted in local tradition and identity(ies) and those that are designed to appeal to broader audiences as being on an internal-external axis. Internally, events can celebrate local culture, whilst externally events are used to promote or market a destination. There is, however, some overlap between these ideas as they both centre upon the concept of local distinctiveness and identity. Internally, events can enhance a sense of identity amongst local communities by celebrating something that is unique or distinctive to that community. Moreover, it is this distinctiveness that appeals to external audiences, as tourists continually seek authentic experiences (Wang, 1999). Event organisers are well aware of this and therefore events are increasingly designed, or redesigned, to appeal to a wide range of audiences as a means of generating income for the host area (Tyrell and Johnston, 2011).

One of the driving forces behind the transformation of previously locally significant events into something that can be marketed to a broader range of audiences is related to the increasing realisation, by a range of policy makers and

other stakeholders, that events can yield significant economic and tourism benefits for the host destination and community (Quinn, 2009). This, in turn, is
related to the concept of place competitiveness, where individual destinations
compete for tourist business by promoting their range of festivals and events to
national and international audiences. Ironically, though, whilst the promotion of
festivals and events is aimed to be a celebration of unique local cultures, the end
result is often a blurring of the distinction between places. Richards (2010)
claims that this lack of local distinctiveness in events is related to what he terms
'hyperfestivity', whereby every place, every organisation and every community
seems compelled to organise events, whether as a tool for social cohesion, a
means of generating economic impact, or boosting an external image.

## The media: presentation and consumption of local 'image' and 'identities'

The media, broadly defined as a communication medium that is designed to
inform or educate an audience (Katz, 2007), has many overlaps with event management. Amongst other things, the media has been responsible for revitalising
certain events and also re-engineering how events are organised and delivered
(Bladen *et al.*, 2012). Local media, such as local newspapers and radio, are
essential to how people receive information about the areas around them, and
can influence how people relate and connect to their local area. The media form
part of a complex cultural process in which meanings are produced and consumed (Avraham and First, 2006). Reality is constructed through shared, culturally specific, symbolic systems of visual and verbal communications, and the
media plays a fundamental role in the construction of this reality by selectively
providing knowledge about the lives, landscapes and cultures of different social
groups (Simon, 2005). Therefore, the media industry(ies) can be seen to be participating in a complex cultural process through which meanings are produced
and consumed (Burgess 1990).

Whilst much has been written about how national and international media
outlets construct images and identities for large-scale events in a particular location (Tajima, 2004; Falkheimer, 2007; Nylund, 2009), much less attention has
been paid to how smaller events are covered by local media sources, whose
readers will already be familiar with many local issues. However, the portrayal
of local identity through local media sources has real social importance. Thompson (1995: 35), for example, uses the concept of 'mediatisation' to explain how

> our sense of the groups and communities with which we share a common
> path through time and space, a common origin and a common fate, is
> altered, we feel ourselves to belong to groups and communities which are
> constituted in part through the media.

As such, local media outlets can be seen as one of the key ways that local identities are established, maintained, and, in some cases, challenged.

In the last decade, local media outlets, such as local daily newspapers, have come under increasing pressure to maintain their readership levels. This is due in large part to the fact that many people are increasingly turning to more instant forms of news. Consequently sales have seen a marked decline in terms of the number of printed copies of newspapers sold. For example, the ABC (Audit Bureau of Circulation) figures for the various local newspapers in the Gloucester area (where this research was based) for the period between July and December 2011 reveal that a reduction in sales of between 6.6 and 7.6 per cent took place in this period alone (Press Gazzette, 2012). One way in which local newspapers have sought to revive their fortunes is through the adoption of an online presence which allows them not only to report the news, but also allows local people to comment upon stories and issues that affect their daily lives. Newspapers such as *Cambridge News* and the *Sunderland Echo*, that have seen a decline in sales of 10 per cent, have also reported an increase in traffic of over 30 per cent to their website during the same period (Moss, 2012; Ponsford, 2012). Therefore, this produces an opportunity for people to openly discuss local issues, their connection to the local area and how meanings are constructed and interpreted.

## A brief introduction to cheese rolling in Gloucestershire

The cheese rolling event takes place on Cooper's Hill in Brockworth, which is approximately three miles south-east of the centre of Gloucester in the south-west of England. The event involves participants chasing a round disc of Double Gloucester cheese, which is released by the Master of Ceremonies, down a steep incline with a gradient ranging between 1:1 and 1:2 (for every one metre travelled horizontally the hill descends between one and two metres vertically). The aim is to be the first one to the bottom to claim the cheese. The cheeses used in the event weigh 7–8 lb (approximately 3.5 kg) and it is estimated that the cheese reaches speeds of 70 mph during its descent down the hill, taking around 12 seconds to reach the bottom (Kemp *et al.*, 2010). Due to the steepness of the descent, the race to the bottom of the hill is fraught with danger for the participants. It is virtually impossible to run down the hill. As such, participants usually lose their footing in the first few metres and are carried down the hill under their own momentum with limbs flailing in all directions. Injuries, mainly to racers, are not uncommon, with the highest number being recorded in 1997 when at least 33 people were injured (Kemp *et al.*, 2010). The race is repeated with a fresh set of participants several times during the day of the event, and special races are also organised for children that involve chasing sweets, but which do not include the perilous descent. The unusual nature of the event, coupled with the risk and element of danger it involves, makes it popular with spectators who crowd the edges of the hill to watch.

As with many events, the origins and early history of the annual cheese rolling event are unclear, but an event of this type has taken place in Gloucestershire for several centuries. Jefferies (2007) traces the history of cheese rolling races back to its first written record in the early 1800s. However, even in this first written record it is noted that it is already a well-established local tradition, and it is believed that the event may have evolved from activities associated with sun worship and other festivities on the site at the mid-summer festival (Jefferies, 2007). The event used to be held at midsummer, but at some undetermined point was moved to Whit Monday. Since 1967 the cheese rolling event has been held annually on the Monday of late Spring Bank Holiday.

The event has received significant attention across many forms of worldwide media, ranging across appearances on television shows such as Rory and Paddy's Great British Adventure (Channel 5, UK), Bert the Conqueror (Travel Channel, US and the UK), Pânico na TV (Panic on TV) (Rede TV, Brazil); references in a number of guide books to the UK, including both the *Lonely Planet* and *Rough Guide* to the UK; and also an iPhone app called 'Cooper's Hill'. Such media exposure has brought this local event to the attention of a worldwide audience which has, in turn, created some significant issues for the organisers. Perhaps the most significant of these is related to its scale of growth. Over the last two decases the audience for the event has grown from less than a thousand people in the 1990s to several thousand by the 2010s.

## Pressures to change the event and the proposed response

Following a 2009 police report that an estimated 15,000 people were trying to get to the event, it became clear that things would have to change, as current structures and procedures were not capable of accommodating such exponential growth. For instance, it is estimated that the hill can only accommodate about 5000 spectators (Kemp *et al.*, 2010). After 2009, the small group of volunteers who formed the organising committee was faced with various demands from the insurance company, police and local authorities. Amongst other things the insurance company required a 'defined area' for the attending public to validate any insurance; the local authority and police required a traffic and parking plan to control the number of vehicles arriving; and the local authorities had concerns over the increasing numbers of visitors, and their negative impact on the daily lives of residents.

The organising committee suggested a number of solutions to the situation. These included creating a 'defined, fenced area' which would control the number of people on the hill with designated entrances to enable attendee numbers to be controlled. For this to happen the event would have to become ticketed, a traffic plan involving road closures devised, and traffic control introduced to ease traffic flow in the surrounding area. Several meetings were held with a variety of stakeholder groups, including: the organising committee; local residents; and parish, town, city and county council representatives. Unfortunately, by the time these issues had come to light there was insufficient time to get agreement on the key issues and thus, in March 2010, the event was cancelled for that year. However, shortly after, a 'rebel cheese rolling' event was announced, and on 31 May 2010 five races were held which were witnessed by 300 spectators. This was in spite of Gloucestershire Constabulary's cordoning off of the event area and surrounding roads in an attempt to prevent access to the site.

Following the cancellation of the official cheese rolling event in 2010, the organising committee decided that a professional event management and marketing company should be consulted. In the main, they wanted these companies to manage the operational issues, raise sponsorship and explore other means of raising money to cover the increased costs that the event would incur. Proposals for the revised event were published in the local newspaper – the *Gloucester Echo* – in January 2011 (*Gloucester Echo*, 2011b). Proposals included suggestions that the event should be spread over a whole weekend, and that an opening ceremony be held on the Friday evening, with the traditional races being held on Saturday morning and afternoon, and again on Sunday. It was also decided that the numbers of people attending the event could only be controlled by making this a ticketed event with tickets only available in advance. It was proposed that the date of the event be changed from the Spring Bank Holiday weekend to Whitsun weekend in an attempt to reduce the costs of policing and any other manpower required. As the event would now be spread over an entire weekend, it was also proposed that facilities for overnight camping – much akin to a 'folk'-style festival – would be provided. This would include music, entertainment and other activities, which had not previously formed a part of the cheese rolling event. As such, these revised proposals represented a significant departure from the existing event, not only in terms of its timescale (one afternoon to three days), but also in its range of activities (one event to several events and associated entertainments) and costs (free to £20 for adults and £15 for children over the age of four).

These proposals were met with some negative feeling amongst the local residents. Residents' views were expressed publicly at Brockworth Parish Council meetings and through letters sent to the event's organising team (*Gloucester Echo*, 2011c). In late March 2011, plans for the revised event were withdrawn following alleged abuse and threats of physical violence to the event organisers. It was reported in the local press that members of the event management team

> have been spat at in the street, received verbal abuse in shops and at school gates. There has even been talk of bricks through windows and houses being burned down. We have also endured a torrent of online criticism and abuse from cowards who failed to identify themselves by hiding behind false identities.
>
> (*Gloucester Echo*, 2011a: 2)

Following the abandonment of the organised cheese rolling 'festival', local people held a second 'rebel cheese rolling' event on the second Bank Holiday Monday in May, organised by a handful of local people (*Gloucester Echo*, 2011d).

## Local reaction to the proposed changes: asserting local identity

In the period between the 2010 event being cancelled in March and the coverage of the 'rebel cheese rolling' event on 30 May 2011, the website operated by the local newspaper, the *Gloucester Echo*, produced 20 separate articles related to the cheese rolling event. These articles received 725 individual comments posted by respondents. These postings provide the research base for this chapter. As Du Gay *et al.* (1997) note, identity is closely tied to issues of production, consumption, regulation and representation. Therefore, exploring the issue of identity through the comments that users have left on a newspaper website offers an opportunity to explore how local people react to the consumption of mediated identities that are connected to issues of production, representation and regulation. Similarly, Sharpley and Stone (2011) note that there is a need to understand how identity is constructed through social constructs of place and to consider how events impact upon place identity from the perspective of local communities, amongst others, as this will reflect their cultural reality.

The use of online sources, such as online forums or blogs, as a research base is an area that has received significant methodological attention in the last five years (Jawecki and Fuller, 2008; Kozinets, 2009; Bowler and Gary, 2010; Holtz *et al.*, 2012; Prior and Miller, 2012; Im and Chee, 2013). Whilst there are issues that are specific to this area of research, such as the broad ethical issues in its use (Rodham and Gavin, 2006), issues surrounding informed consent of participants, and how 'public' users' comments are (Madge, 2007), the core issue of how to analyse the data is largely consistent with the techniques used in other qualitative enquiry. All comments have been anonymised and, in order to ensure clarity, it has been necessary to correct issues of spelling, grammar and punctuation in the original data. In saying this, the meaning(s) of comments have remained unaltered.

This analysis produced a number of distinct themes, which will be elucidated in the following sections: (1) constructions of local history and tradition; (2) tensions between economics and locally situated events; and (3) how local people intend to preserve the traditions and local connections with the event.

## Constructions of local histories and traditions

A recurring theme from the analysis was the event's connection with the 'local'. The idea of 'local' was largely understood in relation to the event's connection with local history, local traditions or local people. For example, it is noted that "It is an event which has been dreamed up and perpetuated by the people of Brockworth over a long period of time. None of the competitors have ever been paid for taking part and the tradition remained steadfastly local" (Comment 1, 2011). The historical roots of the event and its connection to local people were referred to in a number of postings. For example, "locals would make a day of it, having a few beers in a local pub for a bit of Dutch courage (and to raise the pain threshold) before hurling themselves down Coopers Hill" (Comment 2, 2011). Similarly, it was believed that "cheese rolling is very much a local tradition and as such belongs to the local people" (Comment 3, 2011) and that "it was something everybody local looked forward to and was a real nice day out" (Comment 4, 2011).

These comments firmly situate the event as being an important part of how people relate to their local area, its history and traditions and, as such, relate to Sharpley and Stone's (2011) ideas of an internal event that has deep meaning for local people. However, something that is lacking from the ideas of Sharpley and Stone (2011) and from Du Gay *et al.*'s (1997) conceptualisation of the relationship(s) between identity, consumption, representation, production and regulation, is that these ideas are essentially 'static'. In other words, they take no account of how people construct, reconstruct and communicate concepts of identity as events change from those that are internally focused to those that are designed to appeal to a broader range of external audiences. Moreover, there is a need to acknowledge the catalysts that can cause people to re-assess or re-assert local identities. In the case of cheese rolling, this catalyst appears to be economic in nature and has created a clear threat to local ownership and the event's connection to its locality and the local community's identities.

## Tensions between economics and locally situated events

It was the perception of many local people that the proposals for the revised cheese rolling event, including for example, the introduction of an entrance fee, were a mechanism to exploit 'their' event for economic gain. This also had clear implications for the connection that local people had to the event. For example, "turning this old Brockworth custom into a two-day festival of crass commercialism on a different date is a nonsense. It's tantamount to tearing the heart out of an old tradition" (Comment 5, 2011). The economic exploitation of the event is also seen as representing a fundamental shift in the nature of the event. For example, according to one respondent,

> the character of this "managed" event will be so far removed from the authentic local tradition that it won't even be worth visiting. Leave it alone for Cotswold residents to enjoy and stop trying to turn it into a media circus. There won't be anything left of the old traditions if we keep exploiting them for commercial gain.
>
> (Comment 6, 2011)

It is these perceived commercial gains that local people feared would lead to them losing a connection with the ('their') event. For example, it was expressed that "cheese rolling is part of this county's heritage and it is one more thing that is being lost". He/she went on to say that the organisers are trying to "turn this into another Glastonbury" (Comment 7, 2011). A cautionary note is sounded by another respondent who believed that the proposed alterations to the event would "change the tradition into something no longer meaningful, charge more than people can afford and alienate the local community" (Comment 8, 2011).

These comments reveal an engrained and deap-seated tension between local distinctiveness, how local people connect to events and the potential for events to have economic impacts. However, whilst these individual areas have all received significant attention from academics (MacLeod, 2006; Derrett, 2008;

Quinn, 2009; Van Aalst and Van Melik, 2012), the interrelationships between them are far less clear. Locally distinctive events are attractive to a range of audiences, but as more people become aware of these events they have a tendency to become 'sanitised', thereby losing their local distinctiveness and individuality. As such, the distinctiveness that people seek as part of the 'experience economy' (Morgan *et al.*, 2009; Kaplanidou and Vogt, 2010; Mehmetoglu and Engen, 2011) becomes lost and, moreover, the connection between local people and their local event becomes strained.

## Preserving tradition and local connections to the event

Suggestions for preserving traditions and local connections to cheese rolling were based around claims to maintain the event's 'true' or 'real' nature. For example, "the true spirit of our ancient tradition will survive through clandestine cheese rolling in the Spring holiday" (Comment 9, 2011). Similarly,

> who cares about the so-called organised event, it will be a huge flop as it is an ill-conceived, badly thought out, poor man's festival, based loosely on the age old tradition of the cheese rolling and a selection of borrowed medieval pastimes from other places. I will be focusing on the "real" cheese rolling on the last weekend of May.
>
> (Comment 10, 2011)

Following the collapse of the proposed cheese rolling 'festival' in 2011, local people have successfully managed to stage the event in 2011, 2012 and 2013, despite Gloucestershire Constabulary asking the maker of the cheese not to provide anything for the event (*Gloucester Echo*, 2013). The efforts to preserve a locally based event which is organised by and participated in by local people, despite a range of logistical issues, demonstrate how attached local people are to this event and reveal the extent of the bond that is possible between local people and local events.

## Conclusions

The case study of cheese rolling in Gloucestershire raises a number of salient issues for those interested in event management, local identities, and the role of the media in how people relate to and communicate ideas about their locality. Whilst events predate any concept of event management, it is clear that distinctive local events, such as cheese rolling, are an important part of how people relate to their local area, and how fiercely people are willing to defend these traditions and maintain their uniqueness. In this particular case, the event appears to be thoroughly embedded in local tradition(s) and lore(s); it has been run and managed *by* local people *for* local people for decades (even centuries), and this is seen as being fundamental to maintaining its sense of distinctiveness and connection with its locality. In this case study, the proposed changes to the event were seen as a direct challenge to the event's connection with the local area and local people. Many of the criticisms voiced by local people via local media centred around these proposed changes which, it was felt, would fundamentally change the event, and alter its local distinctiveness and meaning.

The case study highlights the importance of the local media as a communication mechanism about local issues, and how local identity can be both constructed and challenged via these media. It also highlights a shift in the way in which people can engage with local media sources. Whereas previously the consumption of local media has been a passive activity, with 'consumers' merely reading printed material, the economic challenges faced by this medium have seen local media sources create opportunities for people to be involved in the stories by having the ability to leave comments, and also to respond to comments left by others. This also provides an excellent source of information for researchers. Reaction to local issues and debates over their meanings and relevance, which may have previously been confined to private conversations between individuals, are now recorded on online databases, and are available for study and analysis.

Overall, what is clearly highlighted here is that distinctive events are very much a part of how people relate to place, and the identities that they construct for the places where they live and work. These identities, however, are neither static nor timebound; they are instead open to debate, discussion and, some would argue, transformation. There is, therefore, a need to revisit existing ideas of how local identities are produced and consumed through events (Du Gay *et al.*, 1997) so that these processes can be situated in a broader context of economic change and the increasing use of events as a key part of the experience economy (Holloway *et al.*, 2010). Moreover, the relationship between local people, local events, local identities and an increasingly diverse set of audiences that are constantly searching for things that are out of the ordinary, is deserving of further attention. This is exemplified in this chapter, as the case study shows how fiercely protective people can be of what they perceive to be 'their' event. Cheese rolling in Gloucester illustrates some of the ways in which local identities and local events are intimately connected – a relationship that becomes increasingly visible and important when traditional identities are perceived to be under threat. The atmosphere created at events is one of the key factors affecting the experience of attendees (Kaplanidou and Vogt, 2010) and this will no doubt be influenced by the attitude of local people to the event, and how engaged they are in its delivery. This makes the issues raised in this chapter of particular salience to event managers and related policy makers engaged in managing and delivering local and community-based events.

## References

Avraham, E. and First, A. (2006) Media, power and space: Ways of constructing the periphery as the "other". *Social and Cultural Geography*, 7(1): 71–86.

Bladen, C., Kennell, J., Abson, E. and Wilde, N. (2012) *Events management: An introduction.* London: Routledge.

Bowdin, G., Allen, J., O'Toole, W., Harris, R. and McDonnell, I. (2011) *Events management*, 3rd edition. Oxford: Butterworth-Heinemann.

Bowler, J. and Gary, J. (2010) Netnography: A method specifically designed to study cultures and communities online. *Qualitative Report*, 15(5): 1270–1275.

Bradley, A. and Hall, T. (2006) The festival phenomenon: Festivals, events and the promotion of small urban areas. In D. Bell and M. Jayne (eds) *Small cities: Urban experience beyond the metropolis.* London: Routledge, 77–89.

Bradley, A. (2011) The media coverage of events. In S. Page and J. Connell (eds) *The Routledge handbook of events.* London: Routledge, 289–303.

Burgess, J. (1990) The production and consumption of environmental meanings in the mass media: A research agenda for the 1990s. *Transactions of the Institute of British Geographers*, 15: 139–161.

De Bres, K. and Davis, J. (2001) Celebrating group and place identity: A case study of a new regional festival. *Tourism Geographies*, 3(3): 326–337.

Derrett, R. (2008) How festivals nurture resilience in regional communities. In J. Ali-Knight, M. Robertson, A. Fyall and A. Ladkin (eds) *International perspectives of festivals and events.* Oxford: Elsevier, 107–124.

Du Gay, P., Hall, S., Janes, L., Mackay, H. and Negus, K. (1997) *Doing cultural studies: The story of the Sony Walkman.* London: Sage.

Falkheimer, J. (2007) Events framed by the mass media: Media coverage and effects of America's Cup Preregatta in Sweden. *Event Management*, 11: 81–88.

Ferdinand, N. and Kitchen, P. (2012) *Events management: An international approach.* London: Sage.

*Gloucester Echo.* (2011a) Cheese rolling in Gloucestershire cancelled. Friday 25 March: 1.

*Gloucester Echo.* (2011b) Gloucestershire cheese rolling is back – but you'll have to buy a ticket. Friday 14 January: 1.

*Gloucester Echo.* (2011c) Cheese rolling bosses challenged by residents over boozing and camping. Friday 4 February: 3.

*Gloucester Echo.* (2011d) Rebel rollers chase cheese. Monday 30 May: 3.

*Gloucester Echo.* (2013) Cheese rolling gran in police Double Gloucester ban. Thursday 23 May: 2.

Holloway, I., Brown, L. and Shipway, R. (2010) Meaning not measurement: Using ethnography to bring a deeper understanding to the participant experience of festivals and events. *International Journal of Event and Festival Management*, 1(1): 74–85.

Holtz, P., Kronberger, N. and Wagner, W. (2012) Analyzing internet forums: A practical guide. *Journal of Media Psychology: Theories, Methods, and Applications*, 24(2): 55–66.

Im, E. and Chee, W. (2012) Practical guidelines for qualitative research using online forums. *Computers, Informatics, Nursing*, 30(11): 604–611.

Janiskee, R. (1996) Historic houses and special events. *Annals of Tourism Research*, 23(2): 398–414.

Jawecki, G. and Fuller, J. (2008) How to use the innovative potential of online communities? Netnography – an unobtrusive research method to absorb the knowledge and creativity of online communities. *International Journal of Business Process Integration and Management*, 3(4): 248–255.

Jefferies, J. (2007) *Cheese rolling in Gloucestershire.* Stroud: Tempus.

Kaplanidou, K. and Vogt, C. (2010) The meaning and measurement of a sport event experience among active sport tourists. *Journal of Sport Management*, 24(5): 544–566.

Katz, H. (2007) *The media handbook: A complete guide to advertising media selection, planning, research, and buying*, 3rd edition. New York: Lawrence Erlbaum Associates.

Kemp, C., Moore, T. and Mellor, P. (2010) *A review of the management of crowd safety at outdoor street/special events.* Norwich: HSE Books.

Kozinets, R.V. (2009) *Netnography: Doing ethnographic research online*. London: Sage.

Macleod, N.E. (2006) The placeless festival: Identity and place in the post-modern festival. In D. Picard and M. Robinson (eds) *Festivals, tourism and social change: Remaking worlds*. Clevedon: Channel View Publications, 222–237.

Madge, C. (2007) Developing a geographers' agenda for online research ethics. *Progress in Human Geography*, 31(5): 654–674.

Mehmetoglu, M. and Engen, M. (2011) Pine and Gilmore's concept of experience economy and its dimensions: An empirical examination in tourism. *Journal of Quality Assurance in Hospitality and Tourism*, 12(4): 237–255.

Morgan, M., Elbe, J. and de Esteban Curiel, J. (2009) Has the experience economy arrived? The views of destination managers in three visitor-dependent areas. *International Journal of Tourism Research*, 11(2): 201–216.

Moss, R. (2012) *Can local newspapers survive in the digital age?* [Online] Available from www.bbc.co.uk/news/uk-england-18032555 [accessed 17 April 2013].

Nylund, M. (2009) Mega sporting events and the media in attention economies: National and international press coverage of the IAAF world championships in Helsinki 2005. *Nordicom Review*, 30(2): 125–140.

Ponsford, D. (2012) *Strong year-on-year growth for most local press websites*. [Online] Available from www.pressgazette.co.uk/node/48862 [accessed 19 September 2013].

Press Gazette (2012) *Regional ABCs: Full breakdown for all titles*. [Online] Available from www.pressgazette.co.uk/node/48861 [accessed 18 April 2013].

Prior, D.D. and Miller, L.M. (2012) Webethnography: Towards a typology for quality in research design. *International Journal of Market Research*, 54(4): 503–520.

Quinn, B. (2009) Festivals, events and tourism. In T. Jamal and M. Robinson (eds) *The Sage handbook of tourism studies*. London: Sage, 483–503.

Richards, G. (2010) *Leisure in the network society: From pseudo events to hyperfestivity*. Inaugural address given at the public acceptance of the appointment of Professor in Leisure Studies at Tilburg University, 8 October. [Online] Available from http://academia.edu/1271795/Leisure_in_the_Network_Society [accessed 2 July 2013].

Rodham, K. and Gavin, J. (2006) The ethics of using the internet to collect qualitative research data. *Research Ethics Review*, 2(3): 92–97.

Sharpley, R. and Stone, P.R. (2011) Socio-cultural impacts of events: Meanings, authorized transgression, and social capital. In S. Page and J. Connell (eds) *The Routledge handbook of events*. London: Routledge, 347–361.

Simon, C. (2005) Commodification of regional identities: The "selling" of Waterland. In G.J. Ashworth and B. Graham (eds) *Senses of place: Senses of time*. Ashgate: London, 31–45.

Tajima, A. (2004) "Amoral universalism": Mediating and staging global and local in the 1998 Nagano Olympic Winter Games. *Critical Studies in Media Communication*, 21(3): 241–260.

Thompson, J. (1995). *The media and modernity: A social theory of the media*. Cambridge: Polity Press.

Tyrell, T.J. and Johnston, R.J. (2011) A spatial extension to a framework for assessing direct economic impacts of tourist events. In S. Page and J. Connell (eds) *The Routledge handbook of events*. London: Routledge, 329–346.

Van Aalst, I. and Van Melik, R. (2012) City festivals and urban development: Does place matter? *European Urban and Regional Studies*, 19(2): 195–206.

Wang, N. (1999) Rethinking authenticity in tourism experiences. *Annals of Tourism Research*, 30(1): 194–215.

# Part IV

# Mega-events

# 12 Sports mega-events and Islam

## An introduction

*Karl Russell, Noëlle O'Connor, Katherine Dashper
and Thomas Fletcher*

## Introduction

Events are embedded within the socio-cultural milieus of their host communities (Ferdinand and Shaw, 2012; Getz, 2012). Many of the world's international sporting events, staged since the Second World War, have predominantly emerged and been hosted within Europe, North America, Japan and Australia. This is, in part, due to the success and growth within these post-war nations' economies. These regions of the world, collectively known as the "developed" or "western" world, have largely adopted or have acknowledged Christianity as their main religion. As such their societies have developed a series of value systems which are based upon Christian-led beliefs witnessed in the worship of Jesus Christ, the adherence of Sunday as a day of worship, modest dress codes, traditional gender roles in both domestic and working situations, and the acknowledgment of Christian significant religious dates and holidays (Weber, 1992). International sports governing bodies for the majority of "major" sports, such as football, rugby and tennis, were founded in western states and so were also loosely based around Christian values. As Gupta (2009: 1779) argues: "Because western nations were the founder members of most international sporting associations they dominated these bodies and set the rules for a sport, dominated its finances, and determined the location of major international events". However, recent global changes, such as shifting economic power, have seen a trend towards many "emerging" regions outside of the western world hosting, and/or actively seeking to host, international sporting events.

One such emerging region is the Middle East which is largely composed of Islamic countries. It is the geographical home to economically powerful nations such as the Kingdom of Saudi Arabia (KSA, a member of the G20), United Arab Emirates (UAE), Qatar and Bahrain, where

> wealth, economic growth and diversification, based on the sale of natural resources such as oil and liquefied gas that "continue to drive the Gulf Economy" (O'Sullivan, 2008: p. 1) has seen their global profiles raised dramatically in terms of their political, economic and socio-cultural influence.
>
> (Russell and O'Connor, 2013: 206)

Today the region plays host to many international sporting events, such as Formula One motor racing staged in Bahrain and Abu Dhabi, international golfing and tennis events staged in Qatar and Dubai, and international cycling road racing staged in Oman. A review of the current literature has focused on examining the economic suitability of Islamic countries in relation to hosting international sporting events (Scharenberg, 1999; Randeree, 2011). However, to date, little attention has been given to examining the socio-cultural beliefs and values within Islam – many of which are fundamental to everyday life within non-secular Islamic countries – and the challenges these may present (to both the host nation and the event) when an international sporting event is staged in a non-secular Islamic country.

In this chapter we begin to consider some of the complexities of hosting major international sporting events in non-secular Islamic countries. We begin by considering the historical relationship between religion and sporting events. We then go on to identify emerging sports events markets, focusing particularly on the Middle East, and consider various ways in which event managers need to be culturally sensitive to the teachings and practices of Islam when staging major sports events in non-secular Islamic countries. We suggest that, due to the imperatives of global sport and the need to attract new audiences and investors, there is a need to expand sporting events into hitherto uncharted territories. This will require a reconsideration of many of the hegemonic ideological assumptions around which international sports events are currently conceptualised. As Maguire (1999) has long argued, the globalisation of sport has led to the domination of the west over non-western countries. However, recent tendencies to award the hosting of major international sports events to non-western nations suggests that the tide is now turning. Therefore, this chapter is a timely introduction to some of the issues and complexities associated with hosting major international sports events outside of the traditional power block of the western world.

## Religion and sporting events

The popularity of modern-day large-scale international sporting events can be traced back to the inter-war period after the First World War (Riordan and Kruger, 1999). During this period (within Europe and the USA) public interest in sport increased, resulting in growth in the popularity and prominence of sporting tournaments. This period also witnessed the expansion of sport as a commercialised product, leading to greater participation and more sporting competitions, as well as growth in the number of international sporting tournaments. This era became known as the period of the "universalisation of sport" (Riordan and Kruger, 1999). As sport and sports events became more popular and prominent, divisions along the lines of class, gender, "race" and – importantly for our discussion here – religion, became increasingly apparent.

The contemporary events literature is dominated by examples of international sporting events staged within the developed (western) world (Riordan and Kruger, 1999; Pfister, 2000; Getz, 2008; Randeree, 2011). A contributing factor towards this relates to the Cold War era when the capitalist west and the communist states of the east used sport, sporting events and sporting victories to emphasise their political ideologies, social dominance and religious right; a propaganda campaign which the west arguably won (Wagg and Andrews, 2006). This politicisation of sport placed it at the top of political and economic agendas (Riordan and Kruger, 1999). During the post-Second World War period, sport and sporting events became increasingly commercialised throughout the western world. Historical accounts of the emergence and development of modern sport and sporting events are strongly rooted in western societies and cultures (e.g. Holt, 1990). As such, the emergence and initial development of international sporting events took place within capitalist states based (sometimes loosely) on Christian ethics and beliefs. It is within this context that popular sport first took shape and developed (Riordan and Kruger, 1999; Scharenberg, 1999). This context shaped the development of sport and sporting events in a number of ways, including: the observance of Sunday as the day of worship and rest throughout most of the twentieth century; the avoidance of Christian dates of celebration, such as Christmas and Easter, within the sporting calendar; and widespread sex-segregation in the organisation of most sporting activities and competitions to reflect western Christian value systems related to traditional gender roles and expectations (Pfister, 2010a, 2010b).

Over the last 100 years the centrality of the Christian church to many western states has diminished, resulting in a number of social changes that have impacted on sport and sports events. The sanctity of Sunday as a day of worship and rest has been called into question, and sporting events are now regularly scheduled on Sundays and close to Christian religious holidays. For example, Formula One, tennis (e.g. the French Open, Wimbledon), FIFA World Cup games, Olympic and Paralympic events, may all take place on Sunday, the traditional Christian day of worship. The role of women in society at large and sport in particular has changed dramatically and, although still lagging far behind that of male sports and athletes, this has resulted in increased female sporting participation and increased visibility and celebration of female athletes (Pfister, 2010a; Dashper, 2012). In addition there has been an increase in sports and sporting governing bodies making rules that ban participants from performing any acts related to "shows of faith" or secularism (Amara, 2012).

All of these changes have contributed to increases in sports participation and attraction of global media audiences. International sporting events have become increasingly commercialised, and (predominantly) western sponsors now use these events to target global audiences. The Olympic Games and FIFA World Cup global sponsors, for example, include companies such as Adidas, Coca Cola, McDonalds, Visa and Kodak, all of which are major western companies. However, recent "shifts" in the world's economic power bases are arguably changing this status quo. The rising prominence of India in sports such as cricket are a prime example of this (see Gupta, 2004; Rumford, 2007).

## Emerging markets and international sporting events

Major international sports events have been staged in non-Western countries for some time, for example: Tokyo Olympics, 1964; Mexico Olympics, 1968; Seoul Olympics, 1988; FIFA World Cup in Uruguay 1930, Brazil, 1950, Mexico 1986, Japan/South Korea, 2002, and South Africa, 2010. However, for many, the Beijing Olympics set in motion a new social and political agenda for considering the role of non-Western nations on the major international sports events circuit (Palmer, 2013: 114). Russell and O'Connor (2013) suggest that Beijing 2008 can be regarded as a major turning point in Olympic history. To iterate this they identify how the Games attracted over 10,000 athletes and millions of 'cultural sports tourists' in person, in addition to billions via many media sources. Moreover, an estimated 4.3 billion people (63 per cent of the world's population) in 220 territories are thought to have viewed the event (Russell and O'Connor, 2013: 207). They also argue that the "success" of Beijing has encouraged other "Eastern" nations/cities to announce to the International Olympic Committee (IOC) their credentials, willingness and readiness to "bid" to be host cities for future Olympics.

Indeed, emerging nations from Asia, South America and the Middle East are now actively seeking, and are being courted by event owners and organisers, to be potential future hosts and venues for all types of international sporting events, many of which attract global media audiences. Countries such as China (Beijing Olympics and Paralympics, 2008; Shanghai Diamond League (track and field, annual), India (Commonwealth Games 2010), Bahrain (Formula One, annual) and Russia (UEFA Champions League Final, 2010) have all recently staged major sporting events. Brazil will also host future mega sporting events, with the FIFA World Cup in 2014 and the Olympic and Paralympic Games in 2016 being staged there.

While the debate is ongoing as to what benefit the staging or hosting of an international sporting event can actually bring to a country or a city, especially one in the "emerging" world, it is clear that in playing host to such sporting events, countries and cities are seeking to elevate their global image (Matheson, 2006; Rein and Shields, 2006; Konrad-Adenauer-Stiftung, 2011). Cornelissen (2012: 78), argues that sporting events are increasingly "seen as opportunities to project or 'show-case' [a country's] achieved levels of modernity to the outside world". Referring specifically to the Global South, Darnell (2012: 105) argues that "sports mega-events ... are used to showcase successful development, particularly for states struggling for legitimacy within competitive globalisation".

This global shift in the hosting of international sporting events outside of the West is set to continue. Bang (2011: 1) suggests that "the biggest events are leaving Europe and North America". Evidence of this dramatic shift can be provided by the Danish Institute for Sports Studies Research, which demonstrates that only 23 per cent of major international events, such as the Olympic and Paralympic Games and world championship tournaments in football, athletics and swimming, will be held within Western countries after 2010. The remaining 77 per cent of these events will be held within countries from the Middle East, Asia, Africa (south of the Sahara Desert) and Central/South America (Bang, 2011).

This shifting pattern can be conceptualised through the idea of "post-Westernisation" (Rumford, 2007). For Rumford this shift is not simply about the decreasing salience of the idea of the West as a reference point for political identification and global leadership, rather, it can be characterised through a series of processes. First, he suggests that post-Westernisation signals the increasing "lack of unity within those countries formerly considered to have a common 'Western' world view" (Rumford, 2007: 205). Second, post-Westernisation signifies the co-existence of multiple "modernities" – Western, post-communist, Islamic – as opposed to an assumed dominance of the West over the rest. Finally, post-Westernisation involves recognition of a "new East" capable of "shaping global affairs previously seen as the preserve of the West" (Rumford, 2007: 206). For example, cricket has witnessed a shift in decision-making power from the West – England in particular – to non-Western former peripheries of the game, principally India. It is our contention here that power shifts within global sport are becoming increasingly visible, which necessitates further consideration and exploration of potential issues arising when events are staged in these regions.

## Middle Eastern countries and international sporting events

Some Islamic states are actively pursuing opportunities to host international sports events. Today, Bahrain, United Arab Emirates (UAE), Oman, Qatar and Iran are proving to be attractive hosts for staging a range of international sporting events. The financial case can be easily made for staging an international sporting event within economically wealthy Islamic countries such as Bahrain, Kingdom of Saudi Arabia (KSA), Qatar and the UAE (Randeree, 2011). However, socio-cultural factors are also important to the success (or otherwise) of international sporting events, and have not hitherto been examined in this context. Arzt (1996: 140) notes that the above-mentioned Middle Eastern states have officially proclaimed Islam to be the state religion. Therefore, the value systems and everyday lives of citizens within these countries are influenced by Islamic values and beliefs, and not by Christianity. The beliefs and values of Islam, which are reflected in the social and cultural practices of Islamic nations, differ in many respects from the Christian-influenced social and cultural environments of Western nations which have traditionally staged international sporting events. Thus, as we argue in this chapter, staging international sporting events in different social and cultural contexts, such as those offered by non-secular Islamic states, may expose conflicts between the Christian-based ethics and values that underpin the ethos of those events, and the Islamic values of host nations.

Some of the social and cultural challenges of hosting international sporting events within non-secular Islamic countries are already coming to the fore and receiving attention within the general media. Recent examples of this are: negative coverage of issues surrounding the availability of alcohol during the Qatar

2022 FIFA World Cup (Wilson, 2010); the use of rose water and not traditional champagne at the celebration of the winners of the Bahrain Grand Prix; the use of inappropriate language by Formula One drivers at the end of the 2013 Abu Dhabi Grand Prix (Duncan, 2012); the participation of female Muslims and the mixing of men and women at international sporting events (Scharenberg, 1999; Pfister, 2000; Pfister, 2010b). On all of these issues there appears to be something of a West-East dichotomy. Many of these examples are, effectively, "non-issues" in the West, but require a certain amount of cultural sensitivity when events take place outside of western contexts. Writing specifically about mega-events in BRIC countries, Palmer (2013: 114–115) argues that research is only now "registering the social, symbolic, political and policy import of these 'other' events in 'other' countries". In the next section we begin to consider some of the key elements of Islam that event managers should consider when staging major international sporting events in non-secular Islamic countries.

## The socio-cultural implications of hosting international sporting events within non-secular Islamic countries

Middle Eastern countries such as Bahrain, Iran, KSA, Oman, Qatar and the UAE are all non-secular Islamic states. Islamic beliefs and values are regarded as a way of life for practicing Muslims. As stated, most international sporting events have evolved from within the Western world, where athletic dress codes are quite relaxed, dietary rules provide for all, alcohol is often served and men and women regularly interact in public. In addition, many of these sporting events observe the Gregorian calendar and are loosely structured around Christian holidays and celebration. Therefore, when these sporting events are hosted by non-secular Islamic countries, it may be that a process of social and cultural understanding and evolution is required to preserve the integrity of the host country and the appeal of the sporting event to both existing Western markets and new markets from within the Islamic world. The question needs to be posed: what potential issues could arise when international sporting events are staged within non-secular Islamic countries? To examine this issue more closely, a brief examination of certain Islamic beliefs and values is required as a basis for understanding what adaptations (if any) may be needed for the hosting and staging of international sporting events within non-secular Islamic countries.

The religious life of Muslims is based on adherence to the Five Pillars of Islam. These are considered to represent the obligations and responsibilities of all Muslims towards God (Allah) and also towards their fellow men. Adherence to the Five Pillars of Islam should be at the forefront of a Muslim's thoughts and actions at all times. The Five Pillars of Islam are:

1   Shahadah (declaration of faith)
2   Salah (daily prayers)
3   Saum (fasting during the lunar month of Ramadan and on other important Islamic dates)

4   Hajj (the pilgrimage to Makkah)
5   Zakah (a share of one's surplus wealth given to those in need of it) (Uddin, 1991).

In accordance with these Five Pillars, Muslims should also adopt a set of beliefs, values and principles in accordance with the teaching of the Qur'an. While many Islamic religious beliefs, values and principles are related to personal (and private) life, some apply to the behaviour of Muslims in public life. Islamic religious beliefs, values and principles that have relevance to international sporting events include (though are not restricted to): gender segregation, dress codes and female modesty, and dietary rules.

It is the combination of three of the Five Pillars – (1) Shahadah, (2) Salah, (3) Saum – and the three Islamic cultural beliefs and values related to gender segregation, dress code and dietary rules, that present particular challenges when international sporting events are hosted and staged within non-secular Islamic countries. Space does not allow for an exhaustive appraisal of the intricacies of Islam and its teachings, and we acknowledge that our discussion is only preliminary and that there is much more research to do on this topic. However, our aim here is to signpost some key areas for future research, and so our analysis is necessarily succinct.

### Shahadah (declaration of faith)

The first of the Five Pillars is the profession of faith, or Shahadah, which is a testimony demonstrated through prayer, to the belief that there is no God other than Allah, and Muhammad (peace be upon him) is the messenger or prophet of Allah (Uddin, 1991; Hattstein, 2006).

### Salah (daily prayers)

The second Pillar is traditionally regarded as prayer (Salah) to be performed five times a day. These prayers are to take place at prescribed times: (1) before sunrise (Fajr); (2) after the sun has passed its zenith or highest point at noon (Zuhr); (3) after mid-afternoon (Asr); (4) after sunset (Maghrib); and (5) after the onset of night (Isha). The community is summoned to prayer by the Muezzin, who calls from the minaret of the mosque. Prior to prayer, the worshippers must perform a series of ritual ablutions called "Wudu", the purpose of which is to prepare the worshipper to approach God in a state of external and internal purity (Hattstein, 2006). Prayer can be performed by Muslims wherever they happen to be at the time. However, crucially, wherever they are in the world, a Muslim must face Makkah – the spiritual home of Islam – and the prayers involve both body and mind in a series of bows and prostrations that are performed together with recitations of the Qur'an and praises to Allah. The Friday midday prayer – Friday is the Islamic Holy day of the week – is regarded as the most important prayer time.

## Saum (fasting during the lunar month of Ramadan and other important Islamic dates)

The ritual of fasting (Saum) is the third Pillar. Fasting is to be observed by Muslims during the Islamic month of Ramadan. This is a lunar month and is the ninth month of the year. During the month of Ramadan Muslims must fast from sunrise until sunset (Uddin, 1991). This fast is an abstinence from eating, drinking, consumption of tobacco, and having sexual relations (Hattstein, 2006). However, certain groups are exempt from fasting, including, for example, the sick, pregnant women, and those who undertake heavy labour, as well as Muslims who have travelled or are travelling. The Islamic calendar and its important dates differ from the Gregorian calendar of Western societies and countries. Key dates and holidays are related to such occasions as Ramadan, Hajj, Eid and the Islamic New Year, all of which are lunar events, and so do not fall on the same dates of the Gregorian calendar each year.

In addition to the three aforementioned Pillars, we have decided to focus on three key issues influenced by Islamic values and beliefs. We acknowledge that there are many more important aspects of Islam, but due to space constraints we have limited our discussion to three issues that have most relevance to sports events.

### Gender segregation

Islam holds that men and women are equal in the sight of God (Badawi, 2011). Some forms of Islam require men and women to maintain their own social groups and gatherings, segregated by gender (Bleher, 2009). Within Islam, in accordance with Sharia Law, the head of the household (the husband) decides on all major issues pertinent to the family. His duty as head of the family extends to economically maintaining his wife or wives and, in return, his wife or wives are committed to obedience (Pfister, 2010b). One of the main points regulated through female deference to the male head of the household is the regulation of sexuality, which is controlled by gender segregation. The degree of segregation may differ between different Muslim societies and countries, and their interpretation of the Qur'an (Russell and O'Connor, 2013). In some interpretations this can prevent women from having any contact with males from outside of the family. The head of the household can also determine what the other members are allowed and not allowed to do outside of the home. This can include sporting participation or being a spectator at sporting events. Sport has long been a masculine-dominated institution and many women have struggled for greater female sporting participation, inclusion and recognition (Hargreaves, 1994). Whilst many people celebrate the gains made by female sports and athletes, for some Muslim women sport can be an unappealing environment that conflicts with religious, cultural and social preferences for female modesty and gender segregation (Zamin, 1997; see also Chapter 9 in this volume).

*Dress code and female modesty*

The London 2012 Olympic Games witnessed for the first time participation of female Muslim athletes from Qatar, Saudi Arabia and Brunei. Their participation illuminated a number of underlying tensions between the IOC (and other sporting bodies) who promote mass participation, and 'home' politics, which had, even in the run up to the Games, actively discouraged participation of females in sport. There is a growing body of literature on Muslim women's experiences of and participation in sport (Hargreaves, 2007; Kay, 2007). This has focused on the following areas: religion; patriarchy and male power; and veiling and the body. Islam advocates that women and girls should adopt a modest dress code when seen in public and to maintain this they may have to cover their bodies, something that works to guarantee gender differences and social hierarchies (Pickthall, 2011). The extent to which female modesty is regulated through dress is a complex issue and beyond the scope of this chapter. However, issues to do with dress code and female modesty may have implications for staging international sports events in non-secular Islamic countries in the following ways: clothing of female athletes; mixing of male and female athletes; spectators – dress and segregated viewing areas; and media images and sponsorship messages associated with the event.

*Dietary rules (food and alcohol consumption)*

Islamic religious beliefs and values related to food and drink dictate what food can be lawfully consumed by Muslims (Bachok *et al.*, 2012). Referring to readings from the Qur'an, Pickthall (2011: 64) states, "Forbidden to (for food) are carrion and blood and swineflesh, and that which has been dedicated to any other than Allah". Muslims will only eat meat where the blood of the animal has been allowed to drain fully from the animal's body (Bleher, 2009). This is known as the Zabiha (halal) method, where the food has been prepared, stored, manufactured, slaughtered and served in a manner prescribed by Sharia Law. Islam also forbids the consumption of anything which might interfere with the perception of the senses or blurring of judgment, like alcohol or mind altering drugs (Bleher, 2009; Bachok *et al.*, 2012). Some more liberal Muslim countries adopt a more relaxed approach to the sale and consumption of alcohol, while in other non-secular Muslim countries like the KSA and Iran it is illegal to possess and to consume alcohol, both by Muslims and non-Muslims.

## Discussion

International sporting events cost millions – and in some cases billions – of pounds to host and stage (Horne and Whannel, 2012). The global economic crisis which started in 2008, and the resulting lack of financial liquidity in much of the Western world, means that Western governments are finding it increasingly hard to justify the spend needed to host and stage major international sporting events.

The recent world global shift in political influence and economic power, and a greater tolerance towards socio-cultural differences, has created a situation where many emerging nations are regarded as financially lucrative potential host cities for international sporting events. Islamic countries such as KSA, Qatar, Bahrain, and the UAE are economically wealthy and have the financial liquidity to stage major international sporting events. According to Russell and O'Connor (2013: 209):

> The financial liquidity available to the emerging countries of the Middle East and East Asia have put these nations, with their mainly Muslim populations, at the forefront of those seeking to stage mega-events, becoming active participants within such events and the opening of new media audiences and markets that have often been untapped.

This has brought into focus a number of potential social, cultural and political challenges and issues associated with non-secular Islamic nations staging major international sporting events.

Many international sporting events, such as those associated with international tennis, athletics, golf, cycling and Formula One, are currently being staged in Qatar, UAE and Bahrain. Most recently, the economic and financial strength of many non-secular Islamic countries has led to the decision to award the FIFA 2022 World Cup to Qatar. This will be the first time that a mega sporting event will be hosted and staged within a non-secular Islamic state. Mindful of this fact, international sporting events may well need to take into account and, in some cases, adapt, elements of the event as a result of some significant issues related to the Islamic world's beliefs and values, as outlined in this chapter. These include: Shahadah (declaration of faith), Salah (daily prayers), Saum (fasting), gender segregation, dress codes and dietary rules. We will now spend some time unpacking each of these.

Today it is common-place for athletes, especially successful ones, to demonstrate signs of their religious faith and beliefs in public. Lionel Messi, when he scores a goal, points towards the sky and offers a prayer in a religious gesture. Mohammed Farrar is often witnessed going to his knees after a race victory to give praise, and Usain Bolt is often seen after a race victory pointing to the sky and mouthing the words 'Thank you God'. Other actions by sports participants include: athletes touching the ground, followed by crossing themselves; pointing to the sky; and openly praying.

In many sports, such as football and judo, shows of religious faith and the wearing of garments determined by religion (such as the headscarf or hijab) are banned (Ferris-Lay, 2012). However, pressure from many quarters has forced some sporting federations to re-visit their rules and regulations. The International Judo Federation (IJF) is one organisation that has recently made changes to its policies. In this instance, the Federation revised its policy towards the Muslim headscarf to allow Saudi Arabian female Judo competitor, Wojdan Ali Seraj Abdulrahim Shaherkanim, to wear one of an approved design during competition at the London 2012 Olympic Games. Originally, the IJF had banned the headscarf on the basis of athlete safety, despite the fact that the Asian Judo Federation has previously allowed Muslim women to wear the headscarf during major competitions (Magnay, 2012). However, such revisions are not necessarily welcomed by all. Some sports bodies have suggested, for instance, that sporting attire, designed to maintain the modesty of female Muslim athletes, may in fact give a competitor an unfair advantage over their rivals. This was the case when Muslim female swimmers began to wear a full body suit, which the swimming federations subsequently banned (Pfister, 2000). These decisions can have significant consequences. FIFA's decision to ban the hijab in 2007 led to the Saudi Arabian women's football team missing out on qualification rounds for the 2012 Olympic Games. Notably, FIFA have changed this rule and now allow female players to wear approved hijabs, although this was too late for the Saudi women's team (Reuters, 2012). As a result, pressure is mounting from both the athletes themselves and concerned governing bodies for rule changes to allow for such garments to be worn in other competitions to preserve the modesty of Muslim females in accordance with their religious beliefs and values.

Certain international sporting events may also offend some Muslims, and it would be deemed culturally unsuitable not only to take part in, but also to watch those events. Here we are referring specifically to the attire of athletes within those sports. Examples of such sports are female beach volleyball, female tennis and female swimming events, which may, due to the dress codes often associated with the sports and worn by athletes taking part in these events, expose certain parts of the body that may cause offence to Muslim viewers. It is not unreasonable to assume that Muslims would boycott such events if they took place in non-secular Islamic countries, thereby discrediting these events, and creating an uneasy atmosphere for athletes and spectators

In respect of the Islamic call to daily prayers, event organisers have to ensure mosques or multi-faith prayer rooms are available for worship. This will allow Muslim athletes the opportunity to join communally to conduct their five daily prayers while taking part in the event itself. However, the call for prayer need not hold up an event. The call does not mean athletes have to pray at that particular moment, as long as they manage to find a time to pray before the next call to prayer goes out. Sports event organisers would thus need to ensure that competition programmes were organised in such a way that allows Muslim competitors sufficient time for prayer, in addition to their sporting activities.

International sporting events that conform to the Gregorian calendar may have to be re-scheduled in accordance with the Islamic calendar and important Islamic dates. This is not necessarily a simple task because many of these 'important' dates are dependent upon the sighting of the moon and are therefore not fixed dates from one year to the next. In addition, important Islamic dates related to holidays, birth celebrations and New Year all differ from the calendar used in the West and could present logistical problems if sports event organisers are not aware of them. The practice of Ramadan is a case in point. Ramadan is a traditional period for fasting and any attempt to host an international sporting event during this holy Islamic month may meet with some resistance. This considera-tion is particularly relevant for non-secular Islamic states, as hosting during this time could be interpreted as a clear disregard of important Islamic dates that are to be respected as holy and as times for religious reflection and practice. Mindful of this, members of the sports and the sports events industry(ies) need to become acquainted with Islamic beliefs and values, and must reflect (and encourage others to reflect) critically on the challenges these present.

As numbers of Muslim female athletes and female spectators are growing, some other aspects of international sporting events may prove problematic. Gender segregation in terms of sport, accommodation, eating areas and within spectating and socialising areas may have to be tolerated and implemented, in accordance with the teachings of Islam. Practically this would require separate areas for females and males, and family areas being implemented in respect of some of the beliefs and values of Islam. Attempts to force gender integration at sports events within non-secular Islamic states could create tensions and fric-tions, and could be considered offensive and a clear breach of Islamic teaching and practices. This could result in (Muslim) females playing no part in the sport-ing event.

In the history of the Western world, modern sports cultures, leisure and alcohol have been intimately linked (Fletcher and Spracklen, 2013). Some sports, namely football, rugby and cricket, are closely associated with alcohol, both in terms of their leisure culture and sponsorship. In Western countries, where alcohol is per-missible by law and tradition, and a part of popular culture, the consumption of alcohol is seen as crucial to human interaction and sociality (Fletcher and Sprack-len, 2013). Indeed, the drinking of alcohol is a key leisure ritual and in sport, as in any other part of leisure where sociality is important, drinking and buying drinks is an accepted part of the subcultural practice. It is common, for example, for spectators to consume alcohol (often to excess) within grounds and stadia where events are staged (Collins and Vamplew, 2002). However, this ritual is not, and cannot, be enjoyed by all. Within non-secular Islamic countries where alcohol is not tolerated this culture of drinking may present conflicts between spectators in and outside the venues and, in some cases, with sponsors, such as Budweiser which has traditionally used sports events like the FIFA World Cup to showcase its products. The lack of availability and tolerance of alcohol in non-secular Islamic countries is an important issue to consider in that it may discourage some (Western) fans from travelling to an Islamic country to actually attend the event. Moreover, there is evidence of Western travellers getting into difficulty – some have been heavily fined and even jailed – for consuming alcohol in non-designated areas (dba, n.d). Some Islamic countries have relaxed their policies towards alcohol consumption. For example, some have established designated areas to allow non-Muslims to enjoy alcohol in public places – events, for example – and in some international hotels. However, general public consump-tion, i.e. in the streets or outside licenced designated bars, will likely not be encouraged, and would result in trouble for Western travellers not necessarily accustomed to local cultural expectations (Widen, 2013).

This debate is timely given the current discussions about the legitimacy of Qatar as host for the 2022 FIFA World Cup (alongside concerns for the staging of the event during the Qatar summer months). While various forms of non-alcoholic products can be used, consumed and promoted, event organisers face challenges from a number of places over how to deal with the questions of alcohol consumption and alcohol sponsors when staging international sporting events in non-secular Islamic countries. In addition, event organisers would have to be mindful not to offer Muslims non-halal foods, and halal foods would have to be clearly signed with suppliers checking to ensure only halal products are used as ingredients.

Thus, some adaptations may be needed when major sports events are hosted in non-secular Islamic countries. There is some evidence to suggest that international sports events rights holders, e.g. FIFA, are willing to make such changes to accommodate Islamic beliefs and values in relation to matters such as public shows of faith, worship, respect of the Islamic calendar and important dates, dress codes and the public consumption of alcohol, in order to ensure international sporting events can be hosted and staged within non-secular Islamic countries. This is important if event organisers, rights holders and partners are seeking greater participation of Muslims in international sporting events, as well as greater spectator bases from within the Muslim world. Furthermore, as the first mega-sports event to be staged within a non-secular Islamic state (FIFA Qatar World Cup, 2022) approaches, factors associated with Islam that may clash with the culture of the event will need to be raised and discussed. Suitable solutions and compromises may need to be found to ensure both the integrity of the host nation and that of the event itself are maintained.

## Conclusions

We acknowledge that the content of this chapter is preliminary. As we have stressed throughout, a critical appraisal of the many intricacies within Islam, and of sporting events too, are beyond the scope of this chapter. Our intention was not necessarily to provide answers to our observations, but rather to provoke others to engage in work on this topic. At the very least, our aim was to shed light on some of the 'back stage' (Goffman, 1959) 'anticipatory concerns' (Palmer, 2013) that surround hosting major sporting events in non-secular Islamic countries. In so doing, we hope these are now 'front stage' (Goffman, 1959) and ready for further interrogation.

Palmer (2013: 150) summarises our main contention by arguing that

as new countries appear on the mega-event circuit, systems, policies and regimes that were previously "closed" become subject to scrutiny ... [meaning that] what were once largely domestic policy concerns are now situated within a wider milieu of exogenous policies, politics and pressures that circulate globally.

Therefore, it is important that individuals and organisations involved in major international sports events become more culturally aware, thus ensuring they can anticipate challenges brought about by local traditions, customs, beliefs and lifestyles of host communities. Adaptations and compromises on the behalf of both the host community and events rights holders may be necessary for the future success and development of major international sporting events, within and beyond non-secular Islamic countries.

## References

Amara, M. (2012) Veiled women athletes in the 2008 Beijing Olympics: Media accounts. *The International Journal of History of Sport*, 29(4): 638–651.

Artz, D.E. (1996) *Religious human rights in Muslim states of the Middle East and North Africa religious human rights in the world today: A report on the 1994 Atlanta conference: Legal perspectives on religious human rights*. Emory International Law Review. Georgia, USA.

Bachok, S., Chik, C.T., Arsat, A., Jamil, J. and Ghani, M.A. (2012) Detection of non-halal ingredients for halal verification in bakery and confectionery in Malaysia. In A. Zainal, S.M. Radzi and R. Hashim (eds) *Current issues in hospitality and tourism research and innovations*. Proceedings of the International Hospitality and Tourism Conference. Kuala Lumpur, Malaysia, 3–5 September.

Badawi, J. (2011) *The position of women in Islam*. Birmingham: Islamic Dawah Centre International.

Bang, S. (2011) *Western countries are losing the race for major sporting events*. [Online] Available from www.playthegame.org/news/detailed/western-countries-are-losing-the-race-for-major-sporting-events-5156.html [accessed 7 May 2013].

Bleher, S.M. (2009) *Islam: A brief guide*. Birmingham: Islamic Dawah Centre International.

Collins, T. and Vamplew, W. (2002) *Mud, sweat and beers: A cultural history of sport and alcohol*. Oxford: Berg.

Cornelissen, S. (2012) A delicate balance: Major sports events and development. In R. Levermore and A. Beacon (eds) *Sport and international development*. Basingstoke: Palgrave Macmillan: 76–97.

Darnell, S. (2012) *Sport for development and peace: A critical sociology*. London: Bloomsbury.

Dashper, K. (2012) Together, yet still not equal? Sex integration in equestrian sport. *Asia-Pacific Journal of Health, Sport and Physical Education*, 3(3): 213–225.

dba. (n.d.) *"Dos and Don'ts" for business visitors to the UAE*. [Online] Available from www.dba.org.uk/aboutdba/newsarticles/documents/DosandDonts.pdf [accessed 6 November 2013].

Duncan, P. (2012) Raikkonen and Vettel turn the air blue on live TV, forcing BBC's Coulthard to apologise. [Online] Available from www.dailymail.co.uk/sport/formulaone/article-2227827/Kimi-Raikkonen-Sebastian-Vettel-swear-Abu-Dhabi-live-TV-forcing-BBCs-David-Coulthard-apologise.html [accessed 3 March 2013].

Ferdinand, N. and Shaw. S.J. (2012) Events in our changing world. In N. Ferdinand and P.J. Kitchen (eds) *Event management: An international approach*. London: Sage, 5–22.

Ferris-Lay, C. (2012) British MP slams Saudi ban on female Olympic athletes. [Online] Available from www.arabianbusiness.com/british-mp-slams-saudi-ban-on-female-olympic-athletes-447330.html [accessed 25 March 2012].

Fletcher, T. and Spracklen, K. (2013) Cricket, drinking and exclusion of British Pakistani Muslims? *Ethnic and Racial Studies.* DOI:10.1080/01419870.2013.790983. Published online 29 April.

Getz, D. (2008) Events tourism: Definition, evolution and research. *Tourism Management*, 29: 403–428.

Getz, D. (2012) Events studies. In S.J. Page and J. Connell (eds) *The Routledge handbook of events*, Abingdon: Routledge, 27–46.

Goffman, E. (1959) *The presentation of self in everyday life*. New York: Anchor Books.

Gupta, A. (2004) The globalization of cricket: The rise of the non-West. *International Journal of the History of Sport*, 21(2): 257–276.

Gupta, A. (2009) The globalisation of sports, the rise of non-western nations, and the impact on international sporting events. *The International Journal of the History of Sport*, 26(2): 1779–1790.

Hargreaves, J. (1994) *Sporting females: Critical issues in the history and sociology of women's sport*. London: Routledge.

Hargreaves, J. (2007) Sport, exercise and the female Muslim body: Negotiating Islam, politics and male power. In J. Hargreaves and P. Vertinsky (eds) *Physical culture, power and the body*. London: Routledge, 74–100.

Hattstein, M. (2006) *Islam: Religion and culture*. Germany: Konemann.

Holt, R. (1990) *Sport and the British: A modern history*. Oxford: Oxford University Press.

Horne, J. and Whannel, G. (2012) *Understanding the Olympics*. London: Routledge.

Kay, T.A. (2007) Daughters of Islam: Family influences on Muslim young women's participation in sport. *International Review for the Sociology of Sport*, 41(3–4): 357–375.

Konrad-Adenauer-Stiftung (2011) *Sustainable mega-events in developing countries: Experiences and insights from host cities in South Africa, India and Brazil*. [Online] Available from www.kas.de/wf/doc/kas_29583–1522–2–30.pdf?111209095524 [accessed 23 July 2012].

Magnay, J. (2012) *London 2012 Olympics: Saudi judo competitor will not be allowed to wear headscarf due to safety concerns*. [Online] Available from www.telegraph.co.uk/sport/olympics/judo/9430190/London-2012-Olympics-Saudi-judo-competitor-will-not-be-allowed-to-wear-headscarf-due-to-safety-concerns.html [accessed 15 November 2013].

Maguire, J. (1999) *Global sport: Identities, societies and civilisations*. Cambridge: Polity.

Matheson, V.A. (2006) *Mega-Events: The effect of the world's biggest sporting events on local, regional, and national economies*. [Online] Available from http://casgroup.fiu.edu/pages/docs/2744/1277904942_matheson_events.pdf [accessed 2 March 2013].

Palmer, C. (2013) *Global sports policy*. London: Sage.

Pfister, G. (2000) Doing sport in a headscarf? German sports and Turkish females. *Journal of Sport History*, 27(3): 497–525.

Pfister, G. (2010a) Women in sport: Gender relations and future perspectives. *Sport in Society*, 13(2): 234–248.

Pfister, G. (2010b) Outsiders: Muslim women and Olympic Games: Barriers and opportunities. *International Journal of the History of Sport*, 27(16–18): 2925–2957.

Pickthall, M.M. (2011) *The glorious Qur'an: An explanatory translation*. Birmingham: Islamic Dawah Centre International.

Randeree, K. (2011) Islam and the Olympics: Seeking a host city in the Muslim world. *International Journal of Islamic and Middle Eastern Finance and Management*, 4(3): 211–226.

Reuters (2012) *FIFA lifts ban on hijab for women footballers*. [Online] Available from http://tribune.com.pk/story/404321/fifa-lifts-ban-on-headscarves-for-women-footballers [accessed 5 November 2013].

Riordan, J. and Kruger, A. (eds) (1999) *The international politics of sport in the 20th century*. London: Routledge.

Rein, I. and Shields, B. (2006) Place branding sports: Strategies for differentiating emerging transitional, negatively viewed and newly industrialised nations. *Place Branding and Public Diplomacy*, 3(1): 73–85.

Rumford, C. (2007) More than a game: Globalization and the post-Westernization of world cricket. *Global Networks*, 7(2): 202–214.

Russell, K.A. and O'Connor, N. (2013) The London 2012 Olympic Games: The cultural tourist as a pillar of sustainability. In R. Raj., K. Griffin and N. Morpeth (eds) *Cultural tourism*. Wallingford, UK: CABI, 204–211.

Scharenberg, S. (1999) Religion and sport. In J. Riordan and A. Kruger (eds) *The international politics of sport in the 20th century*. London: Routledge.

Uddin, R. (1991) *It's about Islam*. London: Islamic Awareness Project.

Wagg, S. and Andrews, D.L. (eds) (2006) *East plays west: Sport and the cold war*. London: Routledge.

Weber, M. (1992) *The Protestant ethic and spirit of capitalism* (translated by T. Parsons). London: Routledge.

Widen, E. (2013) *Qatar in clampdown on alcohol sales in hotels, pools and beaches*. [Online] Available from www.arabianbusiness.com/qatar-in-clampdown-on-alcohol-sales-in-hotel-pools-beaches-525708.html [accessed 10 November 2013].

Wilson, J. (2010) *Qatar's hosting of the 2022 World Cup finals is FIFA's most dangerous move yet*. [Online] Available from www.telegraph.co.uk/sport/football/international/8176966/Qatars-hosting-of-the-2022-World-Cup-finals-is-Fifas-most-dangerous-move-yet.html [accessed 12 March 2012].

Zamin, H. (1997) Islam, well-being and physical activity: Perceptions of Muslim young women. In G. Clarke and B. Humberstone (eds) *Researching women and sport*. Basingstoke: Macmillan Press, 50–67.

# 13 Knowing the rules and understanding the score

## The 2010 FIFA Football World Cup in South Africa

*Suzanne Dowse*

## Introduction

Sports events are established sites of excellence, of competition and generally perceived (rightly or wrongly) to be a good thing; but for whom? The decision to host the FIFA Football World Cup (FWC) or the Olympic Games is a political one, and the competition to host an event is increasing, which suggests that it should be the population of the host country who should benefit. This is certainly indicated in the range of domestic and foreign policy outcomes recognised as drivers for the political commitments made by the host government. Although predominantly justified in financial terms (Matheson, 2006), mega-events are also perceived as political opportunities in relation to nation-building (Kersting, 2007), public diplomacy (Finlay and Xin, 2010) and soft power accrual (Manzenreiter, 2010). However, although these political outcomes are widely recognised, there is far less understanding of the efficacy of mega-events for domestic and foreign policy purposes. There is also limited knowledge regarding the extent to which outcomes align with original ambitions. These knowledge gaps are primarily due to weaknesses in, or the absence of, post-event evaluations (Kasmati, 2003). They are also due to the limited engagement in mega-event research by scholars in the Political Sciences who could add valuable insight(s) to explorations concerning international relations and foreign and domestic policy (Beacom, 2000). There is a pressing need to close this gap – to reduce what Black (2008: 469) observes as "recurrent tendencies towards the fantastical in games bid hyperbole".

Developing countries are hosting mega-events more frequently than they have done previously (see Chapter 12 in this volume). Within developing contexts the cost of hosting and risk of failing to achieve sought outcomes is likely to be far higher than for events held in the 'developed' world (Matheson and Baade, 2004). However, as historically mega-events have predominantly been hosted by developed and industrialised economies, the existing body of research may be unsuitable for informing decision-making and discussions about hosting opportunities in developing contexts (Cornelissen, 2004). This is because the specific challenges and opportunities that are catalysed by lower levels of development may be unclear. The research presented in this chapter concerning the 2010

Football World Cup in South Africa is offered as a means of informing these discussions. The chapter presents the findings of a case study of a developing country's experience of hosting a sport mega-event of the scale of the Football World Cup for the first time. The study sought to explore the extent to which the FWC was politically perceived as a tool for domestic and foreign policy and how successful it was in this role. As such it is distinct from research that focuses on the utility of sport as a medium for international development (Darnell, 2010).

The findings highlight how political support for hosting the 2010 FWC was justified in relation to economic outcomes, but suggest that this support was not motivated primarily by financial considerations. Instead the indications are that the political support given was motivated by the opportunities perceived to demonstrate parity of status with the developed international community, to improve the external image of South Africa, and advance claims for greater influence in international and regional affairs. Perceived opportunities to advance domestic and community interests were also influential. Positive outcomes in relation to these ambitions were evident and, as will be demonstrated, the indications are that hosting events in developing country contexts may provide valuable opportunities, for example, by supporting state-building activities. However, in the South African context the ability to achieve goals established for the event emerged as constrained by a lack of knowledge concerning the true implications of delivering an event on the scale of the FWC. They were also inhibited by the contractual agreements made with the world governing body, FIFA, which carried significant resource implications for the local and national government departments responsible for delivering the event.

In order to place these findings in context the chapter begins with a review of the socio-political environment at the time of the bid application and the narratives that surrounded the political decision to support the hosting ambition. The discussion then moves on to consider the domestic and foreign policy opportunities that were anticipated, the outcomes perceived, and the issues that emerged during the delivery process. The discussion concludes by reflecting on the key messages to emerge from South Africa's experience of hosting the 2010 FIFA FWC and the implications for future hosts.

## Methodology

The findings presented in this chapter are based on semi-structured interviews carried out in South Africa at the time of the 2010 FWC and repeated one year later. These interviews were held with a range of government stakeholders at national, provincial and host city levels who were involved in the planning and delivery of the 2010 project. Foreign country representatives based in South Africa, civil society stakeholders, Trade Union representatives, experts in South African politics and policy and media representatives were also interviewed. The purpose of the interviews was to explore the ambitions for the event, the experience of hosting and the outcomes perceived. This two-phase format provided the opportunity to re-interview many of these stakeholders and explore the sustainability of the outcomes observed and longer-term impacts of the hosting experience. Table 13.1 sets out the referencing for the comments presented on these aspects of the 2010 project.

## South Africa's journey to winning the 2010 Football World Cup

When President Mbeki used the February 2003 State of the Nation Address (SONA) to publicly declare the government's support for the South Africa Football Association's (SAFA) ambition to host the 2010 FWC he presented it as an opportunity for South Africa, and the wider African continent. Within this framing South Africa was positioned as the champion of Africa's regional interests (South Africa: The Presidency, 2003a). The Address also set out the government's domestic and foreign policy priorities. Domestically, these priorities included economic growth, rebalancing an unequal society and improving the quality of life for all. These priorities were to be achieved through nation and state-building supportive measures that included economic infrastructure modernisation, reducing unemployment and improving the efficacy of public sector organisations, particularly in relation to service delivery. The foreign policy priorities set out had a strong regional orientation and included consolidating national and regional relations with the developed world and accelerating the implementation of regional development projects, such as the New Economic Partnership for African Development (NEPAD). The SONA also confirmed the political belief that South Africa's status within the international community would be elevated through activity that presented the country in a regional leadership role and demonstrated leadership capabilities.

It is therefore clear that SAFA's ambition to bid for the 2010 Football World Cup had political backing early in 2003 and this was reaffirmed in a cabinet statement in May (South Africa: The Cabinet, 2003). However, when this

*Table 13.1* Respondent codes

| Prefix | Representation |
| --- | --- |
| NG | National Government Department Officer |
| HC | Host City Government Officer |
| PO | Provincial City Government Officer |
| MP | Member of Parliament |
| SALOC | South Africa's 2010 Local Organising Committee |
| AE | Academic Expert |
| PC | Political Commentator |
| FWC | World Cup Capacity Building Project |
| DR | Foreign Diplomat based in South Africa |
| M | Media representative |

support was re-stated at a press briefing in the following September, the hosting opportunity was presented with an economic justification that predicted "significant direct and indirect benefits for the country's economy" (South Africa, Department of Sport and Recreation, 2003). However, the cost and benefit evaluation (hereafter Grant Thornton Report) that appears to have provided the basis for the economic projections is dated July 2003 and therefore post-dates the initial statement of political support. This suggests that the political value attached to economic opportunities associated with the hosting ambition did not underpin the support given.

The Grant Thornton Report sets out a supportive economic case for the hosting ambition and notes that the benefits to be gained were obtainable at "minimal tangible and intangible costs" (Grant Thornton Kessel Feinstein, 2003: 4/4). In the context of significant unemployment in South Africa, the determination that hosting would generate the equivalent of 159,000 annual jobs highlights the economic value of the event, as does the way in which attention is draw to the importance of the tourism industry within South Africa's economy. Intangible outcomes were also predicted in relation to an improved country profile, increased tourism and Foreign Direct Investment, civic confidence and pride, and support for the welfare state. There is limited consideration of the potential risks, even in relation to common mega-event issues like budget over-runs and post-event under-use of event-focussed infrastructure.[1] These and similar positive predictions subsequently formed the basis of popular and wider political expectations for the event (Cornelissen, 2008).

The 2003 SONA that confirmed political support for the 2010 hosting ambition drew attention to the public diplomacy opportunities that sport events provide to demonstrate regional progress and value within the international community (South Africa: The Presidency, 2003a). This foreign policy capacity is subsequently reflected and repeated in early political speeches on the bid initiative. For example, when the bid application was formally launched, the then Deputy President Jacob Zuma, positioned FIFA's introduction of the policy of rotation which guaranteed the event to an African state as the result of South Africa's efforts on behalf of the continent. He also confirmed the political perception that the inclusion of Africa as hosts of the event for the first time was an important marker for the continent's increased importance in international affairs. This position was maintained in subsequent speeches as demonstrated here: "Bringing the World Cup to our country is not only about playing soccer.... It is about restoring Africa's rightful place on the global stage" (South Africa: The Presidency, 2003b). This theme of equality within the international community is repeated and reinforced by statements made that confirmed the intention to demonstrate alignment with international standards and modernity through the delivery of the 2010 FWC project. This was explicitly set out in the Bid Book submitted in application for the event: "Our mission is to demonstrate our modern stadiums, world-class infrastructure, advanced technology, mature business systems and proven organisational capacity" (South African Football Association, 2003: 3).

It is therefore clear from the bid application stage that hosting the 2010 FWC was presented as a means through which domestic and foreign policy goals could be pursued. It also appears that, despite the justification presented publicly, these motivations were not primarily economic. These goals will be explored thematically in this chapter. However, before this commences, a brief review of contractual agreements undertaken during the bid processes will be outlined as these obligations proved important to the outcomes and experience of the event in South Africa.

## Contractual requirements of the 2010 FIFA Football World Cup

The FWC is one of the world's largest sport events and therefore the use of legally binding agreements designed to ensure its success is to be expected. The Cabinet statement of support for the event in May 2003 establishes that the political elite recognised that meeting a range of agreements with FIFA were implicit in supporting the bid application. How substantively these obligations were understood is unclear as they are not discussed in the statement. They also do not appear to have been publicised or explored in any great detail within Parliament. This notwithstanding, sometime before the Bid Book submission, SAFA signed FIFA's Organising Association Agreement (OAA) and, in so doing, ostensibly bound the government to a series of contractual conditions that governed relations with and obligations to FIFA. Exact details of these conditions within the copy of the document obtained are inconsistently set out (FIFA, 2003). It therefore appears unlikely that the South African government were in a position to meaningfully understand what the terms and conditions they were obliged to meet actually entailed. The fact that the FWC is an established event raises the possibility that more information about the requirements could have been provided. However, whether this is particular to the 2010 FWC is unknown as OAA's for other events have not been obtained.

The political commitment to the FWC hosting ambition in the absence of an understanding of these contractual obligations could be considered as a failure to exercise appropriate oversight over public resources. This is important as the agreements made at the national level formed the basis of the agreements that would later be signed between FIFA and the Host City governments. Crucially, these were unavailable when the bid application was made (CO8, 2011). This implies that neither national nor local government departments responsible for resourcing and delivering the event entered the process in a position to understand the full implications of hosting, and whether, as a result, stated ambitions were realistic. The indeterminate nature of the obligations agreed also meant that the involved stakeholders would be required to negotiate and review the requirements and their respective responsibilities. In this South Africa appeared at a disadvantage in relation to FIFA, due mainly to the political priority attached to obtaining the event, and using a successful delivery to demonstrate regional progress. These ambitions increased the tolerance for additional conditions and all but ensured the subordination of national interests to those of the event (NG3, 2010). They also increased the potential for policy interests to be retro-fitted around the requirements of the event and redefined as the implications of the agreements were clarified.

## 2010 and the South African economy

Justifying political support for hosting ambitions in terms of an economic business case is normal practice in mega-event processes; South Africa was not unusual. The reasons why the economic justification for the event should not be considered as the primary political motivation were explored in the previous section. However, as an economic rationale was maintained in one form or another past the close of the event, it is an important area for consideration.

Representatives of local and national government confirmed that the economic case presented for the event had unrealistically inflated popular expectations. Comments made by government officers, like the one presented below, suggested that managing these expectations at the local level was unfeasible, due to the need to maintain popular support and remain deferential to the political elite:

> There are things we knew that were not true, but if the President and Premier are saying them you can't say something different, you have a job to keep, so you repeat and reinforce their message even though you know that it is not true.
>
> (CO6, 2010)

Despite acknowledging that the economic case presented was unrealistic, government stakeholders still anticipated positive economic outcomes. For example, City of Cape Town government representatives were emphatic that the original intention was for the event to support existing development plans. This was demonstrated in the presentation of Athlone as an alternative match venue to the Newlands site originally presented in the Bid Book, in order to support existing development of a new 'growth nodule' in that area. The potential therefore existed for accelerated development in each of the city host areas to combine and deliver economic development nationally.

However, the national priority attached to delivering a successful FWC and meeting the associated contractual obligations meant that the ability to support local development ambitions through the event became dependent on the degree of congruence that occurred or could be created between local plans and event requirements. For the city of Johannesburg, the host of two match venues, there was much to be gained from the World Cup project because transport infrastructure development – which is a critical factor in the successful delivery of an event – was a pre-existing strategic goal (South Africa, City of Johannesburg, 2006). However, where priorities were unaligned, or resource constraints forced a choice between them, national and sub-national interests were at risk. In Cape

Town this risk was realised in the decision to build the match stadium at Green Point rather than Athlone in line with development priorities.

Despite these tensions, infrastructure development emerged at all levels of government as a perceived primary benefit of hosting, and was described in terms of the opportunity gained to secure national funding to facilitate, or accelerate, planned or sought projects. However, stadium developments dominated this national investment and consequently, as a result of the FWC, South Africa gained a series of international level venues that far exceed current demand. This means that not all of the stadia are self-financing and those that are not will require on-going public subsidisation (CO2, 2011; CO5, 2011). This was a particular concern at the sub-national level of government where management and maintenance responsibility is located.

However, despite the long-term implications, the stadia developments were perceived as positive developments by many of those interviewed because they evidenced South Africa's progress and capacity to deliver complex projects to international standards, within set deadlines (MP1, 2010). Additionally, the stadia provided anchor points for event-led employment outcomes and future tourist or business attractions. For example, one city representative stated that the construction of 'their' stadium had created 1500 employment opportunities and temporarily boosted the 'informal' economy by providing an additional market for local street sellers (CO7, 2010).

Short- and longer-term economic benefits were also anticipated from the tourism catalysed by the event. In the short-term this involved the direct expenditure of those visiting for the event. In the long-term an economic gain was perceived in global profiling of the country's positive tourism attributes catalysed by the event. As one Member of Parliament explained:

> Hosting a world class event will rebrand South Africa as a desirable, safe and welcome destination…. Tourists are ignorant of South Africa; they view it as this exotic place with lions in the street. We want to promote the game reserves, but also that it is very sophisticated. The World Cup has a 34 billion cumulative audience; they will get to see the infrastructure and IT capacity.
>
> (MP1, 2010)

The value attached to this significant and positive exposure is not exclusive to economic purposes. Benefits are also perceived in the opportunities created by this positive exposure to facilitate foreign policy activity (discussed above) in terms of the public diplomacy opportunities that were expected to enhance South Africa's status and reputation in regional and international communities. The possibility that the concentrated media attention generated by the event would highlight the country's negative attributes appeared to receive limited attention, despite the fact that the FWC coincided with the country's traditional strike season and a period of increased service delivery and social housing protests (Media Tenor, 2010). This risk was observed by diplomats based in South Africa as reflected in the comment below. However, misunderstanding the potential of event-led media attention and the predominant expectation of a positive outcome is not unique to South Africa (Dowse, 2010).

> For the business community it is double-edged. They will see a place they can invest in, but also the huge labour problems in the run up and at the heart of the event. It is a push back to Apartheid; the poor are still poor and still poorly paid by essentially white owned businesses.
>
> (DR1, 2010)

The negative media coverage received by South Africa in the pre-event period was implicated as a reason for lower than anticipated tourist attendance. This necessarily depressed economic expectations. However, a more significant negative impact may have resulted from the over-optimistic initial predictions. This is because, as explained by one government officer in the comment below, the figures underpinned event-delivery plans meaning that developments exceeded what was required.

> The Football World Cup was supposed to bring in visitors, 500,000 initially; this has now been reduced to 300,000, a 60% drop. The scale of the upgrades was indexed to the 2003 predictions, but the drop has been influenced by the global recession and negative perceptions.
>
> (NG2, 2010)

Comments made during an interview held with other government officers representing a different national department suggested that there had been some awareness that the figures used for planning were inappropriate. These observations were explored in the context of the responsibility to ensure the appropriate expenditure of public resources. The feedback received, as the comment below illustrates, indicated that the situation was a logical consequence of the use of economic predications designed to facilitate popular support for the hosting initiative. It is therefore a situation that is unlikely to be unique to South Africa, and highlights how the necessity for this support may undermine positive economic outcomes and good governance practices.

> It's not about scoring points, we have no control over ticket sales and accommodation, and to persuade people to sign up you need higher figures....
>
> (NG7, 2010)

Over the course of the event delivery period the economic benefit expected was revised downwards. For example, initial estimates for a GDP impact of 1.9 per cent for 2010 was revised to 0.54 per cent before the event, and it appears that only 0.2–0.3 per cent may have been achieved (Grant Thornton Kessel Feinstein, 2003: 18 of 24; Grant Thornton, 2010; Amato, 2010). However, the failure to achieve the initial economic projections for the event may be considered politically unproblematic as it does not appear to have been the primary motivation for supporting the hosting ambition.

## Nation and state-building opportunities

Nation and state-building considerations are important policy concerns in South Africa (South Africa: The Presidency, 2003a). This made related ambitions very likely for the 2010 FWC. This certainly transpired in relation to expectations concerning nation-building outcomes. However, expectations for state-building were somewhat different because, rather than an ambition, the potential for the hosting process to improve the capacity and legitimacy of national and sub-national government institutions emerged most frequently as surprising by-products of the hosting process.

The 1995 Rugby World Cup hosted in South Africa is frequently cited as evidence of the nation-building potential of sport events (Carlin, 2008). The 2006 FWC in Germany is also recognised as having a positive effect on German national identity (Kersting, 2007). Both events were repeatedly cited as reference points for the nation-building expectations held for the 2010 FWC, and government officers reflected the belief, illustrated in the quote below, that the impact was expected to be proportional to the size of the event. However, as this comment also makes clear, national unity was not expected as a result of a single event. Consequently, the FWC had to be considered as part of a policy process, rather than an independently effective intervention.

> Social mobilisation, social relations and cohesion; to some extent it [the impact] is limited, but it is a process and never going to be achieved via one event. The Football World Cup will do this on a larger scale than previous events and initiatives, but many other things are needed to sustain this else it will fall back.
>
> (NG3, 2010)

One political commentator raised the possibility that the nation-building effect of the FWC could be particularly significant as the award of the event to South Africa could be interpreted as a reward for the black community in the same way that the 1995 Rugby World Cup could be interpreted as a reward for white South Africans' following the acceptance of political reform in 1994 (PC5, 2010). However, this symbolism also generated concerns for democratic accountability because critical debate about the implications of hosting could be inhibited by allegations of racism, or lack of patriotism (M2, 2010). This is not unique to South Africa or developing countries, however. Research into the 2000 Sydney Olympic Games by Nauright (2004: 1329), for example, identified the use of the label 'un-Australian' to manage internal protest. The possibility was also raised that the significant diversion of public funding away from local priorities and public service delivery could undermine nation-building progress by elevating existing social instabilities.

Despite these challenges the 2010 FWC was defined by now-President Zuma as a "powerful nation-building tool" (South Africa, The Presidency, 2010). This claim was echoed in the media and supported by reference to demonstrations of nationalism, such as widespread wearing of the Bafana Bafana national football team shirts by all ethnic groups. The particular importance of this was explained by the Member of Parliament interviewed:

> The event has been very supportive of nation-building; it has exceeded all expectations.... For the average public person they are seeing old white people – part of the Afrikaner regime – wearing the team colours of Bafana Bafana, playing the Vuvuzela and so on.
>
> (MP1, 2010)

Although the displays of positive nationalism described above generally ceased at the close of the tournament, the possibility was raised that because they are relatively rare in South Africa the overall effect could be to move the process of nation-building forward (Ndlovu-Gatsheni, 2011). This suggests that the event presented an aspirational image of unity while concurrently helping to make that image a reality, although additional research is required to explore this possibility.

Governments that agree to host a sport mega-event essentially assume responsibility for delivering a complex national project that requires the efficient operation of public sector organisations. Consequently, the FWC provided South Africa with a variety of opportunities to develop and demonstrate the efficacy of state institutions. Yet, unlike nation-building outcomes, positive state-building benefits,[2] in terms of improving public sector capacity to govern and provide for the civic population, were largely unanticipated. This outcome could be considered particularly valuable in South Africa as a result of the low level of public service delivery which depresses perceptions of government legitimacy and positive national identity (i.e. nation-building) (Alexander, 2010).

The delivery of the FWC was perceived as supporting state-building activity by expanding the skills and capacities of public sector employees and improving organisational processes and inter-governmental relations. Government officers described how delivering the 2010 World Cup had been an important learning experience that had built skills and knowledge in relation to project and performance management in ways that would improve government operations and service delivery. Confidence also emerged as a particular attribute inspired by the visibly successful delivery of the event. This had two inter-related dimensions: first, popular confidence in the capacity of public sector organisations to operate effectively and, second, personal confidence of those working within those organisations that they could be effective within their roles. The importance of these developments was elevated by the broad popular experience of the failure to deliver public services in line with expectations. As indicated in the comment by a national government officer below, this raised the possibility that the event had enhanced the perceived legitimacy of government and the associated structures of governance.

A major spin-off from the event is public confidence in the governance systems. It is very difficult for government institutions to build a profile and redress imbalances. Since 1994 the public have been made lots of promises, but they were rarely delivered on.

(NG5, 2010)

How sustainable these developments were was debated, particularly as interviews with government department representatives indicated the need for support in taking lessons learnt forward and plans for this appeared limited. It was therefore unsurprising that many of those interviewed a year after the event suggested that the opportunities presented had been under-utilised and that previous ways of working had re-emerged in a number of instances. However, this situation was not perceived as wholly negative because, as with the findings concerning nation-building, it was not considered that the operational environment had regressed to the pre-event situation and, moreover, the 2010 experience continued to provide an important organisational reference point.

These findings suggest that mega-event projects offer valuable state-building opportunities because they facilitate the development of operational efficiency within public sector institutions with the possibility for a legacy effect. This benefit is likely to be particularly valuable in contexts like South Africa where social mistrust is pervasive, as progress will support nation-building activities that are required. More research into the state-building potential is required, particularly as the largely unanticipated nature of this impact is potentially both a consequence and a reflection of the relative absence of research into this area.

## International relations

South Africa's foreign policy expectations for the FWC fell into two distinct categories. They related, first, to status and influence within the international community and, second, to specifically regional ambitions. This dual focus of attention was discernible in then Deputy President Zuma's emphasis on South Africa's role in facilitating the introduction of the policy of rotation (discussed earlier) which appeared as intended to promote regional support and international recognition. It is noteworthy that this dual focus reflects the characteristics of an emerging 'Middle Power'[3] in relation to consolidating regional and international positions through the revision of global norms and structures that disadvantage their communities of interest (Jordaan, 2003; Cornelissen, 2009).

President Mbeki, who was also African National Congress (ANC) leader at the time of the bid application, was widely regarded as being foreign policy orientated (Chan, 2011). Policy preferences articulated during his tenure include regional initiatives, like the African Renaissance, which was designed to advance socio-economic and political development and improve how the continent engaged with the international community. Hosting the FWC played to these political aspirations because the event demonstrated the capacity to act decisively, efficiently and in the region's interest(s). This, as demonstrated in the observation made by one national government officer set out below, meant that hosting provided the means to elevate South Africa's position within the international community.

> It [the event] helps to overcome power imbalances. If they [the international community] have confidence in you they will seek your input in the decisions that affect the world.
>
> (NG1, 2010)

South Africa's successful delivery of the 2010 FWC was widely accepted as exceeding international expectations and redressing the negative stereotypes that historically compromised the country's global position (South Africa, The Presidency, 2010). However, those interviewed were unable to draw causal relations between the event impact and particular foreign policy developments. They were also unable to determine whether the new image presented through the event had changed the behaviour of the international political community towards South Africa. This was not unexpected as the event was targeted towards the broader foreign policy environment. However, rather than changing the international community's behaviour towards South Africa, the suggestion was made that the FWC may have contributed to the observed increase in South Africa's foreign policy independence following the event (DR6, 2011). While it would be inappropriate to attribute this development directly to the event, the possibility exists that the hosting experience inspired self-confidence in the policy communities in South Africa, and in the international community's confidence in South Africa. These developments potentially worked together to support a more determined pursuit of foreign policy interests.

The very specific regional dimension to South Africa's foreign policy aims for the FWC was clearly indicated in the unusual promotion of the tournament as a regional event. However, this departure from a nationally grounded presentation of the FWC aligned with the 'African', and regionally focussed foreign policy trend of the post-Apartheid South African government; a trend which is partly driven by the need to redress a regional reputation considered weak enough to inhibit foreign policy ambitions (Nathan, 2005). To improve these relations event-led opportunities were proactively utilised and this appeared successful in a number of instances. For example, African State representatives described how an environment of goodwill had been created by the astute use of opportunities to play host to African leaders. These opportunities were perceived as providing openings to demonstrate that South Africa valued the regional political elite with the positive potential for reciprocity.

> Inviting the African Heads of State and telling them they could watch for free was a masterstroke, great. It makes the regional leaders think "what can we do to help?".
>
> (DR1, 2010)

Overall, it appeared that the 2010 FWC had supported an improvement in South Africa's regional position by providing opportunities for South Africa to demonstrate commitment to shared interests and the competencies of the political elite. As illustrated in the comment made by a national government officer presented below, this was considered as supportive of claims to regional leadership and improved regional relations. However, as with the domestic policy outcomes already discussed, these outcomes were positioned, as part of broader policy process designed towards these ends, which the FWC could not achieve independently.

> Since the World Cup South Africa has been given the NEPAD investment plan to lead, this is no coincidence. South Africa has proven the ability to deliver a mega-event.... Africa is looking to South Africa for this leadership because of the confidence [this has inspired] and because South Africa invited the other African states and recognised the role of the other African states.
>
> (NG3, 2011)

How far these positive international and regional foreign policy outcomes will lead to a sustained and meaningful change in behaviour either towards the continent by the international community or within regional relations is indeterminable.

## Conclusions

Although political support for the 2010 FWC hosting ambition was publicly presented as economically grounded, a closer review of the bid application process and the priority attached to ensuring the successful delivery of the event, whilst also meeting contractual agreements made with FIFA, suggests that this was not in fact the primary motivation. The narrative that surrounded the bid application indicates that more value was attached to the symbolic message perceived in the award of the event to an African state and to South Africa in particular. Evaluating the overall impact of the hosting experience is complicated because the event was invariably positioned as part of an existing programme of activity designed towards broader domestic and foreign policy ends, rather than a transformational tool sufficient to achieve those ends independently. This makes it difficult to determine how far the event was independently influential, especially as the outcomes were generally intangible.

It is difficult to avoid the conclusion that the 2010 FWC was valued by the political elite primarily for the opportunities presented to project images of international status and influence, and internal capacity and cohesion. However, these images were largely aspirational and did not exist on the scale inferred by the successful delivery of the event. This notwithstanding, it appears that the process of delivering the event importantly, and sometimes unexpectedly, catalysed progress in areas that needed to be improved in order for the aspirational image projected to be realised; for example, although the organisational capacity demonstrated through the delivery of the event is unreflective of the broader public sector that fails to deliver public services comprehensively or effectively. The skills and experience and improved organisational capacity catalysed by the delivery process increased the potential for enhanced operational efficiency. This effect was discernible in foreign policy and nation-building outcomes, but the state-building benefit emerged as particularly valuable in the context of South Africa's developing state context. Although more could have been made of these opportunities, the implications are that there is potential in this area for hosts at similar levels of development. More research is required to establish the scope of this potential, but the contemporary relocation of events to developing economies like Brazil and India offers numerous opportunities to bridge this knowledge gap.

While there were many positive benefits gained through the FWC project, there were also areas where negative outcomes were experienced; for example, in relation to the contractual obligations which appear to have been poorly understood at the time of agreement. It could be argued that this reflected a failure on the part of the national government to adequately safeguard national interests. However, in the absence of previous experience or knowledge of lessons learnt governments engaging in mega-event hosting have to take a leap of faith about the processes involved. While they are unlikely to be alert to the extent of their lack of knowledge, the confidence to take this leap is undoubtedly enhanced by the pervasive view that hosting events is beneficial for the host. However, the South African government's decision in 2011 not to support a bid for the 2020 Olympic Games may suggest that the experience of hosting the 2010 FWC has led the political elite to a different conclusion.

## Notes

1  However, the copy of the report obtained is incomplete as it lacks the appendices.
2  State-building relates to activities designed to develop the capacity of state institutions in relation to meeting and managing the demands between state and societal groups. The legitimacy of a political authority is enhanced when this is effective as it is strongly linked to effective public service delivery and fair governance (Van de Walle and Scott, 2011).
3  Middle Powers are recognised as sharing certain traits, including the promotion of trans-national interests and a desire for reform of the international system (Jordaan, 2003; Cornelissen, 2009). They are also recognised for great diversity in terms of their levels of development, access to international decision making and policy preferences (Jordaan, 2003). Established Middle Powers tend to be developed with relatively good access to the channels of international decision making and are orientated towards an international political role. They seek to maintain their position by appeasing the interest groups they purport to represent through their capacity to provide and promote aid. Emerging Middle Powers tend to be developing countries with more limited access to global decision making structures and are defined more by their regional activity. Due to a lower capacity to provide development aid these countries rely on the promotion and pursuit of global governance institutional reform as a means of legitimating their respective positions.

# References

Alexander, P. (2010) Rebellion of the poor: South Africa's service delivery protests – a preliminary analysis. *Review of African Political Economy*, 37(123): 25–40.

Amato, C. (2010) Weighing the World Cup's worth. *The Times Live* [Online] Available from www.timeslive.co.za/business/article615086.ece/Weighing-the-World-Cups-worth [accessed 26 April 2012].

Beacom, A. (2000) Sport in international relations: A case for cross-disciplinary investigation. *The Sport Historian*, 20(2): 1–23.

Black, D. (2008) Dreaming big: The pursuit of 'second order' games as a strategic response to globalisation. *Sport in Society*, 11(4): 467–480.

Carlin, J. (2008) *Playing the enemy: Nelson Mandela and the game that made a nation*. London: Atlantic Books.

Chan, S. (2011) *Southern Africa: Old Treacheries and New Deceits*. London: Yale University Press.

Cornelissen, S. (2004) Sport mega-events in Africa: Processes, impacts and prospects. *Tourism and Hospitality Planning and Development*, 1(1): 39–55.

Cornelissen, S. (2008) Scripting the nation: Sport, mega-events, foreign policy and state building in post-Apartheid South Africa. *Sport in Society*, 11(4): 481–493.

Cornelissen, S. (2009) Awkward embraces: Emerging and established powers and the shifting fortunes of Africa's international relations in the twenty-first century. *Politikon*, 36(1): 5–26.

Darnell, S. (2010) Power, politics and "sport for development and peace": Investigating the utility of sport for international development. *Sociology of Sport Journal*, 27: 54–75.

Dowse, S. (2010) Paralympic potential: Opportunities and risks. In I. Wellard and M.E. Weed (eds) *Wellbeing, health and leisure*. LSA Publications (111). Eastbourne: Leisure Studies Association, 99–119.

FIFA (2003) *Organising Association Agreement: FIFA and the South African Football Association regarding the 2010 FIFA World Cup*. 4 August (electronic copy supplied by interviewee).

Finlay, C. and Xin, X. (2010) Public diplomacy games: A comparative study of American and Japanese responses to the interplay of nationalism, ideology and Chinese soft power strategies around the 2008 Beijing Olympics. *Sport in Society*, 13(5): 876–900.

Grant Thornton Kessel Feinstein (2003) South Africa 2010 Soccer World Cup bid. ("Grant Thornton Report"). *GFS*. July (supplied by interviewee and incomplete as does not contain appendices).

Grant Thornton (2010) *Updated economic impact of the 2010 FIFA World Cup*. [Online] Available from www.gt.co.za/files/grant_thornton_updated_2010_economic_impact_210410.pdf [accessed 21 April 2012].

Jordaan, E. (2003) The concept of a middle power in international relations: Distinguishing between emerging and traditional middle powers. *Politikon*, 30(2): 165–181.

Kasmati, E. (2003) Economic aspects and the Summer Olympics: A review of related research *International Journal of Tourism Research*, 5: 433–444.

Kersting, N. (2007) Sport and national identity: A comparison of the 2006 and 2010 FIFA World Cups. *Politikon*, 34(3): 277–293.

Manzenreiter, W. (2010) The Beijing Games in the western imagination of China: The weak power of soft power. *Journal of Sport and Social Issues*, 34(1): 29–34.

Matheson, V. (2006) Mega-events: The effect of the world's biggest sporting events on local, regional, and national economies. *College of The Holy Cross, Department of*

*Economics Faculty Research Series*. Paper No. 06–10. [Online] Available from http:// college.holycross.edu/RePEc/hcx/Matheson_MegaEvents.pdf [accessed 2 March 2011].

Matheson, V. and Baade, R. (2004) Mega-sporting events in developing nations: Playing the way to prosperity? *The South African Journal of Economics*, 72(5): 1085–1095.

Media Tenor (2010) *World Cup to be used as a platform for protest action: Coverage on strikes, protests and social unrest in South Africa*. South Africa: Media Tenor South Africa.

Nathan, L. (2005) Consistency and inconsistency in South African foreign policy. *International Affairs*, 81(2): 361–372.

Nauright, J. (2004) Global games: Culture, political economy and sport in the globalised world of the 21st century. *Third World Quarterly*, 25(7): 1325–1336.

Ndlovu-Gatsheni, S. (2011) The World Cup, vuvuzelas, flag-waving patriots and the burden of building South Africa. *Third World Quarterly*, 32(2): 279–293.

South Africa, City of Johannesburg (2006) *Growth and Development Strategy "Joberg GDS"*. [Online] Available from www.joburg.org.za/index.php?option=com_content&t ask=view&id=139&Itemid=114 [11 accessed May 2010].

South Africa, Department of Sport and Recreation (2003) *Statement by the Minister of Sports and Recreation, Mr BMN Balfour, MP, during the GCIS Parliamentary Media Briefing, 9 September 2003*. [Online] Available from www.polity.org.za [accessed 3 August 2009].

South Africa, Department of Sport and Recreation (2010) *Media release, 14 July 2010: Government assessment of the 2010 FIFA World Cup*. [Online] Available from www. srsa.gov.za/MediaLib/Home/.../2010-facts-post-event.pdf [accessed 5 May 2011].

South Africa, The Cabinet (2003) *Statement on Cabinet meeting of 14 May 2003*. [Online] Available from www.gcis.gov.za/newsroom/releases/cabstate/2003/030514.htm# [accessed 22 May 2012].

South Africa, The Presidency (2003a) *State of the nation address of the President of South Africa, Thabo Mbeki, Houses of Parliament, Cape Town, 14 February*. [Online] Available from www.info.gov.za/speeches/2003/03021412521001.htm [accessed 5 May 2010].

South Africa, The Presidency (2003b) *J. Zuma: Handover of SA 2010 Bid Book, 29 September 2003*. [Online] Available from www.polity.org.za/article/j-zuma-handover-of-sa-2010-bid-book-26092003-2003–09–26 [accessed 5 May 2010].

South Africa, The Presidency (2010) *Media statement by President Jacob Zuma marking the end of the 2010 FIFA World Cup tournament*. [Online] Available from www.info. gov.za/speech/DynamicAction?pageid=461&sid=11413&tid=11877 [accessed 5 September 2012].

South African Football Association (2003) *South Africa 2010 Bid Book*. [Online] Available from www.mg.co.za/article/2010–06–11-the-bid-book-for-our-bucks [accessed 14 July 2010).

Van de Walle, S. and Scott, Z. (2011) The political role of service delivery in state-building: Exploring the relevance of European history for developing countries. *Development Policy Review*, 29(1): 5–21.

# 14 London 2012

## The rings of exclusion

*Iain Lindsay*

## Introduction

> London's bid was built on a special Olympic vision. A vision of an Olympic
> Games that would not only be a celebration of sport but a force for regener-
> ation. The Games will transform one of the poorest and most deprived areas
> of London. They will create thousands of jobs and homes. They will offer
> new opportunities for business in the immediate area and throughout
> London.
>
> (Jack Straw, House of Commons, 6 July 2005, cited in Hansard, 2005)

Hyperbolic Olympic narratives, as illustrated above, proliferated within the
public consciousness during the era of London's Olympic delivery
(2005–2012). The realities that underpinned such rhetoric were variously consumed, experienced and/or negotiated, largely dependent upon one's proximity to the venues. There has been much academic research that has explored
hosting implications and outcomes from a holistic Games perspective (e.g.
Preuss 2004; Gold and Gold 2007), however there is a distinct lack of academic research pertaining to the ethnographic realities of Olympic hosting
from the local perspective. This chapter intends to go someway to addressing
this omission.

Based on seven years of ethnography, this chapter aims to contribute to discourse surrounding practices of urban regeneration, belonging, displacement,
urban neglect, citizenship and everyday life during mega-event delivery. It
addresses Olympic-delivery issues that revolve around concepts of inclusion,
exclusion, power relations, ideology and identity. The powerful and often all
encompassing positivistic mnemonic 'London 2012' was saturated with regenerative allegory from its outset and loomed large in the British psyche at this
time. However, those that lived through the daily grind of Olympic-delivery,
as a 'local', experienced a reality vastly different from wider media representations of the 2012 transformation. The Olympic locales became contested
realms where Olympic-related discourse predominantly revolved around how
best to 'tame' this part of London (Gibbons and Wolff, 2012: 442).

## Research focus and methodology

The five London 2012 'Olympic Boroughs' housing those that required 'taming' were Newham, Waltham Forest, Tower Hamlets and Hackney in the east of the capital, and Greenwich in the south-east. It was difficult to argue against the necessity of renewal for this part of London. This was illustrated by a 2007 report by the Department of Communities and Local Government (DCLG) that classified three of these pre-Olympic locales as England's most deprived local authority areas. These were the Olympic Boroughs of Hackney, Newham and Tower Hamlets, with the fourth East London Olympic Borough, Waltham Forest, placed fifteenth (DCLG, 2007a).

This ethnography arrived at the conclusion that the most pertinent location to undertake Olympic-delivery research was within the borough of Newham.[1] This supposition proved conducive to insightful research and it was quickly discovered that in this location the regenerative bidding rhetoric of 'benefit for all' was often offset by divisive segregation. This research is in accord with research that evidences societal differentiation between those perceived as emblematic of progression and facilitators for rapid development, and those that are perceived as threats (Chibber, 2005; Peck, 2005; Tomba, 2009). That which can be described as 'London 2012' readily delineated between the generative affluent and the degenerative poor, the societal stimulant and the societal detriment, the socially valorised and the socially pathologised. This process invited all to engage, to varying degrees, yet actually presented very few tangible opportunities for the socio-economic advancement of the host community. This divisiveness also created divisions within and between this deprived but generally tolerant community, all of which will be explored herein.

Due to the transformative nature of Olympic delivery and the ephemeral nature of Newham as a place,[2] this proved to be a study of great transience. This research asserts thus that the use of the term 'community' is by necessity flexible. This flexibility permeates this analysis; indeed the term 'Newham community' does not exclude those that would not define themselves in these terms as such ambivalence toward inclusion is both an inherent and incurable part of any 'community' (Bauman, 1993: 8–10). Therefore – to simplify matters – this analysis does not use the term 'community' as representational of a holistic group against which to evaluate the implications of Olympic-delivery. Rather, it considers 'community' to be the site where Olympic-delivery questions, issues, difficulties and contestations involved could be explored. Therefore, the Newham 'community' was – and is – considered a 'relational space' within which to consider the reality of London 2012.

As a consequence, documenting Newham's Olympic milieu was a highly complex affair, which required a bespoke methodology. At the outset of the research it appeared logical to assume that those living in the area surrounding the building site that was to become the Olympic Park would have a differential experience to that of those living outside the immediate vicinity. An additional Olympic venue, namely the ExCeL that lay to the south of the borough, also required specific attention, as this locale would host many Olympic events and was also expected to undergo a substantial Olympic transition. Furthermore, all residents that populated the rest of the borough would have experiences and lives that would be impacted upon. The fieldwork needed a triple-fronted approach to researching, one where the researcher was embedded in the surrounding areas of Newham's two major Olympic venues and another that facilitated access to key exemplars of the community at large.

This conclusion permitted Newham to become segregated for research purposes into three distinct zones. These research zones (*Stratfordland, ExCeLland* and the *Dispersal Zone*) were geographically defined locations within which ethnographic research was conducted throughout Olympic delivery. Throughout the research Newham's transformation was recorded through personal reflections. The portrayal of *Stratfordland* (the area in the vicinity of the Olympic Park) saw the researcher immersed within a housing estate on the boundaries of the Olympic Park. *ExCeLland* (the area in the vicinity of the ExCeL) was represented by ethnography conducted from within a housing estate on the boundaries of the ExCeL. The remainder of Newham was defined as an Olympic *Dispersal Zone*, and researching within this larger locale involved ethnographic immersion in the borough's third sector within organisations that were tasked with running community engagement activities on a borough wide basis. The success of their endeavours was evaluated upon their abilities to engage with all levels of Newham's diverse community. The particularities of this methodology included such research variances as representing community organisations in Olympic discourse with Olympic deliverers, attending a plethora of community-orientated Olympic meetings, attending anti-Olympic protests, working in community centres, drinking with migrant construction workers, playing sport with local youths, meeting with gang members and voluntary youth work, amongst many, many others.

This chapter argues that the relatively short Olympic-delivery time frame necessitated this divisive segregation between 'Olympic' and 'non-Olympic' peoples, places and perceptions. Furthermore, it argues that 2012 Olympic-delivery was fundamentally orientated towards the needs and goals of the aspirational economic Olympic 'migrant', of various descriptions, rather than enhancing the lives of those already living within a community that was rife with crime, poverty and deprivation. These locals, although invited to engage with Olympic opportunity, were fundamentally lacking in the requirements necessary to engage with opportunities, and so were excluded from its benefits.

## Newham's Olympic reclamation

For London 2012 the starring role belonged to the London borough of Newham. Pre-Games Newham was a deprived place of transition, with the Olympics being utilised as a catalyst to make the borough more appealing. The 2012 Olympic Park that cut across all five Olympic boroughs was primarily located within Newham. The Olympic venues and the plethora of other regenerative projects, which systemically all become Olympic-related during the Olympic period, were expected to do much to allay Newham's deprivation. This was emphasised by the Newham Mayor, Sir Robin Wales, who consistently advocated his desire to dramatically change Newham via the 2012 Olympics. He stated that London was unlike any other Olympic host city because, in his opinion, for the first time in history, the Olympics were being used to completely transform a deprived area. He believed the regeneration of Newham was the primary reason why London won the Games.[3]

The 2012-related regeneration of Newham's locales promised to deliver a range of socio-economic benefits that included employment opportunities, improved housing, and commercial and public facilities. For the Newham residents, opportunity was to arrive in the shape of jobs, particularly within the construction and service industries in the short-term, and through skills training, which promised to enhance longer-term prospects. Notably, the reality of such socio-economic enhancement altered the dynamics of this area. It is in this regard that Newham's Olympic legacy has, and will, become most apparent.

This chapter contends that Newham's primary Olympic outcome can be considered a means of redressing the 'Rent Gap'[4] of a deprived but potentially valuable location that lay within an easy commute of the city. This appraisal fits with neighbourhood modification models that can be categorised by the term 'gentrification'. In a review of gentrification literature Slater *et al.* (2004: 1145) purported that this schema related to all aspects of the "production of space for – and consumption by – a more affluent and very different incoming population". The paradigm of gentrification is deeply rooted in the social dynamics and economic trends of an area and its signifiers and effects are heavily influenced by the nature of economic restructuring and the goals of those charged with urban regeneration (van Weesep, 1984: 80).

It was expected that Newham's profile, as an Olympic host, ensured that the area – during Olympic-delivery and beyond – would yield higher returns from its land in the form of rents and property values. The anticipated result has and will continue to attract new, more affluent residents to the area as a result of the allure of development and opportunity. This poses the question: who are the key recipients of these Olympic benefits? Regardless, the perception of 'development' was an integral part of 'London 2012' from Olympic bid to beyond the Games:

> By staging the Games in this part of the city, the most enduring legacy of the Olympics will be the regeneration of an entire community for the direct benefit of everyone who lives there.
>
> (London 2012 *Candidate File*, 2004: 19)

Crucially, a definition of the 'entire community' that would attain Olympic benefits was never delineated. Also absent was any semblance of precisely what these benefits would entail. Clearly, there is a fundamental difference between orienting Olympic legacy outcomes geographically and sociologically, and the absence of clarity may speak more towards the intent of Olympic legacy – that of over-arching positivistic rhetoric – rather than tangible, planned outcomes.

## Post-Olympic Newham: utopia or bust?

The nature of 2012 Olympic delivery followed an easy-to-understand narrative of reclamation. It has been argued that, during the post-Games period, less afflu-ent and/or minority (multi) ethnic communities who ordered the space of the Olympic Park were likely to become subject to increased regulation, surveil-lance, policing techniques and displacement to ensure the area was suitable for the habitation of the future populace (Gibbons and Wolff, 2012; Paton *et al.*, 2012). However, the reality was that this process began much earlier: during Olympic delivery. The head of the Olympic Park Legacy Company (OPLC), Andrew Altman's, summation that East London's pre-Olympic landscape was a 'gash' that required 'Olympic healing' perhaps best exemplified the underlying methodological orientation of this regeneration (Armstrong *et al.*, 2011).

It was difficult to argue against the fact that Newham required regeneration. Recent figures revealed that approximately 30 per cent of the borough would move internally or externally each year.[5] Such movement translated to a hugely 'root-less' population that saw the borough as a place of transit and transience, little more than a stop on a journey elsewhere. If, as some argue, place-related identities, relations and histories are formed and asserted via uniformity (Korpela, 1989; Johnston *et al.*, 1994) the absence of such identity-affirming uniformity leads to the consideration that the application of Auge's (1995) conceptualisation of the 'non-place' to Newham was pertinent. Auge argued that if a 'place' can be defined as relational, historical and concerned with identity, then a space that cannot be defined as such must be a 'non-place' (Auge, 1995: 77–78).

The diversity of Newham was perhaps best illustrated by the fact that, it was, and remains, one of the most culturally and ethnically diverse places on the planet, with over 300 languages spoken in the borough (Newham Language Shop, 2005). Indeed, throughout the research period, the most common language for communication between the researcher and Newham residents (and com-monly observable between the community members themselves) was English-Creole. Newham's character could only be one inferred to be a culmination of its component transitory parts as the Newham council mantra of the borough being 'a place to live, work and stay' was implicitly created to address.

The tactics adopted for Newham's rebranding provides insight into the nature of how a long-established neighbourhood, synonymous with poverty and depri-vation, can be re-packaged and re-branded on a global scale through the use of the mega-event. Interestingly, attempts to sell this diverse, deprived area, liter-ally and metaphorically, arose at a precarious political juncture wherein the UK housing market was suffering turbulence and the fiscal policy of the UK govern-ment was increasingly intolerant of those citizens who were dependent on state benefits for their housing costs.[6] Focus will now be placed upon the transitional implications and processes of Newham's Olympic rebranding.

## Evaluating Newham's Olympic delivery transition

It may be argued that Olympic-delivery did – as expected – create many employment opportunities within the geographical confines of Newham. This was, to a degree, in accord with the local government's pre-Games orientation:

> The London 2012 Games represent a once-in-a-lifetime opportunity for us to raise the profile of the borough, improve our transport networks and inspire people to participate in sport and healthy lifestyles. They will speed up the regeneration of Newham, East London ... providing hundreds of jobs and business opportunities before, during and after 2012. To ensure that we take full advantage of this opportunity, we have set six objectives [which included the maximisation of] ... the Games delivery process to develop a thriving economic legacy – *where all people share in the growing prosperity.*
>
> (Newham London website, no date, emphasis in original)[7]

However, these opportunities proved inaccessible for much of the pre-bid community, as discussed further below. The practicalities and assumptions that underpinned the notion that Olympic-delivery would provide a plethora of employment opportunities for local people depended upon the assumption that Newham's residents had the pre-requisite skills and motivation to take advantage of Olympic employment opportunities. Statistics published in a 2011 Aston Mansfield document[8] produced by their 'Advance to Deliver' project[9] demonstrated that, statistically, Newham did not see the widespread Olympic-delivery benefits that were expected to accrue.

This above-mentioned report indicated that in 2008/2009 Newham's employment rate was the lowest in London at just 56.2 per cent, significantly below the average London rate of 62.7 per cent. The report commented that over recent years this gap widened with employment rates for women and ethnic minorities being particularly low: for women 46 per cent (compared to the London average of 62 per cent), and ethnic minorities 49 per cent (compared to 59 per cent across London) (Aston Mansfield, 2011: 4). These statistics indicated that Olympic-delivery was not addressing issues of employment; on the contrary the employment gap between Newham and the rest of London was increasing. This begged the question: if someone else seized the opportunities presented, could anything have been done differently to break this destructive cycle?

Mayor of Newham, Sir Robin Wales, argued that nothing could be done to overcome residents' failure to take advantage of the opportunities the Games provided. Indeed, at a conference organised by the Commission for Racial Equality during a debate regarding London 2012 and its benefits for ethnic minorities, Sir Robin launched a scathing attack on the residents of the borough and their inability (and reluctance) to take advantage of Olympic benefits. The Mayor's comments, printed in a national newspaper,[10] described Newham residents as follows. They:

- Were too idle to get jobs on 2012 projects;
- Struggled to get out of bed before 11 a.m.;
- Were used to being unemployed;
- Had the sole aspiration in life to be given a council house;
- Were lazy and the outcome of their laziness was the hiring of Eastern Europeans to fill the employment void.

Responses to the above comments reverberated around Newham's Third Sector organisations and could be surmised accordingly: Robin Wales was dismissed as a heavy drinker and prone to outlandishly foolish comments that he would later seek to retract. Furthermore, such comments validated the commonly held belief throughout Newham's Third Sector that the Mayor was "as much of an arsehole as we thought he was". Whilst there were few, if any, possibilities to get rid of him as a Mayor – because he was publically elected – the only possibility for removal was his standing down or defeat at an election. Somewhat surprisingly, given the comments highlighted above, even the Mayor's staunchest critics commonly held a begrudging deference to him, believing him an incredibly astute politician who would prove very difficult to defeat on any issue.

### Eastern European void fillers

Newham's Albanian population provides an example of Eastern Europeans that could be classed as representative of those vilified during the Olympic-delivery period, by, for example, the Mayor, media, and public opinion.[11] The following narrative is taken from a private interview with a founding member of an Albanian organisation, 'Shpresa'. Shpresa was established in Newham in 2001 by Albanian residents. Its purpose was to fulfil a self-diagnosed community need to facilitate opportunities for Albanians in many aspect of everyday life, including employment and socialisation opportunities:

> We were promised many opportunities for employment by [Sir] Robin Wales if we won the Games. We were invited to community meetings between us, the Mayor of Newham and the Olympic people and were told that there would be free training for the unemployed that would lead to jobs in construction and not just the menial work but skilled positions too. London obviously got the Games and we really pushed education in our community. Many became trained in various fields. However, once the men became qualified they could not find work anywhere. Sub-contractors that we wouldn't even know how to contact to apply for work did a lot of the construction work and hardly any positions were advertised openly. It was a closed shop. Worse than that though, the jobs that were openly advertised were the menial positions and when our members applied for these jobs they were turned down because they were thought to be over-qualified as a result of attending the training courses!
>
> (Private interview, Luljeta, white Albanian, 37, October 2011)

This illustrates the dichotomy between potential and tangible Olympic benefits and opportunities. The belief that Newham residents, of varied backgrounds and origins, could be transformed from unskilled into skilled workers in time to take advantage of Olympic employment illustrates the potentially damaging nature of such assumptions. The widespread perception of Olympic legacy benefiting local people depended upon the assumption that Newham communities' needs were being met through generic Olympic employment opportunities, but what was offered had little applicability to the communities' abilities or aspirations. Attention now turns to another Olympic delivery reality – that of living within a location deemed too unsightly for the Olympic Games. The following account was indicative of the experiences of many residents who lived on the cusp of the Olympic Park in the Carpenters estate.

## The Carpenters estate

The Carpenters estate composed three 23-storey tower blocks and some 700 other units. This estate was located in Stratford at the heart of the Olympic development in the north-east corner of Newham; having been built by Newham council in 1969. It occupied prime development land and lay some four miles east of the City of London and next to Stratford Regional Station, which formed one of the main entry points to the Olympic Park.

Social housing projects, including the Carpenters estate, attempted to alleviate housing issues in deprived and derelict areas. However, the building of such estates did little to address the underlying social issues, such as unemployment, poverty and deprivation. The consequence of their implementation was increased class-based polarisation (Power, 1996). The cumulative effect of such housing policies was spatial and social exclusion and 'area-based poverty' (Power, 1987, 1996; Power and Turnstall, 1991). This was evidently the case in this location, and over the years this estate has become more decrepit and poorly maintained. Those occupying the estate found living hard to manage and the population of the Carpenters estate were habitually categorised as amongst the most deprived in England (Index of Multiple Deprivation, 2007, cited in Department of Communities and Local Government, 2007b).

At the turn of the twenty-first century the estates' three tower blocks were badly in need of repair. In 2004 the Council decided that the worst of the three – James Riley Point – needed to be demolished, and its residents re-housed. Soon after, in 2007/2008, Newham Council evaluated a refurbishment programme for the other two tower blocks – Lund and Dennison Point – and decided that the £50 million needed was prohibitive. These blocks would also be demolished and the population re-housed. Dependent upon perspective it can either be argued that the Olympic Park and stadium shadowed the estate, or that the estate cast a metaphorical shadow over the Games. Indeed the estate became the backdrop to the Games and the poor condition of it threatened to blot an otherwise contemporary Olympic landscape until 'ingenious' masking tactics were adopted that involved blocking sightlines with advertising (see Figure 14.1).

*Figure 14.1* Masking ugly Newham from Olympic view (source: author's personal photographs).

This masking or removing of that which is deemed unsightly or a threat to the 2012 mystique resonates with similar tactics adopted during other mega-events, such as the 2008 Beijing Olympics, the 2010 FIFA World Cup in South Africa and the 2010 Commonwealth Games in Delhi. It appears that regardless of location the masking of poverty and the hosting of a mega-event are becoming synonymous. Examples include the removal of shack dwellers in Cape Town (Miraftab, 2009; Newton, 2009), slum demolitions in Delhi (Dupont, 2008; Bhan, 2009) and the relocation of 300,000 residents in Beijing in 2004 to make way for the 2008 Olympic facilities (Broudehoux, 2007). However, these other mega-events were commonly referred to as 'coming out parties' intended to demonstrate development on a much more significant scale than London 2012 (Tomlinson *et al.*, 2009). Indeed, reports of the erosion of the *favelas* in Brazil in preparation for the FIFA 2014 World Cup and the 2016 Olympic Games would indicate a similar narrative is currently unravelling (Zirin, 2011).

Newham's Olympic-delivery period witnessed a more gradual decanting of the residents of its tower blocks than that of these other mega-events. This decanting correlated with the birth of Olympic Stratford. The Carpenters estate became emblematic of the poverty and deprivation that the Olympics intended to eradicate from the Olympic locales and those that lived within its boundaries were categorised as deprived and in need of saving from their social malady. An indication of the realities of the Carpenters regeneration and life in the shadow of the Olympic Park is encapsulated in a case study of Sylvie.

## Sylvie: the moan that Newham forgot

> As we sat on the sofa in Sylvie's living room she motioned to the TV in the corner. It was covered in dust: 'I can dust the room in the morning and by the afternoon I can write my name on the top of the TV again with all the crap that gets blown in from the Olympics'. Clearly house-proud and conscious of the perceptions of others, Sylvie had lived in this flat for 35 years. She had raised her kids here and as she stated it had 'seen off' her husband too. She was now being offered a £4,000 moving allowance by the local council to relocate.... The amount rankled as she was only offered the same amount as others that had lived on the estate for a lot less time. She suggested that there was no value to be placed upon personal investment, familiarity or sentimentality in relocation.
>
> As we looked out at the emerging Olympic Park, Sylvie commented on what a great 'Panasonic [*sic*] view' she had and how she would miss it when she'd gone, believing, quite correctly, that she would not see the Park complete: 'Life here has been pretty tough since the Olympics came', she said matter of factly. 'The new flats over the road block out the sun and it is a lot harder to get to the shops now because they have shut the gateway through the station, making it off-limits for residents. Now it's just for workers. There's 24-hour drilling and alarms going off at the Station [Stratford] every couple of hours; at 2am and 4am this morning they went off. The other thing

is the tannoy announcements that go on late into the night. It would be understandable if they were important but the last one shouted 'Dave, your tea is ready'. In full flow Sylvie turned from the structural to the persecuted:

'I don't even recognise the place anymore, it's changed so much in the last year or so, it doesn't feel like home. The site-workers are taking over Stratford. The Poles come over with their women for healthcare and having babies. You can tell the women, blonde hair, black roots … Sluts. My son is a construction worker and he was bullied on the site by Poles, Croats and fucking Paddies. It didn't stop until he threatened to put someone in the ground. At the end of the day you can build what you like, you can't make a silk purse from a sow's ear, it'll always be fucking Stratford'.

(Fieldwork notes, December 2010)

Sylvie had lived a solitary life since her grown up children had flown the nest for the leafier climes of suburban Essex. One might argue that a nostalgic longing for times past had caused Sylvie to become bitter and fatalistic and that she would perceive any modification of her locale as further indication that her best years were behind her. Throughout this research the interactions with Sylvie proved frequently paradoxical. In many exchanges Sylvie demonstrated that she was both open and adaptable to Newham's evolution and she demonstrated an, at times, post-racial outlook that appeared a good fit with that which prevailed in this highly diverse borough. Alternatively, as the above indicates, this was sometimes accompanied by parochial and intolerant comments that resonated with frustration and self-pity more than outright bigotry. This was most notably evidenced by her intolerance of Eastern Europeans, which resonates with wider sociological themes that go beyond the remit of this chapter. Eventually Sylvie and the many others like her left the Carpenters, being relocated elsewhere within the borough.

The 2012 London Olympic-delivery period saw a new skyline surround the Carpenters estate as Olympic Newham evolved at a dizzying pace. The Olympic Park rose from the ashes of faded industry and a plethora of other buildings, flats and offices rapidly began to emerge, and dominate the landscape. This regenerative narrative served to reinforce an on-going Olympic predisposition that hosting was orientated:

…toward a greater level of segregation and separation at the micro-community level, as the Olympic Park attracts residential units that serve the needs of young professionals.… This pattern of separation and segregation at the local level has been a feature of regeneration and gentrification schemes in East London over recent years – with stark divisions emerging in the same street between the 'gated' and those without.

(Imrie *et al.*, 2009: 143)

The Olympic Park's gated communities would arrive after the culmination of the Games. During the delivery stage the council gradually emptied the estate of tenants. As demonstrated, the eradication of the Carpenters estate was planned long before the Olympics and this fact enforces the findings of Burbank *et al.* (2001: 7) who argued that the motivations for a host city to enter the Olympic bidding process are underpinned by "the existence of an established growth regime in the city ... [and] a desire to create or change the city's image".

The outcomes of these tactics are still some years away from being determined. The costs of the housing in the Olympic Park have still to be recouped. Selling the housing units to private investors might do this. Alternatively, the return could be delayed, but guaranteed all the same, by long-term renting. Regardless, those occupying the housing have to be earning an income well above the median that currently typifies Newham. Higher average incomes require more jobs. The post-Olympic rhetoric stresses a convergence of social class within the Park through social mixing. Previous research (Lindsay, 2012) has demonstrated that this idealised social mixing blueprint adopted for use in the Olympic Park has been previously implemented elsewhere in the borough. This created a segregated community that fostered an environment of fear and loathing between social classes, a dependence upon private security and gated communities for segregation and, notably, a spike in crime.

## Conclusions

The successful London Olympic bid of 2005 promised legacy and regeneration for the East End of London. All would be winners; housing would improve, accessibility to this locale would progress exponentially, the various medical epidemics that typified the east of the metropolis would be addressed and the sporting chances afforded the multi-cultural youth that made up the borough's population would be without parallel in the UK. Accordingly, legacy was often portrayed as a panacea to address economic, social and political issues. This revolved around the consideration that Olympic hosting would provide a regenerative juncture for a 'better' Newham, a view based upon an assumption that all shared the same opinion of what constituted a 'better life'. Furthermore, one had to assume that all living in the area under consideration had the ability to take advantage of the opportunities presented therein, which proved not to be the case. The local residents' failure to exploit these Olympic opportunities holds resonance with Fussey *et al.*'s (2011) consideration that regional and economic 'legacy' benefits can often be seen to exacerbate social disadvantage and inequality rather than remedy it.

In this regard, Olympic-delivery Newham was – subtly perhaps – enforcing the transition of the borough away from a 'non-place' towards something else. This 'something else' was a re-branded Newham injected with something called 'culture' where collective identity was intended to be delivered in hermetically sealed, Olympically inspired, instalments. This transitional period (2005–2012) saw Newham become something Lefebvre (1991) would conceptualise as a 'differential space'. This, according to Lefebvre (1991: 52), is an essential transition for a new space to be produced. Within this 'differential space' the functions, elements and moments of social practice are restored (or indeed created). This theoretical perspective suited a definition of Newham as did the idea of it being for so many of its dwellers a 'non-place' evidencing a "very peculiar type of abstraction" that was aspiring to be real but was unable to create a holistic identity (Lefebvre, 1991: 53).

The absence of a tangible, definable place-identity contributed to the consideration that Newham was an ideal prospective Olympic host. In toto Newham was a place that lacked inclusion, but the absence of unity or collective identity was not feared because it was never missed, in this regard Auge's (1995) mechanisms of the '*non-place*' exemplified much of this borough. One might argue Olympic regeneration of selected parts of Newham promises only to enhance the sense of differentiation and strangeness of the borough. This research demonstrated such complex, inconsistent interplay between ideology, rhetoric and implementation and, in doing so, it found that wider pro-Olympic discourse of the benefits of hosting Games proved at odds with the experiences of the local communities.

Irrespective of the profile of Newham as a whole, certain components of this reclaimed post-Olympic metropolis are reminiscent of the precursors of many other gentrified urban locales (Jacobs, 1996; Lees, 2003). The post-Olympic properties will inevitably be attractive to those described variously as post-place flaneurs (King, 1993), transnational elites (Friedmann and Wolff, 1982), stateless persons (Wallerstein, 1993), cosmopolites (Hannerz, 1992) and creative classes (Florida, 2005). Such metropolitan migrants might actively seek the nuances of the 'non-place' to satiate their seeking of a vibrant, urban life. This promises to attract a specific affluent populace and result in a dilution of diversity, whereby less economically able residents relocate elsewhere out of financial necessity (Cole, 1987; Hughes, 1990; Smith, 1996; Ley, 2003). Life in refashioned post-Olympic Games Newham will be one wherein governance through gentrification promises to be prevalent. The new revenue streams (particularly the extra council tax) and demographics promise to ensure the local politicians are happy with the results, at least in the short term.

## Notes

1 Despite Olympic events taking place in other parts of the country, including football at Coventry, Manchester, Newcastle, Cardiff and Glasgow, the vast majority of events took place in London, with 61 per cent hosted by Newham. Newham notably hosted the Olympic Park, which constituted an area of $2.5 \text{km}^2$. Its centrepiece was the 80,000-seat Olympic stadium. It also included the Olympic village, which was intended to be converted into residential apartments post-Games. Other occupants included a 6000 seat velodrome, a 12,000 capacity basketball arena, a hockey centre, an aquatics centre, a handball arena, a broadcast centre, a water polo arena, many recreational spaces and the largest urban shopping mall in Europe – Westfield Stratford City.

2 The *leitmotif* of Newham is the exceptional churn of its residents. Recent figures revealed that some 30 per cent of the borough's demographic would change residence in the course of a year. Newham is consistently referred to as one of the most ethnically diverse places on the planet, with over 300 languages spoken (Newham

Language Shop, 2005). At the time of research there was no place of comparable diversity in Europe or indeed the world. As a consequence, the common language of contemporary Newham was English-Creole and comparisons to other research contexts were problematic.

3 For more information, see www.newham.gov.uk/2012Games/MayorSirRobinWaleshailsarrivalofthe2012Games.htm?Printable=true.

4 The term 'Rent Gap' refers to the shortfall between the actual economic return taken from an area of land given its present land use (capitalised ground rent) and the potential return it would yield if it were put to its optimal, highest and best use (potential ground rent). As a rent gap increases, it creates lucrative opportunities for developers, investors, homebuyers and local governments to orchestrate a shift in land use – for instance, from working-class residential to middle or upper-class residential or high-end commercial (Smith, 1979; Lees *et al.*, 2008).

5 See www.gov.uk/government/uploads/system/uploads/attachment_data/file/6331/5231109.pdf.

6 For more, see http://news.sky.com/story/1072240/welfare-reforms-will-make-benefits-fairer and www.dailymail.co.uk/debate/article-2089696/Immigrants-claiming-UK-benefits-report-Stop-abuse-British-hospitality.html.

7 The webpage from which this quotation was taken no longer exists.

8 A Newham based charity, Aston Mansfield (AM) were a long-established community organisation that focused upon facilitating everyday life within the communities that reside in Newham. They were established in 2000, whose purpose was to create social change for the benefit of local people. They accomplished this by campaigning for social justice, which their General Manager defined as "the quest for fairness and respect that ensures the local people are treated within their expectations of human dignity". AM provided services for education and training, capacity building and developing competencies for local people. AM defined themselves as an organisation that "implemented a community development approach" that aimed to resolve issues pertinent to the Newham community, which they defined as an approach where they work alongside the community to identify areas of concern and improvement. They produce a number of Newham based studies. See, for example, www.aston-mansfield.org.uk/pdf_docs/research/newham-key-statistics.PDF.

9 For more information, see also www.aston-mansfield.org.uk/a2d.php.

10 The newspaper account is available at www.dailymail.co.uk/news/article-419161/Mayor-Olympic-borough-says-locals-lazy-jobs-project.html.

11 A personal interview with an Albanian Shpresa organisation leader, October 2011, indicated that despite the fact that the vast majority of this demographic were Newham residents long before the Games were mooted – most having arrived in the early 1990s – many were defined as Olympic-related economic-migrants during this period.

# References

Armstrong, G., Hobbs, R. and Lindsay, I. (2011) Calling the shots: The pre-2012 London Olympic contest. *Urban Studies*, 48(15): 3169–3184.

Aston Mansfield (2011) *A2D: Newham Key Statistics*. [Online] Available from www.aston-mansfield.org.uk/pdf_docs/research/newham-key-statistics.PDF [accessed 3 June 2011].

Auge, M. (1995) *Non-Places: An introduction to supermodernity*. London: Verso.

Bauman, Z. (1993) *Postmodern ethics*. Oxford: Blackwell.

Bhan, G. (2009) "This is no longer the city I once knew": Evictions, the urban poor and the right to the city in millennial Delhi. *Environment and Urbanization*, 21: 127–142.

Broudehoux, A.M. (2007) Delirious Beijing: Euphoria and despair in the Olympic metropolis. In M. Davis and D.B. Monk (eds) *Evil paradises: Dreamworlds of neoliberalism.* New York: New York Press, 87–101.

Burbank, M., Andranovich, G. and Heying, C.H. (2001) *Olympic dreams: The impact of mega-events on local politics.* Boulder, CO: Lynne Rienner Publishers.

Chibber, V. (2005) Reviving the developmental state? The myth of the national bourgeoisie. In L. Panitch and C. Leys (eds) *The empire reloaded: The socialist register.* New York: Monthly Review Press, 144–165.

Cole, D. (1987) Artists and urban development. *Geographical Review*, 77: 391–407.

DCLG (Department of Communities and Local Government) (2007a) *The English Indices of Deprivation 2007: Summary.* [Online] Available from www.communities.gov.uk/documents/communities/pdf/576659.pdf [accessed 10 April 2010].

DCLG (Department of Communities and Local Government) (2007b) *The English Indices of Deprivation 2007.* London: HMSO.

Dupont, V. (2008) Slum demolitions in Delhi since the 1990s: An appraisal. *Economic and Political Weekly*, July 12.

Essex, S. and Chalkley, B. (1998) Olympic Games: Catalyst of urban change. *Leisure Studies*, 17(3): 187–206.

Florida, R. (2005) *The flight of the creative class: The new global competition for talent.* New York: HarperCollins.

Friedmann, J. and Wolff, G. (1982) World city formation: An agenda for research and action. *International Journal of Urban and Regional Research*, 6: 309–344.

Fussey, P., Coafee, J., Armstrong, G. and Hobbs, D. (2011) *Securing and sustaining the Olympic city: Reconfiguring London for 2012 and beyond.* Aldershot: Ashgate.

Gibbons, A. and Wolff, N. (2012) Games monitor: Undermining the hype of the London Olympics. *City: Analysis of Urban Trends, Culture, Theory, Policy, Action*, 16(4): 468–473.

Gold, J.R. and Gold, M.M. (eds) (2007) *Olympic cities: City agendas, planning, and the world's games, 1896–2012.* London: Routledge.

Hannerz, U. (1992) Cosmopolitans and locals in world culture. In M. Featherstone (ed.) *Global culture: Nationalism, globalism and modernity.* London: Sage, 237–251.

Hansard (2005) *House of Commons debates: London 2012 Olympic bid.* [Online] Available from www.theyworkforyou.com/debates/?id=2005–07–06a.404.0 [accessed 8 May 2012].

Hughes, R. (1990) *Nothing if not critical: Selected essays on art.* New York: Knopf.

Imrie, R., Lees, L. and Raco, M. (2009) *Regenerating London: Governance, sustainability and community in a global city.* London: Routledge.

Jacobs, J. (1996) *Edge of empire: Postcolonialism and the city.* London: Routledge.

Johnston, R.J., Gregory, D. and Smith, D.M. (eds) (1994) *The dictionary of human geography*, 3rd edition. Oxford: Blackwell.

King, A.D. (1993) Identity and difference: The internationalization of capital and the globalization of culture. In P.L. Knox (ed.) *The restless urban landscape.* Englewood Cliffs, NJ: Prentice-Hall, 83–110.

Korpela, K.M. (1989) Place-identity as a product of environmental self-regulation. *Journal of Environmental Psychology*, 9: 241–256.

Lees, L. (2003) Visions of urban renaissance: The urban task force report and the urban white paper. In R. Imrie and M. Raco (eds) *Urban renaissance? New Labour, community and urban policy.* Bristol: The Policy Press, 61–82.

Lees, L., Slater, T. and Wyly, E. (eds) (2008) *The gentrification reader.* London: Routledge.

Lefebvre, H. (1991) *The production of space* (translated into English by D. Nicholson-Smith). Oxford: Blackwell.

Ley, D. (2003) Artists, aesthetics and the field of gentrification. *Urban Studies*, 40(12): 2527–2544.

Lindsay, I. (2012). Social mixing: A life of fear. *Urbanities*, 2(2): 25–44.

London 2012 (Bidding Team) (2004) *Candidate File*. [Online] Available from www.london2012.com/documents/candidate-files [accessed 10 January 2008].

Miraftab, F. (2009) Insurgent planning: Situating radical planning in the global south. *Planning Theory*, 8: 32–50.

Newham Language Shop (2005) *Newham council language survey*. [Online] Available from www.languageshop.org.uk [accessed 1 May 2006].

Newton, C. (2009) The reverse side of the medal: About the 2010 FIFA World Cup and the beautification of the N2 in Cape Town. *Urban Forum*, 20: 93–108.

Paton, K., Mooney, G. and McKee, K. (2012) Class, citizenship and regeneration: Glasgow and the Commonwealth Games 2014. *Antipode*, 44(4): 1470–1489.

Peck, J. (2005) Struggling with the creative class. *International Journal of Urban and Regional Research*, 29: 740–770.

Power, A. (1987) *Property before people: The management of twentieth-century council housing*. London: Unwin.

Power, A. (1996) Area-based poverty and residential empowerment. *Urban Studies*, 33: 1535–1564.

Power, A. and Turnstall, R. (1991) *Swimming against the tide: Polarisation or progress on 20 unpopular council estates, 1980–1995*. York: Joseph Rowntree Foundation.

Preuss, H. (2004) *The economics of staging the Olympics: A comparison of the Games 1972–2008*. Cheltenham: Edward Elgar Publishing.

Slater, T., Curran, W. and Lees, L. (2004) Gentrification research: New directions and critical scholarship. *Environment and Planning*, 36: 1141–1150.

Smith, N. (1996) *The new urban frontier*. New York: Routledge.

Tomba, L. (2009) Of quality, harmony, and community: Civilization and the middle class in urban China. *Positions: East Asia Cultures Critiques*, 17: 591–616.

Tomlinson, R., Bass, O. and Pillay, U. (eds) (2009) *Development and dreams: The urban legacy of the 2010 Football World Cup*. Cape Town: HSRC Press.

van Weesep, J. (1984) Condominium conversation in Amsterdam: Boon or burden. *Urban Geography*, 5: 165–177.

Wallerstein, N. (1993) Empowerment and health: The theory and practice of community change. *Community Development Journal*, 28(3): 218–227.

Zirin, D. (2011) Brazil's disappearing favelas. [Online] Available from www.aljazeera.com/indepth/opinion/2011/05/201159123141256818.htm [accessed 10 December 2011].

# Conclusion

## This is just the beginning…

*Katherine Dashper, Thomas Fletcher and
Nicola McCullough*

> That there is a buzz about events and events management can scarcely be
> doubted.
>
> (Rojek, 2013: 100)

As we identified in the introduction to this collection, the field of event-related
studies, including sports events, is entering a critical moment. The increased
prominence of events within everyday life and the proliferation of event-related
degrees and courses both necessitates and justifies their study but, as critical
scholars such as Rojek (2013) are arguing, there remains a need to move beyond
studying the more technocratic aspects and of broad analyses focusing on event
'impacts' to engage more widely in rigorous and critical debate. The technocratic aspects of events and events management are well rehearsed: taxonomies
of events and practicalities related to planning, delivery and, to a lesser extent,
evaluating events are the staple of the mainstream events literature (e.g. Masterman, 2008; Bowdin *et al.*, 2011; Mallen and Adams, 2013). There is also a
growing body of research beginning to question the economic and/or socio-
cultural impacts of events (e.g. Richards *et al.*, 2013). We acknowledge the
importance of this kind of research and what it contributes to the body of knowledge, especially in relation to student learning and preparing them to enter the
labour market. However, for event-related studies to mature, we advocate the
need to move beyond focusing on the 'doing' of (sports) events management, or
the direct impacts of specific events, towards more critical analyses which situate
events within wider discourses pertaining to power, privilege and legitimacy. As
event educators, as well as researchers, we are reminded of the importance of
transferring knowledge from research into teaching. We acknowledge that many
event-related university courses are currently, and justifiably, vocational and
practically orientated, but as Tribe (2002) suggests in relation to tourism degrees,
we also hope to encourage students to become 'philosophical practitioners'.
Indeed, as Getz (2007: 6–7) argues:

> The professional event manager has to have more than skills. Professionals
> must have a broad base of knowledge together with the ability to reflect

upon how it will shape both specific managerial or business decisions, and the wider implications in society and the environment. They also have to possess a well-developed sense of ethics and a professional responsibility which should be based on a solid foundation that includes philosophy and comparative cultural studies.

This volume is a step in this direction. The selection of contributions is deliberately broad in terms of theoretical approach, subject matter, methodology, and the conceptualisation of sports events and their role within society and culture. Our intention is not to plug the gaps in the events-related literature that we have identified, or to advocate any specific approach(es) or framework(s) for future analyses. Rather, this collection is intended to provoke critical thinking about sports events and their roles, significance and meaning(s), and to encourage students and scholars in event-related studies to look beyond the event itself and engage more freely with literature and theory from outside of the currently rather limited event-specific literature, drawing on the more well-established social and political sciences, including the sub-disciplines of sociology of sport and leisure studies. In so doing, over time event-related studies will evolve and mature to not only draw upon these disciplines, but also contribute to the development of new knowledge and theory.

The contributors to this volume are from diverse disciplinary backgrounds, and few would identify explicitly as event scholars, locating themselves more within the fields of sport studies and the social sciences of sport. Their research draws upon these broader fields and shows some ways in which we can begin to bridge the gaps between event-related studies and associated academic fields. Contributors represent scholars at different stages of their careers, from established professors to PhD students, and so illustrate the richness of the field and suggest that there is an exciting future for sports event-related research. There are many possibilities and a lot of work to be done as the field matures. This volume is a contribution towards this bigger project and, in the final section, we pick up on some of the ideas put forth in these chapters and make some suggestions for future research directions.

## Future research directions

The study of sports events is necessarily multi-disciplinary and encompasses events of vastly different scale and size. As we have already identified, contributors to this volume have examined events ranging from the very local level all the way up to mega-events. Contributors to this volume have broached the theme of mega-events from a number of discipline areas, namely sociology and social policy, international relations, and hospitality and events. And whilst they share a number of core themes – power and development for instance – each has applied the concept of sports mega-events in a different way, specific to their subject area. Future analyses of sports mega-events ought to take heed of this. As Dowse argues in Chapter 13, political scientists are yet to embrace sports mega-events as serious topics for research. The same can certainly be said for other fields, as events-related research is often marginalised within mainstream disciplines. Moreover, as sports mega-events begin to be hosted with increasing regularity outside of the traditional power block of the west, future research must begin to entangle a number of emerging issues around power, governance, sustainable development, image management, globalisation, and ethics. Rumford's (2007) conceptualisation of 'post-westernisation' and its associated challenges to western hegemony may be appropriate to these analyses (see Chapter 13 in this volume). In the wake of negative publicity surrounding India's hosting of the 2010 Commonwealth Games, and Rio de Janeiro's struggle to be ready for the 2014 Football World Cup, an important question emerges: is it ethical for developing nations to host sports mega-events? In the context of Rio de Janeiro, Curi *et al.* (2011) allude to the juxtaposition of 'First' and 'Third' world populations in the host city. They argue that the majority of western travellers will likely never have witnessed such contrasting levels of affluence in the same place. It will be interesting to see how event organisers and governing bodies negotiate such issues of poverty. Continuing this theme, research examining the commingling of global and local forces will facilitate a wider understanding of the impact of these events on local communities. Roche (2008: 288) identifies that the political nature of mega-events leads to host cities becoming "transient and 'glocal' urban hubs of international and global political and economic networks". As a result, one of their main roles is to act as "advertising and brand-promotion vehicles". This imperative, coupled with national development and regeneration agendas has, and will likely continue to, lead to conflict and antagonism over event appropriation (see Chapters 11 and 12 in this volume). More broadly, future research must examine issues of power within the wider web of global sport. There is already evidence in some sports, cricket for example, of where governance structures and economic power have shifted to developing eastern nation-states, to the extent that how we conceive the future of the sport has changed irrevocably. The global success of the Indian Premier League (IPL) and its associated 'threat' to traditional formats of the game are cases in point (Rumford, 2007). It will be interesting to see whether emerging economic powers in the east, such as China, Dubai and Qatar, are able to influence particular sports in the same way India has influenced cricket. Moreover, we must also think more critically about the national politics of these countries; specifically, how power is negotiated with and through marginalised groups.

The meaning(s) of sports events are multiple and contested, and depend widely upon the social and cultural significance attached to the event by individuals and groups. As Crawford (2004) argues, while for many sports events matter, for many more they do not. Yet, even for those without an active interest in the event, it can still play an important role in the formation and articulation of their identities. Bains argues in Chapter 9 that lack of involvement in kabaddi was a key marker in the identities of the British Punjabi women involved in her research. The majority of research into non-involvement in sport assumes that barriers prevent sporting participation whereas future research could consider how non-involvement can be an active choice and an important statement of personal identity. Whereas active involvement in sports events, as participants or spectators, at the venue or mediated, is widely understood as a marker of individual identity and wider allegiance (to team, region, nation, etc.) (see Chapters 8, 10 and 11), equally, for some, the decision to not be involved in sports events, as participants or spectators, can also be an empowering experience and expression of self. We acknowledge that the concept of identities in relation to sports events is extremely broad, and the contributions to this collection can only have limited scope in relation to this theme. Currently, therefore, the field is wide open. The localised focus of the sports events discussed by Harkin, Bains and Bradley identify how the 'big' issues of inequality, inclusion and exclusion are not just expressed through large, mediatised events but also via more everyday sporting events, that are embedded in local praxis. Therefore, whilst we understand the importance of mega-event research we also contend that these smaller-scale events may be even more revealing about social inequalities, power and privilege, precisely because they are more mundane and part of our everyday lives, as opposed to the more spectacular, extraordinary and mediatised nature of mega-events.

Advances in technology have transformed the ways in which sports events are produced, delivered and consumed. Information and communication technologies have opened up new possibilities for sport; amongst other things, they create new consumer and spectator markets. The advent of media technology and wider digitisation have opened up channels, such as websites, blogs, podcasts, video streaming and mobile phone applications, which provide an increasing array of sports information and entertainment services 'on demand'. In doing so these advances have changed the way sports events are conceived, planned, mediatised and experienced. Future research into the relationships between sports events and media can usefully build upon the contributions in this volume. As sports events become increasingly mediatised, research will need to consider how such media representations produce, reproduce and, potentially, contest, hegemonic discourses relating to gender, sexuality, 'race' and ethnicity, disability, nationalism and violence (see Rowe, 2009; Chapters 3 and 5 in this volume). The shift in global power relations from west to east which a number of contributions to this collection argue is characterising the contemporary sports events environment will require researchers to address the implications this has for global, national and local sports media (see Chapter 6). The increasing importance of online media, and user-generated material, also marks a 'paradigm shift' in how we think about sports media and fandom (see Wilson, 2007; Chapter 7 in this volume). Analyses of new media technologies require different methodologies than analyses of more traditional media formats, but will offer researchers opportunities to explore "the internet as a site in which global capitalism can simultaneously be entrenched and challenged, and in sometimes contradictory ways" (Millington and Darnell, 2012: 16; Gibbons and Dixon, 2010; Thorpe and Ahmad, 2013). Continuing the theme of how changes in the media landscape may begin to challenge the dominance of traditional corporate global media, the proliferation of internet piracy of live sports events telecasts raises interesting questions relating to commercialisation, cultural citizenship and fan involvement (Mellis, 2008; Birmingham and David, 2011). Perhaps of more concern for event rights holders is whether online piracy will grow and the impact this will have on the viability of spectatorship of the live event at the venue. Moreover, with the increasingly globalised nature of the sports events industry and the concurrent democratisation of media, research assessing the impact of media development on sports events will grow increasingly important. Research focusing on the influences of globalisation and innovative technologies in permitting, transforming (and enhancing) sports events, and how they are experienced and represented globally/glocally will be timely (see Chapter 4). Indeed, Wenner, Turner and Schulze illustrate in Chapters 1, 2 and 3 how certain aspects of sports events are created, packaged and consumed; though, crucially, they argue that consumers of sports events are not just passive receivers but actively contribute to the development of event narratives and discourses. Future research in this area could consider how these dominant narratives are produced and packaged for audiences, as well as examine the role of audiences more closely, considering how dominant narratives are interpreted, consumed and, sometimes, challenged.

These suggestions are by no means exhaustive and are necessarily influenced by the themes and contributions in this volume. Undoubtedly, sports events provide a fruitful space for further research and critical debate within and beyond the above-mentioned areas, and we hope that this collection provokes debate and further critical scholarship within this vibrant and emerging field.

## References

Birmingham, J. and David, M. (2011) Live-streaming: Will football fans continue to be more law abiding than music fans? *Sport in Society*, 14(1): 69–80.

Bowdin, G., Allen, J., O'Toole, W., Harris, R. and McDonnell, I. (2011) *Events management*, 3rd edition. Oxford: Elsevier Butterworth-Heinemann.

Crawford, G. (2004) *Consuming sport*. London: Routledge.

Curi, M., Knijnik, J. and Mascarenhas, G. (2011) The Pan American Games in Rio de Janeiro 2007: Consequences of a sport mega-event on a BRIC country. *International Review for the Sociology of Sport*, 46(2): 140–156.

Getz, D. (2007) *Event studies: Theory, research and policy for planned events*. Oxford: Elsevier.

Gibbons, T. and Dixon, K. (2010) "Surf's up!": A call to take English soccer fan interactions on the internet more seriously. *Soccer in Society*, 11(5): 599–613.

Mallen, C. and Adams, L.J. (eds) (2013) *Event management in sport, recreation and tourism: Theoretical and practical dimensions*, 2nd edition. London: Routledge.

Masterman, G. (2008) *Strategic sports event management: An international approach*. Oxford: Elsevier Butterworth-Heinemann.

Mellis, M.J. (2008) Internet piracy of live sports telecasts. *Marquette Sports Law Review*, 18(2): 259–284.

Millington, R. and Darnell, S.C. (2012) Constructing and contesting the Olympics online: The internet, Rio 2016 and the politics of Brazilian development. *International Review for the Sociology of Sport*. DOI: 10.1177/1012690212455374.

Richards, G., de Brito, M. and Wilks, L. (eds) (2013) *Exploring the social impacts of events*. London: Routledge.

Roche, M. (2008) Putting the London 2012 Olympics into perspective: The challenge of understanding mega-events. *Twenty-First Century Society*, 3(3): 285–290.

Rojek, C. (2013) *Event power: How global events manipulate and manage*. London: Sage.

Rowe, D. (2009) Media and sport: The cultural dynamics of global games. *Sociology Compass*, 3/4: 543–558.

Rumford, C. (2007) More than a game: Globalization and the post-Westernization of world cricket. *Global Networks*, 7(2): 202–214.

Thorpe, H. and Ahmed, N. (2013) Youth, action sports and political agency in the Middle East: Lessons from a grassroots parkour group in Gaza. *International Review for the Sociology of Sport*. DOI: 10.1177/1012690213490521.

Tribe, J. (2002) The philosophic practitioner. *Annals of Tourism Research*, 29(2): 338–357.

Wilson, B. (2007) New media, social movements, and global sport studies: A revolutionary moment in the sociology of sport. *Sociology of Sport Journal*, 24: 457–477.

# Index